Days Of Awe

The Velveteen Rabbi's *Machzor* for the *Yamim Nora'im*

ISBN 9781490977232

Cover artwork by Natalia Moroz www.nataliamoroz.com

Second edition
2015 / 5775

Velveteen Rabbi Press, Lanesboro MA

velveteenrabbi.com

Days Of Awe

The Velveteen Rabbi's *Machzor* for the *Yamim Nora'im*

Rabbi Rachel Barenblat
with Rabbi Jeffrey Goldwasser

לְשֵׁם יִחוּד קוּדְשָׁא בְּרִיךְ הוּא וּשְׁכִינְתֵּיהּ.

For the sake of unity
between the Holy Blessed One & Shekhinah,
God far above and God deep within,
transcendence and immanence.

About the Cover Art

Why a pomegranate?

The pomegranate is a symbol of abundance.
The pomegranate's many seeds can represent
the 613 *mitzvot* (connective-commandments.)

May our blessings in the new year be as plentiful
as pomegranate seeds.

Welcome

L'shanah tovah; happy new year! May the words contained in this book bring you (and me) closer to holy community, to *teshuvah* (repentance / return), and to God.

About Prayer

Prayer is an opportunity to offer gratitude for our blessings, to connect with something greater than ourselves, to link ourselves with ancestors and with community, to reach toward meaning. The Hebrew word להתפלל / *l'hitpallel*, "to pray," connotes self-examination. Through prayer, we discern the subtle ebbs and flows of heart and soul.

Prayer is one form of the spiritual work, or service, which we do to build and strengthen our connection with something beyond ourselves, which we usually name as God.

About God's Name(s)

Jewish tradition teaches that our Creator is beyond language: our words can only approach the Infinite. May our use of different names for God remind us that our names are only substitutes for ultimate reality.

One of our tradition's names for God is *Yud-Hey-Vav-Hey*, which is never pronounced. In ancient times, it was spoken only once a year by the High Priest on Yom Kippur. Rabbi Arthur Waskow teaches that this Name resembles breath. Perhaps every time we breathe with intention, we speak a holy name.

This machzor mostly follows the practice of rendering that Name with the abbreviation יְיָ (*Adonai*), but that Name does appear a few times in full. Please treat this book with respect.

One of the most repeated images of God in Jewish liturgy is God as king. This metaphor is most pervasive during the Days of Awe. Remember that this is a metaphor, intended to help us feel God as a commanding presence in our lives.

For many of us today, the metaphor of kingship is uncomfortable or distancing. For this reason, the Hebrew word מלך ("king") is sometimes translated in this machzor in ways which draw on other images for God.

On Shabbat

When Rosh Hashanah or Yom Kippur fall on Shabbat, certain liturgical changes are traditionally made. Sections that are added on Shabbat are so indicated under the section heading. Words and phrases which are added on Shabbat appear in parentheses.

About transliteration

Not every word in this machzor is transliterated into English characters, but most things are. The appearance of a little box, like so:

□ little box!

marks a place where my community sings something aloud.

Most importantly...

Rabbi Zalman Schachter-Shalomi z"l (of blessed memory) teaches that printed liturgy is like a set of recipe instructions, packaged with a set of freeze-dried ingredients. But in order to turn those ingredients into a sustaining meal, you have to add water and heat, which is to say, spirit / heart / voice / *you*. Bringing yourself to the prayers and to the experience of the Days of Awe is the most important thing.

Take risks. Try new things. (Try old things!) This season is chock-full of liturgy; use that liturgy to help connect you with something greater than yourself. May your Days of Awe be truly filled with awe!

Rabbi Rachel Barenblat
velveteenrabbi.com | velveteenrabbi.blogs.com | @velveteenrabbi

Contents

Rosh Hashanah Evening

Opening Songs

Hineh Mah Tov

Hineh mah tov u-manaim
shevet achim gam yachad!

הִנֵּה מָה טּוֹב וּמָה–נָּעִים
שֶׁבֶת אַחִים גַּם יָחַד!

How good and how pleasant it is to be in community together!

Esa Einai

Esa einai el he-harim.
Me'ayin yavo ezri?
Ezri me'im Adonai,
Oseh shamayim va'aretz.

אֶשָּׂא עֵינַי אֶל הֶהָרִים.
מֵאַיִן יָבֹא עֶזְרִי?
עֶזְרִי מֵעִם יְיָ,
עֹשֵׂה שָׁמַיִם וָאָרֶץ.

I lift my eyes up to the mountains: from where comes my help?
My help is from the Holy Blessed One
Creator of the heavens and the earth. (From Psalm 121)

Ivdu et Hashem B'Simcha

Ivdu et Hashem b'simcha,
Bo'u l'fanav birnanah,
l'fanav birnanah.

עִבְדוּ אֶת-ה' בְּשִׂמְחָה,
בֹּאוּ לְפָנָיו בִּרְנָנָה,
לְפָנָיו בִּרְנָנָה.

Serve God with joy, come before God with gladness.
(From Psalm 100)

Candle Lighting

As we light these candles, we also kindle the lights of our spirits and our hearts. May our observance of Rosh Hashanah bring light into our lives and into the world.

Baruch atah Adonai Eloheinu
melech ha'olam, asher
kideshanu bemitsvotav
vitsivanu lehadlik neir shel
(Shabbat veshel) yom tov.

בָּרוּךְ אַתָּה יְיָ אֱלֹהֵינוּ מֶלֶךְ
הָעוֹלָם, אֲשֶׁר קִדְּשָׁנוּ
בְּמִצְוֹתָיו, וְצִוָּנוּ לְהַדְלִיק נֵר
שֶׁל (שַׁבָּת וְשֶׁל) יום טוב.

Blessed are you, Adonai our God, source of all being, who makes us holy with mitzvot and enjoins us to light the (Shabbat and) holiday candles.

☐ Baruch atah Adonai Eloheinu
melech ha'olam, shehecheyanu
vekiyemanu vehigiyanu
lazeman hazeh.

☐ בָּרוּךְ אַתָּה יְיָ אֱלֹהֵינוּ מֶלֶךְ
הָעוֹלָם, שֶׁהֶחֱיָנוּ וְקִיְּמָנוּ
וְהִגִּיעָנוּ לַזְּמַן הַזֶּה.

Blessed are You,
Source of all being,
who has given us life,
established us
and allowed us to reach
this sacred moment.

Head of the Year

world, they say it is your birthday,
a thousand years for each day of genesis
and we are using you up,
but they have promised
that the next one will be better.

oh end of days, with your new earth
and your eternity spread before us
like a white sabbath cloth,
and your bread shaped like a hand:
how we long to come toward you,
to take that hand in our own.

but we have discarded the white fowl
which our fathers twirled over their heads.
we hold on to our sins, scarlet threads,
and we do not go any longer to the river
whose waters contain the fish without eyelids.

there, where our fathers cast off their sins
we lean down to untie the knot,
we are letting go of the river.

(Myra Sklarew)

On Shabbat (from) Psalm 92

Mizmor shir l'yom ha-Shabbat.	מִזְמוֹר שִׁיר לְיוֹם הַשַּׁבָּת:
Tov l'hodot l'Adonai u-l'zamer l'shimcha elyon. L'hagid baboker chasdecha, v'emunatecha baleilot.	טוֹב לְהֹדוֹת לַייָ וּלְזַמֵּר לְשִׁמְךָ עֶלְיוֹן: לְהַגִּיד בַּבֹּקֶר חַסְדֶּךָ וֶאֱמוּנָתְךָ בַּלֵּילוֹת:

A psalm: a song of Shabbat.

How good it is to praise the One
and to sing to God on high,
To tell of Your love in the morning
and of your faithfulness at night!

Alei asor va'alei navel alei higayon b'chinor. Ki samachtani Adonai b'fo'alecha B'ma'asecha yadecha aranen.	עֲלֵי עָשׂוֹר וַעֲלֵי נָבֶל עֲלֵי הִגָּיוֹן בְּכִנּוֹר: כִּי שִׂמַּחְתַּנִי יְיָ בְּפָעֳלֶךָ בְּמַעֲשֵׂי יָדֶיךָ אֲרַנֵּן:
□ Mah gadlu ma'asecha Yah M'od amku machshevotecha.	□ מַה גָּדְלוּ מַעֲשֶׂיךָ יְיָ מְאֹד עָמְקוּ מַחְשְׁבֹתֶיךָ:

(I sing) to the music of the harp,
to the sound of string and voice
for You have made me rejoice, my God.
I thrill at the beauty of Your world.

How great is Your work, God:
How profound is the world's design!

Psalm 93

Adonai possesses us,
Robed in sublimity.
God is the strength
of a world secure
and unshakable.
From ancient time
we have sought You.
You are from eternity.
The ancient ocean sounds,
Adonai,
The serene ocean
sounds its voice,
The mysterious ocean
sounds its pounding.
Above the thunder
of the mighty waters,
Truer than the breakers
of the sea,
Is Adonai, the most sublime.
Your wisdom is truer than truth.
Holiness is Your presence in the
world, Adonai,
for time without measure.

יְיָ מָלָךְ גֵּאוּת לָבֵשׁ
לָבֵשׁ יְיָ עֹז הִתְאַזָּר
אַף תִּכּוֹן תֵּבֵל בַּל תִּמּוֹט:
נָכוֹן כִּסְאֲךָ מֵאָז
מֵעוֹלָם אָתָּה:
נָשְׂאוּ נְהָרוֹת יְיָ
נָשְׂאוּ נְהָרוֹת
קוֹלָם יִשְׂאוּ נְהָרוֹת דָּכְיָם:
מִקּוֹלוֹת מַיִם רַבִּים אַדִּירִים
מִשְׁבְּרֵי יָם
אַדִּיר בַּמָּרוֹם יְיָ:
עֵדֹתֶיךָ נֶאֶמְנוּ מְאֹד לְבֵיתְךָ
נַאֲוָה קֹדֶשׁ
יְיָ לְאֹרֶךְ יָמִים:

The Shema and Her Blessings

Barchu — Call to Prayer

As we bless the Source of Life, so we are blessed.
And the blessing gives us strength, and makes our visions clear;
And the blessing gives us peace, and the courage to dare.
As we bless the Source of Life, so we are blessed.

(Faith Rogow)

Barchu et Adonai ha-mevorach. בָּרְכוּ אֶת יְיָ הַמְבֹרָךְ:

☐ Baruch Adonai ha-mevorach l'olam va-ed. בָּרוּךְ יְיָ הַמְבֹרָךְ לְעוֹלָם וָעֶד: ☐

Blessed is God, the blessed One.

Blessed is God, the blessed One,
now and forever!

Ma'ariv Aravim: God of Day and Night

בָּרוּךְ אַתָּה יְיָ ,
אֱלֹהֵינוּ מֶלֶךְ הָעוֹלָם,
אֲשֶׁר בִּדְבָרוֹ מַעֲרִיב עֲרָבִים,
בְּחָכְמָה פּוֹתֵחַ שְׁעָרִים
וּבִתְבוּנָה מְשַׁנֶּה עִתִּים,
וּמַחֲלִיף אֶת הַזְּמַנִּים, וּמְסַדֵּר
אֶת הַכּוֹכָבִים, בְּמִשְׁמְרוֹתֵיהֶם
בָּרָקִיעַ כִּרְצוֹנוֹ. בּוֹרֵא יוֹם
וָלָיְלָה, גּוֹלֵל אוֹר מִפְּנֵי חֹשֶׁךְ,
וְחֹשֶׁךְ מִפְּנֵי אוֹר. וּמַעֲבִיר יוֹם
וּמֵבִיא לָיְלָה, וּמַבְדִּיל בֵּין יוֹם
וּבֵין לָיְלָה, יְיָ צְבָאוֹת שְׁמוֹ.

Baruch atah Adonai
Eloheinu melech ha'olam
asher bidvaro ma'ariv
aravim bechochmah
poteach she'arim uvitvunah
meshaneh itim umachalif et
hazemanim umsadeir et
hakochavim b'mish-
meroteihem baraki'ah
kirtsono. Borei yom valaila
goleil or mipnei choshech
vechoshech mipnei or
uma'avir yom umeivi lailah
umavdil bein yom uvein
lailah Adonai tzeva'ot
shemo.

Blessed are You, Adonai our God, Source of all being,
by Whose word the evening falls.
In wisdom You open heaven's gates.
With understanding You make seasons change,
causing the times to come and go,
and ordering the stars on their appointed paths
through heaven's dome, all according to Your will.
Creator of day and night, who rolls back light before dark,
and dark before light, who makes day pass away
and brings on the night, dividing between day and night;
the Leader of Heaven's Multitudes is Your name!

□ Eil chai vekayam tamid yimloch aleinu le'olam va'ed. Baruch atah Adonai hama'ariv aravim.	□ אֵל חַי וְקַיָּם, תָּמִיד יִמְלוֹךְ עָלֵינוּ לְעוֹלָם וָעֶד. בָּרוּךְ אַתָּה יְיָ, הַמַּעֲרִיב עֲרָבִים:

Living and enduring God, be our guide
now and always.
Blessed are You, Source of All being,
Who makes evening fall.

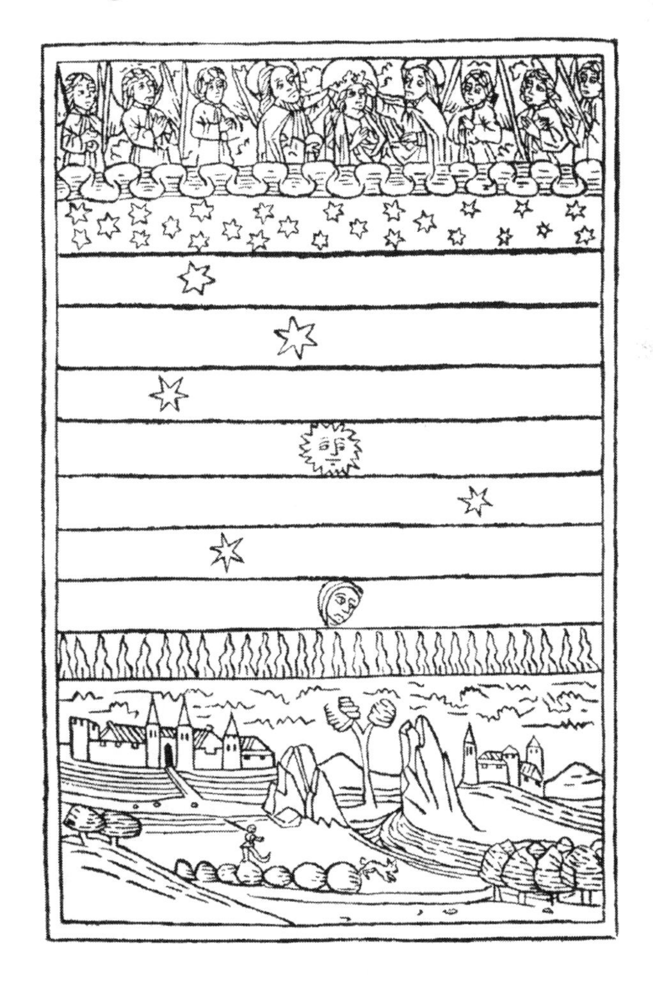

Ahavat Olam: Eternal Love

□ Ahavat olam beit Yisrael
amecha ahavta Torah umitsvot
chukim umishpatim
otanu limadeta.
Al kein Adonai Eloheinu
beshochveinu uvkumeinu
nasiach bechukecha.
Venismach bedivrei Toratecha
Uvmitsvotecha le'olam va'ed.
Kee heim chayeinu
ve'orech yameinu
uvahem negeh
yomam valailah.

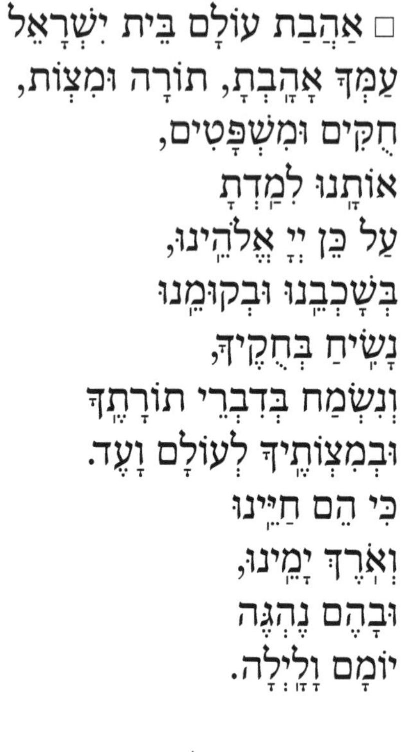
□ אַהֲבַת עוֹלָם בֵּית יִשְׂרָאֵל
עַמְּךָ אָהָבְתָּ, תּוֹרָה וּמִצְוֹת,
חֻקִּים וּמִשְׁפָּטִים,
אוֹתָנוּ לִמַּדְתָּ
עַל כֵּן יְיָ אֱלֹהֵינוּ,
בְּשָׁכְבֵנוּ וּבְקוּמֵנוּ
נָשִׂיחַ בְּחֻקֶּיךָ,
וְנִשְׂמַח בְּדִבְרֵי תוֹרָתֶךָ
וּבְמִצְוֹתֶיךָ לְעוֹלָם וָעֶד.
כִּי הֵם חַיֵּינוּ
וְאֹרֶךְ יָמֵינוּ,
וּבָהֶם נֶהְגֶּה
יוֹמָם וָלָיְלָה.

□ Ve'ahavatcha al tasir
Mimenu le'olamim.
Baruch atah Adonai
oheiv amo Yisrael.

□ וְאַהֲבָתְךָ אַל תָּסִיר
מִמֶּנּוּ לְעוֹלָמִים.
בָּרוּךְ אַתָּה יְיָ,
אוֹהֵב עַמּוֹ יִשְׂרָאֵל:

With eternal love, You love the house of Israel. Torah and mitzvot, laws and justice You have taught us. And so, Adonai, our God, when we lie down and when we rise, we reflect upon Your laws; we take pleasure in Your Torah's words and your mitzvot, now and always. Truly, they are our life, our length of days. On them we meditate by day and night.

Your love will never depart from us as long as worlds endure. Blessed are You, Adonai, who loves Your people Israel.

Unending Love

We are loved by unending love.

We are embraced by arms that find us
even when we are hidden from ourselves.
We are touched by fingers that soothe us
even when we are too proud for soothing.
We are counseled by voices that guide us
even when we are too embittered to hear.

We are loved by unending love.

We are supported by hands that uplift us
even in the midst of a fall.
We are urged on by eyes that meet us
even when we are too weak for meeting.

We are loved by unending love.

Embraced, touched, soothed, and counseled,
ours are the arms, the fingers, the voices;
ours are the hands, the eyes, the smiles;

We are loved by unending love.

(Rabbi Rami Shapiro)

Shema

☐ Shema Yisrael: Adonai Eloheinu Adonai echad! (Baruch shem kvod malchuto l'olam vaed.)

☐ שְׁמַע יִשְׂרָאֵל, יְיָ אֱלֹהֵינוּ, יְיָ אֶחָד:

בָּרוּךְ שֵׁם כְּבוֹד מַלְכוּתוֹ לְעוֹלָם וָעֶד.

Hear, O Israel: Adonai is our God, Adonai is One!
Through time and space Your glory shines, Majestic One!

☐ V'ahavta et Adonai elohecha, b'chol l'vavcha, uv'chol nafshecha, uv'chol me'odecha. V'hayu ha d'varim ha-eileh, asher anochi m'tzv'cha hayom, al levavecha. V'shinantam l'vanecha, v'dibarta bam b'shiv't'cha b'veitecha, uv'lech't'cha vaderech uv'shochb'cha uv'kumecha. Ukshartam l'ot al yadecha, v'hayu l'totafor bein enecha, uchtavtam al mezuzot beitecha uvisharecha.

☐ וְאָהַבְתָּ אֵת יְיָ אֱלֹהֶיךָ, בְּכָל-לְבָבְךָ, וּבְכָל-נַפְשְׁךָ, וּבְכָל-מְאֹדֶךָ. וְהָיוּ הַדְּבָרִים הָאֵלֶּה, אֲשֶׁר אָנֹכִי מְצַוְּךָ הַיּוֹם, עַל-לְבָבֶךָ: וְשִׁנַּנְתָּם לְבָנֶיךָ, וְדִבַּרְתָּ בָּם בְּשִׁבְתְּךָ בְּבֵיתֶךָ, וּבְלֶכְתְּךָ בַדֶּרֶךְ וּבְשָׁכְבְּךָ, וּבְקוּמֶךָ. וּקְשַׁרְתָּם לְאוֹת עַל-יָדֶךָ, וְהָיוּ לְטֹטָפֹת בֵּין עֵינֶיךָ, וּכְתַבְתָּם עַל מְזֻזוֹת בֵּיתֶךָ וּבִשְׁעָרֶיךָ:

You shall love Adonai your God with all your heart, with all your mind, with all your being. Set these words which I enjoin upon you today upon your heart. Teach them faithfully to your children. Speak of them in your home and on your way, when you lie down and when you rise up. Bind them as a sign on your hand. Let them be symbols before your eyes. Inscribe them on the doorposts of your house, and on your gates.

וְהָיָה אִם-שָׁמֹעַ תִּשְׁמְעוּ אֶל-מִצְוֹתַי, אֲשֶׁר אָנֹכִי מְצַוֶּה אֶתְכֶם
הַיּוֹם, לְאַהֲבָה אֶת יְיָ אֱלֹהֵיכֶם, וּלְעָבְדוֹ בְּכָל-לְבַבְכֶם וּבְכָל
נַפְשְׁכֶם. וְנָתַתִּי מְטַר-אַרְצְכֶם בְּעִתּוֹ, יוֹרֶה וּמַלְקוֹשׁ, וְאָסַפְתָּ
דְגָנֶךָ וְתִירֹשְׁךָ וְיִצְהָרֶךָ. וְנָתַתִּי עֵשֶׂב בְּשָׂדְךָ לִבְהֶמְתֶּךָ, וְאָכַלְתָּ
וְשָׂבָעְתָּ. הִשָּׁמְרוּ לָכֶם פֶּן-יִפְתֶּה לְבַבְכֶם, וְסַרְתֶּם וַעֲבַדְתֶּם
אֱלֹהִים אֲחֵרִים וְהִשְׁתַּחֲוִיתֶם לָהֶם. וְחָרָה אַף-יְיָ בָּכֶם, וְעָצַר
אֶת-הַשָּׁמַיִם וְלֹא-יִהְיֶה מָטָר, וְהָאֲדָמָה לֹא תִתֵּן אֶת-יְבוּלָהּ
וַאֲבַדְתֶּם מְהֵרָה מֵעַל הָאָרֶץ הַטֹּבָה אֲשֶׁ יְיָ נֹתֵן לָכֶם: וְשַׂמְתֶּם
אֶת דְּבָרַי אֵלֶּה עַל-לְבַבְכֶם וְעַל-נַפְשְׁכֶם וּקְשַׁרְתֶּם אֹתָם לְאוֹת
עַל-יֶדְכֶם, וְהָיוּ לְטוֹטָפֹת בֵּין עֵינֵיכֶם: וְלִמַּדְתֶּם אֹתָ אֶת-בְּנֵיכֶם,
לְדַבֵּר בָּם, בְּשִׁבְתְּךָ בְּבֵיתֶךָ, וּבְלֶכְתְּךָ בַדֶּרֶךְ, וּבְשָׁכְבְּךָ וּבְקוּמֶךָ:
וּכְתַבְתָּם עַל-מְזוּזוֹת בֵּיתֶךָ וּבִשְׁעָרֶיךָ: לְמַעַן יִרְבּוּ יְמֵיכֶם וִימֵי
בְנֵיכֶם עַל הָאֲדָמָה אֲשֶׁר נִשְׁבַּע יְיָ לַאֲבֹתֵיכֶם לָתֵת לָהֶם, כִּימֵי
הַשָּׁמַיִם עַל-הָאָרֶץ:

If you will listen to Me and know the way to treat each other lovingly that I give you this day, you will be rewarded with fulfillment and always know who you are. You will gather blessings in your life. There will be sustenance for your spirit. But take care not to be lured to ways of selfishness and bow down to injustice, for then you will be far from Me and you will shut the door of blessing. There will be no kindness in a moment of pain, no rejoicing in the world's goodness. You will destroy the love and hope that are My gifts to you. Therefore, impress these words on your heart and mind. Make them the cornerstone of your life and the motto of your being. Teach them to your children; speak them in your home and to your friends, when you begin something new and when you finish. Put them on the mezuzah of your house so that you and your children will live in the hope and justice promised to your ancestors for as long as there is a heaven over the earth.

This is an interpretive translation of the second and third paragraphs of the Shema. *A more literal translation appears on p. 94.*

Vayomer Adonai el Moshe
lemor: daber el-bnei Yisrael
v'amarta aleihem v'asu lahem
tzitzit al kanfei bigdeihem
l'dorotam, v'natnu al tzitzit
ha-kanaf p'til tchelet. V'yaha
lachem l'tzitzit, u'ritem oto,
u'zchartem et-kol-mitzvot
Adonai v'asitem otam. V'lo
taturu acharei l'vavchem
v'acharei eineihem asher-
atem zonim achareihem.

וַיֹּאמֶר יְיָ אֶל-מֹשֶׁה לֵּאמֹר:
דַּבֵּר אֶל-בְּנֵי יִשְׂרָאֵל וְאָמַרְתָּ
אֲלֵהֶם: וְעָשׂוּ לָהֶם צִיצִת עַל-
כַּנְפֵי בִגְדֵיהֶם לְדֹרֹתָם, וְנָתְנוּ
עַל-צִיצִת הַכָּנָף פְּתִיל תְּכֵלֶת.
וְהָיָה לָכֶם לְצִיצִת, וּרְאִיתֶם
אֹתוֹ וּזְכַרְתֶּם אֶת-כָּל-מִצְוֹת יְיָ,
וַעֲשִׂיתֶם אֹתָם, וְלֹא תָתוּרוּ
אַחֲרֵי לְבַבְכֶם וְאַחֲרֵי עֵינֵיכֶם,
אֲשֶׁר-אַתֶּם זֹנִים אַחֲרֵיהֶם:

And God spoke to Moses saying: speak to the children of Israel and say to them that they should make tzitzit on the corners of their garments for all time, and they shall place on the tzitzit a little thread of blue. And these shall be for you as tzitzit, that you may look upon them, that you will remember all of the mitzvot of Adonai and you shall do them, so that you will not go running after the cravings of your heart or the turnings of your eyes which might take you into places where you should not be!

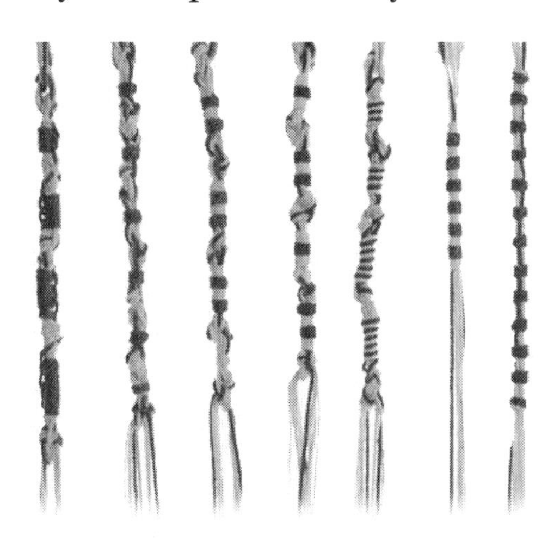

□ לְמַעַן תִּזְכְּרוּ וַעֲשִׂיתֶם אֶת-
כָּל-מִצְוֹתָי, וִהְיִיתֶם קְדֹשִׁים
לֵאלֹהֵיכֶם: אֲנִי יְיָ אֱלֹהֵיכֶם,
אֲשֶׁר הוֹצֵאתִי אֶתְכֶם מֵאֶרֶץ
מִצְרַיִם, לִהְיוֹת לָכֶם
לֵאלֹהִים, אֲנִי יְיָ אֱלֹהֵיכֶם:

□ Lema'an tizkeru va'asitem et kol mitzvotai viheyitem kedoshim l'Eloheichem. Ani Adonai Eloheichem asher hotzeiti etcham me'eretz Mitzrayim lihiyot lachem l'Elohim. Ani Adonai Aloheichem.

This way you will be mindful to actualize my directions
for becoming dedicated to your God;
to be aware that I am your God,
the one who freed you from the oppression
in order to be your God. I am Adonai your God.
That is the truth!

A thread of blue?

On the facing page, we read the ancient instruction to add a thread of *tchelet*, blue, to our tzitzit. But most of us do not have blue threads anymore. Some say this is because we forgot how to identify the *chilazon*, the small sea creature which was crushed to provide the dye, or because we were driving that mollusk extinct. Today some people choose to have blue threads (dyed with commercial dyes) and others choose all white. Practices and interpretations vary. Perhaps the most important thing is that as we daven these words, we remember to think about the choices we make.

יְיָ אֱלֹהֵיכֶם אֱמֶת!

Your God is a true God!

Geulah: Redemption

אֱמֶת וֶאֱמוּנָה כָּל זֹאת, וְקַיָּם עָלֵינוּ, כִּי הוּא יְיָ אֱלֹהֵינוּ וְאֵין
זוּלָתוֹ, וַאֲנַחְנוּ יִשְׂרָאֵל עַמּוֹ. הַפּוֹדֵנוּ מִיַּד מְלָכִים, מַלְכֵּנוּ
הַגּוֹאֲלֵנוּ מִכַּף כָּל הֶעָרִיצִים. הָאֵל הַנִּפְרָע לָנוּ מִצָּרֵינוּ וְהַמְשַׁלֵּם
גְּמוּל לְכָל אֹיְבֵי נַפְשֵׁנוּ. הָעֹשֶׂה גְדֹלוֹת עַד אֵין חֵקֶר, וְנִפְלָאוֹת
עַד אֵין מִסְפָּר. הַשָּׂם נַפְשֵׁנוּ בַּחַיִּים, וְלֹא נָתַן לַמּוֹט רַגְלֵנוּ,
הַמַּדְרִיכֵנוּ עַל בָּמוֹת אוֹיְבֵינוּ, וַיָּרֶם קַרְנֵנוּ, עַל כָּל שׂוֹנְאֵנוּ.
הָעֹשֶׂה לָּנוּ נִסִּים וּנְקָמָה בְּפַרְעֹה, אוֹתוֹת וּמוֹפְתִים בְּאַדְמַת בְּנֵי
חָם. הַמַּכֶּה בְעֶבְרָתוֹ כָּל בְּכוֹרֵי מִצְרָיִם, וַיּוֹצֵא אֶת עַמּוֹ יִשְׂרָאֵל
מִתּוֹכָם, לְחֵרוּת עוֹלָם. הַמַּעֲבִיר בָּנָיו בֵּין גִּזְרֵי יַם סוּף, אֶת
רוֹדְפֵיהֶם וְאֶת שׂוֹנְאֵיהֶם, בִּתְהוֹמוֹת טִבַּע, וְרָאוּ בָנָיו גְּבוּרָתוֹ.
שִׁבְּחוּ וְהוֹדוּ לִשְׁמוֹ. וּמַלְכוּתוֹ בְּרָצוֹן קִבְּלוּ עֲלֵיהֶם, מֹשֶׁה,
מִרְיָם, וּבְנֵי יִשְׂרָאֵל לְךָ עָנוּ שִׁירָה בְּשִׂמְחָה רַבָּה, וְאָמְרוּ כֻלָּם:

All this is true and real and it is up to us:
Adonai is our only God, and we, Israel, are Your people.

You save us from oppression
and make our transformation possible.

You do great deeds beyond measure, wonders beyond counting.
You give our souls life and direct us from death.

You made miracles for us before Pharaoh,
Signs and wonders in the land of Egypt.

You led Your people Israel into freedom.
You led us through the Sea of Reeds.

When we saw Your power,
we thanked You and praised Your name.

Full of joy, Moses, Miriam, and all Israel sang:

□ מִי כָמֹכָה בָּאֵלִים יְיָ,
מִי כָּמֹכָה נֶאְדָּר בַּקֹּדֶשׁ,
נוֹרָא תְהִילֹּת, עֹשֵׂה פֶלֶא:

□ Mi chamocha ba'eilim Adonai, mi camocha nedar bakodesh, nora tehilot oseh feleh.

מַלְכוּתְךָ רָאוּ בָנֶיךָ,
בּוֹקֵעַ יָם לִפְנֵי מֹשֶׁה וּמִרְיַם,
זֶה אֵלִי עָנוּ וְאָמְרוּ:
יְיָ יִמְלוֹךְ לְעוֹלָם וָעֶד.

Malchut'cha ra'u vanecha, bokea yam lifnei Moshe u Miriam. "Zeh eli," anu v'amru; "Adonai yimloch l'olam va'ed!"

וְנֶאֱמַר: כִּי פָדָה יְיָ אֶת יַעֲקֹב,
וּגְאָלוֹ מִיַּד חָזָק מִמֶּנּוּ. בָּרוּךְ
אַתָּה יְיָ גָּאַל יִשְׂרָאֵל:

V'ne'emar: ki fadah Adonai et Ya'akov, u'g'alo miyad chazak mimenu. Baruch atah, Adonai, ga'al Yisrael.

Who is like You, among the gods, Adonai? Who is like You, awesome and doing wonders?

Your children saw your majesty, splitting the sea before Moses and Miriam.

"This is our God," they cried, "Adonai will reign through all space and time!"

And it is said: Adonai has saved the people of Jacob, and redeems the weak from the mighty. Blessed are You, Adonai, who redeems Israel.

Hashkivenu: Shelter of Peace

Hashkivenu Adonai eloheinu l'shalom, v'hamideinu malkeinu l'chayyim, ufros aleinu sukat shlomecha, v'taknenu b'etza tovah milfanecha, v'hoshienu l'ma'an shmecha, v'hagen b'adeinu, v'haser me'aleinu oyev, dever, v'cherev, v'raav v'yagon, v'haser satan milfaneinu u-me'achareinu, u'vtzel canfecha tastireinu. Ki el shomreinu u-matzilenu atah, ki el melech chanun v'rachum atah, ushmor tzeiteinu u-voeinu, l'chayyim u'l'shalom, me'atah v'ad olam.

הַשְׁכִּיבֵנוּ יְיָ אֱלֹהֵינוּ לְשָׁלוֹם,
וְהַעֲמִידֵנוּ מַלְכֵּנוּ לְחַיִּים וּפְרוֹשׂ
עָלֵינוּ סֻכַּת שְׁלוֹמֶךָ, וְתַקְּנֵנוּ
בְּעֵצָה טוֹבָה מִלְּפָנֶיךָ,
וְהוֹשִׁיעֵנוּ לְמַעַן שְׁמֶךָ, וְהָגֵן
בַּעֲדֵנוּ, וְהָסֵר מֵעָלֵינוּ אוֹיֵב,
דֶּבֶר, וְחֶרֶב, וְרָעָב וְיָגוֹן, וְהָסֵר
שָׂטָן מִלְּפָנֵינוּ וּמֵאַחֲרֵנוּ, וּבְצֵל
כְּנָפֶיךָ תַּסְתִּירֵנוּ. כִּי אֵל
שׁוֹמְרֵנוּ וּמַצִּילֵנוּ אָתָּה, כִּי אֵל
מֶלֶךְ חַנּוּן וְרַחוּם אָתָּה, וּשְׁמוֹר
צֵאתֵנוּ וּבוֹאֵנוּ, לְחַיִּים
וּלְשָׁלוֹם, מֵעַתָּה וְעַד עוֹלָם.

Help us to lie down in peace, Adonai our God, and to arise again to life. Spread over the world Your sheltering peace. Direct us with Your guidance and save us. Protect and keep us from enmity, illness, violence, want, and sorrow. Remove envy and recrimination from us. Shelter us in the shadow of Your wings, for You are a protecting, redeeming God. You are God, our source of grace and mercy. Guard our going out and our coming in, for life and for peace, now and forever.

□ U-fros aleinu sukkat shlomecha.
Baruch atah Adonai, shomer amo Yisrael la-ad.

□ וּפְרֹשׂ עָלֵינוּ סֻכַּת שְׁלוֹמֶךָ.
בָּרוּךְ אַתָּה יְיָ, שׁוֹמֵר עַמּוֹ
יִשְׂרָאֵל לָעַד:

Spread your sheltering peace over us. Blessed are you, Adonai, who spreads a shelter of peace over all of your people.

Hashkivenu Chant

Hashkivenu Yah eloheinu
l'shalom.
Ufros aleinu sukkat shlomecha.

הַשְׁכִּיבֵנוּ יָהּ אֱלֹהֵינוּ
לְשָׁלוֹם.
וּפְרֹשׂ עָלֵינוּ סֻכַּת שְׁלוֹמֶךָ.

Help us to lie down in peace, Yah our God.
Spread Your sheltering peace over us.

(Rabbi Hanna Tiferet Siegel)

Veshameru (on Shabbat)

□ Veshameru venei Yisrael
et ha-Shabbat,
la'asot et ha-Shabbat
l'dorotam berit olam.
Beini u-vein b'nei Yisrael
ot hee l'olam.
Ki sheshet yamim asah Adonai
et ha-shamayim v'et ha-aretz,
uvayom ha-shvi'i shavat
vayinafash.

□ וְשָׁמְרוּ בְנֵי יִשְׂרָאֵל
אֶת הַשַּׁבָּת,
לַעֲשׂוֹת אֶת הַשַּׁבָּת
לְדֹרֹתָם בְּרִית עוֹלָם:
בֵּינִי וּבֵין בְּנֵי יִשְׂרָאֵל
אוֹת הִיא לְעוֹלָם,
כִּי שֵׁשֶׁת יָמִים עָשָׂה יְיָ
אֶת הַשָּׁמַיִם וְאֶת הָאָרֶץ, וּבַיּוֹם
הַשְּׁבִיעִי שָׁבַת וַיִּנָּפַשׁ.

The children of Israel shall keep the day of Shabbat and make
Shabbat a perpetual covenant for all their generations.
It shall be a sign between Me and the children of Israel forever.
For in six days, Adonai made the heavens and earth
But on the seventh day, God rested and was refreshed.

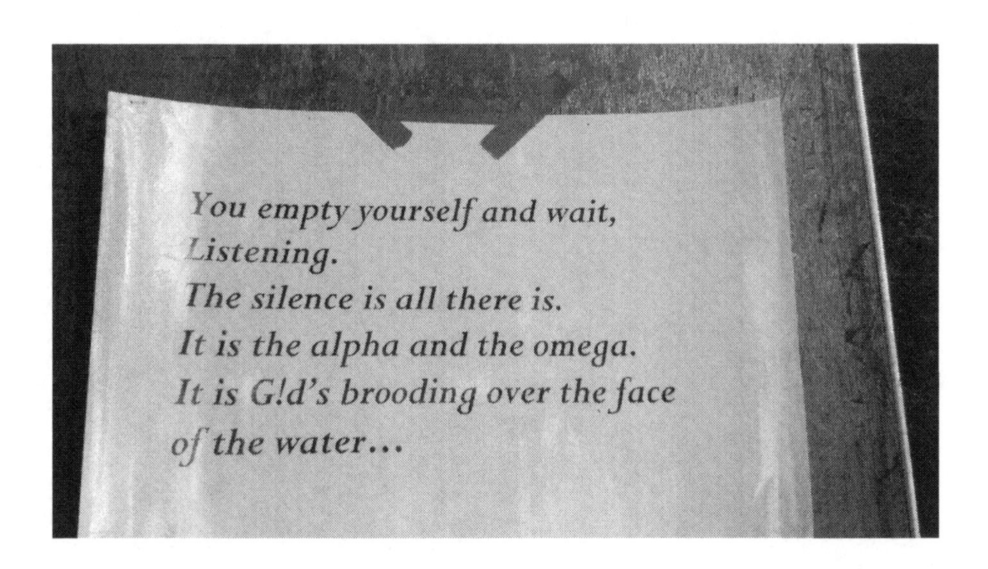

"Sound the Shofar"

תִּקְעוּ בַחֹדֶשׁ שׁוֹפָר, בַּכֶּסֶה לְיוֹם חַגֵּנוּ.
כִּי חֹק לְיִשְׂרָאֵל הוּא, מִשְׁפָּט לֵאלֹהֵי יַעֲקֹב.

Sound the shofar on the new moon
On the day of our celebration, when it is hidden
It is a statute for Israel, a decree of Jacob's God.

(Psalm 91:4)

The Kaddish: A Door

In all of its forms, the Kaddish is a doorway
between one part of the service and the next.

As we move through this door, notice:
what is happening in your heart and mind?

Whatever is arising in you,
bring that into your prayer.

Chatzi Kaddish

Yitgadal v'yitkadash sh'mei rabah. (Amen.) Be'alma div'ra chirutei v'yamlich malchutei. B'chayeichon uv'yomeichon uv'chayei d'chol beit Yisrael. Ba'agala uvizman kariv v'imru Amen.

□Yehei shmei rabah m'vorach l'olam ul'almei almaya.

Yitbarach v'yishtabah v'yitpa'ar v'yitromam v'yitnaseh. V'yithadar v'yitaleh v'yithalal shmeh d'kudsha brich hu. L'eila u-l'eila min kol birchata v'shirata, tushb'chata v'nechemata, d'amiran b'alma, v'imru Amen.

יִתְגַּדַּל וְיִתְקַדַּשׁ שְׁמֵהּ רַבָּא. בְּעָלְמָא דִּי בְרָא כִרְעוּתֵהּ, וְיַמְלִיךְ מַלְכוּתֵהּ בְּחַיֵּיכוֹן וּבְיוֹמֵיכוֹן וּבְחַיֵּי דְכָל בֵּית יִשְׂרָאֵל. בַּעֲגָלָא וּבִזְמַן קָרִיב וְאִמְרוּ אָמֵן:

□ יְהֵא שְׁמֵהּ רַבָּא מְבָרַךְ לְעָולַם וּלְעָלְמֵי עָלְמַיָּא:

יִתְבָּרַךְ וְיִשְׁתַּבַּח, וְיִתְפָּאַר וְיִתְרוֹמַם וְיִתְנַשֵּׂא וְיִתְהַדָּר וְיִתְעַלֶּה וְיִתְהַלָּל שְׁמֵהּ דְּקֻדְשָׁא בְּרִיךְ הוּא לְעֵלָּא וּלְעֵלָּא מִן כָּל בִּרְכָתָא וְשִׁירָתָא, תֻּשְׁבְּחָתָא וְנֶחֱמָתָא, דַּאֲמִירָן בְּעָלְמָא, וְאִמְרוּ אָמֵן:

Magnified and sanctified! Magnified and sanctified! May God's Great Name fill the world God created. May God's splendor be seen in the world in your life, in your days, in the life of all Israel. Quickly and soon! And let us say, Amen.

Forever may the Great Name be blessed!

Blessed and praised! Splendid and supreme! May the holy Name, Bless God, be praised, far beyond all the blessings and songs, comforts and consolations, that can be offered in this world. And let us say: Amen.

Hineni: Here I stand

הִנְנִי הֶעָנִי מִמַּעַשׂ, נִרְעָשׁ וְנִפְחָד מִפַּחַד יוֹשֵׁב תְּהִלּוֹת יִשְׂרָאֵל,
בָּאתִי לַעֲמֹד וּלְהִתְחַנֵּן לְפָנֶיךָ עַל עַמְּךָ יִשְׂרָאֵל אֲשֶׁר שְׁלָחוּנִי,
אַף עַל פִּי שֶׁאֵינִי כְּדַאי וְהָגוּן לְכָךְ...

Here I stand
painfully aware of my flaws
quaking in my shoes
and in my heart.

I'm here on behalf of this *kahal*
even though the part of me
that's quick to knock myself
says I'm not worthy to lead them.

All creation was nurtured
in Your compassionate womb!
God of our ancestors, help me
as I call upon your mercy.

Don't blame this community
for the places where I miss the mark
in my actions or my heart
in my thoughts or in our davening.

Each of us is responsible
for her own *teshuvah*.
Help us remember that
without recriminations.

Accept my prayer
as though I were exactly the leader
this community needs in this moment,
as though my voice never faltered.

Free me from my own baggage
that might get in the way.
See us through the rose-colored glasses
of Your mercy.

Transform our suffering into gladness.
Dear One, may my prayer reach You
wherever You are
for Your name's sake.

All praise is due to You, Dear One
Who hears the prayers of our hearts.

בָּרוּךְ אַתָּה יָהּ שׁוֹמֵעַ תְּפִלָּה.

(Rabbi Rachel Barenblat)

Congregational Hineni

Each of the Biblical figures named in this prayer says הנני*, "Hineni," to God at some point in their story.*

Hineni! Here I am as a poor one standing before You,
in this holy community amidst all Your people Israel,
ready to receive the inner truths of our lives.

Hineni! May I be as Abraham, who answered You by going
according to Your word to do Your will without stumbling.

Hineni! May I be as Abraham, who lovingly answered You
by climbing the mountain together with his son Isaac.

Hineni! May I be as Abraham, who answered You on
Mount Moriah and did not withhold his love from You.

Hineni! May I be as Jacob, who answered You by
returning to his native land under the wings of Your peace.

Hineni! May I be as Joseph, who answered You and
his father by caring for his brothers along his way.

Hineni! May I be as Joseph, who answered You by
descending into Egyptian exile for the sake of Your name.

Hineni! May I be as Moses, who answered You when the bush burned but was not consumed, and his life was changed forever.

Hineni! May I be as Samuel, who answered You by waking from his slumber into the light of Your word.

Hineni! May I be as Isaiah, who answered You saying: Send me to serve Your holiness in truth.

By this merit, may it be Your will that all our travails and sufferings convert into joy and gladness, life and peace. May there be no block to my prayer.

And may it be Your will, Yah, God of Abraham and Sarah, God of Isaac and Rebecca, God of Jacob, Rachel and Leah — the great, mighty and awesome God, I will be what I will be — that Your name be known to all Your people.

Thus on this day may we hear Your voice, as You said: "Even I who speak, *Hineni*—here I am."

Blessed are You, Yah, who hears prayer.

(Rabbi David Markus)

Here I Am

I want to be present to this moment.
What is arising in me?
As I stand before God
    whatever I understand that to mean
    God far above
    or God deep within
As I stand with my community
    whether we are together in person
    connected across the miles
    or linked through the generations
What words pour forth from my heart?
What am I afraid of?
What do I yearn for?
Here I am: me, all that I am.
Here I am: here, and nowhere else.
Here I am: in this very moment
    not remembering yesterday
    not dreaming about tomorrow
    but here and now.
Like Your prophet Isaiah
I yearn to say:
Here I am, God: send me.

(Rabbi Rachel Barenblat)

To gaze at before the amidah...

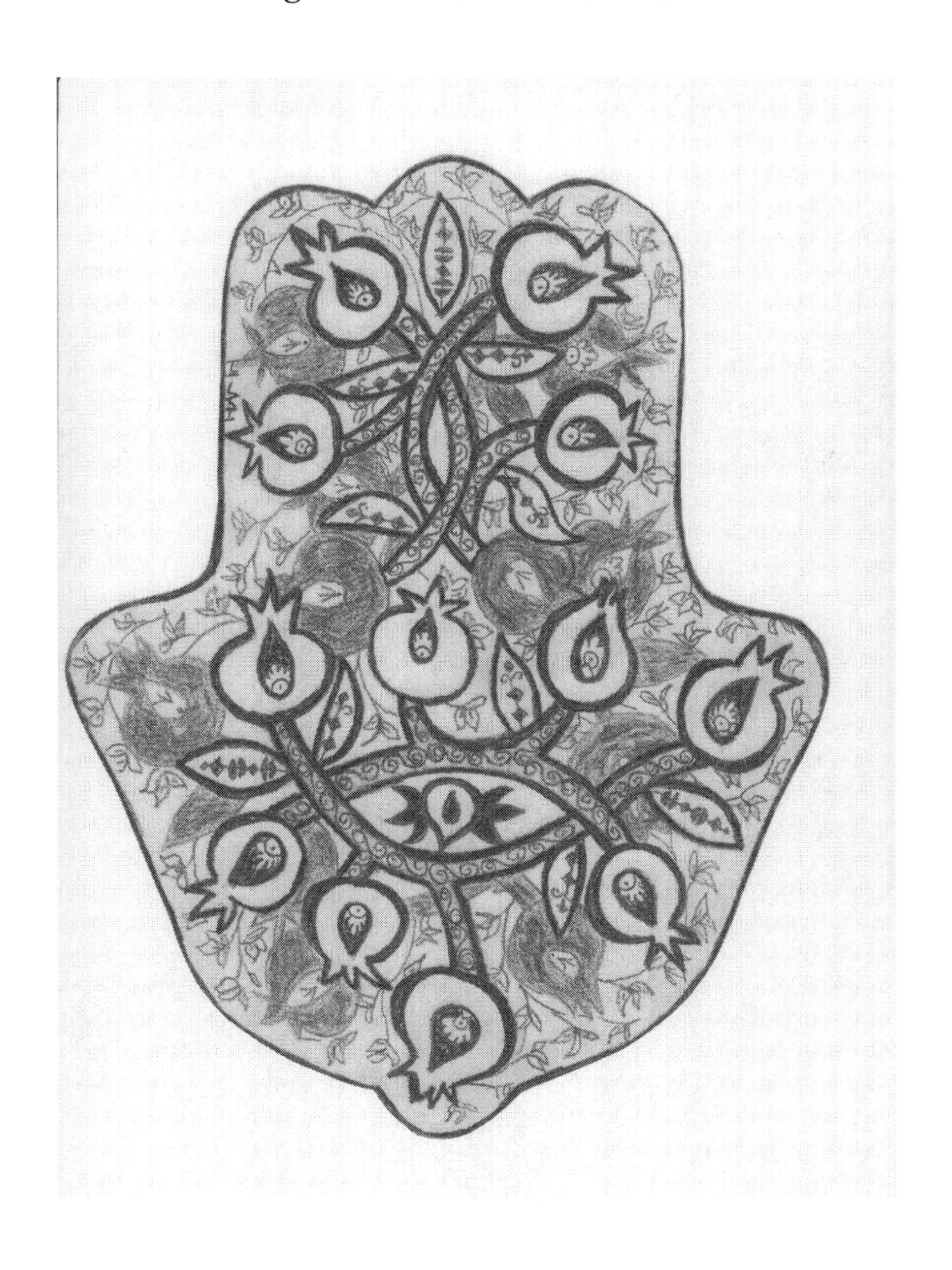

A hamsa is a symbol of peace and compassion.
This one is adorned with pomegranates,
symbols of divine abundance.

Preparing for the Amidah

The Tetragrammaton, God's four-letter name,
is the most holy of all God's names.
By concentrating and meditating upon God's name,
we turn our minds to the highest within us and beyond us.

י The moment before inhaling:
the point of existence which first emerged from nothingness.

ה The universe into which God's healing flows.
We inhale and receive God's blessing.

ו Lungs filled with breath.
God reaches toward us from heaven to earth.

ה We exhale, dedicating ourselves
to bringing blessing into creation.

With every breath, we experience
God reaching out to us in partnership.

Amidah

Adonai sefatai tiftach
ufi yagid tehilatecha.

אֲדֹנָי שְׂפָתַי תִּפְתָּח וּפִי
יַגִּיד תְּהִלָּתֶךָ:

Eternal God, open my lips
that my mouth may declare Your praise.

Avot v'Imahot: Our Ancestors

Baruch atah Adonai Eloheinu
v'Elohei avoteinu v'imoteinu,
elohei Avraham, elohei
Yitzchak, elohei Ya'akov,
elohei Sarah, elohei Rivkah,
elohei Leah, v'elohei Rachel.
Ha'el hagadol hagibor v'hanora
Eil elyon, gomeil chasadim
tovim v'koneh hakol v'zocheir
chasei avot v'imahot, umeivi
go'el livnei veneihem lema'an
shemo b'ahavah.

בָּרוּךְ אַתָּה יְיָ אֱלֹהֵינוּ וֵאלֹהֵי
אֲבוֹתֵינוּ וְאִמּוֹתֵינוּ, אֱלֹהֵי
אַבְרָהָם, אֱלֹהֵי יִצְחָק, וֵאלֹהֵי
יַעֲקֹב, אלֹהֵי שָׂרָה, אלֹהֵי
רִבְקָה, אלֹהֵי לֵאָה, וֵאלֹהֵי
רָחֵל. הָאֵל הַגָּדוֹל הַגִּבּוֹר
וְהַנּוֹרָא, אֵל עֶלְיוֹן, גּוֹמֵל
חֲסָדִים טוֹבִים, וְקוֹנֵה הַכֹּל,
וְזוֹכֵר חַסְדֵי אָבוֹת וְאִמָהוֹת,
וּמֵבִיא גוֹאֵל לִבְנֵי בְנֵיהֶם לְמַעַן
שְׁמוֹ בְּאַהֲבָה:

Blessed are You, Yah our God and God of our ancestors, God of Abraham, God of Isaac, God of Jacob; God of Sarah, God of Rebecca, God of Rachel and God of Leah; the great, mighty, and awesome God, God on high, who does deeds of loving kindness, who is the Source of all, and who remembers the steadfast love of our ancestors, who lovingly brings redemption to their children's children for Your name's sake.

זָכְרֵנוּ לְחַיִּים, מֶלֶךְ חָפֵץ בַּחַיִּים, וְכָתְבֵנוּ בְּסֵפֶר הַחַיִּים, לְמַעַנְךָ אֱלֹהִים חַיִּים.

Zochreinu lechayim melech chafeitz bachayim, vekotveinu beseifer ha-chayyim le ma'ancha Elohim chayyim.

מֶלֶךְ עוֹזֵר וּמוֹשִׁיעַ וּמָגֵן: בָּרוּךְ אַתָּה יְיָ, מָגֵן אַבְרָהָם וְעֶזְרַת שָׂרָה:

Melech ozeir u-moshia u-magen. Baruch Atah Adonai, magein Avraham v'ezrat Sarah.

Remember us for life, creator Who delights in life,
and inscribe us in the book of life for Your own sake, O God of life.

Ruler, helper, redeemer, and protector, blessed are You,
Abraham's shield and Sarah's strength.

Gevurot: God's Strength

אַתָּה גִּבּוֹר לְעוֹלָם אֲדֹנָי, מְחַיֵּה מֵתִים אַתָּה, רַב לְהוֹשִׁיעַ: מוֹרִיד הַטָּל:

Atah gibor l'olam Adonai, mechayeh meitim atah rav l'hoshia. Morid ha-tal.

You are our eternal strength, Adonai. Your saving power gives life that transcends death. You bring the dew of the field.

מְכַלְכֵּל חַיִּים בְּחֶסֶד, מְחַיֵּה
מֵתִים בְּרַחֲמִים רַבִּים, סוֹמֵךְ
נוֹפְלִים, וְרוֹפֵא חוֹלִים, וּמַתִּיר
אֲסוּרִים, וּמְקַיֵּם אֱמוּנָתוֹ
לִישֵׁנֵי עָפָר, מִי כָמוֹךְ בַּעַל
גְּבוּרוֹת וּמִי דּוֹמֶה לָּךְ, מֶלֶךְ
מֵמִית וּמְחַיֶּה וּמַצְמִיחַ יְשׁוּעָה:

Mechalkel chayyim b'chesed, m'chayeh meitim b'rachamim rabim, somech noflim, v'rofeh cholim, umatir asurim, um'kayem emunato lishenei afar. Mi chamocha ba'al gevurot? U-mi domeh lach? Melech meimit u'm'chayeh, umatzmiach yeshuah.

מִי כָמוֹךְ אַב הָרַחֲמִים, זוֹכֵר
יְצוּרָיו לְחַיִּים בְּרַחֲמִים:

Mi chamocha av harachaman, zocheir yetzurav l'chayyim b'rachamim.

וְנֶאֱמָן אַתָּה לְהַחֲיוֹת מֵתִים.
בָּרוּךְ אַתָּה יְיָ, מְחַיֵּה הַמֵּתִים:

V'ne'eman atah le'ha-chayot meitim. Baruch atah Adonai, mechayeh hameitim.

You sustain the living with kindness, in Your great mercy You bestow eternal life. You support the fallen, heal the sick, and free the captive. You keep Your faith with us beyond life and death. There is none like You, our source of strength, the ruler of life and death, the source of our redemption.

Who is like You, source of mercy, Who mercifully remembers Your creatures for life?

Our faith is with You, the God Who brings eternal life.
Blessed are You, Adonai, Who gives life which transcends death.

Kidushat Hashem: Making the Name Holy

You are holy,
and Your name is holy,
and holy ones praise You
always, *selah*.

אַתָּה קָדוֹשׁ וְשִׁמְךָ קָדוֹשׁ
וּקְדוֹשִׁים בְּכָל יוֹם יְהַלְלוּךָ,
סֶלָה.

And so
May fear and concern
be instilled in all living beings,
deep concern for all created.
All creation should be in awe,
all of life humbled before You.
May all of creation form
a single bond to do Your will.
We know that You alone rule
that Your strength is justice
and Your awesome being
transcends all which You
have created.

וּבְכֵן
תֵּן פַּחְדְּךָ יְיָ אֱלֹהֵינוּ, עַל כָּל
מַעֲשֶׂיךָ, וְאֵימָתְךָ עַל כָּל מַה
שֶּׁבָּרָאתָ, וְיִירָאוּךָ כָּל
הַמַּעֲשִׂים וְיִשְׁתַּחֲווּ לְפָנֶיךָ כָּל
הַבְּרוּאִים, וְיֵעָשׂוּ כֻלָּם אֲגֻדָּה
אַחַת לַעֲשׂוֹת רְצוֹנְךָ בְּלֵבָב
שָׁלֵם, כְּמוֹ שֶׁיָּדַעְנוּ יְיָ אֱלֹהֵינוּ,
שֶׁהַשָּׁלְטָן לְפָנֶיךָ, עֹז בְּיָדְךָ
וּגְבוּרָה בִּימִינֶךָ, וְשִׁמְךָ נוֹרָא
עַל כָּל מַה שֶּׁבָּרָאתָ.

And so
May honor be granted
to Your people,
Praise to those who feel awe
and hope
to those who seek You
and voice sincere yearnings.
May there be joy
throughout the land
and joyfulness for the
inhabitants of Your city.
May the light of joy and justice
shine forth in our lifetime.

וּבְכֵן
תֵּן כָּבוֹד, יְיָ לְעַמֶּךָ, תְּהִלָּה
לִירֵאֶיךָ וְתִקְוָה טוֹבָה
לְדוֹרְשֶׁיךָ, וּפִתְחוֹן פֶּה
לַמְיַחֲלִים לָךְ, שִׂמְחָה לְאַרְצֶךָ
וְשָׂשׂוֹן לְעִירֶךָ, וּצְמִיחַת קֶרֶן
לְדָוִד עַבְדֶּךָ, וַעֲרִיכַת נֵר
לְבֶן־יִשַׁי מְשִׁיחֶךָ, בִּמְהֵרָה
בְיָמֵינוּ.

וּבְכֵן
צַדִּיקִים יִרְאוּ וְיִשְׂמָחוּ, וִישָׁרִים
יַעֲלֹזוּ, וַחֲסִידִים בְּרִנָּה יָגִילוּ,
וְעוֹלָתָה תִּקְפָּץ־פִּיהָ, וְכָל
הָרִשְׁעָה כֻּלָּהּ כְּעָשָׁן תִּכְלֶה, כִּי
תַעֲבִיר מֶמְשֶׁלֶת זָדוֹן מִן
הָאָרֶץ.

And so
When such a day arrives
those who struggled for justice
will be first to rejoice;
the upright will be glad;
the faithful will sing with joy;
injustice will close its mouth;
evil will vanish like smoke;
falsehoods will depart from the
earth.

וְתִמְלֹךְ, אַתָּה יְיָ לְבַדֶּךָ, עַל כָּל
מַעֲשֶׂיךָ, בְּהַר צִיּוֹן מִשְׁכַּן
כְּבוֹדֶךָ, וּבִירוּשָׁלַיִם עִיר
קָדְשֶׁךָ, כַּכָּתוּב בְּדִבְרֵי קָדְשֶׁךָ:
יִמְלֹךְ יְיָ לְעוֹלָם, אֱלֹהַיִךְ צִיּוֹן
לְדֹר וָדֹר: הַלְלוּיָהּ.

Sacred Oneness will govern
all things; Mount Zion
will be among Your resting-
places, as will Your holy city,
the city of Shalom, Jerusalem.
As it is written in these holy
words: "Adonai will reign
forever, Your God, O Zion, for
all generations, halleluyah."

קָדוֹשׁ אַתָּה וְנוֹרָא שְׁמֶךָ, וְאֵין
אֱלוֹהַּ מִבַּלְעָדֶיךָ, כַּכָּתוּב:
וַיִּגְבַּהּ יְיָ צְבָאוֹת בַּמִּשְׁפָּט,
וְהָאֵל הַקָּדוֹשׁ נִקְדַּשׁ בִּצְדָקָה.
בָּרוּךְ אַתָּה, יְיָ, הַמֶּלֶךְ הַקָּדוֹשׁ.

You are holy,
Your name is holy
And there is no God besides
You, as it is written:
"The Eternal, the power of all
creation, is elevated through
justice, God's holiness
sanctified through
acts of justice."
Blessed is the Ineffable One,
the sacred Power.

Kidushat Hayom: Sanctifying This Day

אַתָּה בְחַרְתָּֽנוּ עִם כָּל הָעַמִּים,
אָהַֽבְתָּ אוֹתָֽנוּ וְרָצִֽיתָ בָּֽנוּ,
וְרוֹמַמְתָּֽנוּ מִכָּל הַלְּשׁוֹנוֹת,
וְקִדַּשְׁתָּֽנוּ בְּמִצְוֹתֶֽיךָ, וְקֵרַבְתָּֽנוּ
מַלְכֵּֽנוּ לַעֲבוֹדָתֶֽךָ, וְשִׁמְךָ הַגָּדוֹל
וְהַקָּדוֹשׁ עָלֵֽינוּ קָרָֽאתָ.

You have delighted in us
among all of the peoples,
loving us, desiring us,
elevating us and sanctifying us
with mitzvot, drawing us near
to serve You,
that Your great holy Presence
might be known to us.

וַתִּתֶּן לָֽנוּ, יְיָ אֱלֹהֵֽינוּ, בְּאַהֲבָה
אֶת יוֹם (הַשַּׁבָּת הַזֶּה וְאֶת
יוֹם) הַזִּכָּרוֹן הַזֶּה, מִקְרָא
קֹֽדֶשׁ, זֵֽכֶר לִיצִיאַת מִצְרָֽיִם.

With love, we have been given
(on Shabbat: this Shabbat and)
This Day of Remembering,
for renouncing our wrongs,
for asking for forgiveness,
for cleansing, for
reconciliation.

A day of holy gathering
reminding us of our liberation
from enslavement.

Preserving the Spark of Prayer
Likutim Yekarim 15b

When you pray, you are like a bed of coals.
After prayer, as long as a single spark remains,
A great fire can be kindled again.
But if that spark dies, there can be no fire.
Cling to God always,
Even at times when you feel unable to reach God.
This is how you may preserve that single spark,
So that the fire of your soul is never extinguished.

(Rabbi Dov Baer of Mezritch)

Ya'aleh v'yavo: May These Ascend

Our God
and God of our ancestors:
allow memory to ascend,
to come, to reach us.
May our memory
and our ancestors' memory
and the memory of the dream
of a messianic time,
and the memory of the vision
of Jerusalem as a city of peace,
and the memories of all of Your
people of the House of Israel,
be before You.
On this day
may these memories,
these dreams of redemption,
inspire graciousness,
lovingkindness,
and compassion in us,
for life and for peace,
on this Rosh Hashanah.

אֱלֹהֵינוּ
וֵאלֹהֵי אֲבוֹתֵינוּ וְאִמּוֹתֵינוּ,
יַעֲלֶה וְיָבֹא, וְיַגִּיעַ וְיֵרָאֶה,
וְיֵרָצֶה וְיִשָּׁמַע, וְיִפָּקֵד וְיִזָּכֵר
זִכְרוֹנֵנוּ וּפִקְדוֹנֵנוּ,
וְזִכְרוֹן אֲבוֹתֵינוּ וְאִמּוֹתֵינוּ,
וְזִכְרוֹן מָשִׁיחַ בֶּן־דָּוִד עַבְדֶּךָ,
וְזִכְרוֹן יְרוּשָׁלַיִם עִיר קָדְשֶׁךָ,
וְזִכְרוֹן כָּל עַמְּךָ
בֵּית יִשְׂרָאֵל לְפָנֶיךָ
לִפְלֵיטָה וּלְטוֹבָה,
לְחֵן וּלְחֶסֶד וּלְרַחֲמִים, לְחַיִּים
וּלְשָׁלוֹם, בְּיוֹם הַזִּכָּרוֹן הַזֶּה.

זָכְרֵנוּ, יְיָ אֱלֹהֵינוּ בּוֹ לְטוֹבָה,
וּפָקְדֵנוּ בוֹ לִבְרָכָה, וְהוֹשִׁיעֵנוּ
בוֹ לְחַיִּים; וּבִדְבַר יְשׁוּעָה
וְרַחֲמִים חוּס וְחָנֵּנוּ, וְרַחֵם
עָלֵינוּ וְהוֹשִׁיעֵנוּ, כִּי אֵלֶיךָ
עֵינֵינוּ, כִּי אֵל מֶלֶךְ חַנּוּן וְרַחוּם
אָתָּה.

Remember us, Adonai our
God, for goodness. Count us in
for blessing. Save us with life.
Shower us with salvation
and with compassion;
be merciful to us; enfold us
in the compassion we knew
before we were born.
For You are our merciful
parent and our sovereign.

אֱלֹהֵינוּ וֵאלֹהֵי אֲבוֹתֵינוּ, מְלוֹךְ
עַל כָּל הָעוֹלָם כֻּלּוֹ בִּכְבוֹדֶךָ,
וְהִנָּשֵׂא עַל כָּל הָאָרֶץ בִּיקָרֶךָ,
וְהוֹפַע בַּהֲדַר גְּאוֹן עֻזֶּךָ, עַל כָּל
יוֹשְׁבֵי תֵבֵל אַרְצֶךָ, וְיֵדַע כָּל
פָּעוּל כִּי אַתָּה פְעַלְתּוֹ, וְיָבִין
כָּל יָצוּר כִּי אַתָּה יְצַרְתּוֹ,
וְיֹאמַר כֹּל אֲשֶׁר נְשָׁמָה בְּאַפּוֹ,
יְיָ אֱלֹהֵי יִשְׂרָאֵל מֶלֶךְ, וּמַלְכוּתוֹ
בַּכֹּל מָשָׁלָה.

Our God and God of our
generations:
shine Your glory on creation.
Remind us that You cherish
all who live on this earth,
here and everywhere.
You are our Creator;
You formed us; You breathe
life into us in every moment.
You are King/Queen
of all creation.

אֱלֹהֵינוּ וֵאלֹהֵי אֲבוֹתֵינוּ, (רְצֵה
בִמְנוּחָתֵנוּ) קַדְּשֵׁנוּ בְּמִצְוֹתֶיךָ
וְתֵן חֶלְקֵנוּ בְּתוֹרָתֶךָ, שַׂבְּעֵנוּ
מִטּוּבֶךָ וְשַׂמְּחֵנוּ בִּישׁוּעָתֶךָ
(וְהַנְחִילֵנוּ, יְיָ אֱלֹהֵינוּ, בְּאַהֲבָה
וּבְרָצוֹן שַׁבַּת קָדְשֶׁךָ, וְיָנוּחוּ
בָהּ יִשְׂרָאֵל מְקַדְּשֵׁי שְׁמֶךָ.)

Our God and God of our
generations (*Shabbat:* accept
our rest with mercy)
help us make ourselves holy
with Your mitzvot; give us
a portion of Your Torah's
sweetness; grant us
Your goodness, help us rejoice
in Your salvation
(*Shabbat:* and on this Shabbat
which is also a holiday, help us
be mindful of both, and to
wholly rest as befits Your
people who yearn to sanctify
Your name.)

Purify our hearts
to serve You in truth,
for You are God of truth
and Your truth endures
forever. Blessed are You,
Adonai, ruler over all the earth,
Who sanctifies (Shabbat and)
Israel and this Day of
Remembrance.

וְטַהֵר לִבֵּנוּ לְעָבְדְךָ בֶּאֱמֶת, כִּי
אַתָּה אֱלֹהִים אֱמֶת, וּדְבָרְךָ
אֱמֶת וְקַיָּם לָעַד. בָּרוּךְ אַתָּה,
יְיָ, מֶלֶךְ עַל כָּל הָאָרֶץ, מְקַדֵּשׁ
(הַשַּׁבָּת וְ) יִשְׂרָאֵל וְיוֹם
הַזִּכָּרוֹן.

Avodah: Worship

May it be Your will, Adonai our
God, that You accept our rest
and take pleasure in our
prayers. Accept the service of
our hearts and our lips
which we mean to offer in love.
May the offerings of our hearts
always bring You joy in Your
people.

רְצֵה, יְיָ אֱלֹהֵינוּ, בְּעַמְּךָ
יִשְׂרָאֵל וּבִתְפִלָּתָם, בְּאַהֲבָה
תְקַבֵּל וּתְהִי לְרָצוֹן תָּמִיד
עֲבוֹדַת יִשְׂרָאֵל עַמֶּךָ.

May Your presence return to
Zion speedily and with
compassion. Blessed are You,
Adonai, Whose presence
returns to Zion and fills all
creation.

וְתֶחֱזֶינָה עֵינֵינוּ בְּשׁוּבְךָ לְצִיּוֹן
בְּרַחֲמִים. בָּרוּךְ אַתָּה יְיָ,
הַמַּחֲזִיר שְׁכִינָתוֹ לְצִיּוֹן.

Hoda'ah: Giving Thanks

מוֹדִים אֲנַחְנוּ לָךְ, שָׁאַתָּה
הוּא, יְיָ אֱלֹהֵינוּ וֵאלֹהֵי
אֲבוֹתֵינוּ, לְעוֹלָם וָעֶד, צוּר
חַיֵּינוּ, מָגֵן יִשְׁעֵנוּ, אַתָּה הוּא
לְדוֹר וָדוֹר נוֹדֶה לְּךָ וּנְסַפֵּר
תְּהִלָּתֶךָ. עַל חַיֵּינוּ הַמְּסוּרִים
בְּיָדֶךָ, וְעַל נִשְׁמוֹתֵינוּ הַפְּקוּדוֹת
לָךְ, וְעַל נִסֶּיךָ שֶׁבְּכָל יוֹם עִמָּנוּ,
וְעַל נִפְלְאוֹתֶיךָ וְטוֹבוֹתֶיךָ
שֶׁבְּכָל עֵת, עֶרֶב וָבֹקֶר
וְצָהֳרָיִם, הַטּוֹב כִּי לֹא כָלוּ
רַחֲמֶיךָ, וְהַמְרַחֵם כִּי לֹא תַמּוּ
חֲסָדֶיךָ מֵעוֹלָם קִוִּינוּ לָךְ.

We are grateful before You, that You are our God and God of our generations, for ever. You are the rock of our lives, the shield of our salvation; You, only You, from generation to generation we sing praises. For our lives which are in Your keeping; for our souls of which You take daily account; for all of the miracles which You perform for us, and all of the wonders and goodnesses which You bring forth in every era and in every day, evening and morning and afternoon; for the goodness of Your compassion; for all of these things we could never thank You enough.

וְעַל כֻּלָּם יִתְבָּרַךְ וְיִתְרוֹמַם
שִׁמְךָ מַלְכֵּנוּ תָּמִיד לְעוֹלָם וָעֶד.

For all of these we bless and elevate Your name, our Sovereign and Source, forever and ever.

וּכְתוֹב לְחַיִּים טוֹבִים כָּל בְּנֵי
בְרִיתֶךָ.

And we thank You for inscribing us, the children of Your covenant, into the book of life.

וְכֹל הַחַיִּים יוֹדוּךָ סֶּלָה, וִיהַלְלוּ
אֶת שִׁמְךָ בֶּאֱמֶת, הָאֵל
יְשׁוּעָתֵנוּ וְעֶזְרָתֵנוּ סֶלָה. בָּרוּךְ
אַתָּה יְיָ, הַטּוֹב שִׁמְךָ וּלְךָ נָאֶה
לְהוֹדוֹת.

All that lives praises Your name in truth, our God and our help. Blessed are You, Adonai, for Your goodness and for the many wonders which merit our thanks.

Birkat Shalom: Peace

שָׁלוֹם רָב עַל יִשְׂרָאֵל עַמְּךָ
תָּשִׂים לְעוֹלָם, כִּי אַתָּה הוּא
מֶלֶךְ אָדוֹן לְכָל הַשָּׁלוֹם.
וְטוֹב בְּעֵינֶיךָ לְבָרֵךְ אֶת עַמְּךָ
יִשְׂרָאֵל, בְּכָל עֵת וּבְכָל שָׁעָה
בִּשְׁלוֹמֶךָ.

Shalom rav al Yisrael amcha
tasim le'olam, ki atah
hu melech adon l'chol
hashalom. V'tov
b'einecha levarech et amcha
Yisrael, b'chol eit
u'vchol sha'ah bishlomecha.

בְּסֵפֶר חַיִּים, בְּרָכָה וְשָׁלוֹם
וּפַרְנָסָה טוֹבָה, נִזָּכֵר וְנִכָּתֵב
לְפָנֶיךָ, אֲנַחְנוּ וְכָל עַמְּךָ בֵּית
יִשְׂרָאֵל, לְחַיִּים טוֹבִים
וּלְשָׁלוֹם.

B'sefer chayyim, bracha
v'shalom, ufarnasah tovah,
n'zacher v'nikatev l'fanecha,
anachnu v'chol amcha beit
Yisrael, l'chayyim tovim
u'l'shalom.

בָּרוּךְ אַתָּה יְיָ, עוֹשֵׂה הַשָּׁלוֹם.

Baruch atah, Adonai, oseh
ha-shalom.

May there be abundant peace for Israel Your people, always; for You are the sovereign of peace. Let it be good in Your eyes to bless Your people Israel, in every time and in every hour, with Your peace.

In the book of life, blessing, and peace, and of making a good living may we be remembered and written before You: us, and all of Your people in our many communities, for a good life and for peace.

Blessed are You, Adonai, maker of peace.

Meditations After Prayer

אֱלֹהַי, נְצוֹר לְשׁוֹנִי מֵרָע.
וּשְׂפָתַי מִדַּבֵּר מִרְמָה:
וְלִמְקַלְלַי נַפְשִׁי תִדֹּם, וְנַפְשִׁי
כֶּעָפָר לַכֹּל תִּהְיֶה. פְּתַח לִבִּי
בְּתוֹרָתֶךָ, וּבְמִצְוֹתֶיךָ תִּרְדּוֹף
נַפְשִׁי.

Elohai n'tzor l'shoni mera
usfatai m'daber mirmah
v'limkallelai nafshi tidom
v'nafshi ke'afar l'kol tihiyeh.
Petach libi ba-Toratecha,
uv'mitzvotecha tirdof nafshi.

God, keep my tongue from evil
and my lips from speaking deceit.
Before those who slander me, I will hold my tongue;
I will practice humility.
Open my heart to Your Torah,
and connect my heart to Your mitzvot.

יִהְיוּ לְרָצוֹן אִמְרֵי פִי וְהֶגְיוֹן לִבִּי
לְפָנֶיךָ, יְיָ צוּרִי וְגוֹאֲלִי.

Yihiyu l'ratzon imrei fi
v'hegyon libi l'fanecha
Adonai tzuri v'goali.

עֹשֶׂה שָׁלוֹם בִּמְרוֹמָיו הוּא
יַעֲשֶׂה שָׁלוֹם עָלֵינוּ וְעַל כָּל
יִשְׂרָאֵל, וְעַל כָּל יוֹשְׁבֵי תֵבֵל,
וְאִמְרוּ אָמֵן:

Oseh shalom bimromav, hu
ya'aseh shalom, aleinu v'al kol
yisrael, v'al kol yoshvei tevel,
v'imru Amen.

May the words of my mouth
and the meditations of my heart
be acceptable to You, O God,
my rock and my redeemer.

May the One who makes peace in the heavens
make peace for us, for all Israel, and for all who dwell on earth.
And let us say: Amen.

The Kaddish: A Doorway in Prayer

The Kaddish which follows
—known as *Kaddish shalem* (whole Kaddish)—
is the doorway
between the amidah
and our concluding prayers.

Where have tonight's prayers taken you?
Whatever you're feeling in this moment,
bring that into your prayer.

Kaddish Shalem

Yitgadal v'yitkadash, shmeh rabah. B'alma divra chiruteh, v'yamlich malchuteh b'chayyeichon u'v'yomeichon u'vchayyei d'chol beit Yisrael. Ba'agala u-vizman kariv v'imru amen.

יִתְגַּדַּל וְיִתְקַדַּשׁ שְׁמֵהּ רַבָּא.
בְּעָלְמָא דִּי בְרָא כִרְעוּתֵהּ,
וְיַמְלִיךְ מַלְכוּתֵהּ בְּחַיֵּיכוֹן
וּבְיוֹמֵיכוֹן וּבְחַיֵּי דְכָל בֵּית
יִשְׂרָאֵל. בַּעֲגָלָא וּבִזְמַן קָרִיב
וְאִמְרוּ אָמֵן:

☐ Y'hei sh'mei raba m'varakh l'olam ol'almey almaya.

☐ יְהֵא שְׁמֵהּ רַבָּא מְבָרַךְ
לְעָלַם וּלְעָלְמֵי עָלְמַיָּא:

Magnified and sanctified! Magnified and sanctified! May God's Great Name fill the world God created. May God's splendor be seen in the world in your life, in your days, in the life of all Israel. Quickly and soon! And let us say, Amen.

Forever may the Great Name be blessed!

Yitbarach v'yishtabach, v'yitpa'ar v'yit-romam v'yit-naseh. V'yithadar v'yitaleh v'yithallal shmeh d'kud'sha b'rich hu. L'eyla u'leyla min kol birchata v'shirata, tushbechata v'nechemata, damiran b'alma, v'imru amen.

יִתְבָּרַךְ וְיִשְׁתַּבַּח, וְיִתְפָּאַר
וְיִתְרוֹמַם וְיִתְנַשֵּׂא וְיִתְהַדָּר
וְיִתְעַלֶּה וְיִתְהַלָּל שְׁמֵהּ
דְּקֻדְשָׁא בְּרִיךְ הוּא לְעֵלָּא
וּלְעֵלָּא מִכָּל בִּרְכָתָא
וְשִׁירָתָא, תֻּשְׁבְּחָתָא
וְנֶחֱמָתָא, דַּאֲמִירָן בְּעָלְמָא,
וְאִמְרוּ אָמֵן:

Blessed and praised! Splendid and supreme! May the holy name, Bless God, be praised, beyond all the blessings and songs, comforts and consolations, that can be offered in this world. And let us say: Amen.

Titkabel tzlo'uthon uva-ut'hon d'chol beit Yisrael kadam avuhon di vishmaia v'imru Amen.

תִּתְקַבֵּל צְלוֹתְהוֹן וּבָעוּתְהוֹן דְּכָל
(בֵּית) יִשְׂרָאֵל קֳדָם אֲבוּהוֹן דִּי
בִשְׁמַיָּא וְאִמְרוּ אָמֵן:

Y'hei shlama raba min shemaya v'chayyim tovim aleinu v'al kol Yisrael, v'imru amen.

יְהֵא שְׁלָמָא רַבָּא מִן שְׁמַיָּא
וְחַיִּים עָלֵינוּ וְעַל כָּל יִשְׂרָאֵל,
וְאִמְרוּ אָמֵן:

Oseh shalom bimromav, hu ya'aseh shalom, aleinu v'al kol yisrael, v'al kol yoshvei tevel, v'imru Amen.

עֹשֶׂה שָׁלוֹם בִּמְרוֹמָיו הוּא יַעֲשֶׂה
שָׁלוֹם עָלֵינוּ וְעַל כָּל יִשְׂרָאֵל,
וְעַל כָּל יוֹשְׁבֵי תֵבֵל, וְאִמְרוּ אָמֵן:

May our prayers, and the prayers of the entire community, be accepted before You, our Parent.

May there be peace and life, great peace and life from heaven above for us and all Israel. And let us say, Amen!

May the One who makes peace in the high heavens make peace for us, for our whole community, and for all the peoples of the world. And let us say: Amen.

Closing Prayers

And Then, And Then

And then, and then
Both men and women will be gentle
And then, and then
Both women and men will be strong
And then all will be
So varied, rich, and free
And everywhere will be
Called Eden once again.

(Judy Chicago)

About the Aleinu

There has long been dispute in American Jewish communities about the particularistic language of the traditional Aleinu. For some of us, the idea of chosenness is a beacon and a source of pride. For others, it smacks of an outmoded particularism.

Jews are both a unique family, and part of the human family. And divergent opinions have always been part of our culture; our sages teach that both "these and those are the words of the living God."

During these Days of Awe, we honor both impulses: the yearning to experience chosenness, and the yearning to see ourselves as part of the family of all humanity.

In the first paragraph of the Aleinu which follows, there are three asterisks, each marking a place where you may choose to daven either לֹא or לוֹ. The two Hebrew words sound the same *("lo")*, but carry different meanings. In including both options on the page, we aspire toward the day which the Aleinu describes: when God will be One and God's Name One.

Aleinu

☐ Aleinu l'shabe'ach la'adon hakol, latet gedulah l'yotzer breshit. Shelo asanu k'goyei ha'aratzot, v'lo samanu k'mishpachot ha-adamah. Shelo sam chelkenu kahem, v'goralenu k'chol hamonam.

☐ עָלֵינוּ לְשַׁבֵּחַ לַאֲדוֹן הַכֹּל,
לָתֵת גְּדֻלָּה לְיוֹצֵר בְּרֵאשִׁית,
שֶׁלֹּא/שֶׁלּוֹ* עָשָׂנוּ כְּגוֹיֵי
הָאֲרָצוֹת, וְלֹא/וְלוֹ* שָׂמָנוּ
כְּמִשְׁפְּחוֹת הָאֲדָמָה, שֶׁלֹּא/
שֶׁלּוֹ* שָׂם חֶלְקֵנוּ כָּהֶם,
וְגֹרָלֵנוּ כְּכָל הֲמוֹנָם.

It is up to us to praise the Source of all, to exalt the Molder of creation.

We are:		
	made for God like all nations.	not made like other nations.
We are:		
	placed here for God like all humanity.	unlike other peoples.
Our portion and our fate are:		
	for God's own sake.	not like those of other peoples.

☐ Va-anachnu korim, u-mishtachavim u-modim, lifnei melech malchei ham'lachim, hakadosh baruch hu.

☐ וַאֲנַחְנוּ כּוֹרְעִים וּמִשְׁתַּחֲוִים
וּמוֹדִים, לִפְנֵי מֶלֶךְ, מַלְכֵי
הַמְּלָכִים, הַקָּדוֹשׁ בָּרוּךְ הוּא.

We bow low and prostrate in thanks before the Source of all sources, the Holy One, blessed is God.

☐ Shehu noteh shamayim v'yosed aretz, u-moshav yekaro bashamayim mima'al, uschinat uzo b'gavheh meromim. Hu eloheinu, ein od.

☐ שֶׁהוּא נוֹטֶה שָׁמַיִם וְיֹסֵד
אָרֶץ, וּמוֹשַׁב יְקָרוֹ בַּשָּׁמַיִם
מִמַּעַל, וּשְׁכִינַת עֻזּוֹ בְּגָבְהֵי
מְרוֹמִים, הוּא אֱלֹהֵינוּ אֵין
עוֹד.

**Pray either לא, pronounced lo ("not"), or לו, also pronounced lo ("for God"). One articulates Jewish chosenness; the other, post-triumphalism.*

□ אֱמֶת מַלְכֵּנוּ אֶפֶס זוּלָתוֹ,
כַּכָּתוּב בְּתוֹרָתוֹ: וְיָדַעְתָּ הַיּוֹם
וַהֲשֵׁבֹתָ אֶל לְבָבֶךָ, כִּי יְיָ הוּא
הָאֱלֹהִים בַּשָּׁמַיִם מִמַּעַל, וְעַל
הָאָרֶץ מִתָּחַת, אֵין עוֹד:

□ Emet malkenu efes zulato. Kakatuv b'torato: v'yadata hayom vahashevota el levavecha. Ki adonai hu ha-elohim, bashamayim mima'al, v'al ha-aretz mitachat ein od.

God sets out the heavens and establishes the earth. God's honored place is in the heights of our aspirations; God's powerful presence is in the heavens of our hopes. This is our God, there is none else. There is nothing that God is not.

עַל כֵּן נְקַוֶּה לְךָ יְיָ אֱלֹהֵינוּ,
לִרְאוֹת מְהֵרָה בְּתִפְאֶרֶת עֻזֶּךָ,
לְהַעֲבִיר גִּלּוּלִים מִן הָאָרֶץ
וְהָאֱלִילִים כָּרוֹת יִכָּרֵתוּן. לְתַקֵּן
עוֹלָם בְּמַלְכוּת שַׁדַּי, וְכָל בְּנֵי
בָשָׂר יִקְרְאוּ בִשְׁמֶךָ. לְהַפְנוֹת
אֵלֶיךָ כָּל רִשְׁעֵי אָרֶץ. יַכִּירוּ
וְיֵדְעוּ כָּל יוֹשְׁבֵי תֵבֵל, כִּי לְךָ
תִּכְרַע כָּל בֶּרֶךְ תִּשָּׁבַע כָּל לָשׁוֹן:

Al kein nekaveh lecha Adonai Eloheinu, lirot meheirah betiferet uzecha, leha'avir gilulim min ha'arets veha'elilim karot yikareitun letakein olam bemalchut shadai. Vechol benei asar yikre'u vishmecha. Lehafnot eilecha kol rishei arets. Yakiru veyeidu kol yoshvei teiveil kee lecha tichra kol berech tishava kol lashon.

Therefore we hope in You, Adonai our God, to see soon the power of Your beauty wipe away false gods from the earth and sweep away idolatry, so that the truth of Your sovereign presence will repair the world. Then will all humanity call Your name and then all that had been dark will turn to Your light. All who dwell on earth will feel in their hearts and know in their minds that You are our source—the true object of devotion and loyalty.

Lefanecha Adonai Eloheinu yichre'u veyipolu velichvod shimcha yekar yiteinu. Vikabelu chulam et ol malchutecha. Vetimloch aleihem meheirah le'olam va'ed. Kee hamalchut shelcha hee, ulolmei ad timloch bechavod.	לְפָנֶיךָ יְיָ אֱלֹהֵינוּ יִכְרְעוּ וְיִפֹּלוּ. וְלִכְבוֹד שִׁמְךָ יְקָר יִתֵּנוּ. וִיקַבְּלוּ כֻלָּם אֶת עוֹל מַלְכוּתֶךָ. וְתִמְלֹךְ עֲלֵיהֶם מְהֵרָה לְעוֹלָם וָעֶד. כִּי הַמַּלְכוּת שֶׁלְּךָ הִיא, וּלְעוֹלְמֵי עַד תִּמְלוֹךְ בְּכָבוֹד:

Before You, Adonai our God, will they bend low and pay homage to glorify Your name. Then all will accept the obligations of living in Your world— obligations of hope, love and duty to heaven and humanity. Then You will surely rule forever and ever. For the earth is Yours and Your glory fills it forever.

□ Kakatuv b'toratecha, Adonai yimloch leolam vaed. V'ne-emar, v'haya Adonai l'melech al kol ha-aretz. Bayom hahu yiheh Adonai echad, ushmo echad!	□ כַּכָּתוּב בְּתוֹרָתֶךָ, יְיָ יִמְלֹךְ לְעוֹלָם וָעֶד: וְנֶאֱמַר, וְהָיָה יְיָ לְמֶלֶךְ עַל כָּל הָאָרֶץ, בַּיּוֹם הַהוּא יִהְיֶה יְיָ אֶחָד, וּשְׁמוֹ אֶחָד.

As it is written in God's sacred teaching: "You shall know this day and place upon your heart that Adonai is God in heaven above and earth below; there is none else."

Then shall your realm be established on earth, and the word of Your prophet fulfilled: "Adonai will reign forever and ever. On that day, Adonai shall be One, and God's name shall be One."

Every Person Has a Name

Every person has a name
given by God
given by her parents

Every person has a name
given by his appearance
given by her clothes

Every person has a name
given by the mountains
and given by his walls.

Every person has a name
given by the stars
given by her neighbors

Every person has a name
given by his sins
given by her yearning

Every person has a name
given by his enemies,
given by her love.

Every person has a name
given by his holidays,
given by her toil.

Every person has a name
given by the seasons,
given by his blindness.

Every person has a name
given by the sea,
given by her death.

(Zelda Schneersohn Mishkovsky)

לְכָל אִישׁ יֵשׁ שֵׁם
שֶׁנָּתַן לוֹ אֱלֹהִים
וְנָתְנוּ לוֹ אָבִיו וְאִמּוֹ

לְכָל אִישׁ יֵשׁ שֵׁם
שֶׁנָּתְנוּ לוֹ קוֹמָתוֹ וְאֹפֶן חִיּוּכוֹ
וְנָתַן לוֹ הָאָרִיג

לְכַל אִישׁ יֵשׁ שֵׁם
שֶׁנָּתְנוּ לוֹ הֶהָרִים
וְנָתְנוּ לוֹ כְּתָלָיו

לְכָל אִישׁ יֵשׁ שֵׁם
שֶׁנָּתְנוּ לוֹ הַמַּזָּלוֹת
וְנָתְנוּ לוֹ שְׁכֵנָיו

לְכָל אִישׁ יֵשׁ שֵׁם
שֶׁנָּתְנוּ לוֹ חֲטָאָיו
וְנָתְנָה לוֹ כְּמִיהָתוֹ

לְכַל אִישׁ יֵשׁ שֵׁם
שֶׁנָּתְנוּ לוֹ שׂוֹנְאָיו
וְנָתְנָה לוֹ אַהֲבָתוֹ

לְכַל אִישׁ יֵשׁ שֵׁם
שֶׁנָּתְנוּ לוֹ חַגָּיו
וְנָתְנָה לוֹ מְלַאכְתּוֹ

לְכַל אִישׁ יֵשׁ שֵׁם
שֶׁנָּתְנוּ לוֹ תְּקוּפוֹת הַשָּׁנָה
וְנָתַן לוֹ עִוְרוֹנוֹ

לְכָל אִישׁ יֵשׁ שֵׁם
שֶׁנָּתַן לוֹ הַיָּם
וְנָתַן לוֹ מוֹתוֹ.

Mourner's *Kaddish*

Yitgadal v'yitkadash, shmeh rabah. B'alma di vra chiruteh, v'yamlich malchuteh b'chayyeichon u'v'yomeichon u'vchayyei d'chol beit Yisrael. Ba'agala u-vizman kariv v'imru amen.

□Y'hei sh'mei raba m'varakh l'olam ol'almey almaya.

Yitbarach v'yishtabach, v'yitpa'ar v'yit-romam v'yit-naseh. V'yithadar v'yitaleh v'yithallal shmeh d'kudh'sha b'rich hu. L'eyla u-l'eyla min kol birchata v'shirata, tushbechata v'nechemata, damiran b'alma, v'imru amen.

Y'hei shlama raba min shemaya v'chayyim tovim aleinu v'al kol Yisrael, v'imru amen.
Oseh shalom bimromav, hu ya'aseh shalom, aleinu v'al kol yisrael, v'al kol yoshvei tevel, v'imru Amen.

יִתְגַּדַּל וְיִתְקַדַּשׁ שְׁמֵהּ רַבָּא. בְּעָלְמָא דִּי בְרָא כִרְעוּתֵהּ, וְיַמְלִיךְ מַלְכוּתֵהּ בְּחַיֵּיכוֹן וּבְיוֹמֵיכוֹן וּבְחַיֵּי דְכָל בֵּית יִשְׂרָאֵל.
בַּעֲגָלָא וּבִזְמַן קָרִיב וְאִמְרוּ אָמֵן:

□ יְהֵא שְׁמֵהּ רַבָּא מְבָרַךְ לְעָלַם וּלְעָלְמֵי עָלְמַיָּא:

יִתְבָּרַךְ וְיִשְׁתַּבַּח, וְיִתְפָּאַר וְיִתְרוֹמַם וְיִתְנַשֵּׂא וְיִתְהַדָּר וְיִתְעַלֶּה וְיִתְהַלָּל שְׁמֵהּ דְּקֻדְשָׁא בְּרִיךְ הוּא לְעֵלָּא וּלְעֵלָּא מִן כָּל בִּרְכָתָא וְשִׁירָתָא, תֻּשְׁבְּחָתָא וְנֶחֱמָתָא, דַּאֲמִירָן בְּעָלְמָא, וְאִמְרוּ אָמֵן:

יְהֵא שְׁלָמָא רַבָּא מִן שְׁמַיָּא וְחַיִּים עָלֵינוּ וְעַל כָּל יִשְׂרָאֵל, וְאִמְרוּ אָמֵן:
עֹשֶׂה שָׁלוֹם בִּמְרוֹמָיו הוּא יַעֲשֶׂה שָׁלוֹם עָלֵינוּ וְעַל כָּל יִשְׂרָאֵל, וְעַל כָּל יוֹשְׁבֵי תֵבֵל, וְאִמְרוּ אָמֵן:

Magnified and sanctified! Magnified and sanctified! May God's Great Name fill the world God created. May God's splendor be seen in the world in your life, in your days, in the life of all Israel. Quickly and soon! And let us say, Amen.

Forever may the Great Name be blessed!

Blessed and praised! Splendid and supreme! May the holy name, Bless God, be praised, far beyond all the blessings and songs, comforts and consolations, that can be offered in this world. And let us say: Amen.

May there be peace and life, great peace and life from heaven above for us and all Israel. And let us say, Amen!

May the One who makes peace in the high heavens make peace for us, for our whole community, and for all the peoples of the world. And let us say: Amen.

from Psalm 27

□ Achat sha'alti me'eit Adonai,
otah avakesh

Shivti b'veit Adonai,
kol y'mei chayyay

Lachazot b'noam Adonai,
u'l'vaker b'heikhalo

□ אַחַת שָׁאַלְתִּי מֵאֵת-יְיָ
אוֹתָהּ אֲבַקֵּשׁ:

שִׁבְתִּי בְּבֵית-יְיָ,
כָּל-יְמֵי חַיַּי;

לַחֲזוֹת בְּנֹעַם-יְיָ,
וּלְבַקֵּר בְּהֵיכָלוֹ.

□ One thing I ask, I ask of You
I earnestly pray for:
That I might dwell in Your house
all the days of my life
Knowing the beauty, the beauty of You
and to dwell in Your holy place!

This is an abbreviated psalm 27. The full psalm can be found on p.246.

from Psalm 34

□ Mi ha-ish hechafeitz chayim,
oheiv yamim lirot tov.
Netzor leshoncha meira
usfatecha midabeir mirmah.
Sur meirah va'aseih tov
bakeish shalom veradfeihu.

□ מִי-הָאִישׁ, הֶחָפֵץ חַיִּים;
אֹהֵב יָמִים, לִרְאוֹת טוֹב.
נְצֹר לְשׁוֹנְךָ מֵרָע;
וּשְׂפָתֶיךָ מִדַּבֵּר מִרְמָה.
סוּר מֵרָע וַעֲשֵׂה-טוֹב;
בַּקֵּשׁ שָׁלוֹם וְרָדְפֵהוּ.

Who shall delight in life?
Those who love every day and see the good.
Guard your tongue from evil,
Your lips from speaking deceit.
Shun evil and do good.
Seek peace and pursue it.

Kiddush

Baruch atah, Adonai, eloheynu melech ha'olam, asher bakhar banu im kol ha-amim, v'rom'manu im kol lashon, v'kidshanu b'mitzvotav. Va-titen lanu Adonai eloheynu, b'ahavah (shabatot limnucha u-) mo'adim l'simkha, hagim u-z'manim l'sason, et yom (ha-(shabbat hazeh v'et yom) ha-zikaron hazeh, z'man cheruteinu, (b'ahavah) mikra kodesh, zecher l'tziat mitzrayim. Ki vanu vacharta, v'otanu kidashta, im kol ha'amim u-moadim kadshekha (b'ahavah uvratzon) v'simcha uv-sason hin-khaltanu. Baruch atah, melech al kol ha-aretz, m'kadesh (ha-shabbat v') Yisrael v'yom ha-zikaron.

בָּרוּךְ אַתָּה יְיָ, אֱלֹהֵינוּ מֶלֶךְ
הָעוֹלָם, אֲשֶׁר בָּחַר בָּנוּ עִם
כָּל הָעַמִּים, וְרוֹמְמָנוּ עִם כָּל-
לָשׁוֹן, וְקִדְּשָׁנוּ בְּמִצְוֹתָיו,
וַתִּתֶּן-לָנוּ יְיָ אֱלֹהֵינוּ בְּאַהֲבָה
(שַׁבָּתוֹת לִמְנוּחָה וּ)מוֹעֲדִים
לְשִׂמְחָה, חַגִּים וּזְמַנִּים לְשָׂשׂוֹן
אֶת-יוֹם (הַשַּׁבָּת הַזֶּה וְאֶת
יוֹם) הַזִּכָּרוֹן הַזֶּה. זְמַן
חֵרוּתֵנוּ, (בְּאַהֲבָה,) מִקְרָא
קֹדֶשׁ, זֵכֶר לִיצִיאַת מִצְרָיִם.
כִּי בָנוּ בָחַרְתָּ וְאוֹתָנוּ קִדַּשְׁתָּ
עִם כָּל-הָעַמִּים. (וְשַׁבָּת)
וּמוֹעֲדֵי קָדְשֶׁךָ (בְּאַהֲבָה
וּבְרָצוֹן) בְּשִׂמְחָה וּבְשָׂשׂוֹן
הִנְחַלְתָּנוּ: בָּרוּךְ אַתָּה יְיָ,
מֶלֶךְ עַל כָּל הָאָרֶץ, מְקַדֵּשׁ
(בשבת הַשַּׁבָּת וְ) יִשְׂרָאֵל
וְיוֹם הַזִּכָּרוֹן.

We praise You, Sovereign of Existence! You have called us for service along with other peoples, and have hallowed our lives with commandments. In love You have given us (Shabbat and) festivals for rejoicing, seasons of celebration, including this (Shabbat and this) Day of Remembrance, the time of our freedom, a commemoration of the Exodus from Egypt. Praised are You, our Eternal God, Who gave us this joyful heritage, sovereign of all Who sanctifies (Shabbat and) Israel and this Day of Remembrance.

□ Baruch atah, Adonai, eloheinu melech ha'olam, borei p'ri hagafen.	□ בָּרוּךְ אַתָּה יְיָ, אֱלֹהֵינוּ מֶלֶךְ הָעוֹלָם, בּוֹרֵא פְּרִי הַגָּפֶן.

Blessed are you, Adonai our God, Ruler of the Universe, creator of the fruit of the vine.

When the first or second Rosh Hashanah evening falls on Saturday night, the kiddush continues with modified havdalah. We bless the lights of fire, looking at the holiday candles we already lit this evening. We do not inhale sweet spices, nor do we extinguish the candle in juice or wine.

בָּרוּךְ אַתָּה יְיָ אֱלֹהֵינוּ מֶלֶךְ
הָעוֹלָם, בּוֹרֵא מְאוֹרֵי הָאֵשׁ.

Baruch Atah Adonai eloheinu melech ha-olam borei me-orey ha-esh.

Blessed are you, Adonai our God, the sovereign of all worlds, who creates the lights of fire.

בָּרוּךְ אַתָּה יְיָ, אֱלֹהֵינוּ מֶלֶךְ
הָעוֹלָם, הַמַּבְדִּיל בֵּין קֹדֶשׁ
לְחוֹל, בֵּין אוֹר לְחֹשֶׁךְ, בֵּין
יִשְׂרָאֵל לָעַמִּים, בֵּין יוֹם
הַשְּׁבִיעִי, לְשֵׁשֶׁת יְמֵי הַמַּעֲשֶׂה:
בֵּין קְדֻשַּׁת שַׁבָּת לִקְדֻשַּׁת יוֹם
טוֹב הִבְדַּלְתָּ, וְאֶת יוֹם
הַשְּׁבִיעִי מִשֵּׁשֶׁת יְמֵי הַמַּעֲשֶׂה
קִדַּשְׁתָּ, הִבְדַּלְתָּ וְקִדַּשְׁתָּ אֶת
עַמְּךָ יִשְׂרָאֵל בִּקְדֻשָּׁתֶךָ. בָּרוּךְ
אַתָּה יְיָ הַמַּבְדִּיל בֵּין קֹדֶשׁ
לְקֹדֶשׁ.

Baruch Atah Adonai eloheinu melech ha-olam hamavdil beyn kodesh lechol, beyn or le choshech, beyn kedushat Shabbat likdushat Yom Tov hivdalta, v'et yom ha-shvi'i misheshet y'mei ha-ma'aseh kidashta, hivdalta v'kidashta et amecha Yisrael bikdushatecha. Baruch Atah Adonai eloheinu melech ha-olam hamavdil beyn kodesh l'kodesh.

Blessed are You, Adonai our God, the sovereign of all worlds, who separates between holy and ordinary, light and dark, the holiness of Shabbat and the holiness of holidays, and between Shabbat and ordinary time: You have created these divisions and have made us holy through the commandment to notice them. Blessed are you, Adonai, who separates holy time from other holy time.

Rosh Hashanah

Rosh HaShanah never comes at the right time;
It is always too early or too late.
Who can remember exactly when
The wheels of our Jewish year
Intersect the cycles of secular time
And interrupt our worldly life?

Rosh HaShanah never comes at the right time;
Sneaking in right at the end of summer
After vacation and as school begins,
Or hanging around in the background
Only to arrive just after our autumnal schedule has been set.

Rosh HaShanah always comes before we are ready
To put aside our past and lay our burdens down.
There is always something else to do:
Another job, another client, laundry to fold, a room to paint.
Rosh HaShanah always catches us by surprise.
Showing up with a Shofar blast
And a chorus of angels proclaiming,
"*Hinei Yom HaDin!*"
"The New Year is here – Judgment Day has arrived."
An unexpected summons,
Like being called to the principal's office
Or an audit from the IRS.

So we stop, turn and listen
To the arresting voice within and around us
And gather together and pray
For peace and for blessings.

(Rabbi Lewis Eron)

Yigdal

יִגְדַּל אֱלֹהִים חַי וְיִשְׁתַּבַּח,
נִמְצָא, וְאֵין עֵת אֶל מְצִיאוּתוֹ:
אֶחָד וְאֵין יָחִיד כְּיִחוּדוֹ, נֶעְלָם,
וְגַם אֵין סוֹף לְאַחְדּוּתוֹ:

Yigdal Elohim chai ve-yishtabach / nimtsah ve'ein eit el metsi'uto / Echad ve'ein yachid keyichudo / nelam vegam ein sof le'achduto.

Exalt the living God, who is unbounded by time.
God is One—unique, unknowable and endless.

אֵין לוֹ דְּמוּת הַגּוּף וְאֵינוֹ גוּף, לֹא
נַעֲרוֹךְ אֵלָיו קְדֻשָּׁתוֹ: קַדְמוֹן לְכָל
דָּבָר אֲשֶׁר נִבְרָא, רִאשׁוֹן וְאֵין
רֵאשִׁית לְרֵאשִׁיתוֹ:

Ein lo damut haguf ve'eino guf / lo na'aroch eilav ke-dushato. / Kadmon lechol davar asher nivra / rishon ve'ein reishit lereishito.

God has no body or form, only holiness beyond measure.
God existed uniquely before a single thing was created.

הִנּוֹ אֲדוֹן עוֹלָם, לְכָל נוֹצָר.
יוֹרֶה גְדֻלָּתוֹ וּמַלְכוּתוֹ:
שֶׁפַע נְבוּאָתוֹ נְתָנוֹ, אֶל
אַנְשֵׁי סְגוּלָּתוֹ וְתִפְאַרְתּוֹ:

Hino adon olam lechol not-sar, / yoreh gedulato umalchuto. / Shefa nevu'ato netano, el / anshei segulato vetifarto.

Behold, the universe is God's, and everything in it.
God's wisdom flows to those who seek God's splendor.

לֹא קָם בְּיִשְׂרָאֵל כְּמֹשֶׁה עוֹד,
נָבִיא וּמַבִּיט אֶת תְּמוּנָתוֹ:
תּוֹרַת אֱמֶת נָתַן לְעַמּוֹ, אֵל,
עַל יַד נְבִיאוֹ נֶאֱמַן בֵּיתוֹ:

Lo kam b'Yisrael k'Mosheh od, / navi umabit et temuna-to. / Torat emet natan le'amo Eil, / al yad nevi'o ne'eman beito.

No prophet like Moses shall ever come again,
Through him God gave us the Torah of truth.

Lo yachalif ha'eil velo yamir dato, / le'olamim lezulato. / Tzofeh veyodei'a setareinu, / mabit lesof davar b'kadmato.

לֹא יַחֲלִיף הָאֵל וְלֹא יָמִיר דָּתוֹ.
לְעוֹלָמִים, לְזוּלָתוֹ:
צוֹפֶה וְיוֹדֵעַ סְתָרֵינוּ,
מַבִּיט לְסוֹף דָּבָר בְּקַדְמָתוֹ:

God's truth is eternal and God's law is irreplaceable.
God knows our hidden places and sees from beginning to end.

Gomeil le'ish chesed kemifalo, / notein lerasha ra kerishato. / Yishlach lekeits hayamin meshicheinu, / lifdot mechakei keits yeshuato.

גּוֹמֵל לְאִישׁ חֶסֶד כְּמִפְעָלוֹ, נוֹתֵן
לְרָשָׁע רָע כְּרִשְׁעָתוֹ:
יִשְׁלַח לְקֵץ הַיָּמִין מְשִׁיחֵנוּ,
לִפְדּוֹת מְחַכֵּי קֵץ יְשׁוּעָתוֹ:

God accords good and bad according to our deeds,
God will send redemption to all who yearn to be redeemed.

Meitim yechayeh Eil
berov chasdo.
Baruch adei ad
sheim tehilato!

מֵתִים יְחַיֶּה אֵל
בְּרוֹב חַסְדּוֹ,
בָּרוּךְ עֲדֵי עַד
שֵׁם תְּהִלָּתוֹ!

With love, God gives life which transcends death.
Blessed is God's name, God be blessed for all eternity.

This hymn is based on Maimonides' 13 Articles of Faith; this version was written by Daniel ben Judah Dayan, and was completed in 1404.

Blessing

יְהִי רָצוֹן מִלְּפָנֶיךָ, יְיָ אֱלֹהֵינוּ וֵאלֹהֵי אֲבוֹתֵינוּ,
שֶׁתְּחַדֵּשׁ עָלֵינוּ שָׁנָה טוֹבָה וּמְתוּקָה.

May it be Your will, Adonai our God and God of our ancestors,
that this new year be renewed for us as a year of sweetness.

Amen!

May it be Your will that _____ be a year of joy!

Amen!

May this be a year of deep connections
Between us and each other, and between us and You.

Amen!

May this be a year of learning, new insights, new ideas.
May this be a year of transformation, healing, and compassion.

Amen!

May our hearts be opened to receive Your blessing,
Today and every day. And we say together:

Amen!

Closing chant

L'shanah tovah
tikatevu v'techatemu!

לְשָׁנָה טוֹבָה
תִּכָּתֵבוּ וְתֵחָתֵמוּ!

May we all be inscribed for a good and sweet year!

Apples and honey

Baruch atah Adonai eloheinu melech ha'olam, borei pri ha-etz.

בָּרוּךְ אַתָּה יְיָ אֱלֹהֵינוּ מֶלֶךְ
הָעוֹלָם, בּוֹרֵא פְּרִי הָעֵץ.

Blessed are You, Adonai our God, source of all being, creator of the fruit of the tree.

Morning Service for Rosh Hashanah and Yom Kippur

Blessing for Gratitude

□ Modeh/modah* ani lefanecha, melech chai vekayam, shehechezarta bee nishmati bechemlah. Raba emunatecha.

□ מודה* אֲנִי לְפָנֶיךָ, מֶלֶךְ חַי וְקַיָּם, שֶׁהֶחֱזַרְתָּ בִּי נִשְׁמָתִי בְּחֶמְלָה. רַבָּה אֱמוּנָתֶךָ!

I am grateful before You,
living and enduring God:
You have restored my soul to me.
Great is Your faithfulness!

**Hebrew is a gendered language; men say* modeh *and women say* modah.

Putting on the Tallit

בָּרְכִי נַפְשִׁי אֶת יְיָ, יְיָ אֱלֹהַי
גָּדַלְתָּ מְּאֹד. הוֹד וְהָדָר לָבָשְׁתָּ,
עֹטֶה אוֹר כַּשַּׂלְמָה. נוֹטֶה
שָׁמַיִם כַּיְרִיעָה.

Barchi nafshi et Adonai,
Adonai Elohai gedalta me'od.
Hod vehadar lavashta, oteh or kasalmah.
Noteh shamayim kayeri'ah.

בָּרוּךְ אַתָּה יְיָ אֱלֹהֵינוּ מֶלֶךְ
הָעוֹלָם אֲשֶׁר קִדְּשָׁנוּ בְּמִצְוֹתָיו
וְצִוָּנוּ לְהִתְעַטֵּף
בַּצִּיצִת.

Baruch atah Adonai Eloheinu
melech ha'olam asher
kideshanu bemitsvotav
vetsivanu lehitateif batsitsit.

My soul will bless Adonai!
Adonai, my God, You are very great.
You are dressed in glory and splendor,
Wearing light like a gown.
You spread out the heavens like a cloth.

Blessed are You, Adonai our God, source of all being,
Who sanctifies us with mitzvot
and Who enjoins us to wrap ourselves with tzitzit.

Shekhinah, wrap Your arms around me
like a mother's embrace

stroke my hair, press a kiss
to my tender forehead

settle around my shoulders
like a royal mantle

help me remember
You are as close as my beating heart

(Rabbi Rachel Barenblat)

Mah Tovu : How Lovely Are Your Tents!

□ Mah tovu ohalecha Ya'akov, mishkenotecha Yisrael. // Va'ani berov chasdecha avo veitecha, eshtachaveh el heichal kodshecha beyiratecha. // Adonai ahavti me'od beitecha, umkom mishkan kevodecha. // Va'ani eshtachaveh ve'echra'ah, evrechah lifnei Adonai osi. // Va'ani tefilati lecha Adonai eit ratson, // Elohim berov chasdecha, aneini be'emet yishecha.

□ מַה טֹּבוּ אֹהָלֶיךָ יַעֲקֹב, מִשְׁכְּנֹתֶיךָ
יִשְׂרָאֵל.

וַאֲנִי בְּרֹב חַסְדְּךָ אָבוֹא בֵיתֶךָ,
אֶשְׁתַּחֲוֶה אֶל הֵיכַל קָדְשְׁךָ בְּיִרְאָתֶךָ.

יְיָ אָהַבְתִּי מְעוֹן בֵּיתֶךָ,
וּמְקוֹם מִשְׁכַּן כְּבוֹדֶךָ.

וַאֲנִי אֶשְׁתַּחֲוֶה וְאֶכְרָעָה,
אֶבְרְכָה לִפְנֵי יְיָ עֹשִׂי.

וַאֲנִי, תְפִלָּתִי לְךָ יְיָ, עֵת רָצוֹן,
אֱלֹהִים בְּרָב חַסְדֶּךָ, עֲנֵנִי בֶּאֱמֶת
יִשְׁעֶךָ.

How lovely are your tents, O Jacob;
your dwellings, O Israel.

I enter Your house, filled with Your overflowing love.
I bow down to Your holy Temple in awe.

Adonai, how much do I love Your house,
the place where Your glory dwells.

I bow low and prostrate myself,
blessing Adonai, my maker.

I offer this prayer at this moment
to You, Adonai.

God, abundant in love,
answer me with Your redemption!

Asher Yatzar : Blessing for the Body

בָּרוּךְ אַתָּה יְיָ אֱלֹהֵינוּ מֶלֶךְ
הָעוֹלָם, אֲשֶׁר יָצַר אֶת הָאָדָם
בְּחָכְמָה, וּבָרָא בוֹ נְקָבִים
נְקָבִים, חֲלוּלִים חֲלוּלִים, גָּלוּי
וְיָדוּעַ לִפְנֵי כִסֵּא כְבוֹדֶךָ שֶׁאִם
יִפָּתֵחַ אֶחָד מֵהֶם, אוֹ יִסָּתֵם
אֶחָד מֵהֶם, אִי אֶפְשַׁר
לְהִתְקַיֵּם וְלַעֲמוֹד לְפָנֶיךָ:

Baruch atah Adonai Eloheinu melech ha'olam, asher yatzar et ha'adam bechochmah uvara vo nekavim nekavim chalulim chalulim. Galui veyadua lifnei chisei chevodecha she'im yipate'ach echad meihem o yisateim echad meihem ee efshar lehitkayeim vela'amod lefanecha.

בָּרוּךְ אַתָּה יְיָ, רוֹפֵא כָל בָּשָׂר,
וּמַפְלִיא לַעֲשׂוֹת:

Baruch atah Adonai rofei chol basar umafli la'asot.

Blessed are You, Adonai our God, source of all being,
Who formed the human body with wisdom
and Who placed within us a miraculous combination
of organs and arteries, tissues and sinews.
Clearly, we would not be able to praise Your miracles
were it not for the miracle within us.
Blessed are You, Adonai,
healer of all flesh and worker of miracles.

Elohai Neshama: Blessing for the Soul

□ Elohai neshamah shenatata bee tehorah hee!

□ אֱלֹהַי, נְשָׁמָה שֶׁנָּתַתָּ בִּי
טְהוֹרָה הִיא.

Atah veratah atah yetsartah atah nefachtah bee ve'atah meshamerah bekirbi ve'atah atid litelah mimeni ulhachazirah bee le'atid lavo. Kol zeman shehaneshamah vekirbi modeh/modah* ani lefanecha Adonai Elohai v'Elohei avotai ve'imotai ribon kol hama'asim adon kol haneshamot.

אַתָּה בְרָאתָהּ, אַתָּה יְצַרְתָּהּ,
אַתָּה נְפַחְתָּהּ בִּי, וְאַתָּה
מְשַׁמְּרָהּ בְּקִרְבִּי, וְאַתָּה עָתִיד
לִטְּלָהּ מִמֶּנִּי, וּלְהַחֲזִירָהּ בִּי
לֶעָתִיד לָבוֹא. כָּל זְמַן
שֶׁהַנְּשָׁמָה בְקִרְבִּי, מודה* אֲנִי
לְפָנֶיךָ, יְיָ אֱלֹהַי וֵאלֹהֵי אֲבוֹתַי
וְאִמּוֹתַי, רִבּוֹן כָּל הַמַּעֲשִׂים,
אֲדוֹן כָּל הַנְּשָׁמוֹת.

Baruch atah Adonai hamachazir neshamot lifgarim meitim.

בָּרוּךְ אַתָּה יְיָ, הַמַּחֲזִיר נְשָׁמוֹת
לִפְגָרִים מֵתִים.

My God, the soul that You have placed within me is pure!

You created it, You formed it, You breathed it into me, You protect it within me, and, someday, You will take it from me to return it in a time beyond time. As long as this soul is within me I shall thank You, Adonai my God and God of my ancestors, author of every action, creator of every soul.

Blessed are You, Adonai, who protects our souls beyond life and death.

**Hebrew is a gendered language; men say* modeh *and women say* modah.

from Daily Miracles

You teach me to distinguish waking life from dreaming.
You press the wooden floor against the soles of my feet.

You slip my eyeglasses into my questing hand
and the world comes into focus again.

Every morning you remake me in your image
and free me to push back against my fears.

You are the balance that holds up my spine,
the light in my gritty, grateful eyes.

(*Rabbi Rachel Barenblat*)

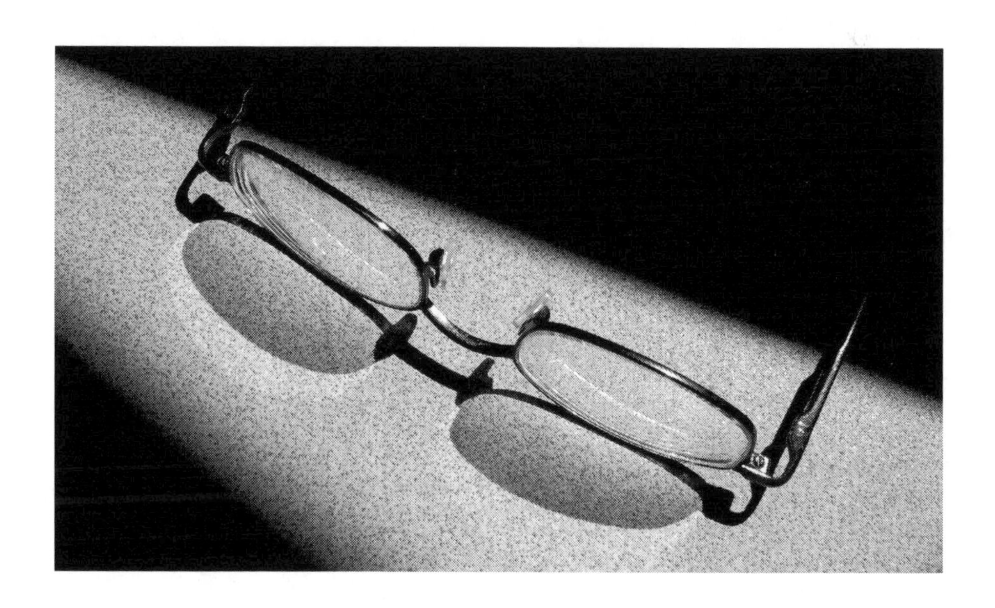

Blessings for Each Day

Baruch atah Adonai, eloheinu
melech ha'olam:

בָּרוּךְ אַתָּה יְיָ אֱלֹהֵינוּ
מֶלֶךְ הָעוֹלָם:

Blessed are You, Adonai our God, Source of all being:

...asher natan l'sechvei vinah
l'havchin bein yom u-vein laila.

...אֲשֶׁר נָתַן לַשֶּׂכְוִי בִינָה,
לְהַבְחִין בֵּין יוֹם וּבֵין לָיְלָה:

...Who gives the bird of dawn discernment to tell day from night;

...she'asani Yisrael.

...שֶׁעָשַׂנִי יִשְׂרָאֵל:

... Who made me a Jew;

...she'asani ben/bat chorin.

...שֶׁעָשַׂנִי בֵּן/בַּת חורין:

... Who made me free;

...she'asani b'tzalmo/ah.

...שֶׁעָשַׂנִי בְּצַלְמוֹ/ה:

... Who made me in Your image;

...poke'ach ivrim.

...פּוֹקֵחַ עִוְרִים:

... Who opens the eyes of the blind;

...malbish arumim.

...מַלְבִּישׁ עֲרֻמִּים:

... Who clothes the naked;

...matir asurim.

...מַתִּיר אֲסוּרִים:

... Who frees the captive;

...zokef kefufim.

...זוֹקֵף כְּפוּפִים:

... Who lifts up the fallen;

...roka ha-aretz al ha-mayim.

...רוֹקַע הָאָרֶץ עַל הַמָּיִם:

... Who stretches the earth over the waters;

...she'asa li kol tzorki.

...שֶׁעָשָׂה לִּי כָּל צָרְכִּי:

... Who gives me all I need;

...hamechin mitzadei gaver.

...הַמֵּכִין מִצְעֲדֵי גָבֶר:

... Who straightens the bent;

...ozer Yisrael bigvurah.

...אוֹזֵר יִשְׂרָאֵל בִּגְבוּרָה:

... Who enfolds Israel in strength;

...oter Yisrael b'tifarah.

...אוֹזֵר יִשְׂרָאֵל בִּגְבוּרָה:

... Who crowns Israel in splendor;

...hanotein la-ya'ef ko'ach.

...הַנּוֹתֵן לַיָּעֵף כֹּחַ:

... Who gives strength to the weary;

...hame'avir sheina mei'einai
u-tnumah me-afapai.

...הַמַּעֲבִיר שֵׁנָה מֵעֵינָי
וּתְנוּמָה מֵעַפְעַפָּי:

... Who wipes sleep from the eyes, and slumber from the eyelids;

(You may add more blessings in your own words.)

...for whatever unspoken blessings are in our hearts.

Psukei D'Zimra: Poems & Psalms of Praise

Baruch She'amar: Blessed is the One Who Speaks (1)

1) Baruch hu, baruch shemo
Brucha hee, baruch shema

בָּרוּךְ הוּא, בָּרוּךְ שְׁמוֹ
בְּרוּכָה הִיא, בָּרוּךְ שְׁמָה

2) Baruch she'amar
v'haya ha-olam

בָּרוּךְ שֶׁאָמַר וְהָיָה הָעוֹלָם

(Blessed is He, blessed is His Name;
Blessed is She, blessed is Her Name.
Blessed is the One who speaks and the world comes into being!)

"Baruch She'Amar."

Baruch She'amar: Blessed is the One Who Speaks (2)

Baruch she'amar vehayah ha'olam. Baruch hu.
Baruch oseh vereisheet.
Baruch omeir ve'oseh.
Baruch gozeir umkayeim.
Baruch meracheim al ha'arets.
Baruch meracheim al habriot.
Baruch meshaleim sachar tov lirei'av. Baruch chai la'ad vekayam lanetsach.
Baruch podeh umatsil, baruch shemo.

בָּרוּךְ שֶׁאָמַר וְהָיָה הָעוֹלָם,
בָּרוּךְ הוּא, בָּרוּךְ עֹשֶׂה
בְרֵאשִׁית, בָּרוּךְ אוֹמֵר וְעֹשֶׂה,
בָּרוּךְ גּוֹזֵר וּמְקַיֵּם,בָּרוּךְ מְרַחֵם
עַל הָאָרֶץ, בָּרוּךְ מְרַחֵם עַל
הַבְּרִיּוֹת,
בָּרוּךְ מְשַׁלֵּם שָׂכָר טוֹב
לִירֵאָיו, בָּרוּךְ חַי לָעַד וְקַיָּם
לָנֶצַח, בָּרוּךְ פּוֹדֶה וּמַצִּיל,
בָּרוּךְ שְׁמוֹ.

Blessed is the One who speaks
and the universe comes into being.
Blessed is the One whose thought sustains the world's existence.
Blessed is the One whose mercy is the womb of the world.
Blessed is the One who rewards! Blessed is the One who is eternal! Blessed is the One who saves! Blessed is the Name!

בָּרוּךְ אַתָּה יְיָ אֱלֹהֵינוּ מֶלֶךְ
הָעוֹלָם, הָאֵל הָאָב הָרַחֲמָן,
הַמְהֻלָּל בְּפִי עַמּוֹ, מְשֻׁבָּח
וּמְפֹאָר בִּלְשׁוֹן חֲסִידָיו
וַעֲבָדָיו, וּבְשִׁירֵי דָוִד עַבְדֶּךָ.
נְהַלֶּלְךָ יְיָ אֱלֹהֵינוּ בִּשְׁבָחוֹת
וּבִזְמִרוֹת, נְגַדֶּלְךָ וּנְשַׁבֵּחֲךָ
וּנְפָאֶרְךָ וְנַזְכִּיר שִׁמְךָ,
וְנַמְלִיכְךָ, מַלְכֵּנוּ אֱלֹהֵינוּ,
יָחִיד, חֵי הָעוֹלָמִים, מֶלֶךְ
מְשֻׁבָּח וּמְפֹאָר עֲדֵי עַד שְׁמוֹ
הַגָּדוֹל: בָּרוּךְ אַתָּה יְיָ, מֶלֶךְ
מְהֻלָּל בַּתִּשְׁבָּחוֹת:

Baruch atah Adonai Eloheinu
melech ha'olam, ha'Eil ha'av
harachaman hamhulal befee
amo meshubach umfo'ar
bilshon chasidav va'avodav
uvshirei David avdecha.
Nehalelcha Adonai Eloheinu
bishvachot uvizmirot
ungadelcha unshebeichacha
unfa'ercha venazkir shimcha
venamlichecha malkeinu
Eloheinu yachid chei
ha'olamim melech meshubach
umfo'ar adei ad shemo
hagadol. Baruch atah Adonai
melech mehulal batishbachot.

Blessed are You, Adonai our God, Source of all that is, Source of mercy, whose praises are sung in every mouth. With the songs of David, Your servant, we will praise You, Adonai our God. You alone are the life of the universe. You are our Eternal Source. Blessed are You, Adonai our God, praised in song.

From Psalm 30

אֵלֶיךָ יְיָ אֶקְרָא,
וְאֶל אֲדֹנָי אֶתְחַנָּן:
שְׁמַע יְיָ וְחָנֵּנִי, יְיָ הֱיֵה עֹזֵר לִי:

Eleicha Adonai ekra,
v'el Adonai etchanan.
Shema, Adonai, v'choneini
Adonai heyeh ozer li.

Answer me, God, when I cry.
Hear me and be merciful; You are my help!

On Shabbat (from Psalm 92)

Mizmor shir l'yom ha-Shabbat:
Tov l'hodot l'Adonai
u-l'zamer l'shimcha elyon.

מִזְמוֹר שִׁיר לְיוֹם הַשַּׁבָּת:
טוֹב לְהֹדוֹת לַיְיָ
וּלְזַמֵּר לְשִׁמְךָ עֶלְיוֹן:

L'hagid baboker chasdecha,
v'emunatecha baleilot.
Alei asor va'alei navel
alei higayon b'chinor.

לְהַגִּיד בַּבֹּקֶר חַסְדֶּךָ
וֶאֱמוּנָתְךָ בַּלֵּילוֹת:
עֲלֵי עָשׂוֹר וַעֲלֵי נָבֶל
עֲלֵי הִגָּיוֹן בְּכִנּוֹר:

A psalm. A song of the day Shabbat.
How good it is to praise Adonai
and to sing to God on high:

To tell of Your love in the morning
and of your faithfulness at night!
I sing to the music of the harp,
to the sound of string and voice

Ki samachtani Adonai
b'fo'alecha
B'ma'asecha yadecha aranen.
Mah gadlu ma'asecha Yah
M'od amku machshevotecha.

כִּי שִׂמַּחְתַּנִי יְיָ בְּפָעֳלֶךָ
בְּמַעֲשֵׂי יָדֶיךָ אֲרַנֵּן:
מַה גָּדְלוּ מַעֲשֶׂיךָ יְיָ
מְאֹד עָמְקוּ מַחְשְׁבֹתֶיךָ:

for You have made me rejoice, Adonai.
I thrill at the beauty of Your world.
How great is Your work, Adonai:
How profound is the world's design!

from the *Ashrei*

Ashrei yoshvei veitecha
Od y'hallelucha selah

אַשְׁרֵי יוֹשְׁבֵי בֵיתֶךָ,
עוֹד יְהַלְלוּךָ סֶּלָה:

Joyous, dwelling in the One!

Home is in my heart.

(English words, melody by Rabbi Hanna Tiferet Siegel)

Psalm 150

□ Halleluyah!
Halelu Eil bekodsho,
haleluhu birkia uzo.
Haleluhu bigvurotav,
haleluhu kerov gudlo.
Haleluhu beteika shofar,
haleluhu beneivel vechinor.
Haleluhu betof umachol,
haleluhu beminim ve'ugav.
Haleluhu betsiltselei shama,
haleluhu betsiltselei teru'ah.
Kol haneshamah tehaleil Yah,
halleluyah.

□ הַלְלוּיָהּ, הַלְלוּ אֵל בְּקָדְשׁוֹ,
הַלְלוּהוּ בִּרְקִיעַ עֻזּוֹ: הַלְלוּהוּ
בִגְבוּרֹתָיו, הַלְלוּהוּ כְּרֹב
גֻּדְלוֹ: הַלְלוּהוּ בְּתֵקַע שׁוֹפָר,
הַלְלוּהוּ בְּנֵבֶל וְכִנּוֹר: הַלְלוּהוּ
בְּתֹף וּמָחוֹל, הַלְלוּהוּ בְּמִנִּים
וְעֻגָב: הַלְלוּהוּ בְצִלְצְלֵי
שָׁמַע, הַלְלוּהוּ בְּצִלְצְלֵי
תְרוּעָה: כֹּל הַנְּשָׁמָה תְּהַלֵּל
יָהּ הַלְלוּיָהּ.

Hallelujah.
Praise God in holy places, praise God in the sky.
Praise God for might, praise God for greatness.
Praise God with shofar blasts, praise God with harp and lyre.
Praise God with song and dance, praise God with lute and pipe.
Praise God with cymbals, praise God with their crash.
Let all that breathes praise God. Hallelujah.
Let all that breathes praise God. Hallelujah.

Singable English Psalm 150

Let us praise the Mystery,
of celestial awe and majesty
with shofar, lute and timbrels, halleluYah.

As wonders of life go on and on
we praise as our awareness dawns
with flutes, drums and cymbals, halleluYah

Refrain: halleluYah (4x)

Your drum beats out our every breath
each living thing to life says: *Yes!*
of Your Great Name we sing out, halleluYah

This Glory fills the earth with joy,
with eyes of wonder we deploy
ourselves to dance & praise in halleluYah.

Refrain: halleluYah (4x)

(Rabbi Goldie Milgram)

Nishmat Kol Chai: The Breath of All Life

Nishmat kol chai, t'varech et shimcha Adonai eloheinu. V'ruach kol basar, t'far u-tromem zichrecha malkeinu tamid, min ha-olam v'ad ha-olam atah el.

נִשְׁמַת כָּל חַי, תְּבָרֵךְ אֶת שִׁמְךָ
יְיָ אֱלֹהֵינוּ. וְרוּחַ כָּל בָּשָׂר,
תְּפָאֵר וּתְרוֹמֵם זִכְרְךָ מַלְכֵּנוּ
תָּמִיד, מִן הָעוֹלָם וְעַד הָעוֹלָם
אַתָּה אֵל.

The breath of all life will bless Your name, Adonai our God, the spirit of our bodies. We praise and exalt You, from one reality to the next: You are God.

□Ilu finu maleh shirah kayam...

□ אִלּוּ פִינוּ מָלֵא שִׁירָה כַּיָּם...

Were our mouths filled with song as the sea
our tongues joyful like the waves
our lips filled with praise as the heavens
our eyes brilliant like the sun and the moon
our hands outspread as eagle's wings
our feet as swift as deer's,
it would not be enough to thank You,
our God of eternity and eternities.

On the word מלך (*Melech*, "King")

The letter מ stands for *mayim* (water), which flows like blessing; the shape of the ל evokes the coursing path which blessing takes to reach us; and the כ represents hands cupped to receive blessing.

(*Rabbi Marcia Prager*)

Hamelech: God Rules

Hamelech
yosheiv al kisei ram venisa.
Shochein ad marom
vekadosh shemo.
Vechatuv: ranenu tzadikim
b'Adonai, la-yesharim nava
tehilah.

הַמֶּלֶךְ
יוֹשֵׁב עַל כִּסֵּא רָם וְנִשָּׂא.
שׁוֹכֵן עַד מָרוֹם וְקָדוֹשׁ שְׁמוֹ:
וְכָתוּב, רַנְּנוּ צַדִּיקִים בַּייָ,
לַיְשָׁרִים נָאוָה תְהִלָּה.

Befee yesharim titromam,
uvdivrei tzadikim titbarach,
uvilshon chasidim titkadash,
uvkerev kedoshim tit-halal.

בְּפִי יְשָׁרִים תִּתְרוֹמָם.
וּבְדִבְרֵי צַדִּיקִים תִּתְבָּרַךְ.
וּבִלְשׁוֹן חֲסִידִים תִּתְקַדָּשׁ.
וּבְקֶרֶב קְדוֹשִׁים תִּתְהַלָּל:

Majestic One
who presides over all destiny!
Eternal Shekhinah, Holy Beyond:
Saints sing Your name
In harmony with the upright.

Good people exalt You
Saints are Your blessing
Devotees sanctify You
You delight in our inner holiness.

In the second stanza, the enlarged Hebrew letters highlight an acrostic which spells "Yitzchak" and "Rivkah," Isaac and Rebecca. If we add the numerical values (gematria) of those two Hebrew names, we get the numerical value of the word "tefilah," prayer. Perhaps this teaches that our prayer reaches its highest form when our communities are gender-inclusive.

Yishtabach: Blessing Ending *Psukei D'Zimrah*

Yishtabach shimcha la'ad malkeinu, ha'eil hamelech hagadol vehakadosh bashamayim uva'arets. Kee lecha na'eh Adonai Eloheinu v'Elohei avoteinu ve'imoteinu shir ushvachah haleil vezimrah oz umemshalah netzach gedulah ugvurah tehilah vetiferet kedushah umalchut berachot vehoda'ot me'atah ve'ad olam.

יִשְׁתַּבַּח שִׁמְךָ לָעַד מַלְכֵּנוּ, הָאֵל הַמֶּלֶךְ הַגָּדוֹל וְהַקָּדוֹשׁ בַּשָּׁמַיִם וּבָאָרֶץ. כִּי לְךָ נָאֶה יְיָ אֱלֹהֵינוּ וֵאלֹהֵי אֲבוֹתֵינוּ וְאִמּוֹתֵינוּ שִׁיר וּשְׁבָחָה הַלֵּל וְזִמְרָה עֹז וּמֶמְשָׁלָה נֶצַח גְּדֻלָּה וּגְבוּרָה תְּהִלָּה וְתִפְאֶרֶת קְדֻשָּׁה וּמַלְכוּת בְּרָכוֹת וְהוֹדָאוֹת מֵעַתָּה וְעַד עוֹלָם.

□ Baruch atah Adonai Eil melech gadol batishbachot Eil hahoda'ot adon hanifla'ot habocheir beshirei zimrah melech Eil chei ha'olamim.

□ בָּרוּךְ אַתָּה יְיָ אֵל מֶלֶךְ גָּדוֹל בַּתִּשְׁבָּחוֹת אֵל הַהוֹדָאוֹת אֲדוֹן הַנִּפְלָאוֹת הַבּוֹחֵר בְּשִׁירֵי זִמְרָה מֶלֶךְ אֵל חֵי הָעוֹלָמִים.

May Your name be forever blessed, our source of being,
great and holy God, in heaven and on earth.
Songs and praise, adulation and melody,
strength and power, eternity, greatness and might,
blessing and thanks are the words we can use
to speak of Adonai, our God and God of our ancestors,
for now and evermore.

Blessed are You, Adonai, God who is greatly praised,
God who is thanked, master of miracles
who chooses songs of praise, the God of eternal life.

The Kaddish: A Door

In all of its forms, the Kaddish is a door in the service
between one part of the service and the next.
As we move through this door, be attentive:
What is happening in your heart and mind?
Whatever you're feeling, bring that into your prayer.

Chatzi Kaddish

Yitgadal v'yitkadash sh'mei rabah. (Amen.) Be'alma div'ra chirutei v'yamlich malchutei. B'chayeichon uv'yomeichon uv'chayei d'chol beit Yisrael. Ba'agala uvizman kariv v'imru Amen.

יִתְגַּדַּל וְיִתְקַדַּשׁ שְׁמֵהּ רַבָּא.
בְּעָלְמָא דִּי בְרָא כִרְעוּתֵהּ,
וְיַמְלִיךְ מַלְכוּתֵהּ בְּחַיֵּיכוֹן
וּבְיוֹמֵיכוֹן וּבְחַיֵּי דְכָל בֵּית
יִשְׂרָאֵל. בַּעֲגָלָא וּבִזְמַן קָרִיב
וְאִמְרוּ אָמֵן:

□ Yehei shmei rabah m'vorach l'olam ul'almei almaya.

□ יְהֵא שְׁמֵהּ רַבָּא מְבָרַךְ
לְעָלַם וּלְעָלְמֵי עָלְמַיָּא:

Yitbarach v'yishtabah v'yitpa'ar v'yitromam v'yitnaseh. V'yithadar v'yitaleh v'yithalal shmeh d'kudsha brich hu. L'eila u-l'eila min kol birchata v'shirata, tushb'chata v'nechemata, d'amiran b'alma, v'imru Amen.

יִתְבָּרַךְ וְיִשְׁתַּבַּח, וְיִתְפָּאַר
וְיִתְרוֹמַם וְיִתְנַשֵּׂא וְיִתְהַדָּר
וְיִתְעַלֶּה וְיִתְהַלָּל שְׁמֵהּ
דְּקֻדְשָׁא בְּרִיךְ הוּא לְעֵלָּא
וּלְעֵלָּא מִן כָּל בִּרְכָתָא
וְשִׁירָתָא, תֻּשְׁבְּחָתָא
וְנֶחֱמָתָא, דַּאֲמִירָן בְּעָלְמָא,
וְאִמְרוּ אָמֵן:

Magnified and sanctified! Magnified and sanctified! May God's Great Name fill the world God created. May God's splendor be seen in the world in your life, in your days, in the life of all Israel. Quickly and soon! And let us say, Amen.

Forever may the Great Name be blessed!

Blessed and praised! Splendid and supreme! May the holy name, Bless God, be praised, beyond all the blessings and songs, comforts and consolations, that can be offered in this world. And let us say: Amen.

The Shema and Blessings

Barchu: Call to Prayer

As we bless the source of life, so we are blessed.
And our blessings give us strength
And make our vision clear
And our blessings give us peace and the courage to dare.
As we bless the source of life, so we are blessed.

(Faith Rogow)

בָּרְכוּ אֶת יְיָ הַמְבֹרָךְ:

Barchu et Adonai
ha-mevorach.

☐ בָּרוּךְ יְיָ הַמְבֹרָךְ לְעוֹלָם וָעֶד:

☐ Baruch Adonai ha-mevorach
l'olam va-ed.

Blessed is Adonai, the blessed one.

Blessed is Adonai, the blessed one,
now and forever!

Yotzer Or: Creator of Light

בָּרוּךְ אַתָּה יְיָ, אֱלֹהֵינוּ מֶלֶךְ
הָעוֹלָם, יוֹצֵר אוֹר, וּבוֹרֵא
חֹשֶׁךְ, עֹשֶׂה שָׁלוֹם וּבוֹרֵא אֶת
הַכֹּל: הַמֵּאִיר לָאָרֶץ וְלַדָּרִים
עָלֶיהָ בְּרַחֲמִים. וּבְטוּבוֹ מְחַדֵּשׁ
בְּכָל יוֹם תָּמִיד מַעֲשֵׂה
בְרֵאשִׁית:

Baruch atah Adonai, Eloheinu melech ha'olam, yotser or uvorei choshech osei shalom uvorei et hakol. Hamei'ir la'arets veladarim aleyah berachamim. Uvtuvo mechadeish bechol yom tamid ma'aseih vereishit.

Blessed are You, Adonai our God, source of all being, who forms light and creates darkness, who makes peace and creates all. It is God who illumines the earth and all upon it with mercy, and who every day continually renews the work of Creation.

מָה רַבּוּ מַעֲשֶׂיךָ יְיָ. כֻּלָּם
בְּחָכְמָה עָשִׂיתָ, מָלְאָה הָאָרֶץ
קִנְיָנֶךָ: תִּתְבָּרַךְ יְיָ אֱלֹהֵינוּ עַל
שֶׁבַח מַעֲשֵׂה יָדֶיךָ. וְעַל מְאוֹרֵי
אוֹר שֶׁעָשִׂיתָ יְפָאֲרוּךָ סֶּלָה.

Mah rabu ma'asecha Adonai, kulam b'chochmah asitah, malah ha'aretz kinyanecha. Titbarach Adonai Eloheinu al shevach ma'aseih yadecha, ve'al me'orei or she'asita, yefa'arucha sela.

How magnificent is Your world, Adonai! You made it all with wisdom. The world is full of Your presence. Let all bless You, our Saving Power, for the work of Your hands and the heavenly lights You have made. Let them glorify You forever.

□ אוֹר חָדָשׁ עַל צִיּוֹן תָּאִיר
וְנִזְכֶּה כֻלָּנוּ מְהֵרָה לְאוֹרוֹ:
בָּרוּךְ אַתָּה יְיָ יוֹצֵר
הַמְּאוֹרוֹת:

□ Or chadash al Tzion ta'ir venizkeh chulanu meheirah le'oro. Baruch atah Adonai yotseir hamorot.

May You shine a new light upon Zion, and may we all soon be worthy of its radiance. Blessed are You, Adonai, creator of light.

Ahavah Rabbah: More Love

When you love not one another in daily communion
How can you love God, whom you have never seen?

More love! More love!
The heavens are calling, the angels are singing,
O Zion, more love, more love.

If you love one another then God is within you
And you are made pure to walk in the light.

More love! More love!
The heavens are calling, the angels are singing,
O Zion, more love, more love.

Ahavah rabbah	אַהֲבָה רַבָּה
Ahavah ba-eynayim Ahavah ba-shamayim	אַהֲבָה בְּעֵינַיִם, אַהֲבָה בַּשָּׁמַיִם
Ahavah, ahavah rabbah.	אַהֲבָה, אַהֲבָה רַבָּה.

(More love! Love in our eyes; love from the heavens; more love.)

(English words: from a Shaker hymn)

Ahavah Rabbah: Your Love for Us (2)

אַהֲבָה רַבָּה אֲהַבְתָּנוּ, יְיָ
אֱלֹהֵינוּ, חֶמְלָה גְדוֹלָה וִיתֵרָה
חָמַלְתָּ עָלֵינוּ. בַּעֲבוּר אֲבוֹתֵינוּ
וְאִמּוֹתֵינוּ, שֶׁבָּטְחוּ בְךָ,
וַתְּלַמְּדֵם חֻקֵּי חַיִּים, כֵּן תְּחָנֵּנוּ
וּתְלַמְּדֵנוּ, הַמְרַחֵם, רַחֵם
עָלֵינוּ, וְתֵן בְּלִבֵּנוּ לְהָבִין
וּלְהַשְׂכִּיל, לִשְׁמֹעַ, לִלְמֹד
וּלְלַמֵּד, לִשְׁמֹר וְלַעֲשׂוֹת וּלְקַיֵּם
אֶת כָּל דִּבְרֵי תַלְמוּד תּוֹרָתֶךָ
בְּאַהֲבָה.

Ahavah raba ahavtanu Adonai
Eloheinu chemlah gedolah
viteirah chamalta aleinu.
Ba'avur avoteinu ve'imoteinu
shebatchu vecha,vatelamdeim
chukei chayim kein techoneinu
utlamdeinu, harachaman
hamracheim racheim aleinu
vetein belibeinu lehavin
ulhaskil lishmo'a lilmod
ul'lameid lishmor vela'asot
ulkayeim et kol divrei talmud
Toratecha be'ahavah.

You have loved us with a great love, Adonai our God.
With great compassion you have cared for us.
Our ancestors trusted in You and learned from You laws of life.
For their sake, have mercy on us and teach us.
You are our source and our womb—be gracious with us.
Give our hearts understanding
to hear, learn, teach and do
all the words of Your teaching with love.

Like a parent, God loves us so much
that S/He gives us stories to learn from and rules to live by.
This is Torah: our ancestors' experiences,
our sages' yearnings toward wisdom,
our Parent's instructions for a mindful life.

Veha'eir eineinu be'Toratecha vedabek libeinu bemitsvotecha veyacheid levaveinu le'ahavah ulyirah et shemecha. Velo neivosh velo nikaleim velo nikasheil le'olam va'ed, kee vesheim kodshecha hagadol vehanora batachnu. Nagilah venismechah bishuatecha.

וְהָאֵר עֵינֵינוּ בְּתוֹרָתֶךָ, וְדַבֵּק
לִבֵּנוּ בְּמִצְוֹתֶיךָ, וְיַחֵד לְבָבֵנוּ
לְאַהֲבָה וּלְיִרְאָה אֶת שְׁמֶךָ,
וְלֹא נֵבוֹשׁ וְלֹא נִכָּלֵם וְלֹא
נִכָּשֵׁל לְעוֹלָם וָעֶד: כִּי בְשֵׁם
קָדְשְׁךָ הַגָּדוֹל וְהַנּוֹרָא
בָּטָחְנוּ, נָגִילָה וְנִשְׂמְחָה
בִּישׁוּעָתֶךָ.

Enlighten our eyes with Your Torah; attach us to Your mitzvot. Unite our hearts to the love and awe of Your name. Then we shall never be shamed or humiliated, nor shall we stumble. We will trust in Your great, wondrous and holy name. We will rejoice and exult in Your saving power.

Vehavi'einu leshalom mei'arba kanefot ha'arets vetolicheinu komemiyut la'artseinu, kee Eil po'eil yeshu'ot ata, uvanu vacharta mikol am velashon. Vekeiravtanu leshimcha hagadol sela be'emet lehodot lecha ulyachdecha be'ahavah. Baruch atah Adonai, habocheir be'amo Yisrael be'ahavah.

וַהֲבִיאֵנוּ לְשָׁלוֹם מֵאַרְבַּע
כַּנְפוֹת הָאָרֶץ, וְתוֹלִיכֵנוּ
קוֹמְמִיּוּת לְאַרְצֵנוּ, כִּי אֵל פּוֹעֵל
יְשׁוּעוֹת אָתָּה, וּבָנוּ בָחַרְתָּ
מִכָּל עַם וְלָשׁוֹן. וְקֵרַבְתָּנוּ
לְשִׁמְךָ הַגָּדוֹל סֶלָה בֶּאֱמֶת
לְהוֹדוֹת לְךָ וּלְיַחֶדְךָ בְּאַהֲבָה.
בָּרוּךְ אַתָּה יְיָ, הַבּוֹחֵר בְּעַמּוֹ
יִשְׂרָאֵל בְּאַהֲבָה.

Bring us in peace from the four corners of the earth and lead us upright to our home, for You are the God of redemptive power who has chosen us as a people. Draw us close to Your great name in truth, to praise You and unify Your name. Blessed are You, Adonai, who has in love chosen Your people.

Meditation Before the *Shema*

Shhh.... ש

(silence your mind)

Mmmmm.... מ

(sink into this moment)

Ahhh! ע

(God is One!)

Shema

On Yom Kippur, we recite "Baruch shem..." aloud.

☐ שְׁמַע יִשְׂרָאֵל, יְיָ אֱלֹהֵינוּ, יְיָ אֶחָד:

☐ Shema Yisrael: Adonai Eloheinu Adonai echad!

בָּרוּךְ שֵׁם כְּבוֹד מַלְכוּתוֹ לְעוֹלָם וָעֶד.

Baruch shem kevod malchuto le'olam va'ed!

Hear, O Israel: Adonai is our God, Adonai is One!
Through time and space Your glory shines, Majestic One!

☐ וְאָהַבְתָּ אֵת יְיָ אֱלֹהֶיךָ,
בְּכָל-לְבָבְךָ, וּבְכָל-נַפְשְׁךָ,
וּבְכָל-מְאֹדֶךָ. וְהָיוּ הַדְּבָרִים
הָאֵלֶּה, אֲשֶׁר אָנֹכִי מְצַוְּךָ
הַיּוֹם, עַל-לְבָבֶךָ: וְשִׁנַּנְתָּם
לְבָנֶיךָ, וְדִבַּרְתָּ בָּם בְּשִׁבְתְּךָ
בְּבֵיתֶךָ, וּבְלֶכְתְּךָ בַדֶּרֶךְ
וּבְשָׁכְבְּךָ, וּבְקוּמֶךָ. וּקְשַׁרְתָּם
לְאוֹת עַל-יָדֶךָ, וְהָיוּ לְטֹטָפֹת
בֵּין עֵינֶיךָ, וּכְתַבְתָּם עַל
מְזֻזוֹת בֵּיתֶךָ וּבִשְׁעָרֶיךָ:

☐ V'ahavta et Adonai elohecha, b'chol l'vavcha, uv'chol nafshecha, uv'chol me'odecha. V'hayu ha-d'varim ha-eileh, asher anochi m'tzv'cha hayom, al-levavecha. V'shinantam l'vanecha, v'dibarta bam b'shiv't'cha b'veitecha, uv'lech't'cha vaderech uv'shochb'cha uv'kumecha. Ukshartam l'ot al yadecha, v'hayu l'totafot bein enecha, uchtavtam al mezuzot beitecha uvisharecha.

You shall love Adonai your God with all your heart, with all your mind, with all your being. Set these words which I enjoin upon you today upon your heart. Teach them faithfully to your children. Speak of them in your home and on your way, when you lie down and when you rise up. Bind them as a sign on your hand. Let them be symbols before your eyes. Inscribe them on the doorposts of your house, and on your gates.

וְהָיָה אִם-שָׁמֹעַ תִּשְׁמְעוּ אֶל-מִצְוֹתַי, אֲשֶׁר אָנֹכִי מְצַוֶּה אֶתְכֶם הַיּוֹם, לְאַהֲבָה אֶת יְיָ אֱלֹהֵיכֶם, וּלְעָבְדוֹ בְּכָל-לְבַבְכֶם וּבְכָל נַפְשְׁכֶם. וְנָתַתִּי מְטַר-אַרְצְכֶם בְּעִתּוֹ, יוֹרֶה וּמַלְקוֹשׁ, וְאָסַפְתָּ דְגָנֶךָ וְתִירֹשְׁךָ וְיִצְהָרֶךָ. וְנָתַתִּי עֵשֶׂב בְּשָׂדְךָ לִבְהֶמְתֶּךָ, וְאָכַלְתָּ וְשָׂבָעְתָּ. הִשָּׁמְרוּ לָכֶם פֶּן-יִפְתֶּה לְבַבְכֶם, וְסַרְתֶּם וַעֲבַדְתֶּם אֱלֹהִים אֲחֵרִים וְהִשְׁתַּחֲוִיתֶם לָהֶם. וְחָרָה אַף-יְיָ בָּכֶם, וְעָצַר אֶת-הַשָּׁמַיִם וְלֹא-יִהְיֶה מָטָר, וְהָאֲדָמָה לֹא תִתֵּן אֶת-יְבוּלָהּ וַאֲבַדְתֶּם מְהֵרָה מֵעַל הָאָרֶץ הַטֹּבָה אֲשֶׁר יְיָ נֹתֵן לָכֶם: וְשַׂמְתֶּם אֶת דְּבָרַי אֵלֶּה עַל-לְבַבְכֶם וְעַל-נַפְשְׁכֶם וּקְשַׁרְתֶּם אֹתָם לְאוֹת עַל-יֶדְכֶם, וְהָיוּ לְטוֹטָפֹת בֵּין עֵינֵיכֶם: וְלִמַּדְתֶּם אֹתָם אֶת-בְּנֵיכֶם, לְדַבֵּר בָּם, בְּשִׁבְתְּךָ בְּבֵיתֶךָ, וּבְלֶכְתְּךָ בַדֶּרֶךְ, וּבְשָׁכְבְּךָ וּבְקוּמֶךָ: וּכְתַבְתָּם עַל-מְזוּזוֹת בֵּיתֶךָ וּבִשְׁעָרֶיךָ: לְמַעַן יִרְבּוּ יְמֵיכֶם וִימֵי בְנֵיכֶם עַל הָאֲדָמָה אֲשֶׁר נִשְׁבַּע יְיָ לַאֲבֹתֵיכֶם לָתֵת לָהֶם, כִּימֵי הַשָּׁמַיִם עַל-הָאָרֶץ:

If you will truly listen to My words and keep My mitzvot which I command you today, to love your God and to serve God with all of your heart and soul, then I will give you rains in season, autumn and spring, and you will have an ample harvest of grain, wine, and oil. There will be abundance in your fields for your cattle; you will eat and be satisfied. But take care lest you turn your heart away from Me and turn to serve false gods in worship. Then God's anger will face you. God will close back the heavens and hold back the rain; the earth will not yield its fruits; and you will disappear from this good earth which Adonai is giving you. Therefore keep these words close to you; impress them on your heart. Bind them as a sign upon your hand; carve them in your consciousness. Teach them to your children. Repeat them at home and away, morning and night. Inscribe them on the doorposts of your house and on your gates. Then your days and your childrens' days will endure, on this land which God promised to you, as the days of the heavens are long over the earth.

This is a faithful translation; an interpretive translation appears on p. 19.

Vayomer Adonai el Moshe lemor: daber el-bnei Yisrael v'amarta aleihem v'asu lahem tzitzit al kanfei bigdeihem l'dorotam, v'natnu al tzitzit ha-kanaf p'til tchelet. V'haya lachem l'tzitzit, u'ritem oto, u'zchartem et-kol-mitzvot Adonai v'asitem otam. V'lo taturu acharei l'vavchem v'acharei eineihem asher-atem zonim achareihem.

וַיֹּאמֶר יְיָ אֶל-מֹשֶׁה לֵּאמֹר:
דַּבֵּר אֶל-בְּנֵי יִשְׂרָאֵל וְאָמַרְתָּ
אֲלֵהֶם: וְעָשׂוּ לָהֶם צִיצִת עַל-
כַּנְפֵי בִגְדֵיהֶם לְדֹרֹתָם, וְנָתְנוּ
עַל-צִיצִת הַכָּנָף פְּתִיל תְּכֵלֶת.
וְהָיָה לָכֶם לְצִיצִת, וּרְאִיתֶם
אֹתוֹ וּזְכַרְתֶּם אֶת-כָּל-מִצְוֹת
יְיָ, וַעֲשִׂיתֶם אֹתָם, וְלֹא תָתוּרוּ
אַחֲרֵי לְבַבְכֶם וְאַחֲרֵי עֵינֵיכֶם,
אֲשֶׁר-אַתֶּם זֹנִים אַחֲרֵיהֶם:

And God spoke to Moses saying: speak to the children of Israel and say to them that they should make tzitzit on the corners of their garments for all time, and they shall place on the tzitzit a little thread of blue. And these shall be for you as tzitzit, that you may look upon them, that you will remember all of the mitzvot of Adonai and you shall do them, so that you will not go running after the cravings of your heart or the turnings of your eyes which might take you into places where you should not be!

The knots and windings in our tzitzit have mystical significance. The numerical value of the word 'tzitzit' is 600. Add the eight strands plus the five knots, and you get 613: the number of mitzvot.

□ לְמַעַן תִּזְכְּרוּ וַעֲשִׂיתֶם אֶת-כָּל-מִצְוֹתָי, וִהְיִיתֶם קְדֹשִׁים לֵאלֹהֵיכֶם: אֲנִי יְיָ אֱלֹהֵיכֶם, אֲשֶׁר הוֹצֵאתִי אֶתְכֶם מֵאֶרֶץ מִצְרַיִם, לִהְיוֹת לָכֶם לֵאלֹהִים, אֲנִי יְיָ אֱלֹהֵיכֶם:

□ Lema'an tizkeru va'asitem et kol mitzvotai viheyitem kedoshim l'Eloheichem. Ani Adonai Eloheichem asher hotzeiti etcham me'eretz Mitzrayim lihiyot lachem l'Elohim. Ani Adonai Eloheichem.

This way you will be mindful to actualize my directions
for becoming dedicated to your God;
to be aware that I am your God,
the one who freed you from the oppression
in order to be your God. I am Adonai your God.
That is the truth!

יְיָ אֱלֹהֵיכֶם אֱמֶת!

Your God is a true God!

The morning [Zalman Schachter-Shalomi] led the davening, he came up to me during the last part of the *Shema*, touched me on the shoulder, looked straight into my eyes, and said, "Your God is a true God." I found that a powerful challenge.

I usually felt as I prayed in a group that I was assenting to ideas and images that were very foreign to me or that I didn't have time to check out. Zalman's gesture had cut through that in a very personal way.... My God is a true God? Whch God was he talking about? Long white beard, old Daddy in the sky? Autocrat, general, father, king? Master of the Universe, doyen of regulations and punishments? These were the images that made me reject the very idea of God.

But in a funny mental jujitsu, the more I struggled with these images, the more what Zalman said came through. "Your God is a true God" meant to me that the images and the language weren't going to be supplied in advance. I would have to find them for myself out of my own experience....

(Rodger Kamenetz, from The Jew In the Lotus)

Ge'ulah: Redemption

Redemption

Redemption is not a time, is not a place.
Redemption is the Promised Land that has no boundaries.
It is the World to Come that is already here.
Redemption is the discovery that within you
Is the ability to become, and to keep becoming.
It is now without knowing and here without being.
Redemption is reaching beyond self and into eternity.

(Rabbi Jeffrey Goldwasser)

אֱמֶת וְיַצִּיב וְנָכוֹן וְקַיָּם
וְיָשָׁר וְנֶאֱמָן וְאָהוּב וְחָבִיב
וְנֶחְמָד וְנָעִים וְנוֹרָא וְאַדִּיר
וּמְתֻקָּן וּמְקֻבָּל וְטוֹב וְיָפֶה
הַדָּבָר הַזֶּה עָלֵינוּ לְעוֹלָם וָעֶד.

Emet v'yatziv v'nachon v'kayam
v'yashar v'ne'eman v'ahuv
v'chaviv v'nechmad v'na'im
v'nora v'adir u-m'tukan u'mkubal
v'tov v'yafeh hadavar hazeh
aleinu l'olam vaed!

True and enduring, right and real, just and faithful,
good and beautiful is this eternal teaching:

God is our protection and our redemption,
from generation to generation.

God's words live and endure forever,
faithfully and beautifully.

For us as for our parents, for our children as for ourselves,
we have no God but You.

You were our help in ages past, and will be in years to come.
We hope in You, our God far above and deep within.

Through Your truth and justice we dare hope
for our lives fulfilled and our world redeemed.

Happy are they who hear Your teachings
and take them to heart.

You are our guide, mighty and merciful.
You are first and You are last.

Moses, Miriam and the children of Israel sang out in joy
this song of praise to the God of blessings:

□ Mi chamocha ba'eilim Adonai, mi camocha nedar bakodesh, nora tehilot oseh feleh.	□ מִי כָמֹכָה בָּאֵלִים יְיָ, מִי כָּמֹכָה נֶאְדָּר בַּקֹּדֶשׁ, נוֹרָא תְהִילֹּת, עֹשֵׂה פֶלֶא:
Shirah chadashah shibechu ge'ulim leshimcha al sefat hayam, yachad kulam hodu vehimlichu ve'amru: Adonai yimloch le'olam va'ed.	שִׁירָה חֲדָשָׁה שִׁבְּחוּ גְאוּלִים לְשִׁמְךָ עַל שְׂפַת הַיָּם, יַחַד כֻּלָּם הוֹדוּ וְהִמְלִיכוּ וְאָמְרוּ: יְיָ יִמְלֹךְ לְעוֹלָם וָעֶד.
Tzur Yisrael, kumah be'ezrat Yisrael, ufdei chinumecha yehudah v'Yisrael. Go'aleinu Adonai tzeva'ot shemo, kedosh Yisrael. Baruch atah Adonai ga'al Yisrael.	צוּר יִשְׂרָאֵל, קוּמָה בְּעֶזְרַת יִשְׂרָאֵל, וּפְדֵה כִנְאֻמֶךָ יְהוּדָה וְיִשְׂרָאֵל. גֹּאֲלֵנוּ יְיָ צְבָאוֹת שְׁמוֹ, קְדוֹשׁ יִשְׂרָאֵל. בָּרוּךְ אַתָּה יְיָ גָּאַל יִשְׂרָאֵל.

Who is like You, among the gods, Adonai? Who is like You, awesome and doing wonders? On the shores of the sea, the redeemed sang a new song of praise to Your name. As one, they thanked You and declared You ruler, crying, "Adonai will reign forever and ever."

Rock of Israel, arise and come to the aid of Israel! Redeem us as You have promised. We know you as the God of hosts; sanctify us. Blessed are You, Who redeems Your people Israel.

Without Ceasing

The wash of dawn across the sky
reveals your signature.

Cicadas drone your praise
through the honey-slow afternoon.

The angular windmills on the ridge
recite your name with every turn.

And I, who can barely focus on breath
without drifting into story:

what can I say to you,
author of wisteria and sorrel,

you who shaped these soft hills
with glaciers' slow passage?

You fashioned me as a gong:
your presence reverberates.

Help me to open my lips
that I may sing your praise.

(Rabbi Rachel Barenblat)

Amidah meditation

For those who wish to daven the full text of the amidah, it follows, beginning on page 101. For those who prefer to reflect in their own time on the prayer's themes, instead of using pre-existing words on the page, the themes are below:

1. *Avot v'imahot*: connections with our ancestors
both Biblical and personal / familial;

2. *Gevurot*: God's strength; we thank God Who keeps us alive
and who enlivens the deadened;

3. *Kidushat Hashem*: God is holy; we ask God
to strengthen our awe and amazement;

4. *Kidushat Hayom*: today is holy; reflect on today's themes
(includes *Ya'aleh v'yavo*: may our prayers ascend,
including prayers for a world perfected and at peace);

5. *Avodah*: may our prayers be acceptable,
may God receive our words with love;

6. *Hoda'ah*: gratitude for the many blessings of each day;

7. *Shalom*: may God bless us with peace
and with wholeness; may peace come to all who live on earth.

Amidah

□ Adonai sefatai tiftach
ufi yagid tehilatecha.

□ אֲדֹנָי שְׂפָתַי תִּפְתָּח
וּפִי יַגִּיד תְּהִלָּתֶךָ:

Eternal God, open my lips
that my mouth may declare Your praise.

Avot v'Imahot: Our Ancestors

□ Baruch atah Adonai Eloheinu v'Elohei avoteinu v'imoteinu, elohei Avraham, elohei Yitzchak, elohei Ya'akov, elohei Sarah, elohei Rivkah, elohei Leah, v'elohei Rachel. Ha'el hagadol hagibor v'hanora Eil elyon, gomeil chasadim tovim v'koneh hakol v'zocheir chasei avot v'imahot, umeivi go'el livnei veneihem lema'an shemo b'ahavah.

□ בָּרוּךְ אַתָּה יְיָ אֱלֹהֵינוּ וֵאלֹהֵי אֲבוֹתֵינוּ וְאִמּוֹתֵינוּ, אֱלֹהֵי אַבְרָהָם, אֱלֹהֵי יִצְחָק, וֵאלֹהֵי יַעֲקֹב, אלֹהֵי שָׂרָה, אלֹהֵי רִבְקָה, אלֹהֵי לֵאָה, וֵאלֹהֵי רָחֵל. הָאֵל הַגָּדוֹל הַגִּבּוֹר וְהַנּוֹרָא, אֵל עֶלְיוֹן, גּוֹמֵל חֲסָדִים טוֹבִים, וְקוֹנֵה הַכֹּל, וְזוֹכֵר חַסְדֵי אָבוֹת ואמהות, וּמֵבִיא גוֹאֵל לִבְנֵי בְנֵיהֶם לְמַעַן שְׁמוֹ בְּאַהֲבָה:

Blessed are You, Adonai our God and God of our ancestors, God of Abraham, God of Isaac, God of Jacob; God of Sarah, God of Rebecca, God of Rachel and God of Leah; the great, mighty, and awesome God, God on high, who does deeds of loving kindness, who is the Source of all, and who remembers the steadfast love of our ancestors, who lovingly brings redemption to their children's children for Your name's sake.

מִסּוֹד חֲכָמִים וּנְבוֹנִים, וּמִלֶּמֶד
דַּעַת מְבִינִים, אֶפְתְּחָה פִּי
בִּתְפִלָּה וּבְתַחֲנוּנִים, לְחַלּוֹת
וּלְחַנֵּן פְּנֵי מֶלֶךְ מַלְכֵי הַמְּלָכִים
וַאֲדוֹנֵי הָאֲדוֹנִים.

Misod chachamim unevonim,
u-melech da'at m'vinim, eft'cha
pi bitfilah uvtachanunim,
l'chalot ul'chanen pnei melech
malchei hamlachim v'adonei
ha-adonim.

Drawing on secret wisdom, with all the learning and discernment I can muster, I open my mouth in prayer and supplication to bring forth grace from the Source of all Sources.

זָכְרֵנוּ לְחַיִּים, מֶלֶךְ חָפֵץ
בַּחַיִּים, וְכָתְבֵנוּ בְּסֵפֶר הַחַיִּים,
לְמַעַנְךָ אֱלֹהִים חַיִּים.

Zochreinu lechayim melech
chafeitz bachayim, vekotveinu
beseifer ha-chayyim le
ma'ancha Elohim chayyim.

מֶלֶךְ עוֹזֵר וּמוֹשִׁיעַ וּמָגֵן: בָּרוּךְ
אַתָּה יְיָ, מָגֵן אַבְרָהָם וְעֶזְרַת
שָׂרָה:

Melech ozeir u-moshia u-
magen. Baruch Atah Adonai,
magein Avraham v'ezrat
Sarah.

Remember us for life, creator Who delights in life,
and inscribe us in the book of life for Your own sake, O God of life. Ruler, helper, redeemer, and protector, blessed are You Adonai, Abraham’s shield and Sarah’s strength.

Gevurot: God's Strength

□ אַתָּה גִּבּוֹר לְעוֹלָם אֲדֹנָי,
מְחַיֵּה מֵתִים אַתָּה, רַב
לְהוֹשִׁיעַ: מוֹרִיד הַטָּל:

□ Atah gibor l'olam Adonai,
mechayeh meitim atah rav
l'hoshia. Morid ha-tal.

You are our eternal strength, Adonai. Your saving power gives life that transcends death. You bring the dew of the field.

□ Mechalkel chayyim b'chesed, m'chayeh meitim b'rachamim rabim, somech noflim, v'rofeh cholim, umatir asurim, um'kayem emunato lishenei afar. Mi chamocha ba'al gevurot? U-mi domeh lach? Melech meimit u'm'chayeh, umatzmiach yeshuah.

□ מְכַלְכֵּל חַיִּים בְּחֶסֶד, מְחַיֵּה
מֵתִים בְּרַחֲמִים רַבִּים, סוֹמֵךְ
נוֹפְלִים, וְרוֹפֵא חוֹלִים,
וּמַתִּיר אֲסוּרִים, וּמְקַיֵּם
אֱמוּנָתוֹ לִישֵׁנֵי עָפָר, מִי
כָמוֹךָ בַּעַל גְּבוּרוֹת וּמִי דוֹמֶה
לָּךְ, מֶלֶךְ מֵמִית וּמְחַיֶּה
וּמַצְמִיחַ יְשׁוּעָה:

Mi chamocha av harachaman, zocheir yetzurav l'chayyim b'rachamim.

מִי כָמוֹךָ אַב הָרַחֲמִים, זוֹכֵר
יְצוּרָיו לְחַיִּים בְּרַחֲמִים:

V'ne'eman atah le'ha-chayot meitim. Baruch atah Adonai, mechayeh hameitim.

וְנֶאֱמָן אַתָּה לְהַחֲיוֹת מֵתִים.
בָּרוּךְ אַתָּה יְיָ, מְחַיֵּה הַמֵּתִים:

You sustain the living with kindness, in Your great mercy You bestow eternal life. You support the fallen, heal the sick, and free the captive. You keep Your faith with us beyond life and death. There is none like You, our source of strength, the ruler of life and death, the source of our redemption.

Who is like You, source of mercy, Who mercifully remembers Your creatures for life?

Our faith is with You, the God Who brings eternal life.
Blessed are You, Adonai, Who gives life which transcends death.

Kidushat Hashem: Making the Name Holy

Nekadesh et shimcha ba'olam keshem shemakdishim oto bishmei marom. Kakatuv al yad nevi'echa vekara zeh el zeh ve'amar:

נְקַדֵּשׁ אֶת שִׁמְךָ בָּעוֹלָם כְּשֵׁם
שֶׁמַּקְדִּישִׁים אוֹתוֹ בִּשְׁמֵי
מָרוֹם. כַּכָּתוּב עַל יַד נְבִיאֶךָ
וְקָרָא זֶה אֶל זֶה וְאָמַר:

May Your name be sanctified in the world as the angels sanctify it in the heavens above. As Your prophet wrote, they cry out to one another:

Kadosh kadosh kadosh Adonai tzeva'ot! Melo chol ha'arets kevodo!

קָדוֹשׁ קָדוֹשׁ יְיָ צְבָאוֹת!
מְלֹא כָל הָאָרֶץ כְּבוֹדוֹ!

Holy, holy, holy is Adonai Tzevaot! The whole earth is filled with Your glory!

Adir adireinu, Adonai adoneinu, mah adir shimcha bechol ha'aretz. Baruch kevod Adonai mimkomo!

אַדִּיר אַדִּירֵנוּ, יְיָ אֲדוֹנֵנוּ,
מָה אַדִּיר שִׁמְךָ בְּכָל הָאָרֶץ
בָּרוּךְ כְּבוֹד יְיָ מִמְּקוֹמוֹ!

Wondrous of all wonders, Adonai our strength, how majestic is Your name in all the earth. Blessed is Adonai's glory wherever God dwells!

אֶחָד הוּא אֱלֹהֵינוּ, הוּא אָבִינוּ,
הוּא מַלְכֵּנוּ, הוּא מוֹשִׁיעֵנוּ
וְהוּא יַשְׁמִיעֵנוּ בְּרַחֲמָיו לְעֵינֵי
כָּל חָי. אֲנִי יְיָ אֱלֹהֵיכֶם. יִמְלֹךְ
יְיָ לְעוֹלָם אֱלֹהַיִךְ צִיּוֹן לְדֹר
וָדֹר. הַלְלוּיָהּ!

Echad hu Eloheinu, hu avinu,
hu malkeinu, hu moshi'einu
vehu yashmi'einu berachamav
le'einei kol chai. Ani Adonai
Eloheichem. Yimloch Adonai
le'olam Elohayich Tziyon ledor
vador. Haleluyah!

God is our One—our parent, our ruler, our redeemer. With compassion, God is revealed before the sight of all that live. May Adonai, your God, O Zion, rule eternally from generation to generation. Hallelujah!

לְדוֹר וָדוֹר נַגִּיד גָּדְלֶךָ.
וּלְנֵצַח נְצָחִים קְדֻשָּׁתְךָ
נַקְדִּישׁ, וְשִׁבְחֲךָ אֱלֹהֵינוּ מִפִּינוּ
לֹא יָמוּשׁ לְעוֹלָם וָעֶד.

Ledor vador, nagid godlecha.
Ulneitsach netsachim,
kedushatecha nakdish,
veshivchacha Eloheinu mipinu
lo yamush le'olam va'ed.

May each generation speak of Your greatness to the next. For all eternity, may we sanctify Your holiness. May Your praise, our God, never depart from our lips.

And so
May fear and concern
be instilled in all living beings,
deep concern for all created.
All creation should be in awe,
all of life humbled before You.
May all of creation form
a single bond to do Your will.
We know that You alone rule
that Your strength is justice
and Your awesome being
transcends all which You
have created.

וּבְכֵן
תֵּן פַּחְדְּךָ יְיָ אֱלֹהֵינוּ, עַל כָּל
מַעֲשֶׂיךָ, וְאֵימָתְךָ עַל כָּל מַה
שֶּׁבָּרָאתָ, וְיִירָאוּךָ כָּל
הַמַּעֲשִׂים וְיִשְׁתַּחֲווּ לְפָנֶיךָ כָּל
הַבְּרוּאִים, וְיֵעָשׂוּ כֻלָּם אֲגֻדָּה
אַחַת לַעֲשׂוֹת רְצוֹנְךָ בְּלֵבָב
שָׁלֵם, כְּמוֹ שֶׁיָּדַעְנוּ יְיָ אֱלֹהֵינוּ,
שֶׁהַשָּׁלְטָן לְפָנֶיךָ, עֹז בְּיָדְךָ
וּגְבוּרָה בִּימִינֶךָ, וְשִׁמְךָ נוֹרָא
עַל כָּל מַה שֶּׁבָּרָאתָ.

And so
May honor be granted
to Your people,
Praise to those who feel awe
and hope to those
who seek You
and voice sincere yearnings.
May there be joy
throughout the land
and joyfulness for the
inhabitants of Your city.
May the light of joy and justice
shine forth in our lifetime.

וּבְכֵן
תֵּן כָּבוֹד, יְיָ לְעַמֶּךָ, תְּהִלָּה
לִירֵאֶיךָ וְתִקְוָה טוֹבָה
לְדוֹרְשֶׁיךָ, וּפִתְחוֹן פֶּה
לַמְיַחֲלִים לָךְ, שִׂמְחָה לְאַרְצֶךָ
וְשָׂשׂוֹן לְעִירֶךָ, וּצְמִיחַת קֶרֶן
לְדָוִד עַבְדֶּךָ, וַעֲרִיכַת נֵר
לְבֶן־יִשַׁי מְשִׁיחֶךָ, בִּמְהֵרָה
בְיָמֵינוּ.

And so
When such a day arrives
those who struggled for justice
will be first to rejoice;
the upright will be glad;
the faithful will sing with joy;
injustice will close its mouth;
evil will vanish like smoke;
falsehoods will depart
from the earth.

וּבְכֵן
צַדִּיקִים יִרְאוּ וְיִשְׂמָחוּ, וִישָׁרִים
יַעֲלֹזוּ, וַחֲסִידִים בְּרִנָּה יָגִילוּ,
וְעוֹלָתָה תִּקְפָּץ־פִּיהָ, וְכָל
הָרִשְׁעָה כֻּלָּהּ כְּעָשָׁן תִּכְלֶה, כִּי
תַעֲבִיר מֶמְשֶׁלֶת זָדוֹן מִן
הָאָרֶץ.

Sacred Oneness will govern
all things; Mount Zion
will be among Your resting-
places, as will Your holy city,
the city of Shalom, Jerusalem.
As it is written in these holy
words: "Adonai will reign
forever, Your God, O Zion, for
all generations, halleluyah."

וְתִמְלֹךְ, אַתָּה יְיָ לְבַדֶּךָ, עַל כָּל
מַעֲשֶׂיךָ, בְּהַר צִיּוֹן מִשְׁכַּן
כְּבוֹדֶךָ, וּבִירוּשָׁלַיִם עִיר
קָדְשֶׁךָ, כַּכָּתוּב בְּדִבְרֵי קָדְשֶׁךָ:
יִמְלֹךְ יְיָ לְעוֹלָם, אֱלֹהַיִךְ צִיּוֹן
לְדֹר וָדֹר: הַלְלוּיָהּ.

You are holy, Your name is
holy, and there is no God
besides You, as it is written:
"The Eternal, the power of all
creation, is elevated through
justice, God's holiness
sanctified through
acts of justice."

קָדוֹשׁ אַתָּה וְנוֹרָא שְׁמֶךָ, וְאֵין
אֱלוֹהַּ מִבַּלְעָדֶיךָ, כַּכָּתוּב:
וַיִּגְבַּהּ יְיָ צְבָאוֹת בַּמִּשְׁפָּט,
וְהָאֵל הַקָּדוֹשׁ נִקְדַּשׁ בִּצְדָקָה.

Baruch Atah Adonai, hamelech
hakadosh.

בָּרוּךְ אַתָּה יְיָ, הַמֶּלֶךְ הַקָּדוֹשׁ.

Blessed is the Ineffable One, the sacred Power.

Kidushat Hayom: Sanctifying This Day

You have delighted in us
among all of the nations,
loving us, desiring us,
elevating us and sanctifying us
with mitzvot,
drawing us near to serve You,
that Your great holy Presence
might be known to us.

אַתָּה בְחַרְתָּנוּ עִם כָּל הָעַמִּים,
אָהַבְתָּ אוֹתָנוּ וְרָצִיתָ בָּנוּ,
וְרוֹמַמְתָּנוּ עִם כָּל הַלְּשׁוֹנוֹת,
וְקִדַּשְׁתָּנוּ בְּמִצְוֹתֶיךָ, וְקֵרַבְתָּנוּ
מַלְכֵּנוּ לַעֲבוֹדָתֶךָ, וְשִׁמְךָ הַגָּדוֹל
וְהַקָּדוֹשׁ עָלֵינוּ קָרָאתָ.

With love, we have been given:

וַתִּתֶּן לָנוּ, יְיָ אֱלֹהֵינוּ, בְּאַהֲבָה
אֶת יוֹם

(on Shabbat) this Shabbat and

(הַשַּׁבָּת הַזֶּה וְאֶת יוֹם)

(on Rosh Hashanah)
this Day of Remembering /

(on Yom Kippur)
this Day of Atonement

הַזִּכָּרוֹן הַזֶּה,
or
הַכִּפּוּרִים הַזֶּה,

for renouncing our wrongs,
for asking for forgiveness,
for cleansing, for
reconciliation.

יוֹם (זִכְרוֹן) תְּרוּעָה
(בְּאַהֲבָה) מִקְרָא קֹדֶשׁ,

A day of holy gathering
reminding us of our liberation
from the straits of
enslavement.

זֵכֶר לִיצִיאַת מִצְרָיִם.

Ya'aleh v'yavo: May These Ascend

Our God, God of our ancestors:
allow memory to ascend,
to come, to reach us.
May our memory
and our ancestors' memory
and the memory of the dream
of a messianic time,
and the memory of the vision
of Jerusalem as a city of peace,
and the memories of all of Your
people of the House of Israel,
be before You. On this day
may these memories,
these dreams of redemption,
inspire graciousness,
lovingkindness,
and compassion in us,
for life and for peace,
on this (R"H) Rosh Hashanah
(or Y"K) Yom Kippur.

אֱלֹהֵינוּ
וֵאלֹהֵי אֲבוֹתֵינוּ וְאִמּוֹתֵינוּ,
יַעֲלֶה וְיָבֹא, וְיַגִּיעַ וְיֵרָאֶה,
וְיֵרָצֶה וְיִשָּׁמַע, וְיִפָּקֵד וְיִזָּכֵר
זִכְרוֹנֵנוּ וּפִקְדוֹנֵנוּ,
וְזִכְרוֹן אֲבוֹתֵינוּ וְאִמּוֹתֵינוּ,
וְזִכְרוֹן מָשִׁיחַ בֶּן־דָּוִד עַבְדֶּךָ,
וְזִכְרוֹן יְרוּשָׁלַיִם עִיר קָדְשֶׁךָ,
וְזִכְרוֹן כָּל עַמְּךָ
בֵּית יִשְׂרָאֵל לְפָנֶיךָ
לִפְלֵיטָה וּלְטוֹבָה,
לְחֵן וּלְחֶסֶד וּלְרַחֲמִים, לְחַיִּים
וּלְשָׁלוֹם,
(on R"H) בְּיוֹם הַזִּכָּרוֹן הַזֶּה.
(on Y"K) בְּיוֹם הַכִּפּוּרִים הַזֶּה.

זָכְרֵנוּ, יְיָ אֱלֹהֵינוּ בּוֹ לְטוֹבָה,
וּפָקְדֵנוּ בוֹ לִבְרָכָה, וְהוֹשִׁיעֵנוּ
בוֹ לְחַיִּים; וּבִדְבַר יְשׁוּעָה
וְרַחֲמִים חוּס וְחָנֵּנוּ, וְרַחֵם
עָלֵינוּ וְהוֹשִׁיעֵנוּ, כִּי אֵלֶיךָ
עֵינֵינוּ, כִּי אֵל מֶלֶךְ חַנּוּן וְרַחוּם
אָתָּה.

Remember us, Adonai our
God, for goodness. Count us in
for blessing. Save us with life.
Shower us with salvation
and with compassion;
be merciful to us; enfold us
in the compassion we knew
before we were born.
For You are our merciful
parent and sovereign.

אֱלֹהֵינוּ וֵאלֹהֵי אֲבוֹתֵינוּ, מְלוֹךְ
עַל כָּל הָעוֹלָם כֻּלּוֹ בִּכְבוֹדֶךָ,
וְהִנָּשֵׂא עַל כָּל הָאָרֶץ בִּיקָרֶךָ,
וְהוֹפַע בַּהֲדַר גְּאוֹן עֻזֶּךָ, עַל כָּל
יוֹשְׁבֵי תֵבֵל אַרְצֶךָ, וְיֵדַע כָּל
פָּעוּל כִּי אַתָּה פְעַלְתּוֹ, וְיָבִין
כָּל יָצוּר כִּי אַתָּה יְצַרְתּוֹ,
וְיֹאמַר כֹּל אֲשֶׁר נְשָׁמָה בְאַפּוֹ,
יְיָ אֱלֹהֵי יִשְׂרָאֵל מֶלֶךְ, וּמַלְכוּתוֹ
בַּכֹּל מָשָׁלָה.

Our God, and God of our
generations:
shine Your glory on all.
Remind us that You cherish
all who live on this earth,
here and everywhere.
You are our Creator;
You formed us; You breathe
life into us in every moment.
You are King/Queen
of all creation.

אֱלֹהֵינוּ וֵאלֹהֵי אֲבוֹתֵינוּ, (רְצֵה
בִמְנוּחָתֵנוּ) קַדְּשֵׁנוּ בְּמִצְוֹתֶיךָ
וְתֵן חֶלְקֵנוּ בְּתוֹרָתֶךָ, שַׂבְּעֵנוּ
מִטּוּבֶךָ וְשַׂמְּחֵנוּ בִּישׁוּעָתֶךָ
(וְהַנְחִילֵנוּ, יְיָ אֱלֹהֵינוּ, בְּאַהֲבָה
וּבְרָצוֹן שַׁבַּת קָדְשֶׁךָ, וְיָנוּחוּ
בָהּ יִשְׂרָאֵל מְקַדְּשֵׁי שְׁמֶךָ).

Our God
and God of our generations
(accept our rest with mercy)
help us make ourselves holy
with Your mitzvot; give us
a portion of Your Torah's
sweetness; grant us
Your goodness, help us rejoice
in Your salvation
(and on this Shabbat which is
also a holiday, help us be
mindful of both, and to wholly
rest as befits Your people
who yearn to sanctify Your
name).

Purify our hearts to serve You in truth, for You are God of truth and your truth endures forever. Blessed are You, Adonai, ruler over all the earth, Who sanctifies (Shabbat and) Israel and this:

(on R"H) Day of Remembrance
(or on Y"K) Yom Kippur.

וְטַהֵר לִבֵּנוּ לְעָבְדְךָ בֶּאֱמֶת, כִּי אַתָּה אֱלֹהִים אֱמֶת, וּדְבָרְךָ אֱמֶת וְקַיָּם לָעַד. בָּרוּךְ אַתָּה, יְיָ, מֶלֶךְ עַל כָּל הָאָרֶץ, מְקַדֵּשׁ (הַשַּׁבָּת וְ) יִשְׂרָאֵל וְיוֹם:

(on R"H) הַזִּכָּרוֹן
(or on Y"K) הַכִּפּוּרִים.

Avodah: Worship

May it be Your will, Adonai our God, that You accept our rest and take pleasure in our prayers. Accept the service of our hearts and our lips which we mean to offer in love. May the offerings of our hearts always bring You joy in Your people.

רְצֵה, יְיָ אֱלֹהֵינוּ, בְּעַמְּךָ יִשְׂרָאֵל וּבִתְפִלָּתָם, בְּאַהֲבָה תְקַבֵּל וּתְהִי לְרָצוֹן תָּמִיד עֲבוֹדַת יִשְׂרָאֵל עַמֶּךָ.

May Your presence return to Zion speedily and with compassion. Blessed are You, Adonai, Whose presence returns to Zion and fills all creation.

וְתֶחֱזֶינָה עֵינֵינוּ בְּשׁוּבְךָ לְצִיּוֹן בְּרַחֲמִים. בָּרוּךְ אַתָּה יְיָ, הַמַּחֲזִיר שְׁכִינָתוֹ לְצִיּוֹן.

Hoda'ah: Giving Thanks

We are grateful before You, that You are our God and God of our generations, for ever. You are the rock of our lives, the shield of our salvation; You, only You, from generation to generation we sing praises. For our lives which are in Your keeping; for our souls of which You take daily account; for all of the miracles which You perform for us, and all of the wonders and goodnesses which You bring forth in every era and in every day, evening and morning and afternoon; for the goodness of Your compassion; for all of these things we could never thank You enough.

מוֹדִים אֲנַחְנוּ לָךְ, שָׁאַתָּה הוּא, יְיָ אֱלֹהֵינוּ וֵאלֹהֵי אֲבוֹתֵינוּ, לְעוֹלָם וָעֶד, צוּר חַיֵּינוּ, מָגֵן יִשְׁעֵנוּ, אַתָּה הוּא לְדוֹר וָדוֹר נוֹדֶה לְּךָ וּנְסַפֵּר תְּהִלָּתֶךָ. עַל חַיֵּינוּ הַמְּסוּרִים בְּיָדֶךָ, וְעַל נִשְׁמוֹתֵינוּ הַפְּקוּדוֹת לָךְ, וְעַל נִסֶּיךָ שֶׁבְּכָל יוֹם עִמָּנוּ, וְעַל נִפְלְאוֹתֶיךָ וְטוֹבוֹתֶיךָ שֶׁבְּכָל עֵת, עֶרֶב וָבֹקֶר וְצָהֳרָיִם, הַטּוֹב כִּי לֹא כָלוּ רַחֲמֶיךָ, וְהַמְרַחֵם כִּי לֹא תַמּוּ חֲסָדֶיךָ מֵעוֹלָם קִוִּינוּ לָךְ.

For all of these we bless and elevate Your name, our Sovereign and Source, forever and ever.

וְעַל כֻּלָּם יִתְבָּרַךְ וְיִתְרוֹמַם שִׁמְךָ מַלְכֵּנוּ תָּמִיד לְעוֹלָם וָעֶד.

And we thank You for inscribing us, the children of Your covenant, into the book of life.

וּכְתוֹב לְחַיִּים טוֹבִים כָּל בְּנֵי בְרִיתֶךָ.

All that lives praises Your name in truth, our God and our help. Blessed are You, Adonai, for Your goodness and for the many wonders which merit our thanks.

וְכֹל הַחַיִּים יוֹדוּךָ סֶּלָה, וִיהַלְלוּ אֶת שִׁמְךָ בֶּאֱמֶת, הָאֵל יְשׁוּעָתֵנוּ וְעֶזְרָתֵנוּ סֶלָה. בָּרוּךְ אַתָּה יְיָ, הַטּוֹב שִׁמְךָ וּלְךָ נָאֶה לְהוֹדוֹת.

Birkat Shalom: Peace

שָׁלוֹם רָב עַל יִשְׂרָאֵל עַמְּךָ
תָּשִׂים לְעוֹלָם, כִּי אַתָּה הוּא
מֶלֶךְ אָדוֹן לְכָל הַשָּׁלוֹם. וְטוֹב
בְּעֵינֶיךָ לְבָרֵךְ אֶת עַמְּךָ
יִשְׂרָאֵל, בְּכָל עֵת וּבְכָל שָׁעָה
בִּשְׁלוֹמֶךָ.

Shalom rav al Yisrael amcha
tasim le'olam, ki atah hu
melech adon l'chol hashalom.
V'tov b'einecha levarech et
amcha Yisrael, b'chol eit
u'vchol sha'ah bishlomecha.

בְּסֵפֶר חַיִּים, בְּרָכָה וְשָׁלוֹם
וּפַרְנָסָה טוֹבָה, נִזָּכֵר וְנִכָּתֵב
לְפָנֶיךָ, אֲנַחְנוּ וְכָל עַמְּךָ בֵּית
יִשְׂרָאֵל, לְחַיִּים טוֹבִים
וּלְשָׁלוֹם.

B'sefer chayyim, bracha
v'shalom, ufarnasah tovah,
n'zacher v'nikatev l'fanecha,
anachnu v'chol amcha beit
Yisrael, l'chayyim tovim
u'l'shalom.

בָּרוּךְ אַתָּה יְיָ, עוֹשֵׂה הַשָּׁלוֹם.

Baruch atah, Adonai,
oseh ha-shalom.

May there be abundant peace for Israel Your people, always; for You are the sovereign of peace. Let it be good in Your eyes to bless Your people Israel, in every time and in every hour, with Your peace.

In the book of life, blessing, peace, and of making a good living may we be remembered and written before You: us, and all of Your people in our many communities, for a good life and for peace.

Blessed are You, Adonai, maker of peace.

On **Yom Kippur morning**, we continue
with **Selichot** prayers, beginning on **p. 222**.

Meditations After Prayer

אֱלֹהַי, נְצוֹר לְשׁוֹנִי מֵרָע.
וּשְׂפָתַי מִדַּבֵּר מִרְמָה:
וְלִמְקַלְלַי נַפְשִׁי תִדֹּם, וְנַפְשִׁי
כֶּעָפָר לַכֹּל תִּהְיֶה. פְּתַח לִבִּי
בְּתוֹרָתֶךָ, וּבְמִצְוֹתֶיךָ תִּרְדּוֹף
נַפְשִׁי.

Elohai n'tzor l'shoni mera
usfatai m'daber mirmah
v'limkallelai nafshi tidom
v'nafshi ke'afar l'kol tihiyeh.
Petach libi ba-Toratecha,
uv'mitzvotecha tirdof nafshi.

God, keep my tongue from evil
and my lips from speaking deceit.
Before those who slander me, I will hold my tongue;
I will practice humility.
Open my heart to Your Torah,
and connect my heart to Your mitzvot.

יִהְיוּ לְרָצוֹן אִמְרֵי פִי וְהֶגְיוֹן לִבִּי
לְפָנֶיךָ, יְיָ צוּרִי וְגוֹאֲלִי.

Yihiyu l'ratzon imrei fi
v'hegyon libi l'fanecha
Adonai tzuri v'goali.

עֹשֶׂה שָׁלוֹם בִּמְרוֹמָיו הוּא
יַעֲשֶׂה שָׁלוֹם עָלֵינוּ וְעַל כָּל
יִשְׂרָאֵל, וְעַל כָּל יוֹשְׁבֵי תֵבֵל,
וְאִמְרוּ אָמֵן:

Oseh shalom bimromav,
hu ya'aseh shalom, aleinu
v'al kol yisrael, v'al kol
yoshvei tevel, v'imru Amen.

May the words of my mouth
and the meditations of my heart
be acceptable to You, O God,
my rock and my redeemer.
May the One who makes peace on high
make peace for us
and for all the children of Israel
and for all who dwell on this earth
and let us say: Amen.

On Yom Kippur morning we continue as a community with Selichot beginning on p. 222.

Avinu Malkeinu

We address the Parent of the Universe,
the Majesty of Life. There is no other.

We pray for renewal this year:
that harsh decrees be annulled,

that the plans of our enemies be thwarted,
every oppressor and adversary be gone

that pestilence, guns, famine, captivity
and destruction be removed from our midst.

Through *teshuvah*, personal and social change,
we hope for a return to the Sacred.

We ask for complete healing for the sick.
We ask that our guilt be removed:

that we be inscribed in the Book of Life,
inscribed in the Book of Liberation and Wholeness,

in the Book of Sustenance, the Book of Merits
in the Book of Pardon and Forgiveness.

Though we have been lacking in deeds,
please answer us, and help us become whole.

This is abridged to fit the Janowski melody; full text on p. 336.

Avinu malkeinu, sh'ma koleinu.
Avinu malkeinu,
chatanu l'fanecha.
Avinu malkeinu, chamol aleinu
v'al olaleinu v'tapeinu.

אָבִינוּ מַלְכֵּנוּ, שְׁמַע קוֹלֵנוּ.
אָבִינוּ מַלְכֵּנוּ, חָטָאנוּ לְפָנֶיךָ.
אָבִינוּ מַלְכֵּנוּ, חֲמוֹל עָלֵינוּ
וְעַל עוֹלָלֵינוּ וְטַפֵּנוּ.

Avinu malkeinu, chaleh dever
v'cherev v'ra'av me'aleinu.
Avinu malkeinu, chaleh
kol-tzar u-masteen me'aleinu.

אָבִינוּ מַלְכֵּנוּ, כַּלֵּה דֶּבֶר
וְחֶרֶב וְרָעָב מֵעָלֵינוּ.
אָבִינוּ מַלְכֵּנוּ, כַּלֵּה כָּל-צַר
וּמַשְׂטִין מֵעָלֵינוּ.

Avinu malkeinu!
Cotveinu b'sefer
chayyim tovim.
Avinu malkeinu,
chadesh aleinu shanah tovah.

אָבִינוּ מַלְכֵּנוּ ,אָבִינוּ מַלְכֵּנוּ
כָּתְבֵנוּ בְּסֵפֶר חַיִּים טוֹבִים.
אָבִינוּ מַלְכֵּנוּ, חַדֵּשׁ עָלֵינוּ,
חַדֵּשׁ עָלֵינוּ שָׁנָה טוֹבָה.

Avinu malkeinu, hear our prayer.
Avinu malkeinu, we have sinned before You.
Avinu malkeinu, have mercy on us and on our children.
Avinu Malkeinu, rid us of sickness, sword, hunger, destruction.
Avinu Malkeinu, rid us of persecution. *Avinu Malkeinu,*
inscribe us in the book of a good life.
Avinu Malkeinu, renew us; renew us for a good year.

☐ Avinu malkeinu, chanenu
va'anenu, ki ein banu ma'asim,
aseh imanu tzedakah
vachesed v'hoshienu.

☐אָבִינוּ מַלְכֵּנוּ, חָנֵּנוּ וַעֲנֵנוּ, כִּי
אֵין בָּנוּ מַעֲשִׂים, עֲשֵׂה עִמָּנוּ
צְדָקָה וָחֶסֶד וְהוֹשִׁיעֵנוּ.

Avinu malkeinu, be gracious, answer us, for we have little merit.
Treat us generously and with kindness, and be our help.

The Kaddish: A Doorway in Prayer

The Kaddish which follows
known as *Kaddish shalem*
(the "whole Kaddish")

is the doorway
between Avinu Malkeinu
and our Torah service.

Where have today's prayers taken you?
Whatever you're feeling in this moment,
bring that into your prayer.

Kaddish Shalem

Yitgadal v'yitkadash, shmeh
rabah. B'alma divra chiruteh,
v'yamlich malchuteh
b'chayyeichon u'v'yomeichon
u'vchayyei d'chol beit
Yisrael. Ba'agala u-vizman
kariv v'imru amen.

יִתְגַּדַּל וְיִתְקַדַּשׁ שְׁמֵהּ רַבָּא.
בְּעָלְמָא דִּי בְרָא כִרְעוּתֵהּ,
וְיַמְלִיךְ מַלְכוּתֵהּ בְּחַיֵּיכוֹן
וּבְיוֹמֵיכוֹן וּבְחַיֵּי דְכָל בֵּית
יִשְׂרָאֵל. בַּעֲגָלָא וּבִזְמַן קָרִיב
וְאִמְרוּ אָמֵן:

□ Y'hei sh'mei raba m'varakh
l'olam ol'almey almaya.

□ יְהֵא שְׁמֵהּ רַבָּא מְבָרַךְ
לְעָלַם וּלְעָלְמֵי עָלְמַיָּא:

Magnified and sanctified! Magnified and sanctified! May God's Great Name fill the world God created. May God's splendor be seen in the world in your life, in your days, in the life of all Israel. Quickly and soon! And let us say, Amen.

Forever may the Great Name name be blessed!

Yitbarach v'yishtabach,
v'yitpa'ar v'yit-romam
v'yit-naseh. V'yithadar
v'yitaleh v'yithallal shmeh
d'kud'sha b'rich hu. L'eyla
u'leyla min kol birchata
v'shirata, tushbechata
v'nechemata, damiran
b'alma, v'imru amen.

יִתְבָּרַךְ וְיִשְׁתַּבַּח, וְיִתְפָּאַר
וְיִתְרוֹמַם וְיִתְנַשֵּׂא וְיִתְהַדָּר
וְיִתְעַלֶּה וְיִתְהַלָּל שְׁמֵהּ
דְּקֻדְשָׁא בְּרִיךְ הוּא לְעֵֽלָּא
וּלְעֵֽלָּא מִכָּל בִּרְכָתָא
וְשִׁירָתָא, תֻּשְׁבְּחָתָא
וְנֶחֱמָתָא, דַּאֲמִירָן בְּעָלְמָא,
וְאִמְרוּ אָמֵן:

Titkabel tzlot'hon uva-ut'hon d'chol beit Yisrael kadam avuhon di vishmaia v'imru Amen.

תִּתְקַבֵּל צְלוֹתְהוֹן וּבָעוּתְהוֹן דְּכָל (בֵּית) יִשְׂרָאֵל קֳדָם אֲבוּהוֹן דִּי בִשְׁמַיָּא וְאִמְרוּ אָמֵן:

Y'hei shlama raba min shemaya v'chayyim tovim aleinu v'al kol Yisrael, v'imru amen.

יְהֵא שְׁלָמָא רַבָּא מִן שְׁמַיָּא וְחַיִּים עָלֵינוּ וְעַל כָּל יִשְׂרָאֵל, וְאִמְרוּ אָמֵן:

Oseh shalom bimromav, hu ya'aseh shalom, aleinu v'al kol yisrael, v'al kol yoshvei tevel, v'imru Amen.

עֹשֶׂה שָׁלוֹם בִּמְרוֹמָיו הוּא יַעֲשֶׂה שָׁלוֹם עָלֵינוּ וְעַל כָּל יִשְׂרָאֵל, וְעַל כָּל יוֹשְׁבֵי תֵבֵל, וְאִמְרוּ אָמֵן:

Blessed and praised! Splendid and supreme! May the holy name, Bless God, be praised, beyond all the blessings and songs, comforts and consolations, that can be offered in this world. And let us say: Amen.

May our prayers, and the prayers of the entire community, be accepted before You, our Parent.

Accept them! Accept them! May our words of prayer and pleading from all the people of Israel be accepted before God in heaven. And let us say, Amen!

May there be peace and life, great peace and life from heaven above for us and all Israel. And let us say, Amen!

May the One who makes peace in the high heavens make peace for us, for our whole community, and for all the peoples of the world. And let us say: Amen.

Torah Service

Removing the Scroll from the Ark

□ אֵין כָּמוֹךָ בָאֱלֹהִים, יְיָ, וְאֵין כְּמַעֲשֶׂיךָ. מַלְכוּתְךָ מַלְכוּת כָּל עֹלָמִים, וּמֶמְשַׁלְתְּךָ בְּכָל דֹּר וָדֹר. יְיָ מֶלֶךְ, יְיָ מָלָךְ, יְיָ יִמְלֹךְ לְעֹלָם וָעֶד. יְיָ עֹז לְעַמּוֹ יִתֵּן יְיָ יְבָרֵךְ אֶת עַמּוֹ בַשָּׁלוֹם.

□ Ein kamocha va'Elohim, Adonai, ve'ein kema'asecha. Malchutecha malchut kol olamim umemshaltecha bechol dor vador. Adonai melech, Adonai malach, Adonai yimloch le'olam va'ed. Adonai oz le'amo yitein, Adonai yevareich et amo vashalom.

There is none like You among the gods, Adonai,
and there are no deeds like Yours.
You are sovereign over all worlds,
and Your dominion is in all generations.
Adonai reigns, Adonai has reigned,
Adonai will reign forever and ever!
Adonai will give strength to our people;
Adonai will bless our people with peace.

□ אַב הָרַחֲמִים, הֵיטִיבָה בִרְצוֹנְךָ אֶת צִיּוֹן, תִּבְנֶה חוֹמוֹת יְרוּשָׁלָיִם. כִּי בְךָ לְבַד בָּטָחְנוּ, מֶלֶךְ אֵל רָם וְנִשָּׂא, אֲדוֹן עוֹלָמִים.

□ Av harachamim, heitivah virtsonecha et tziyon. Tivneh chomot Yerushalayim. Kee vecha levad batachnu, melech Eil ram venisa, adon olamim.

Source of mercy: favor Zion with Your goodness; rebuild Jerusalem. In You alone do we trust, God of space and time.

□ וַיְהִי בִּנְסוֹעַ הָאָרֹן וַיֹּאמֶר
מֹשֶׁה, קוּמָה יְיָ, וְיָפֻצוּ
אֹיְבֶיךָ, וְיָנֻסוּ מְשַׂנְאֶיךָ
מִפָּנֶיךָ: כִּי מִצִּיּוֹן תֵּצֵא
תוֹרָה , וּדְבַר יְיָ
מִירוּשָׁלָיִם: בָּרוּךְ שֶׁנָּתַן
תּוֹרָה לְעַמּוֹ יִשְׂרָאֵל
בִּקְדֻשָּׁתוֹ:

□ Vayehi binso'a ha'aron vayomer Mosheh, Kumah Adonai, veyafutsu oyvecha,veyanusu mesanecha mipanecha. Kee mitsiyon teitsei Torah, udvar Adonai mirushalayim.

Baruch shenatan Torah, le'amo Yisrael bikdushato.

When the ark went forth, Moshe used to call out: Arise, Adonai, and scatter what is inimical to You, scatter it from before Your face. For from out of Zion will come the Torah, and the word of Adonai from Jerusalem. Blessed is the One who gives Torah to Your people Israel, in holy connection!

יְיָ, יְיָ, אֵל רַחוּם וְחַנּוּן, אֶרֶךְ
אַפַּיִם, וְרַב חֶסֶד וֶאֱמֶת: נֹצֵר
חֶסֶד לָאֲלָפִים, נֹשֵׂא עָוֹן וָפֶשַׁע
וְחַטָּאָה, וְנַקֵּה:

Adonai, Adonai, El rachum vechanun, erech apayim, verav chesed ve'emet, notseir chesed la'alafim, nosei avon, vafesha, vechata'ah, venakeih.

Adonai, Adonai, God of mercy and grace, patient, loving and faithful. Who extends love to the thousandth generation, forgiving transgression, rebellion and sin, and granting pardon.

Singable English:

Yod Hay, Vav Hay, Compassion and Tenderness,
Patience, Forebearance, Kindness, Awareness.
Bearing love from age to age,
Lifting guilt and mistakes and making us free.

Va'ani tefilati lecha, Adonai, eit ratzon, elohim b'rov chas-decha, aneni b'emet yishecha.	וַאֲנִי, תְפִלָּתִי לְךָ יְיָ, עֵת רָצוֹן, אֱלֹהִים בְּרָב חַסְדֶּךָ, עֲנֵנִי בֶּאֱמֶת יִשְׁעֶךָ.

And I: I am my prayer before You, Adonai!
May my words reach You in a good time.
God, with Your great mercy, answer me truly with Your help.

Repeat the next two lines after the prayer-leader:

□ Shema Yisrael, Adonai eloheinu, Adonai echad.	□ שְׁמַע יִשְׂרָאֵל, יְיָ אֱלֹהֵינוּ, יְיָ אֶחָד.
□ Echad eloheinu, gadol adoneinu, kadosh v'nora shemo.	□ אֶחָד אֱלֹהֵינוּ, גָּדוֹל אֲדוֹנֵנוּ, קָדוֹשׁ וְנוֹרָא שְׁמוֹ.
Gadlu l'Adonai iti, u'n'rome-mah shemo yachdav.	גַּדְּלוּ לַייָ אִתִּי, וּנְרוֹמְמָה שְׁמוֹ יַחְדָּו.

Hear, O Israel; Adonai is our God; Adonai is One.
One is our God, great, holy, and awesome!
Magnify God with me, and together let us elevate the Name.

Lecha Adonai hagedulah vehagevurah vehatiferet vehaneitsach vehahod, kee chol bashamayim uva'arets.	לְךָ יְיָ הַגְּדֻלָּה וְהַגְּבוּרָה וְהַתִּפְאֶרֶת וְהַנֵּצַח וְהַהוֹד, כִּי כֹל בַּשָּׁמַיִם וּבָאָרֶץ:

Yours, Adonai, are greatness, might, splendor, triumph, and majesty: yes, all that is in heaven and on earth.

Lecha Adonai hamamlachah
vehamitnasei lechol lerosh.
Romemu Adonai Eloheinu,
vehishtachavu lahadom
raglav kadosh hu.
Romemu Adonai Eloheinu
vehishtachavu lehar kodsho
kee kadosh Adonai Eloheinu.

לְךָ יְיָ הַמַּמְלָכָה וְהַמִּתְנַשֵּׂא
לְכֹל לְרֹאשׁ: רוֹמְמוּ יְיָ אֱלֹהֵינוּ
וְהִשְׁתַּחֲווּ לַהֲדֹם רַגְלָיו קָדוֹשׁ
הוּא: רוֹמְמוּ יְיָ אֱלֹהֵינוּ,
וְהִשְׁתַּחֲווּ לְהַר קָדְשׁוֹ, כִּי
קָדוֹשׁ יְיָ אֱלֹהֵינוּ:

To You, Adonai, belong sovereignty and preeminence above all, for You are holy, Adonai our God! Exalt Adonai with me, let us extol God's name together.

Blessing before Torah

Traditional: highlights the uniqueness of the Jewish people

Baruch atah Adonai Eloheinu
melech ha'olam, asher bachar
banu mikol ha'amim venatan
lanu et Torato. Baruch atah
Adonai, notein ha-Torah.

בָּרוּךְ אַתָּה יְיָ
אֱלֹהֵינוּ מֶלֶךְ הָעוֹלָם,
אֲשֶׁר בָּחַר בָּנוּ מִכָּל הָעַמִּים
וְנָתַן לָנוּ אֶת תּוֹרָתוֹ:
בָּרוּךְ אַתָּה יְיָ, נוֹתֵן הַתּוֹרָה:

Holy One of Blessing, Your presence fills creation. You have chosen us from among all the peoples to receive Your Torah. Blessed are You, Adonai, giver of the Torah.

Alternative version: revised wording emphasizes inclusivity

Baruch atah Adonai Eloheinu
melech ha'olam,asher bachar
banu im kol ha-amim venatan
lanu et Torato. Baruch atah
Adonai, notein ha-Torah.

בָּרוּךְ אַתָּה יְיָ
אֱלֹהֵינוּ מֶלֶךְ הָעוֹלָם,
אֲשֶׁר בָּחַר בָּנוּ עִם כָּל הָעַמִּים
וְנָתַן לָנוּ אֶת תּוֹרָתוֹ:
בָּרוּךְ אַתָּה יְיָ, נוֹתֵן הַתּוֹרָה:

Holy One of Blessing, Your presence fills creation. You have chosen us along with all peoples to receive Your Torah. Blessed are You, Adonai, giver of the Torah.

Blessing after Torah

Baruch atah, Adonai, eloheinu
melech haolam. Asher natan
lanu Torat emet, v'chayyei
olam nata b'tocheinu. Baruch
atah, Adonai, notein haTorah!

בָּרוּךְ אַתָּה יְיָ אֱלֹהֵינוּ מֶלֶךְ הָעוֹלָם,
אֲשֶׁר נָתַן לָנוּ תּוֹרַת אֱמֶת, וְחַיֵּי עוֹלָם
נָטַע בְּתוֹכֵנוּ: בָּרוּךְ אַתָּה יְיָ, נוֹתֵן
הַתּוֹרָה:

Holy One of Blessing, Your Presence fills creation. This Torah is a teaching of truth, and from it comes eternal life for the people who embrace it. Blessed are You, Merciful One, giver of the Torah!

Blessing for Healing

May the One who blessed our ancestors, Abraham, Isaac and Jacob, Sarah, Rebecca, Leah and Rachel, bless those in need of healing of body, mind and spirit. May the compassion of the Holy One be upon them and watch over them. Strengthen them with courage in each day, along with all who are ill, now and swiftly. And let us say: Amen.

מִי שֶׁבֵּרַךְ אֲבוֹתֵינוּ אַבְרָהָם
יִצְחָק וְיַעֲקֹב וְאִמּוֹתֵינוּ שָׂרָה
רִבְקָה לֵאָה וְרָחֵל הוּא יְבָרֵךְ
אֶת-חוֹלֵי הַנֶּפֶשׁ חוֹלֵי הָרוּחַ
וְחוֹלֵי הַגּוּף. הַקָּדוֹשׁ · בָּרוּךְ
הוּא יִהְיֶה עִמָּהֶם · וּשְׁמַר לָהֶם.
חַזֵּק אֶת יָדָם · בְּאוֹמֶץ לֵב
בְּכָל יוֹם, · בְּתוֹךְ שְׁאָר חוֹלֵי
יִשְׂרָאֵל הַשְׁתָּא · בַּעֲגָלָא
וּבִזְמַן קָרִיב. וְנֹאמַר אָמֵן.

מִי שֶׁבֵּרַךְ אֲבוֹתֵינוּ, מְקוֹר הַבְּרָכָה לְאִמּוֹתֵינוּ
Mi sheberach avoteinu, m'kor ha-brakha l'imoteinu
May the source of strength
Who blessed the ones before us
Help us find the courage
To make our lives a blessing
And let us say: Amen.

מִי שֶׁבֵּרַךְ אִמּוֹתֵינוּ, מְקוֹר הַבְּרָכָה לַאֲבוֹתֵינוּ
Mi sheberach imoteinu, m'kor ha-brakha l'avoteinu
Bless those in need of healing
With refuah shleimah
A renewal of body
A renewal of spirit
And let us say: Amen

(Debbie Friedman)

On Rosh Hashanah: *continue with the Torah readings beginning on p. 126 (First Day) or 129 (Second Day.)*

On Yom Kippur: *continue with the Yom Kippur morning Torah reading on p. 248, or with Yizkor on p. 259.*

Torah Readings

For the First Day of Rosh Hashanah

Genesis 21:1-21

First aliyah

Adonai took note of Sarah, as God had promised, and did for her as God had spoken. Sarah conceived and bore a son when Abraham was in his old age, just at the time that God had told him. Abraham named the son whom Sarah had given birth. He named him Isaac—meaning, "he shall laugh." Abraham circumcised Isaac on the eighth day, as God had told him. Abraham was one hundred years old when Isaac was born. Sarah said, "God has brought me laughter! All who hear will laugh with me!" She said, "Who would have thought that Sarah would suckle children for Abraham? For I have given him a child in his old age!" The boy grew and was weaned. Abraham made a great feast on the day that Isaac was weaned. However, Sarah saw the son of Hagar the Egyptian, the boy whom Hagar had borne for Abraham, playing.

וַיְיָ֛ פָּקַ֥ד אֶת־שָׂרָ֖ה כַּאֲשֶׁ֣ר
אָמָ֑ר וַיַּ֧עַשׂ יְיָ֛ לְשָׂרָ֖ה כַּאֲשֶׁ֥ר
דִּבֵּֽר׃ וַתַּ֩הַר֩ וַתֵּ֨לֶד שָׂרָ֧ה
לְאַבְרָהָ֛ם בֵּ֖ן לִזְקֻנָ֑יו לַמּוֹעֵ֕ד
אֲשֶׁר־דִּבֶּ֥ר אֹת֖וֹ אֱלֹהִֽים׃
וַיִּקְרָ֨א אַבְרָהָ֜ם אֶֽת־שֶׁם־בְּנ֧וֹ
הַנּֽוֹלַד־ל֛וֹ אֲשֶׁר־יָלְדָה־לּ֥וֹ שָׂרָ֖ה
יִצְחָֽק׃ וַיָּ֤מָל אַבְרָהָם֙
אֶת־יִצְחָ֣ק בְּנ֔וֹ בֶּן־שְׁמֹנַ֖ת יָמִ֑ים
כַּאֲשֶׁ֛ר צִוָּ֥ה אֹת֖וֹ
אֱלֹהִֽים׃ וְאַבְרָהָ֖ם בֶּן־מְאַ֣ת
שָׁנָ֑ה בְּהִוָּ֣לֶד ל֔וֹ אֵ֖ת יִצְחָ֥ק
בְּנֽוֹ׃ וַתֹּ֣אמֶר שָׂרָ֔ה צְחֹ֕ק עָ֥שָׂה
לִ֖י אֱלֹהִ֑ים כָּל־הַשֹּׁמֵ֖עַ
יִֽצְחַק־לִֽי׃ וַתֹּ֗אמֶר מִ֤י מִלֵּל֙
לְאַבְרָהָ֔ם הֵינִ֥יקָה בָנִ֖ים שָׂרָ֑ה
כִּֽי־יָלַ֥דְתִּי בֵ֖ן לִזְקֻנָֽיו׃ וַיִּגְדַּ֥ל
הַיֶּ֖לֶד וַיִּגָּמַ֑ל וַיַּ֤עַשׂ אַבְרָהָם֙
מִשְׁתֶּ֣ה גָד֔וֹל בְּי֖וֹם הִגָּמֵ֥ל
אֶת־יִצְחָֽק׃ וַתֵּ֨רֶא שָׂרָ֜ה
אֶֽת־בֶּן־הָגָ֧ר הַמִּצְרִ֛ית
אֲשֶׁר־יָלְדָ֥ה לְאַבְרָהָ֖ם מְצַחֵֽק׃

Second aliyah

She said to Abraham, “Send away that slave- woman and her son, for the son of that slave shall not share the inheritance of my son Isaac.” The matter distressed Abraham greatly, for it concerned his son. But God said to Abraham, “Do not be distressed over the boy or your slave. Obey whatever Sarah tells you to do, for it is through Isaac that your lineage shall be known. But I also will make the descendants of the son of the slave-woman into a great nation, for he, too, is your son.” Abraham got up early in the morning and took some bread and a container of water and gave them to Hagar and put them on her shoulder. He gave her the boy and sent them away. She wandered about in the desert of Beer-Sheba. When the water was gone, she sent the boy off under one of the bushes.

וַתֹּ֙אמֶר֙ לְאַבְרָהָ֔ם גָּרֵ֛שׁ
הָאָמָ֥ה הַזֹּ֖את וְאֶת־בְּנָ֑הּ כִּ֣י
לֹ֤א יִירַשׁ֙ בֶּן־הָאָמָ֣ה הַזֹּ֔את
עִם־בְּנִ֖י עִם־יִצְחָֽק׃ וַיֵּ֧רַע
הַדָּבָ֛ר מְאֹ֖ד בְּעֵינֵ֣י אַבְרָהָ֑ם
עַ֖ל אוֹדֹ֥ת בְּנֽוֹ׃ וַיֹּ֨אמֶר
אֱלֹהִ֜ים אֶל־אַבְרָהָ֗ם אַל־יֵרַ֤ע
בְּעֵינֶ֙יךָ֙ עַל־הַנַּ֣עַר וְעַל־אֲמָתֶ֔ךָ
כֹּל֩ אֲשֶׁ֨ר תֹּאמַ֥ר אֵלֶ֛יךָ שָׂרָ֖ה
שְׁמַ֣ע בְּקֹלָ֑הּ כִּ֣י בְיִצְחָ֔ק
יִקָּרֵ֥א לְךָ֖ זָֽרַע׃ וְגַ֥ם
אֶת־בֶּן־הָאָמָ֖ה לְג֣וֹי אֲשִׂימֶ֑נּוּ
כִּ֥י זַרְעֲךָ֖ הֽוּא׃ וַיַּשְׁכֵּ֣ם
אַבְרָהָ֣ם בַּבֹּ֡קֶר וַיִּֽקַּח־לֶחֶם֩
וְחֵ֨מַת מַ֜יִם וַיִּתֵּ֣ן אֶל־הָ֠גָר שָׂ֨ם
עַל־שִׁכְמָ֛הּ וְאֶת־הַיֶּ֖לֶד
וַֽיְשַׁלְּחֶ֑הָ וַתֵּ֣לֶךְ וַתֵּ֔תַע
בְּמִדְבַּ֖ר בְּאֵ֥ר שָֽׁבַע׃ וַיִּכְל֥וּ
הַמַּ֖יִם מִן־הַחֵ֑מֶת וַתַּשְׁלֵ֣ךְ
אֶת־הַיֶּ֔לֶד תַּ֖חַת אַחַ֥ד
הַשִּׂיחִֽם׃

Third aliyah

She went and sat a bowshot away, for she thought, “Let me not see the boy die.” As she sat, she burst into tears. But God heard the cry of the boy, and an angel called to Hagar from heaven and said to her, “What is the matter, Hagar? Do not fear, for God has heard the cry of the boy where he is. Get up and pick up the boy. Take him by the hand, for I will make his descendants a great nation. God opened her eyes and she saw a well full of water. She went and filled her container and gave it to the boy to drink. God was with the boy as he grew. He settled in the desert and was a great archer and hunter. He dwelled in the desert of Paran and his mother chose a wife for him from the land of Egypt.

וַתֵּ֨לֶךְ וַתֵּ֤שֶׁב לָהּ֙ מִנֶּ֔גֶד הַרְחֵק֙
כִּמְטַחֲוֵ֣י קֶ֔שֶׁת כִּ֣י אָֽמְרָ֔ה
אַל־אֶרְאֶ֖ה בְּמ֣וֹת הַיָּ֑לֶד
וַתֵּ֣שֶׁב מִנֶּ֔גֶד וַתִּשָּׂ֥א אֶת־קֹלָ֖הּ
וַתֵּֽבְךְּ׃ וַיִּשְׁמַ֣ע אֱלֹהִים֮
אֶת־ק֣וֹל הַנַּ֒עַר֒ וַיִּקְרָא֩ מַלְאַ֨ךְ
אֱלֹהִ֤ים אֶל־הָגָר֙ מִן־הַשָּׁמַ֔יִם
וַיֹּ֥אמֶר לָ֖הּ מַה־לָּ֣ךְ הָגָ֑ר
אַל־תִּ֣ירְאִ֔י כִּֽי־שָׁמַ֧ע אֱלֹהִ֛ים
אֶל־ק֥וֹל הַנַּ֖עַר בַּאֲשֶׁ֥ר
הוּא־שָֽׁם׃ ק֚וּמִי שְׂאִ֣י
אֶת־הַנַּ֔עַר וְהַחֲזִ֥יקִי אֶת־יָדֵ֖ךְ
בּ֑וֹ כִּֽי־לְג֥וֹי גָּד֖וֹל
אֲשִׂימֶֽנּוּ׃ וַיִּפְקַ֤ח אֱלֹהִים֙
אֶת־עֵינֶ֔יהָ וַתֵּ֖רֶא בְּאֵ֣ר מָ֑יִם
וַתֵּ֜לֶךְ וַתְּמַלֵּ֤א אֶת־הַחֵ֙מֶת֙
מַ֔יִם וַתַּ֖שְׁקְ אֶת־הַנָּֽעַר׃ וַיְהִ֧י
אֱלֹהִ֛ים אֶת־הַנַּ֖עַר וַיִּגְדָּ֑ל
וַיֵּ֙שֶׁב֙ בַּמִּדְבָּ֔ר וַיְהִ֖י רֹבֶ֥ה
קַשָּֽׁת׃ וַיֵּ֖שֶׁב בְּמִדְבַּ֣ר פָּארָ֑ן
וַתִּקַּח־ל֥וֹ אִמּ֛וֹ אִשָּׁ֖ה מֵאֶ֥רֶץ
מִצְרָֽיִם׃

For the Second Day of Rosh Hashanah

Genesis 22:1-19

First aliyah

Later on, God tested Abraham. God said to him, “Abraham,” and he answered, “Here I am.” God said, “Please take your son, your only son, your beloved son Isaac. Go to the land of Moriah and offer him there as an offering on one of the mountains that I will point out to you.” Abraham got up early the next morning, saddled his donkey and took two of his servants and his son Isaac. He split wood for the offering. He set out for the place of which God had told him. On the third day, Abraham looked and saw the place from afar. Abraham said to the servants, “Make camp here with the donkey. The boy and I will go thus far, make our offering, and come back to you.” Abraham took the wood for the offering, put it on his son Isaac, and took the fire and the knife in his hand. The two of them went off together.

וַיְהִ֗י אַחַר֙ הַדְּבָרִ֣ים הָאֵ֔לֶּה
וְהָ֣אֱלֹהִ֔ים נִסָּ֖ה אֶת־אַבְרָהָ֑ם
וַיֹּ֣אמֶר אֵלָ֔יו אַבְרָהָ֖ם וַיֹּ֥אמֶר
הִנֵּֽנִי׃ וַיֹּ֡אמֶר קַח־נָ֠א אֶת־בִּנְךָ֨
אֶת־יְחִֽידְךָ֤ אֲשֶׁר־אָהַ֨בְתָּ֙
אֶת־יִצְחָ֔ק וְלֶךְ־לְךָ֔ אֶל־אֶ֖רֶץ
הַמֹּרִיָּ֑ה וְהַעֲלֵ֤הוּ שָׁם֙ לְעֹלָ֔ה עַ֚ל
אַחַ֣ד הֶֽהָרִ֔ים אֲשֶׁ֖ר אֹמַ֥ר אֵלֶֽיךָ׃
וַיַּשְׁכֵּ֨ם אַבְרָהָ֜ם בַּבֹּ֗קֶר וַֽיַּחֲבֹשׁ֙
אֶת־חֲמֹר֔וֹ וַיִּקַּ֞ח אֶת־שְׁנֵ֤י נְעָרָיו֙
אִתּ֔וֹ וְאֵ֖ת יִצְחָ֣ק בְּנ֑וֹ וַיְבַקַּע֙ עֲצֵ֣י
עֹלָ֔ה וַיָּ֣קָם וַיֵּ֔לֶךְ אֶל־הַמָּק֖וֹם
אֲשֶׁר־אָֽמַר־ל֥וֹ הָאֱלֹהִֽים׃ בַּיּ֣וֹם
הַשְּׁלִישִׁ֗י וַיִּשָּׂ֨א אַבְרָהָ֧ם
אֶת־עֵינָ֛יו וַיַּ֥רְא אֶת־הַמָּק֖וֹם
מֵרָחֹֽק׃ וַיֹּ֨אמֶר אַבְרָהָ֜ם
אֶל־נְעָרָ֗יו שְׁבוּ־לָכֶ֥ם פֹּה֙
עִֽם־הַחֲמ֔וֹר וַאֲנִ֣י וְהַנַּ֔עַר נֵלְכָ֖ה
עַד־כֹּ֑ה וְנִֽשְׁתַּחֲוֶ֖ה וְנָשׁ֥וּבָה
אֲלֵיכֶֽם׃ וַיִּקַּ֨ח אַבְרָהָ֜ם אֶת־עֲצֵ֣י
הָעֹלָ֗ה וַיָּ֙שֶׂם֙ עַל־יִצְחָ֣ק בְּנ֔וֹ
וַיִּקַּ֣ח בְּיָד֔וֹ אֶת־הָאֵ֖שׁ
וְאֶת־הַֽמַּאֲכֶ֑לֶת וַיֵּלְכ֥וּ שְׁנֵיהֶ֖ם
יַחְדָּֽו׃

Second aliyah

Isaac spoke to Abraham his father. He said, “Father?” And Abraham answered, “Yes, my son.” He said, “I see the fire and the wood, but where is the sheep for the offering?” Abraham said, “God will see to the sheep for the offering, my son.” And the two of them walked on together. They came to the place of which God had spoken and there Abraham built an altar. He laid out the wood; he bound his son Isaac; he placed him on the altar, on top of the wood. Abraham picked up the knife to slay his son.

וַיֹּ֨אמֶר יִצְחָ֜ק אֶל־אַבְרָהָ֤ם
אָבִיו֙ וַיֹּ֣אמֶר אָבִ֔י וַיֹּ֖אמֶר הִנֶּ֣נִּֽי
בְנִ֑י וַיֹּ֗אמֶר הִנֵּ֤ה הָאֵשׁ֙ וְהָ֣עֵצִ֔ים
וְאַיֵּ֥ה הַשֶּׂ֖ה לְעֹלָֽה: וַיֹּ֙אמֶר֙
אַבְרָהָ֔ם אֱלֹהִ֞ים יִרְאֶה־לּ֥וֹ הַשֶּׂ֛ה
לְעֹלָ֖ה בְּנִ֑י וַיֵּלְכ֖וּ שְׁנֵיהֶ֥ם
יַחְדָּֽו: וַיָּבֹ֗אוּ אֶֽל־הַמָּקוֹם֮ אֲשֶׁ֣ר
אָֽמַר־ל֣וֹ הָאֱלֹהִים֒ וַיִּ֨בֶן שָׁ֤ם
אַבְרָהָם֙ אֶת־הַמִּזְבֵּ֔חַ וַֽיַּעֲרֹ֖ךְ
אֶת־הָעֵצִ֑ים וַֽיַּעֲקֹד֙ אֶת־יִצְחָ֣ק
בְּנ֔וֹ וַיָּ֤שֶׂם אֹתוֹ֙ עַל־הַמִּזְבֵּ֔חַ
מִמַּ֖עַל לָעֵצִֽים: וַיִּשְׁלַ֤ח אַבְרָהָם֙
אֶת־יָד֔וֹ וַיִּקַּ֖ח אֶת־הַֽמַּאֲכֶ֑לֶת
לִשְׁחֹ֖ט אֶת־בְּנֽוֹ:

Third aliyah

An angel called down from heaven, “Abraham! Abraham!” Abraham answered, “Here I am.” The voice said, “Do not raise your hand against the boy. Do nothing to him. For now I know that you revere God, since you have not withheld your son, your only one, from Me.”

וַיִּקְרָ֨א אֵלָ֜יו מַלְאַ֤ךְ יְהוָה֙
מִן־הַשָּׁמַ֔יִם וַיֹּ֖אמֶר אַבְרָהָ֣ם
אַבְרָהָ֑ם וַיֹּ֖אמֶר הִנֵּֽנִי: וַיֹּ֗אמֶר
אַל־תִּשְׁלַ֤ח יָֽדְךָ֙ אֶל־הַנַּ֔עַר
וְאַל־תַּ֥עַשׂ ל֖וֹ מְא֑וּמָה כִּ֣י עַתָּ֣ה
יָדַ֗עְתִּי כִּֽי־יְרֵ֤א אֱלֹהִים֙ אַ֔תָּה
וְלֹ֥א חָשַׂ֛כְתָּ אֶת־בִּנְךָ֥
אֶת־יְחִידְךָ֖ מִמֶּֽנִּי:

When Abraham looked up, he saw, lo and behold, a lone ram, caught in the thicket by its horns. Abraham went and took the ram and offered it as a burnt offering in place of his son. Abraham named that place "Adonai-Sees," as it is said to this day, "On the mount Adonai is seen." The angel called to Abraham from heaven a second time. The voice said, "By Myself, I swear, Adonai declares, as you have done this thing and did not withhold your son, your only one, I will bless you and greatly increase your descendants as the stars of the heavens and as the sands of the seashore. Your descendants shall take the cities of their enemies! All the nations of the earth will bless themselves by your descendants, because you obeyed My voice!" Abraham returned to his servants. They broke camp and went together to Beer-Sheva and Abraham dwelled in Beer-Sheva.

וַיִּשָּׂא אַבְרָהָם אֶת־עֵינָיו
וַיַּרְא וְהִנֵּה־אַיִל אַחַר נֶאֱחַז
בַּסְּבַךְ בְּקַרְנָיו וַיֵּלֶךְ אַבְרָהָם
וַיִּקַּח אֶת־הָאַיִל וַיַּעֲלֵהוּ
לְעֹלָה תַּחַת בְּנוֹ׃ וַיִּקְרָא
אַבְרָהָם שֵׁם־הַמָּקוֹם הַהוּא
יְיָ יִרְאֶה אֲשֶׁר יֵאָמֵר הַיּוֹם
בְּהַר יְיָ יֵרָאֶה׃ וַיִּקְרָא מַלְאַךְ
יְיָ אֶל־אַבְרָהָם שֵׁנִית
מִן־הַשָּׁמָיִם׃ וַיֹּאמֶר בִּי
נִשְׁבַּעְתִּי נְאֻם־יְיָ כִּי יַעַן אֲשֶׁר
עָשִׂיתָ אֶת־הַדָּבָר הַזֶּה וְלֹא
חָשַׂכְתָּ אֶת־בִּנְךָ
אֶת־יְחִידֶךָ׃ כִּי־בָרֵךְ אֲבָרֶכְךָ
וְהַרְבָּה אַרְבֶּה אֶת־זַרְעֲךָ
כְּכוֹכְבֵי הַשָּׁמַיִם וְכַחוֹל אֲשֶׁר
עַל־שְׂפַת הַיָּם וְיִרַשׁ זַרְעֲךָ
אֵת שַׁעַר אֹיְבָיו׃ וְהִתְבָּרְכוּ
בְזַרְעֲךָ כֹּל גּוֹיֵי הָאָרֶץ עֵקֶב
אֲשֶׁר שָׁמַעְתָּ בְּקֹלִי׃ וַיָּשָׁב
אַבְרָהָם אֶל־נְעָרָיו וַיָּקֻמוּ
וַיֵּלְכוּ יַחְדָּו אֶל־בְּאֵר שָׁבַע
וַיֵּשֶׁב אַבְרָהָם בִּבְאֵר שָׁבַע׃

For reflection...

Here are some poems and meditations arising out of the fertile ground of this holiday's holy stories.

Inheritance

The ram came last.
And Abraham did not know
that it came to answer
the boy's question,
first of his strength
and now his day was waning.

The old man raised his head.
Seeing that he dreamed no dream,
that the angel stood there
the knife slipped from his hand.

The boy, released from his bonds
saw his father's back.

Isaac, it is said,
was not offered up.
He lived for many years,
and saw goodness,
until his eyes dimmed.

But he bequeathed that hour
to his offspring.
They are born
with a knife in their hearts.

(Haim Gouri,
translated by Rabbi Rachel Barenblat)

from The Ram's Horn

The ram encodes the hidden spiral of all things. The ram's horn we sound represents the double fallopian tubes; also the power of the male; also the space-time continuum with its startling curves and hollows. Also it represents the *tzimtzum*: the empty space at the beginning of creation; the space that allows creatures to come into being.

Or, the ram's horn is the winding serpent of everything, the life-leviathan, the universe-umblicus. It dances in space and in song, filled with our voices, yet alien, vast, gorgeously terrible. This is why we blow the spiral horn during Elul: to teach us that everything is connected. Every action reverberates through the web; no string is plucked in isolation. The sound vibrations of the shofar lap against our ears like the great mother sea, murmuring: *Thou art not alone.*

There are two horns that come from the primordial ram: one that was sounded at Sinai, and one to be sounded at the time of the Messiah. We never know which one we are hearing: the wisdom of the past, or the truths of the future. We stand listening, trying to hear a sound so multiple it is like the waves of the ocean. We, the present, stand listening for past and future. For a moment, the ancestors whisper; ova and spermatozoa sing; words we have woven from our memories slip between these two books of life to write our names.

The shofar is the crying child entering the world. The shofar is the cry of the one who leaves the world. The shofar is the breath, running and returning while life lasts. We who know we are all this: we are the ram, emerging from the hairy thicket onto the altar, voicing the long ache of the soul-sound.

(Rabbi Jill Hammer)

For I Will Consider Your Dog Molly

For it was the first day of Rosh Ha'shanah, New Year's Day, day of remembrance, of ancient sacrifices and averted calamities.
For I started the day by eating an apple dipped in honey, as ritual required.
For I went to the local synagogue to listen to the ram's horn blown.
For I asked Our Father, Our King, to save us for his sake if not for ours, for the sake of his abundant mercies, for the sake of his right hand, for the sake of those who went through fire and water for the sanctification of his name.
For despite the use of a microphone and other gross violations of ceremony, I gave myself up gladly to the synagogue's sensual insatiable vast womb.
For what right have I to feel offended?
For I communed with my dead father, and a conspicuous tear rolled down my right cheek, and there was loud crying inside me.
For I understood how that tear could become an orb.
For the Hebrew melodies comforted me.
For I lost my voice.
For I met a friend who asked "is this a day of high seriousness" and when I said yes he said "it has taken your voice away."
For he was right, for I felt the strong lashes of the wind lashing me by the throat.
For I thought there shall come a day that the watchmen upon the hills of Ephraim shall cry, Arise and let us go up to Zion unto the Lord our God.
For the virgin shall rejoice in the dance, and the young and old in each other's arms, and their soul shall be as a watered garden, and neither shall they learn war any more.
For God shall lower the price of bread and corn and wine and oil, he shall let our cry come up to him.
For it is customary on the first day of Rosh Ha'shanah to cast a stone into the depths of the sea, to weep and pray to weep no more.
For the stone represents all the sins of the people.
For I asked you and Molly to accompany me to Cascadilla Creek, there being no ocean nearby.

For we talked about the Psalms of David along the way, and the story of Hannah, mother of Samuel, who sought the most robust bard to remedy her barrenness.
For Isaac said "I see the fire and the wood, but where is the lamb for the offering?"
For as soon as I saw the stone, white flat oblong and heavy, I knew that it had summoned me.
For I heard the voice locked inside that stone, for I pictured a dry wilderness in which, with a wave of my staff, I could command sweet waters to flow forth from that stone.
For I cast the stone into the stream and watched it sink to the bottom where dozens of smaller stones, all of them black, gathered around it.
For the waterfall performed the function of the chorus.
For after the moment of solemnity dissolved, you playfully tossed Molly into the stream.
For you tossed her three times, and three times she swam back for her life.
For she shook the water off her body, refreshed.
For you removed the leash from her neck and let her roam freely.
For she darted off into the brush and speared a small gray moving thing in the neck.
For this was the work of an instant.
For we looked and behold! the small gray thing was a rat.
For Molly had killed the rat with a single efficient bite, in conformance with Jewish law.
For I took the rat and cast him into the stream, and both of us congratulated Molly.
For now she resumed her noble gait.
For she does not lie awake in the dark and weep for her sins, and whine about her condition, and discuss her duty to God.
For I'd as lief pray with your dog Molly as with any man.
For she knows that God is her savior.

(David Lehman)

from The Akedah Cycle

Acharei ha-dvarim ha-eileh / After these things

—the hidden ache of infertility,
their marriage straining at the seams
beneath everything unspoken—

Sarai's desperate play for control,
claiming she wouldn't mind
if Avram slept with the maid

—then watching Hagar's belly swell,
how she carried unborn Ishmael
as though she were dancing—

after jealousy arose between them
like brackish water, after Hagar
spoke with the Almighty

—after Avram changed their names
and circumcised his heart,
after the angels came—

after Avraham argued with God
and Lot offered his own daughters
to a mob of angry men

—after Avraham and Sarah moved
to Abimelech's lands, desperate
to escape their own story—

after they returned home
and Sarah became pregnant
and they named their son Laughter

—after Sarah had laughed
to think of milk flowing
from her withered breasts—

after Sarah saw the boys at play
        and fury overwhelmed her
                and she sent Hagar away

—after Avraham, distraught,
        accused Abimelech of stealing
                his source of inspiration—

after the men made a treaty
        and planted a tamarisk
                and they stayed there a while

—after Avraham had forgotten
        Sarah's exhausted radiance
                when she first held their son—

after these things
        the sweet and the bitter
                God tested Avraham

Acharei ha-dvarim ha-eileh / After these words

The adversary stood before God
like a prosecutor before a judge
and said, My Lord, with all due respect
this guy you've chosen isn't worthy
if you demanded a real sacrifice
he would balk like a frightened mule.

No, that's not right:
it was Yitzchak and Ishmael arguing
as brothers do, and one said
my circumcision is better than yours
I was thirteen, and you were eight days old
and the other said, so what, I'd do anything for God.

Actually the conversation was between God
and Avraham: God said take your son.
Avraham asked, which one? God tried your only son
but Avraham said one is Sarah's, one is Hagar's.

Whom you love, God said, and Avraham said
so help me, I love them both.

When it was all over God said
I never meant for you to kill him.
I only wanted you to raise him up.
But Avraham had forgotten
how to hear God's voice
and he never replied.

Meanwhile, back at the ranch

Their dwelling is quiet.
Sarah wakes early,
has to remind herself
that no one needs her.

After Hagar left
(after Sarah sent her:
not her finest moment,
she blames depression)

Sarah never sought
another handmaid
preferring to wrangle
her son alone.

For months Avraham slept
in his own tent, or
under the spread of stars
while Sarah woke

and nursed, woke and nursed.
She crooned Yitzchak
back to sleep
five times a night.

When he learned to walk
their camp was his.
He waddled from one tent
to the next, from goats

to firepit, even
to the well his father
covered hastily
with a woven net.

But always Yitzchak returned
to his mother, peeking
around her loom.
Now his absence echoes.

On the third night
Sarah dreams a visitor
who tells her
Avraham wields a knife,

their son is bound
and she wakes screaming
as though the blade
pierced her own chest.

The angels say

Avraham failed the test.
For Sodom and Gomorrah he argued
but when it came to his son
no protest crossed his lips.

God was mute with horror.
Avraham, smasher of idols
and digger of wells
was meant to talk back.

Sarah would have been wiser
but Avraham avoided her tent,
didn't lay his head in her lap
to unburden his secret heart.

In stricken silence God watched
as Avraham saddled his ass
and took Yitzchak on their last hike
to the place God would show him.

The angel had to call him twice.
Avraham's eyes were red, his voice hoarse
he wept like a man pardoned
but God never spoke to him again.

Possibilities

Maybe Avraham was testing God,
walking slowly, stalling for time.

Maybe God wanted obedience
and Yitzchak yearned to submit.

Yitzchak might have been
old enough to understand

maybe he was sixteen, maybe thirty-seven
in the moment when God saw him.

Avraham might have been crazy.
He might have misunderstood.

Maybe the angel who said
Now I know that you fear God

was a literalist, unable to imagine
how this story sticks in our throats.

Maybe the angel's speech
wasn't originally part of the story.

Maybe Sarah got wind of the plan
and her soul departed, or

maybe she was ready with a feast
when Yitzchak came home.

Maybe Avraham's tears
made Yitzchak go blind.

Maybe Yitzchak was killed, then spent
three years in Eden before returning.

Maybe we need to accept
we too are bound.

Prepare ourselves every day to die,
to offer God what we most prize.

Maybe there's always a ram
waiting just outside the frame.

Together

The two of them walked together
Yitzchak and Ishmael
they never spoke again
after their mothers quarreled

Yitzchak and Ishmael
beneath the cloudless sky
after their mothers quarreled
exchanged one last embrace

beneath the cloudless sky
Sarah and her son
exchanged one last embrace
before the three-day journey

Sarah and her son
drew water from the well
before the three-day journey
barefoot in the dust

drawing water from the well
Avraham plumbed the depths
barefoot in the dust
asking God for insight

Avraham plumbed the depths
he looked up to the mountain
asking God for insight
his heart afire with fear

he looked up to the mountain
they never spoke again
his heart afire with fear
the two of them walked together

And here we are

But what about us
again, wishing
that our ancestors

listening to this tale
for the hundredth time
weren't so familiar

sometimes petty   and sometimes kind
walking awestruck   through a world
where God's presence   is always manifest

In this season of turning   and returning
we long for heroes   we want to be able to say
I take after my parents   with uncomplicated pride

But that's not how it goes   our forebears had
marriages and children   relationships and arguments
sometimes they missed   even the widest of marks

All we can do   is tell their stories
around our campfire   around our festival table
with the polished cup   and challah round as the moon

all we can do is pray   for a year as sweet
as mother's milk, a year   when we don't make
the same mistakes   for the millionth time

or, when we do,   resolve not to wait
until next year   to seek forgiveness
All we can do   is remember

(Rabbi Rachel Barenblat)

Haftarah Reading

Blessing Before the Reading

Blessed are You, Adonai our God, Source of all, who has chosen good prophets and has delighted in the faithful words they have spoken. Blessed are You, Adonai, who continues to choose Torah, Moses, the people Israel, and prophets of truth and justice.

בָּרוּךְ אַתָּה יְיָ אֱלֹהֵינוּ מֶלֶךְ הָעוֹלָם, אֲשֶׁר בָּחַר בִּנְבִיאִים טוֹבִים, וְרָצָה בְדִבְרֵיהֶם הַנֶּאֱמָרִים בֶּאֱמֶת, בָּרוּךְ אַתָּה יְיָ, הַבּוֹחֵר בַּתּוֹרָה וּבְמֹשֶׁה עַבְדּוֹ, וּבְיִשְׂרָאֵל עַמּוֹ, וּבִנְבִיאֵי הָאֱמֶת וָצֶדֶק.

First day: First Samuel 1:1-28

There was a man from Ramah-Zuph, in the hill country of Ephraim, whose name was Elkanah son of Jeroham son of Elihu son of Tohu son of Zuph. He had two wives, one named Hannah and the other Peninnah. Peninnah had children, but Hannah was childless.

This man used to go up from his town every year to worship and to offer sacrifice to Adonai Tzevaot at Shiloh. Hophni and Phinehas, the two sons of Eli, were priests of Adonai there.

וַיְהִי אִישׁ אֶחָד מִן־הָרָמָתַיִם צוֹפִים מֵהַר אֶפְרָיִם וּשְׁמוֹ אֶלְקָנָה בֶּן־יְרֹחָם בֶּן־אֱלִיהוּא בֶּן־תֹּחוּ בֶן־צוּף אֶפְרָתִי׃ וְלוֹ שְׁתֵּי נָשִׁים שֵׁם אַחַת חַנָּה וְשֵׁם הַשֵּׁנִית פְּנִנָּה וַיְהִי לִפְנִנָּה יְלָדִים וּלְחַנָּה אֵין יְלָדִים׃ וְעָלָה הָאִישׁ הַהוּא מֵעִירוֹ מִיָּמִים יָמִימָה לְהִשְׁתַּחֲוֺת וְלִזְבֹּחַ לַיהוָה צְבָאוֹת בְּשִׁלֹה וְשָׁם שְׁנֵי בְנֵי־עֵלִי חָפְנִי וּפִנְחָס כֹּהֲנִים לַיְיָ.

One such day, Elkanah offered a sacrifice. He gave portions to his wife Peninnah and to all her sons and daughters. However, he gave only one portion to Hannah—even though she was his favorite—because Adonai had made her barren. Her rival, Peninnah, to make her miserable, would taunt Hannah, saying that Adonai had made her barren. This happened year after year. Every time Hannah went up to the Temple, Peninnah would taunt her, to the point that she wept and would not eat.

Her husband, Elkanah, said to her, "Hannah, why are you crying and why aren't you eating? Why are you so sad? Am I not more devoted to you than ten sons?"

After they had eaten and drunk at Shiloh, Hannah rose. The priest Eli was sitting on the seat next to the entrance to the Temple. In her misery, she prayed to Adonai, weeping all the while. She made this vow: "Adonai Tzevaot, if You will look upon the suffering of Your servant and will remember me and not forget me, and if You will grant me a baby boy, I will dedicate him to You for all the days of his life, and no razor shall ever touch his head."

וַיְהִי הַיּוֹם וַיִּזְבַּח אֶלְקָנָה וְנָתַן
לִפְנִנָּה אִשְׁתּוֹ וּלְכָל־בָּנֶיהָ
וּבְנוֹתֶיהָ מָנוֹת׃ וּלְחַנָּה יִתֵּן
מָנָה אַחַת אַפָּיִם כִּי
אֶת־חַנָּה אָהֵב וַיהֹוָה סָגַר
רַחְמָהּ׃ וְכִעֲסַתָּה צָרָתָהּ
גַּם־כַּעַס בַּעֲבוּר הַרְּעִמָהּ
כִּי־סָגַר יְהֹוָה בְּעַד
רַחְמָהּ׃ וְכֵן יַעֲשֶׂה שָׁנָה
בְשָׁנָה מִדֵּי עֲלֹתָהּ בְּבֵית יְיָ
כֵּן תַּכְעִסֶנָּה וַתִּבְכֶּה וְלֹא
תֹאכַל׃ וַיֹּאמֶר לָהּ אֶלְקָנָה
אִישָׁהּ חַנָּה לָמֶה תִבְכִּי
וְלָמֶה לֹא תֹאכְלִי וְלָמֶה יֵרַע
לְבָבֵךְ הֲלוֹא אָנֹכִי טוֹב לָךְ
מֵעֲשָׂרָה בָּנִים׃ וַתָּקָם חַנָּה
אַחֲרֵי אָכְלָה בְשִׁלֹה וְאַחֲרֵי
שָׁתֹה וְעֵלִי הַכֹּהֵן יֹשֵׁב
עַל־הַכִּסֵּא עַל־מְזוּזַת הֵיכַל
יְיָ׃ וְהִיא מָרַת נָפֶשׁ וַתִּתְפַּלֵּל
עַל־יְיָ וּבָכֹה תִבְכֶּה׃ וַתִּדֹּר
נֶדֶר וַתֹּאמַר יְיָ צְבָאוֹת
אִם־רָאֹה תִרְאֶה בָּעֳנִי
אֲמָתֶךָ וּזְכַרְתַּנִי וְלֹא־תִשְׁכַּח
אֶת־אֲמָתֶךָ וְנָתַתָּה לַאֲמָתְךָ
זֶרַע אֲנָשִׁים וּנְתַתִּיו לַיהֹוָה
כָּל־יְמֵי חַיָּיו וּמוֹרָה לֹא־יַעֲלֶה
עַל־רֹאשׁוֹ׃

As she prayed before Adonai, Eli watched her mouth. Now Hannah was praying silently. Only her lips moved, but her voice could not be heard. So Eli thought that she was drunk. Eli said to her, “How long will you make a drunken spectacle of yourself? Sober up!”

Hannah replied, “Oh no, my lord! I am a very unhappy woman. I have drunk no wine or other strong drink, but I have been pouring out my heart to Adonai. Do not take me for a worthless woman. All this time I only have been praying out of my great anguish and distress.”

“Then go in peace,” said Eli, “and may the God of Israel grant you what you have asked.”

She answered, “You are most kind.” So the woman left, and she ate, and was no longer downcast. Early next morning they worshipped before Adonai, and they went back home to Ramah.

Elkanah slept with his wife Hannah, and Adonai remembered her. Hannah conceived, and at the turn of the year, she bore a son. She named him Samuel, meaning, “I asked Adonai for him.”

וְהָיָה֙ כִּ֣י הִרְבְּתָ֔ה לְהִתְפַּלֵּ֖ל
לִפְנֵ֣י יְיָ֑ וְעֵלִ֖י שֹׁמֵ֥ר אֶת־פִּֽיהָ׃
וְחַנָּ֗ה הִ֚יא מְדַבֶּ֣רֶת עַל־לִבָּ֔הּ
רַ֚ק שְׂפָתֶ֣יהָ נָּע֔וֹת וְקוֹלָ֖הּ לֹ֣א
יִשָּׁמֵ֑עַ וַיַּחְשְׁבֶ֥הָ עֵלִ֖י
לְשִׁכֹּרָֽה׃ וַיֹּ֚אמֶר אֵלֶ֙יהָ֙ עֵלִ֔י
עַד־מָתַ֖י תִּשְׁתַּכָּרִ֑ין הָסִ֥ירִי
אֶת־יֵינֵ֖ךְ מֵעָלָֽיִךְ׃ וַתַּ֨עַן חַנָּ֤ה
וַתֹּ֙אמֶר֙ לֹ֣א אֲדֹנִ֔י אִשָּׁ֤ה
קְשַׁת־ר֙וּחַ֙ אָנֹ֔כִי וְיַ֥יִן וְשֵׁכָ֖ר
לֹ֣א שָׁתִ֑יתִי וָאֶשְׁפֹּ֥ךְ
אֶת־נַפְשִׁ֖י לִפְנֵ֥י יְיָ׃ אַל־תִּתֵּן֙
אֶת־אֲמָ֣תְךָ֔ לִפְנֵ֖י בַּת־בְּלִיָּ֑עַל
כִּֽי־מֵרֹ֥ב שִׂיחִ֛י וְכַעְסִ֖י דִּבַּ֥רְתִּי
עַד־הֵֽנָּה׃ וַיַּ֧עַן עֵלִ֛י וַיֹּ֖אמֶר
לְכִ֣י לְשָׁל֑וֹם וֵאלֹהֵ֣י יִשְׂרָאֵ֗ל
יִתֵּן֙ אֶת־שֵׁ֣לָתֵ֔ךְ אֲשֶׁ֥ר שָׁאַ֖לְתְּ
מֵעִמּֽוֹ׃ וַתֹּ֕אמֶר תִּמְצָ֧א
שִׁפְחָתְךָ֛ חֵ֖ן בְּעֵינֶ֑יךָ וַתֵּ֨לֶךְ
הָאִשָּׁ֤ה לְדַרְכָּהּ֙ וַתֹּאכַ֔ל
וּפָנֶ֥יהָ לֹא־הָיוּ־לָ֖הּ
עֽוֹד׃ וַיַּשְׁכִּ֣מוּ בַבֹּ֗קֶר
וַיִּֽשְׁתַּחֲווּ֙ לִפְנֵ֣י יְיָ֔ וַיָּשֻׁ֖בוּ
וַיָּבֹ֥אוּ אֶל־בֵּיתָ֖ם הָרָמָ֑תָה
וַיֵּ֤דַע אֶלְקָנָה֙ אֶת־חַנָּ֣ה
אִשְׁתּ֔וֹ וַיִּֽזְכְּרֶ֖הָ יְיָ׃ וַיְהִי֙
לִתְקֻפ֣וֹת הַיָּמִ֔ים וַתַּ֥הַר חַנָּ֖ה
וַתֵּ֣לֶד בֵּ֑ן וַתִּקְרָ֤א אֶת־שְׁמוֹ֙
שְׁמוּאֵ֔ל כִּ֥י מֵיְהוָ֖ה שְׁאִלְתִּֽיו׃

The next year, when Elkanah and his family went to offer the annual sacrifices to Adonai, Hannah did not go. She said to her husband, “When the child is weaned, I will bring him. For when he has appeared before Adonai, he must remain there for good.”

Her husband Elkanah said to her, “Do as you think best. Stay home until you have weaned him. May Adonai’s word be fulfilled.” So Hannah stayed home and nursed her son until she weaned him.

When she had weaned him, she took him to the Temple, along with three bulls, a measure of flour, and a jar of wine. And though the boy was still very young, she brought him to the Temple of Adonai at Shiloh. After slaughtering the bull, they brought the boy to Eli. She said, “Please, my lord! As you live, I am the woman who stood here beside you and prayed to Adonai. It was this boy whom I prayed for, and now Adonai has granted me what I asked. I, in turn, hereby lend him to Adonai. For as long as he lives he is lent to Adonai.” And they bowed low there before Adonai.

וַיַּעַל הָאִישׁ אֶלְקָנָה וְכָל־בֵּיתוֹ
לִזְבֹּחַ לַייָ אֶת־זֶבַח הַיָּמִים
וְאֶת־נִדְרוֹ: וְחַנָּה לֹא עָלָתָה
כִּי־אָמְרָה לְאִישָׁהּ עַד יִגָּמֵל
הַנַּעַר וַהֲבִאֹתִיו וְנִרְאָה אֶת־פְּנֵי
יְיָ וְיָשַׁב שָׁם עַד־עוֹלָם: וַיֹּאמֶר
לָהּ אֶלְקָנָה אִישָׁהּ עֲשִׂי הַטּוֹב
בְּעֵינַיִךְ שְׁבִי עַד־גָּמְלֵךְ אֹתוֹ
אַךְ יָקֵם יְיָ אֶת־דְּבָרוֹ וַתֵּשֶׁב
הָאִשָּׁה וַתֵּינֶק אֶת־בְּנָהּ
עַד־גָמְלָהּ אֹתוֹ: וַתַּעֲלֵהוּ עִמָּהּ
כַּאֲשֶׁר גְּמָלַתּוּ בְּפָרִים שְׁלֹשָׁה
וְאֵיפָה אַחַת קֶמַח וְנֵבֶל יַיִן
וַתְּבִאֵהוּ בֵית־יְיָ שִׁלוֹ וְהַנַּעַר
נָעַר: וַיִּשְׁחֲטוּ אֶת־הַפָּר וַיָּבִיאוּ
אֶת־הַנַּעַר אֶל־עֵלִי: וַתֹּאמֶר בִּי
אֲדֹנִי חֵי נַפְשְׁךָ אֲדֹנִי אֲנִי
הָאִשָּׁה הַנִּצֶּבֶת עִמְּכָה בָּזֶה
לְהִתְפַּלֵּל אֶל־יְיָ: אֶל־הַנַּעַר
הַזֶּה הִתְפַּלָּלְתִּי וַיִּתֵּן יְיָ לִי
אֶת־שְׁאֵלָתִי אֲשֶׁר שָׁאַלְתִּי
מֵעִמּוֹ: וְגַם אָנֹכִי הִשְׁאִלְתִּהוּ
לַייָ כָּל־הַיָּמִים אֲשֶׁר הָיָה הוּא
שָׁאוּל לַייָ וַיִּשְׁתַּחוּ שָׁם לַייָ:

Second day: Isaiah 55:6-12

Seek God when God can be found. Call out to God when God is near. Let the wicked give up their ways and the evil their schemes. Let them return to Adonai, who will be compassionate to them. Let them come back to God, for our God is abounding in forgiveness.

דִּרְשׁוּ יי בְּהִמָּצְאוֹ קְרָאֻהוּ
בִּהְיוֹתוֹ קָרוֹב׃ יַעֲזֹב רָשָׁע
דַּרְכּוֹ וְאִישׁ אָוֶן מַחְשְׁבֹתָיו
וְיָשֹׁב אֶל־יי וִירַחֲמֵהוּ
וְאֶל־אֱלֹהֵינוּ כִּי־יַרְבֶּה
לִסְלוֹחַ׃ כִּי לֹא מַחְשְׁבוֹתַי
מַחְשְׁבוֹתֵיכֶם וְלֹא דַרְכֵיכֶם
דְּרָכָי נְאֻם יי׃

"For My thoughts are not like your thoughts, and My ways are not like your ways," says Adonai. "As the skies are far above the earth, so are My ways far beyond your ways and My thoughts beyond yours. The rain and snow fall from the heavens, and do not return until they have watered the earth, making the plants grow and blossom, spreading life and providing food for all to eat. Just so are My words, which go from My mouth and do not return to Me empty until they have done the work I sent them to do. They complete their assignments."

כִּי־גָבְהוּ שָׁמַיִם מֵאָרֶץ כֵּן
גָּבְהוּ דְרָכַי מִדַּרְכֵיכֶם
וּמַחְשְׁבֹתַי מִמַּחְשְׁבֹתֵיכֶם׃ כִּי
כַּאֲשֶׁר יֵרֵד הַגֶּשֶׁם וְהַשֶּׁלֶג
מִן־הַשָּׁמַיִם וְשָׁמָּה לֹא יָשׁוּב
כִּי אִם־הִרְוָה אֶת־הָאָרֶץ
וְהוֹלִידָהּ וְהִצְמִיחָהּ וְנָתַן זֶרַע
לַזֹּרֵעַ וְלֶחֶם לָאֹכֵל׃ כֵּן יִהְיֶה
דְבָרִי אֲשֶׁר יֵצֵא מִפִּי
לֹא־יָשׁוּב אֵלַי רֵיקָם כִּי
אִם־עָשָׂה אֶת־אֲשֶׁר חָפַצְתִּי
וְהִצְלִיחַ אֲשֶׁר שְׁלַחְתִּיו׃

"You shall go out in joy and return in wholeness and peace. Before you, the mountains and hills will shout aloud with joyful song. All the trees of the forest will clap their hands in approval."

כִּי־בְשִׂמְחָה תֵצֵאוּ וּבְשָׁלוֹם
תּוּבָלוּן הֶהָרִים וְהַגְּבָעוֹת
יִפְצְחוּ לִפְנֵיכֶם רִנָּה וְכָל־עֲצֵי
הַשָּׂדֶה יִמְחֲאוּ־כָף׃

Blessings After the Haftarah

בָּרוּךְ אַתָּה יְיָ אֱלֹהֵינוּ מֶלֶךְ הָעוֹלָם, צוּר כָּל הָעוֹלָמִים, צַדִּיק בְּכָל הַדּוֹרוֹת, הָאֵל הַנֶּאֱמָן הָאוֹמֵר וְעֹשֶׂה, הַמְדַבֵּר וּמְקַיֵּם, שֶׁכָּל דְּבָרָיו אֱמֶת וָצֶדֶק.

Blessed are You, Adonai our God, source of all, rock of all time and space, righteous in every generation, the faithful God whose word is deed, who speaks and establishes, whose every word is truth and justice.

נֶאֱמָן אַתָּה הוּא יְיָ אֱלֹהֵינוּ, וְנֶאֱמָנִים דְּבָרֶיךָ, וְדָבָר אֶחָד מִדְּבָרֶיךָ אָחוֹר לֹא יָשׁוּב רֵיקָם, כִּי אֵל מֶלֶךְ נֶאֱמָן (וְרַחֲמָן) אָתָּה. בָּרוּךְ אַתָּה יְיָ, הָאֵל הַנֶּאֱמָן בְּכָל דְּבָרָיו.

You are faithful, Adonai our God, and faithful is Your word. Not a single word You have spoken goes unfulfilled, for You are God, faithful, just (and merciful). Blessed are You, Adonai our God, faithful in all ways.

רַחֵם עַל צִיּוֹן כִּי הִיא בֵּית חַיֵּינוּ, וְלַעֲלוּבַת נֶפֶשׁ תּוֹשִׁיעַ בִּמְהֵרָה בְיָמֵינוּ. בָּרוּךְ אַתָּה יְיָ מְשַׂמֵּחַ צִיּוֹן בְּבָנֶיהָ.

Be compassionate upon Zion, for it is a life-giving home for our people. Restore her soon. Blessed are You, Adonai, who brings rejoicing to Zion and her children.

שַׂמְּחֵנוּ יְיָ אֱלֹהֵינוּ בְּאֵלִיָּהוּ הַנָּבִיא עַבְדֶּךָ, וּבְמַלְכוּת בֵּית דָּוִד מְשִׁיחֶךָ, בִּמְהֵרָה יָבֹא וְיָגֵל לִבֵּנוּ, עַל כִּסְאוֹ לֹא יֵשֵׁב זָר וְלֹא יִנְחֲלוּ עוֹד אֲחֵרִים אֶת כְּבוֹדוֹ, כִּי בְשֵׁם קָדְשְׁךָ נִשְׁבַּעְתָּ לוֹ, שֶׁלֹּא יִכְבֶּה נֵרוֹ לְעוֹלָם וָעֶד. בָּרוּךְ אַתָּה יְיָ, מָגֵן דָּוִד.

Adonai our God, let us rejoice in the fulfillment of our dream of Elijah and David. Let messianic redemption come soon and bring joy to our hearts. Let us not be misled by false prophets, for You have promised that redemption's light shall never be extinguished. Blessed are You, Adonai, shield of David.

We thank You for the Torah and worship, for the prophets, (for this Shabbat), and for this Day of Remembrance that You have given us, Adonai our God (for holiness and rest,) for honor and splendor. We thank You for everything, Adonai our God. Let Your name ever be blessed by all that lives. Your word is true forever. Blessed are You, Adonai, source of all the earth, who sanctifies (Shabbat,) the people Israel and the Day of Remembrance.	עַל הַתּוֹרָה, וְעַל הָעֲבוֹדָה, וְעַל הַנְּבִיאִים, (וְעַל יוֹם הַשַּׁבָּת הַזֶּה,) וְעַל יוֹם הַזִּכָּרוֹן הַזֶּה, שֶׁנָּתַתָּ לָּנוּ יְיָ אֱלֹהֵינוּ, (לִקְדֻשָּׁה וְלִמְנוּחָה,) לְכָבוֹד וּלְתִפְאָרֶת. עַל הַכֹּל יְיָ אֱלֹהֵינוּ, אֲנַחְנוּ מוֹדִים לָךְ, וּמְבָרְכִים אוֹתָךְ, יִתְבָּרַךְ שִׁמְךָ בְּפִי כָּל חַי תָּמִיד לְעוֹלָם וָעֶד וּדְבָרְךָ אֱמֶת וְקַיָּם לָעַד. בָּרוּךְ אַתָּה יְיָ, מְקַדֵּשׁ (הַשַּׁבָּת וְ) יִשְׂרָאֵל וְיוֹם הַזִּכָּרוֹן.

Blessings, Abridged:

Blessed source
of all time and space:

You have promised
light.

in every generation
You are faithful.

Thank You for
remembrance

Be compassionate,
life-giving, home.

thank You
for everything.

Bring joy to our hearts.
Let us not be misled.

Let Your name be blessed
source of all the earth.

Lifting and Dressing the Torah

□ V'zot ha-Torah asher sam moshe, lifnei b'nei Yisrael al pi Adonai b'yad Moshe.

□ וְזֹאת הַתּוֹרָה אֲשֶׁר שָׂם
מֹשֶׁה לִפְנֵי בְּנֵי יִשְׂרָאֵל עַל
פִּי יְיָ בְּיַד מֹשֶׁה:

This is the Torah which was given to us, before our very eyes, from God's mouth and Moshe's hand!

□ Yisrael v'oraita
v'kud'sha brich hu, chad hu!
Torah ora, hallelujah!

□ יִשְׂרָאֵל וְאוֹרַיְיתָא
וְקוּדְשָׁא בְּרִיךְ הוּא חַד הוּא
תּוֹרָה אוֹרָה, הַלְלוּיָהּ!

Israel, and Torah, and the Holy Blessed One, are one!

Torah is a light: halleluyah!

Many communities keep the scroll
out of the ark until after the shofar service.

Before *Unetaneh Tokef*

Who By Fire

And who by fire, who by water,
who in the sunshine, who in the night time,
who by high ordeal, who by common trial,
who in your merry merry month of May,
who by very slow decay,
and who shall I say is calling?

And who in her lonely slip, who by barbiturate,
who in these realms of love, who by something blunt,
and who by avalanche, who by powder,
who for his greed, who for his hunger,
and who shall I say is calling?

And who by brave assent, who by accident,
who in solitude, who in this mirror,
who by his lady's command, who by his own hand,
who in mortal chains, who in power,
and who shall I say is calling?

(Leonard Cohen)

Many of us struggle with the notion of a God Who decides "who [shall die] by fire and who [shall die] by water" in the year to come.

But perhaps this prayer is more about us than about God. We decide what kind of year we will author. The book of life opens itself, and we write deeds of the coming year in our own handwriting: will we be cruel, or will we be kind?

Teshuvah (repentance / turning-toward-God), *tefilah* (prayer), and *tzedakah* (righteous giving) have the power to temper even the harshest decree. We always have the power to choose these as our guiding lights.

Unetaneh Tokef

וּנְתַנֶּה תֹּקֶף קְדֻשַּׁת הַיּוֹם, כִּי
הוּא נוֹרָא וְאָיוֹם: וּבוֹ תִנָּשֵׂא
מַלְכוּתֶךָ, וְיִכּוֹן בְּחֶסֶד כִּסְאֶךָ,
וְתֵשֵׁב עָלָיו בֶּאֱמֶת. אֱמֶת כִּי
אַתָּה הוּא דַיָּן וּמוֹכִיחַ, וְיוֹדֵעַ
וָעֵד, וְכוֹתֵב וְחוֹתֵם, וְסוֹפֵר
וּמוֹנֶה, וְתִזְכּוֹר כָּל הַנִּשְׁכָּחוֹת:
וְתִפְתַּח אֶת סֵפֶר הַזִּכְרוֹנוֹת,
וּמֵאֵלָיו יִקָּרֵא, וְחוֹתַם יַד כָּל
אָדָם בּוֹ.

Unetaneh tokef kedushat
hayom, kee hu nora ve'ayom;
uvo tinasei malchutecha,
veyikon bechesed kisecha,
veteisheiv alav be'emet. Emet
kee atah hu dayan umochi'ach,
veyodei'a va'eid, vechoteiv
vechoteim, vesofeir umoneh,
vetizkor kol hanishkachot;
vetiftach et sefer hazichronot,
umei'eilav yikarei, vechotam
yad kol adam bo.

Let us declare the sacred power of this day, for it is awesome and dreadful. On this day, Your rule is exalted, Your throne is established with love, and You sit upon it in truth. For it is truth that You judge and determine, know and witness, write and seal, count and account. You remember all that was forgotten. You open the Book of Memory. It reads from itself and the signature of every human being is in it.

> The Moving Finger writes; and, having writ,
> Moves on: nor all thy Piety nor Wit,
> Shall lure it back to cancel half a Line,
> Nor all thy Tears wash out a Word of it...
>
> *(Omar Khayyám, transl. Edward Fitzgerald)*

וּבְשׁוֹפָר גָּדוֹל יִתָּקַע, וְקוֹל דְּמָמָה דַקָּה יִשָּׁמַע: וּמַלְאָכִים יֵחָפֵזוּן, וְחִיל וּרְעָדָה יֹאחֵזוּן, וְיֹאמְרוּ הִנֵּה יוֹם הַדִּין, לִפְקוֹד עַל צְבָא מָרוֹם בַּדִּין, כִּי לֹא יִזְכּוּ בְעֵינֶיךָ בַּדִּין. וְכָל בָּאֵי עוֹלָם יַעַבְרוּן לְפָנֶיךָ כִּבְנֵי מָרוֹן. כְּבַקָּרַת רוֹעֶה עֶדְרוֹ, מַעֲבִיר צֹאנוֹ תַּחַת שִׁבְטוֹ, כֵּן תַּעֲבִיר וְתִסְפּוֹר וְתִמְנֶה, וְתִפְקוֹד נֶפֶשׁ כָּל חַי, וְתַחְתּוֹךְ קִצְבָה לְכָל בְּרִיָּה, וְתִכְתּוֹב אֶת גְּזַר דִּינָם.

The great shofar sounds—the still, small voice is heard. Even the angels are seized by trembling and fear as they declare, "This is the day of judgment when even the hosts of heaven are judged." Nothing can evade Your eyes in judgment. All who live must pass before You like flocks before the shepherd. Just as a shepherd inspects the sheep and makes them pass under the staff, so do You account for the souls of all who live. You weigh the measure of each life and inscribe the verdict of their judgment.

בְּרֹאשׁ הַשָּׁנָה יִכָּתֵבוּן, וּבְיוֹם צוֹם כִּפּוּר יֵחָתֵמוּן.

B'Rosh Hashanah yikateivun, uv'Yom tzom Kippur eichateimun.

For on Rosh Hashanah it is written,
and on Yom Kippur it is sealed:

"On Rosh Hashanah it is inscribed, and on Yom Kippur it is sealed...." From this we can intuit that while the heart may be solid on Rosh Hashanah (so words can be inscribed on it), it must be soft like wax in order to be sealed on Yom Kippur. It is incumbent on us to soften our hearts during these ten days.

כַּמָּה יַעַבְרוּן, וְכַמָּה יִבָּרֵאוּן: מִי יִחְיֶה, וּמִי יָמוּת: מִי בְקִצּוֹ, וּמִי לֹא בְקִצּוֹ: מִי בָאֵשׁ, וּמִי בַמַּיִם: מִי בַחֶרֶב, וּמִי בַחַיָּה: מִי בָרָעָב, וּמִי בַצָּמָא: מִי בָרַעַשׁ, וּמִי בַמַּגֵּפָה: מִי בַחֲנִיקָה, וּמִי בִסְקִילָה: מִי יָנוּחַ, וּמִי יָנוּעַ: מִי יִשָּׁקֵט, וּמִי יִטָּרֵף: מִי יִשָּׁלֵו, וּמִי יִתְיַסָּר: מִי יֵעָנִי, וּמִי יֵעָשֵׁר: מִי יִשָּׁפֵל, וּמִי יָרוּם.

Kamah ya'avrun, vechamah yibarei'un; mi yichyeh, umi yamut; mi vekitso, umi lo vekitso; mi va'eish, umi vamayim; mi vacherev umi vachayah; mi vara'av, umi vatsama; mi varei'ash, umi vamageifah; mi vachanikah, umi viskilah; mi yanu'ach, umi yanu'a; mi yishakeit umi yitareif; mi yishaleiv, umi yityasar; mi yei'ani, umi yei'asheir; mi yishafeil, umi yarum.

How many will pass from this life and how many will be created; who shall live and who shall die; who in old age, and who in youth; who by fire and who by water; who by sword and who by beast; who by famine and who by stoning; who shall find rest and who shall wander; who shall be torn and who shall be whole; who shall be tranquil and who shall be driven; who shall be impoverished and who shall be enriched; who shall be laid low and who shall be exalted.

□ וּתְשׁוּבָה וּתְפִלָּה וּצְדָקָה מַעֲבִירִין אֶת רֹעַ הַגְּזֵרָה.

□ Uteshuvah utefilah utzedakah ma'avirin et ro'a hagezeirah.

But *teshuvah*, *tefilah*, and *tzedakah*
(repentance, prayer, and righteous giving)
temper the harshness of the decree.

כִּי כְּשִׁמְךָ כֵּן תְּהִלָּתֶךָ, קָשֶׁה לִכְעוֹס וְנוֹחַ לִרְצוֹת: כִּי לֹא תַחְפּוֹץ בְּמוֹת הַמֵּת, כִּי אִם בְּשׁוּבוֹ מִדַּרְכּוֹ וְחָיָה. וְעַד יוֹם מוֹתוֹ תְּחַכֶּה לוֹ, אִם יָשׁוּב מִיַּד תְּקַבְּלוֹ.

For as Your name is mercy, so is Your mercy praised. You are slow to anger and ready to forgive. You do not seek our death, rather that we turn from our ways and live. Even until the day of our death You wait for us, to take us back the moment we turn to You.

אֱמֶת כִּי אַתָּה הוּא יוֹצְרָם, וְאַתָּה יוֹדֵעַ יִצְרָם, כִּי הֵם בָּשָׂר וָדָם.אָדָם יְסוֹדוֹ מֵעָפָר וְסוֹפוֹ לֶעָפָר: בְּנַפְשׁוֹ יָבִיא לַחְמוֹ: מָשׁוּל כְּחֶרֶס הַנִּשְׁבָּר, כְּחָצִיר יָבֵשׁ, וּכְצִיץ נוֹבֵל, כְּצֵל עוֹבֵר, וּכְעָנָן כָּלָה, וּכְרוּחַ נוֹשָׁבֶת, וּכְאָבָק פּוֹרֵחַ, וְכַחֲלוֹם יָעוּף.

Truly, You are our creator and You know our ways—good and bad—for we are but flesh and blood. Our origin is dust and to dust is our end. Our sustenance is bought with peril. We are a broken urn, withering grass, a fading flower, a passing shadow, a vanishing cloud, a blowing wind, settling dust, a fleeting dream.

וְאַתָּה הוּא מֶלֶךְ אֵל חַי וְקַיָּם.

Ve'atah hu melech Eil chai vekayam.

But You are the ruler,
the God of life and all that exists.

The Sounding of the Shofar

Once the Baal Shem Tov commanded Rabbi Zev Kitzes to learn the secret meanings behind the blasts of the ram's-horn, because Rabbi Zev was to be his caller on Rosh Ha-Shanah. So Rabbi Zev learned the secret meanings and wrote them down on a slip of paper to look at during the service, and laid the slip of paper in his breast pocket.

When the time came for the blowing of the shofar, he searched everywhere for the slip of paper, but it was gone; and he did not know on what meanings to concentrate. He was greatly saddened. Broken-hearted, he wept bitter tears, and called the blasts of the ram's-horn without concentrating on the secret meanings behind them.

Afterward, the Baal Shem Tov said to him: "In the palace of the king are many rooms and apartments, and there are different keys for every lock, but the master key is the axe, with which it is possible to open all the locks on all the gates. So it is with the shofar: the secret meanings are the keys; every gate has its own meaning; but the master key is the broken heart. When a person truthfully breaks his heart before God, then they can enter into all the gates of all the rooms of the Holy Blessed One!"

A word about prostration

The prayer we know as the *Aleinu,* which closes every service, originated here, in the Rosh Hashanah liturgy. The Aleinu we're about to recite is known as the Great Aleinu. There is a custom of praying this prayer with our whole bodies.

When we recite the words *va-anachnu kor'im,* "We bow low and prostrate ourselves in thanks before the Source of all sources, the Holy One, blessed is God," I invite you to experience prostration: dropping to the knees and placing the forehead on the floor.

Traditionally, this is done only on the Days of Awe. Some experience it as a posture of submission; others as a posture of relief and release. It is very like the posture which our cousins, the spiritual descendants of Ishmael, adopt in daily prayer. It is also very like the yoga pose known as *balasana* or child's pose.

If this is not comfortable for you, please remain standing.

I. *Malchuyot*: God, the Ruler of All

What does it mean
to proclaim Your sovereignty
when we don't understand kings?
Before the Big Bang, there was You.

In the old year
we allowed habits to rule us.
Help us throw off that yoke
so our best selves may serve You.

Help us surrender. The cosmos
is not under our control.
Help us fall to our knees
and find home in Your embrace.

Let Your power increase in the world.
Help us be unashamed of yearning.
Strengthen our awe and our love
so our prayers will soar.

(Rabbi Rachel Barenblat)

□ עָלֵֽינוּ לְשַׁבֵּֽחַ לַאֲדוֹן הַכֹּל,
לָתֵת גְּדֻלָּה לְיוֹצֵר בְּרֵאשִׁית,
שֶׁלֹּא עָשָׂנוּ כְּגוֹיֵי הָאֲרָצוֹת,
וְלֹא שָׂמָנוּ כְּמִשְׁפְּחוֹת
הָאֲדָמָה, שֶׁלֹּא שָׂם חֶלְקֵנוּ
כָּהֶם, וְגֹרָלֵנוּ כְּכָל הֲמוֹנָם.

□ Aleinu l'shabe'ach la'adon hakol, latet gedulah l'yotzer breshit. Shelo asanu k'goyei ha'aratzot, v'lo samanu k'mishpachot ha-adamah. Shelo sam chelkenu kahem, v'goralenu k'chol hamonam.

It is up to us to praise the Source of all, to exalt the Molder of creation. We are made for God, like the nations of the earth; we are placed here for God, like the families of humanity. For God's own sake is our portion here and our fate here.

□ וַאֲנַחְנוּ* כּוֹרְעִים* וּמִשְׁתַּחֲוִים וּמוֹדִים*, לִפְנֵי מֶלֶךְ, מַלְכֵי הַמְּלָכִים, הַקָּדוֹשׁ בָּרוּךְ הוּא.

□ Va-anachnu* korim*, u-mishtachavim u-modim*, lifnei melech malchei ham'lachim, hakadosh baruch hu.

We bow low and prostrate in thanks before the Source of all sources, the Holy One, blessed is God.

□ שֶׁהוּא נוֹטֶה שָׁמַיִם וְיֹסֵד אָרֶץ, וּמוֹשַׁב יְקָרוֹ בַּשָּׁמַיִם מִמַּעַל, וּשְׁכִינַת עֻזּוֹ בְּגָבְהֵי מְרוֹמִים, הוּא אֱלֹהֵינוּ אֵין עוֹד. אֱמֶת מַלְכֵּנוּ אֶפֶס זוּלָתוֹ, כַּכָּתוּב בְּתוֹרָתוֹ: וְיָדַעְתָּ הַיּוֹם וַהֲשֵׁבֹתָ אֶל לְבָבֶךָ, כִּי יְיָ הוּא הָאֱלֹהִים בַּשָּׁמַיִם מִמַּעַל, וְעַל הָאָרֶץ מִתָּחַת, אֵין עוֹד:

□ Shehu noteh shamayim v'yosed aretz, u-moshav yekaro bashamayim mima'al, uschinat uzo b'gavheh meromim. Hu eloheinu, ein od. Emet malkenu efes zulato. Kakatuv b'torato: v'yadata hayom vahashevota el levavecha. Ki adonai, hu ha-elohim, bashamayim mima'al, v'al ha-aretz mitachat ein od.

God sets out the heavens and establishes the earth. God's honored place is in the heights of our aspirations; God's powerful presence is in the heavens of our hopes. This is our God, there is none else. God is the world's truth; there is nothing that God is not.

** On these three words, many people 1) drop down to their knees, 2) place their hands on the floor, and 3) touch their foreheads to the ground. See more about this custom on the note on p. 157.*

☐ בָּרוּךְ אַתָּה, יְיָ אֱלֹהֵינוּ, מֶלֶךְ הָעוֹלָם, אֲשֶׁר קִדְּשָׁנוּ בְּמִצְוֹתָיו, וְצִוָּנוּ לִשְׁמוֹעַ קוֹל שׁוֹפָר.

☐ Baruch atah Adonai Eloheinu melech ha'olam, asher kideshanu bemitsvotav vetsivanu lishmo'a kol shofar.

☐ בָּרוּךְ אַתָּה, יְיָ אֱלֹהֵינוּ, מֶלֶךְ הָעוֹלָם, שֶׁהֶחֱיָנוּ וְקִיְּמָנוּ וְהִגִּיעָנוּ לַזְּמַן הַזֶּה.

☐ Baruch atah Adonai Eloheinu melech ha'olam, shehecheyanu vekiyemanu vehigiyanu lazeman hazeh

Blessed are You, Adonai our God, source of all being, who sanctifies us with mitzvot and enjoins us to hear the sound of the shofar.

Blessed are You, Adonai our God, source of all being, who has given us life, established us and allowed us to reach this holy moment.

תקיעה שברים תרועה תקיעה

TEKIAH SHEVARIM-TERUAH TEKIAH

תקיעה שברים תקיעה

TEKIAH SHEVARIM TEKIAH

תקיעה תרועה תקיעה

TEKIAH TERUAH TEKIAH

אֲרֶשֶׁת שְׂפָתֵינוּ יֶעֱרַב לְפָנֶיךָ, אֵל רָם וְנִשָּׂא, מֵבִין וּמַאֲזִין, מַבִּיט וּמַקְשִׁיב לְקוֹל תְּקִיעָתֵנוּ; וּתְקַבֵּל בְּרַחֲמִים וּבְרָצוֹן סֵדֶר מַלְכֻיּוֹתֵנוּ.

Areshet sefateinu ye'erav lefanecha Eil ram, ram venisa, meivin uma'azin mabit umakshiv lekol teki'ateinu; utkabeil berachamim, berachamim uvratzon seider, seider malchuyoteinu.

May You accept the expression of our lips, God on high and deep within, who notes and hears the sound of our shofar blasts. May You mercifully hear us as we acclaim Your rule.

Where we are

It was like the special bow
reserved for my karate teacher's teacher —
knees first, then head — but this time
a prayerbook instead of fists, tallis
instead of crisp white uniform.
Forehead pressed to carpet

I realized we looked, for that moment,
like a different congregation
descended from Abraham's other son,
the one we'd just read was cast out
until God heard his cries
where he was, and saved him.

(Rabbi Rachel Barenblat)

II. *Zichronot*: God of Remembrance

One of the first questions we are asked as children is, "What do you want to be when you grow up?"

But what if we asked our children, "Who are you? Do you remember? Where do you come from? Please remind us."

(*Rabbi Daniel Siegel*)

God, remember us—
not only our mistakes
but our good intentions
and our tender hearts.

Remember our ancestors
who for thousands of years
have asked forgiveness
with the wail of the ram's horn.

Today again we open ourselves
to the calls of the shofar
reminding us *sleepers, awake!*
We remember what matters most in our lives.

Help us shed old memories
which no longer serve us.
Help us instead
to always remember You.

(Rabbi Rachel Barenblat)

Baruch atah, Adonai, zocheir ha-brit.	בָּרוּךְ אַתָּה יְיָ, זוֹכֵר הַבְּרִית.

Blessed are You, Adonai, Who remembers the covenant.

תקיעה שברים תרועה תקיעה

TEKIAH SHEVARIM-TERUAH TEKIAH

תקיעה שברים תקיעה

TEKIAH SHEVARIM TEKIAH

תקיעה תרועה תקיעה

TEKIAH TERUAH TEKIAH

אֲרֶשֶׁת שְׂפָתֵינוּ יֶעֱרַב לְפָנֶיךָ, אֵל רָם וְנִשָּׂא, מֵבִין וּמַאֲזִין, מַבִּיט וּמַקְשִׁיב לְקוֹל תְּקִיעָתֵנוּ; וּתְקַבֵּל בְּרַחֲמִים וּבְרָצוֹן סֵדֶר זִיכְרוֹנוֹתֵינוּ.

Areshet sefateinu ye'erav lefanecha Eil ram, ram venisa, meivin uma'azin mabit umakshiv lekol teki'ateinu; utkabeil berachamim, berachamim uvratzon seider, seider zichronoteinu.

May You accept the expression of our lips, God on high and deep within, who notes and hears the sound of our shofar blasts. May You mercifully hear us as we acclaim Your remembrance.

III. *Shofarot*: God of Forgiveness

The shofar reminds us
of the ram in the thicket.
Where are we, too, ensnared?
Can our song set us free?

The sound of the shofar
shatters our complacency.
It wails with our grief
and stutters with our inadequacy.

The shofar calls us to teshuvah.
The shofar cries out
I was whole, I was broken,
I will be whole again.

Make shofars of us, God!
Breathe through us: make of us
resonating chambers
for Your love.

(Rabbi Rachel Barenblat)

תקיעה שברים תרועה תקיעה

TEKIAH SHEVARIM-TERUAH TEKIAH

תקיעה שברים תקיעה

TEKIAH SHEVARIM TEKIAH

תקיעה שברים תרועה... תקיעה **גדולה!**

TEKIAH TERUAH...TEKIAH GEDOLAH!

אֲרֶשֶׁת שְׂפָתֵינוּ יֶעֱרַב לְפָנֶיךָ, אֵל רָם וְנִשָּׂא, מֵבִין וּמַאֲזִין, מַבִּיט וּמַקְשִׁיב לְקוֹל תְּקִיעָתֵנוּ; וּתְקַבֵּל בְּרַחֲמִים וּבְרָצוֹן סֵדֶר שׁוֹפְרוֹתֵינוּ.

Areshet sefateinu ye'erav lefanecha Eil ram, ram venisa, meivin uma'azin mabit umakshiv lekol teki'ateinu; utkabeil berachamim, berachamim uvratzon seider, seider shofaroteinu.

May You accept the expression of our lips, God on high and deep within, who notes and hears the sound of our shofar blasts. May You mercifully hear us as we acclaim You through the shofar.

Said the Baal Shem Tov
Tekiah—
a simple scream
Abba, Abba have pity!
Abba, Abba save!
And this simple scream
needs no words
no further modulation
only to scream
so as to unite
with the sound of Creation
and the thunder of Revelation
and the calling of Redemption
the great AMEN.

(Rabbi Zalman Schachter-Shalomi z"l / of blessed memory)

Returning the Torah to the ark:

Ki lekach tov natati lahem: Torati, al taazovu.	כִּי לֶקַח טוֹב נָתַתִּי לָכֶם תּוֹרָתִי אַל תַּעֲזֹבוּ.
□ Etz chayyim hee, l'machazikim ba V'tomche'ha me'ushar. D'racheha darchei noam V'chol n'tivotecha, shalom. Hashivenu Adonai elecha v'nashuva! Chadesh yameinu k'kedem!	□ עֵץ חַיִּים הִיא לַמַּחֲזִיקִים בָּהּ, וְתֹמְכֶיהָ מְאֻשָּׁר. דְּרָכֶיהָ דַרְכֵי נֹעַם, וְכָל נְתִיבוֹתֶיהָ שָׁלוֹם. הֲשִׁיבֵנוּ יְיָ, אֵלֶיךָ וְנָשׁוּבָה, חַדֵּשׁ יָמֵינוּ כְּקֶדֶם.

I have given you my Torah: do not forsake it. It is a tree of life to those who hold it fast. All its paths are paths of pleasantness, and its ways are ways of peace. Turn us, O God, and we will return to You! Renew, renew our days as of old!

Kaddish: a doorway in prayer

The Kaddish in all of its forms
(half-Kaddish, whole Kaddish, mourner's Kaddish)
is a doorway.

As you move through this door
from the shofar service
to concluding prayers

notice what you're experiencing
in body, heart, mind, and soul
and bring that into your prayer.

Kaddish Shalem

Yitgadal v'yitkadash, shmeh rabah. B'alma divra chiruteh, v'yamlich malchuteh b'chayyeichon u'v'yomeichon u'vchayyei d'chol beit Yisrael. Ba'agala u-vizman kariv v'imru amen.

יִתְגַּדַּל וְיִתְקַדַּשׁ שְׁמֵהּ רַבָּא.
בְּעָלְמָא דִּי בְרָא כִרְעוּתֵהּ,
וְיַמְלִיךְ מַלְכוּתֵהּ בְּחַיֵּיכוֹן
וּבְיוֹמֵיכוֹן וּבְחַיֵּי דְכָל בֵּית
יִשְׂרָאֵל. בַּעֲגָלָא וּבִזְמַן קָרִיב
וְאִמְרוּ אָמֵן:

□ Y'hei sh'mei raba m'varakh l'olam ol'almey almaya.

□ יְהֵא שְׁמֵהּ רַבָּא מְבָרַךְ
לְעָלַם וּלְעָלְמֵי עָלְמַיָּא:

Magnified and sanctified! Magnified and sanctified! May God's Great Name fill the world God created. May God's splendor be seen in the world in your life, in your days, in the life of all Israel. Quickly and soon! And let us say, Amen.

Forever may the Great Name be blessed!

Yitbarach v'yishtabach, v'yitpa'ar v'yit-romam v'yit-naseh. V'yithadar v'yitaleh v'yithallal shmeh d'kud'sha b'rich hu. L'eyla u'leyla min kol birchata v'shirata, tushbechata v'nechemata, damiran b'alma, v'imru amen.

יִתְבָּרַךְ וְיִשְׁתַּבַּח, וְיִתְפָּאַר
וְיִתְרוֹמַם וְיִתְנַשֵּׂא וְיִתְהַדָּר
וְיִתְעַלֶּה וְיִתְהַלָּל שְׁמֵהּ
דְּקֻדְשָׁא בְּרִיךְ הוּא לְעֵלָּא
וּלְעֵלָּא מִכָּל בִּרְכָתָא
וְשִׁירָתָא, תֻּשְׁבְּחָתָא
וְנֶחֱמָתָא, דַּאֲמִירָן בְּעָלְמָא,
וְאִמְרוּ אָמֵן:

Titkabel tzlo'uthon
uva-ut'hon d'chol beit
Yisrael kadam avuhon di
vishmaia v'imru Amen.

תִּתְקַבֵּל צְלוֹתְהוֹן וּבָעוּתְהוֹן דְּכָל
בֵּית יִשְׂרָאֵל קֳדָם אֲבוּהוֹן דִּי
בִשְׁמַיָּא וְאִמְרוּ אָמֵן:

Y'hei shlama raba min
shemaya v'chayyim tovim
aleinu v'al kol Yisrael,
v'imru amen.

יְהֵא שְׁלָמָא רַבָּא מִן שְׁמַיָּא
וְחַיִּים עָלֵינוּ וְעַל כָּל יִשְׂרָאֵל,
וְאִמְרוּ אָמֵן:

Oseh shalom bimromav,
hu ya'aseh shalom, aleinu
v'al kol yisrael, v'al kol
yoshvei tevel, v'imru
Amen.

עֹשֶׂה שָׁלוֹם בִּמְרוֹמָיו הוּא יַעֲשֶׂה
שָׁלוֹם עָלֵינוּ וְעַל כָּל יִשְׂרָאֵל,
וְעַל כָּל יוֹשְׁבֵי תֵבֵל, וְאִמְרוּ אָמֵן:

Blessed and praised! Splendid and supreme! May the holy name, Bless God, be praised, beyond all the blessings and songs, comforts and consolations, that can be offered in this world. And let us say: Amen.

May our prayers, and the prayers of the entire community, be accepted before You, our Parent.

Accept them! Accept them! May our words of prayer and pleading from all the people of Israel be accepted before God in heaven. And let us say, Amen!
May there be peace and life, great peace and life from heaven above for us and all Israel. And let us say, Amen!

May the One who makes peace in the high heavens make peace for us, for our whole community, and for all the peoples of the world. And let us say: Amen.

Prayer For Our Country

O God and God of our ancestors
receive our prayer for this land which we love.
Pour out Your blessing on this nation and its government.

Give those who serve our country
appreciation for the Torah's principles of justice and peace.
Help them to see Your face in every constituent.

Cultivate in them, and in us,
awareness that we are all one family
obligated to care for each other with compassion.

Banish hatred from our hearts
and from the hearts of our elected officials.
Help us to make this country a light unto the nations.

May it be Your will
our God and God of our generations
that this nation be a blessing to all who dwell on earth.

Help us to enact the words of Your prophet:
"Nation shall not lift up sword against nation.
Neither shall they learn war anymore." And let us say: Amen.

(Rabbi Rachel Barenblat)

Prayer For Israel

Sovereign of the Universe, accept in lovingkindness and with favor our prayers for the State of Israel, her government and all who dwell within her boundaries and under her authority.

Reopen our eyes and our hearts to the wonder of Israel and strengthen our faith in Your power to work redemption in every human soul. Grant us also the fortitude to keep ever before us those ideals to which Israel dedicated herself in her Declaration of Independence, so that we may be true partners with the people of Israel in working toward her as yet not fully fulfilled vision.

Grant those entrusted with guiding Israel's destiny the courage, wisdom and strength to do Your Will. Guide them in the paths of peace and give them the insight to see Your Image in every human being. Be with those charged with Israel's safety and defend them from all harm. May they have the strength to protect their country and the spiritual fortitude never to abuse the power placed in their hands.

Spread Your blessings over the Land. May justice and human rights abound for all her inhabitants. Guide them "To do justice, love mercy and walk humbly with your God" (Micah 6:8), and "May justice well up like water, righteousness like a mighty stream" (Amos 5:24).

Implant tolerance and mutual respect in every heart, and may all realize that, "We were not brought into this world for conflict and dissension, nor for hatred, jealousy, harassment or bloodshed. Rather, we were brought into this world in order to recognize You, may You be blessed forever" (R. Nahman of Bratzlav). Spread over Israel and all the world Your shelter of peace.

(Rabbi Arik Ascherman)

Aleinu (option 1)

This Aleinu is abbreviated; the full text can be found on p. 53.

□ Aleinu l'shabe'ach la'adon hakol, latet gedulah l'yotzer breshit. Shelo asanu k'goyei ha'aratzot, v'lo samanu k'mishpachot ha-adamah. Shelo sam chelkenu kahem, v'goralenu k'chol hamonam.

□ עָלֵינוּ לְשַׁבֵּחַ לַאֲדוֹן הַכֹּל,
לָתֵת גְּדֻלָּה לְיוֹצֵר בְּרֵאשִׁית,
שֶׁלֹּא/שֶׁלּוֹ* עָשָׂנוּ כְּגוֹיֵי
הָאֲרָצוֹת, וְלֹא/וְלוֹ* שָׂמָנוּ
כְּמִשְׁפְּחוֹת הָאֲדָמָה, שֶׁלֹּא/
שֶׁלּוֹ* שָׂם חֶלְקֵנוּ כָּהֶם,
וְגֹרָלֵנוּ כְּכָל הֲמוֹנָם.

It is up to us to praise the Source of all, to exalt the Molder of creation. We are:

made for God like all nations.	not made like other nations.

We are:

placed here for God like all humanity.	unlike other peoples.

Our portion and our fate are:

for God's own sake.	not like those of other peoples.

□ Va-anachnu korim, u-mishtachavim u-modim, lifnei melech malchei ham'lachim, hakadosh baruch hu.

□ וַאֲנַחְנוּ כּוֹרְעִים וּמִשְׁתַּחֲוִים
וּמוֹדִים, לִפְנֵי מֶלֶךְ, מַלְכֵי
הַמְּלָכִים, הַקָּדוֹשׁ בָּרוּךְ הוּא.

We bow low and prostrate in thanks before the Source of all sources, the Holy One, blessed is God.

**Pray either לא, pronounced lo ("not"), or לו, also pronounced lo ("for God"). One articulates Jewish chosenness; the other, post-triumphalism.*

☐ שֶׁהוּא נוֹטֶה שָׁמַיִם וְיֹסֵד
אָרֶץ, וּמוֹשַׁב יְקָרוֹ בַּשָּׁמַיִם
מִמַּעַל, וּשְׁכִינַת עֻזּוֹ בְּגָבְהֵי
מְרוֹמִים, הוּא אֱלֹהֵינוּאֵין
עוֹד. אֱמֶת מַלְכֵּנוּ אֶפֶס
זוּלָתוֹ, כַּכָּתוּב בְּתוֹרָתוֹ:
וְיָדַעְתָּ הַיּוֹם וַהֲשֵׁבֹתָ אֶל
לְבָבֶךָ, כִּי יְיָ הוּא הָאֱלֹהִים
בַּשָּׁמַיִם מִמַּעַל, וְעַל הָאָרֶץ
מִתָּחַת, אֵין עוֹד:

☐ Shehu noteh shamayim v'yosed aretz, u-moshav yekaro bashamayim mima'al, uschinat uzo b'gavheh meromim. Hu eloheinu, ein od. Emet malkenu efes zulato. Kakatuv b'torato: v'yadata hayom vahashevota el levavecha. Ki adonai, hu ha-elohim, bashamayim mima'al, v'al ha-aretz mitachat ein od.

God sets out the heavens and establishes the earth. God's honored place is in the heights of our aspirations; God's powerful presence is in the heavens of our hopes. This is our God, there is none else. God is the world's truth; there is nothing that God is not.

☐ כַּכָּתוּב בְּתוֹרָתֶךָ, יְיָ יִמְלֹךְ
לְעֹלָם וָעֶד: וְנֶאֱמַר, וְהָיָה יְיָ
לְמֶלֶךְ עַל כָּל הָאָרֶץ, בַּיּוֹם
הַהוּא יִהְיֶה יְיָ אֶחָד, וּשְׁמוֹ אֶחָד.

☐ Kakatuv b'toratecha, Adonai yimloch leolam vaed. V'ne-emar, v'haya Adonai l'melech al kol ha-aretz. Bayom hahu yiheh Adonai echad, ushmo echad!

As it is written in God's sacred teaching: "You shall know this day and place upon your heart that Adonai is God in heaven above and earth below; there is none else."

Then shall your realm be established on earth, and the word of Your prophet fulfilled: "Adonai will reign forever and ever. On that day, Adonai shall be One, and God's name shall be One."

Aleinu (2): It's Upon Us

May we feel Your holy power
May we feel Your holy strength
May we feel Your holy presence
Surround us in this holy place!

May we feel the earth beneath our feet
As we bend and bow to You
May our bodies rise to greet You
As we feel Your presence pouring through!

1) It's upon us, it's upon us
To feel Your holy ground
It's upon us, it's upon us
To hear Your holy sound

2) It's upon us, it's upon us
To feel the love inside
It's upon us, it's upon us
To face You and not hide

3) It's upon us, it's upon us
To think, to act, to do
It's upon us, it's upon us
To do what's right and true

4) It's upon us, it's upon us
To reach up to the sky
It's upon us, it's upon us
To take our wings and fly!

Aleinu l'shabe'ach la-adon hakol! (4 times)

May we feel Your holy power
May we feel Your holy strength
May we feel Your holy presence
Surround us in this holy place!

(Rabbinic Pastor Shayndel Kahn)

Aleinu (3): Od Yavo Shalom

□ Od yavo shalom aleinu
Od yavo shalom aleinu
Od yavo shalom aleinu,
v'al kulam.

□ עוֹד יָבֹא שָׁלוֹם עָלֵינוּ
עוֹד יָבֹא שָׁלוֹם עָלֵינוּ
עוֹד יָבֹא שָׁלוֹם
עָלֵינוּ וְעַל כֻּלָּם.

Shalom, aleinu v'al kol ha-olam!
Shalom, shalom!
Salaam, aleinu v'al kol ha-olam!
Salaam, salaam!

שָׁלוֹם עָלֵינוּ וְעַל כֹּל הָעוֹלָם
שָׁלוֹם, שָׁלוֹם!
سلم עָלֵינוּ וְעַל כֹּל הָעוֹלָם
سلم سلم

Kakatuv b'Toratecha: Adonai yimloch l'olam va'ed. V'ne'emar v'yaha Adonai l'melech al kol ha-aretz, bayom hahu yihyeh Adonai echad ushmo echad.

כַּכָּתוּב בְּתוֹרָתֶךָ, יְיָ יִמְלֹךְ לְעוֹלָם וָעֶד: וְנֶאֱמַר, וְהָיָה יְיָ לְמֶלֶךְ עַל כָּל הָאָרֶץ, בַּיּוֹם הַהוּא יִהְיֶה יְיָ אֶחָד, וּשְׁמוֹ אֶחָד.

May there be peace for us, may there be peace for us, may there be peace for us and for everyone. Peace, for us and for all the world! Peace, peace!

As it is written in Your Torah: Adonai will reign forever and ever. And it is said: on that day Adonai will be God over all the earth, and on that day God will be One and God's Name will be One.

Mourner's *Kaddish*

Yitgadal v'yitkadash,
shmeh rabah. B'alma di vra
chiruteh, v'yamlich
malchuteh b'chayyeichon
u'v'yomeichon u'vchayyei
d'chol beit Yisrael.
Ba'agala u-vizman kariv
v'imru amen.

יִתְגַּדַּל וְיִתְקַדַּשׁ שְׁמֵהּ רַבָּא.
בְּעָלְמָא דִּי בְרָא כִרְעוּתֵהּ,
וְיַמְלִיךְ מַלְכוּתֵהּ בְּחַיֵּיכוֹן
וּבְיוֹמֵיכוֹן וּבְחַיֵּי דְכָל בֵּית
יִשְׂרָאֵל.
בַּעֲגָלָא וּבִזְמַן קָרִיב וְאִמְרוּ אָמֵן:

□ Y'hei sh'mei raba
m'varakh l'olam ol'almey
almaya.

□יְהֵא שְׁמֵהּ רַבָּא מְבָרַךְ לְעָלַם
וּלְעָלְמֵי עָלְמַיָּא:

Yitbarach v'yishtabach,
v'yitpa'ar v'yit-romam
v'yit-naseh. V'yithadar
v'yitaleh v'yithallal shmeh
d'kudh'sha b'rich hu. L'eyla
u l'eyla min kol birchata
v'shirata, tushbechata
v'nechemata, damiran
b'alma, v'imru amen.

יִתְבָּרַךְ וְיִשְׁתַּבַּח, וְיִתְפָּאַר
וְיִתְרוֹמַם וְיִתְנַשֵּׂא וְיִתְהַדָּר
וְיִתְעַלֶּה וְיִתְהַלָּל שְׁמֵהּ דְּקֻדְשָׁא
בְּרִיךְ הוּא לְעֵלָּא וּלְעֵלָּא מִן כָּל
בִּרְכָתָא וְשִׁירָתָא, תֻּשְׁבְּחָתָא
וְנֶחֱמָתָא, דַּאֲמִירָן בְּעָלְמָא,
וְאִמְרוּ אָמֵן:

Y'hei shlama raba min
shemaya v'chayyim tovim
aleinu v'al kol Yisrael,
v'imru amen.

יְהֵא שְׁלָמָא רַבָּא מִן שְׁמַיָּא
וְחַיִּים עָלֵינוּ וְעַל כָּל יִשְׂרָאֵל,
וְאִמְרוּ אָמֵן:

Oseh shalom bimromav,
hu ya'aseh shalom, aleinu
v'al kol yisrael, v'al kol
yoshvei tevel, v'imru
Amen.

עֹשֶׂה שָׁלוֹם בִּמְרוֹמָיו הוּא יַעֲשֶׂה
שָׁלוֹם עָלֵינוּ וְעַל כָּל יִשְׂרָאֵל,
וְעַל כָּל יוֹשְׁבֵי תֵבֵל, וְאִמְרוּ אָמֵן:

Magnified and sanctified! Magnified and sanctified! May God's Great Name fill the world God created. May God's splendor be seen in the world in your life, in your days, in the life of all Israel. Quickly and soon! And let us say, Amen.

Forever may the Great Name be blessed!

Blessed and praised! Splendid and supreme! May the holy name, Bless God, be praised, far beyond all the blessings and songs, comforts and consolations, that can be offered in this world. And let us say: Amen.

May there be peace and life, great peace and life from heaven above for us and all Israel. And let us say, Amen!

May the One who makes peace in the high heavens make peace for us, for our whole community, and for all the peoples of the world. And let us say: Amen.

elul: psalm 27

we are told to say the following
every day for a month
in preparation for the days of awe:

you are my light my help
when I'm with you I'm not afraid
I want to live in your house

the enemies that chew my heart
the enemies that break my spine
I'm not afraid of them when I'm with you

all my life I have truly trusted you
save me from the liars
let me live in your house

(Alicia Ostriker)

from Psalm 27: *Achat Sha'alti*

□ Achat sha'alti me'eit Adonai,
otah avakesh
Shivti b'veit Adonai,
kol y'mei chayyay
Lachazot b'noam, b'noam
Adonai, u'l'vaker b'heikhalo

□ אַחַת שָׁאַלְתִּי מֵאֵת-יְיָ
אוֹתָהּ אֲבַקֵּשׁ:
שִׁבְתִּי בְּבֵית-יְיָ, כָּל-יְמֵי חַיַּי;
לַחֲזוֹת בְּנֹעַם-יְיָ,
וּלְבַקֵּר בְּהֵיכָלוֹ.

□ One thing I ask, I ask of You, I earnestly pray for:
That I might dwell in Your house all the days of my life
Knowing the beauty, the beauty of You
and to dwell in Your holy place!

Lach Amar Libi (Ps. 27:8)

Lach — לָךְ — You
Amar libi — אָמַר לִבִּי — Called to my heart:
Bakshu fanai — בַּקְּשׁוּ פָנָי — Come seek My face,
Bakshu fanai — בַּקְּשׁוּ פָנָי — Come seek My grace.

Et panayich — אֶת פָּנַיִךְ — For Your love,
Havayah — הוי"ה — Source of all,
Avakeish — אֲבַקֵּשׁ — I will seek.

(singable English by Rabbi David Markus)

The full text of this psalm can be found on p. 246.

Tashlich: Casting our Sins Upon the Waters

A Prayer for *Tashlich*

Here I am again
ready to let go of my mistakes.

Help me to release myself
from all the ways I've missed the mark.

Help me to stop carrying
the karmic baggage of my poor choices.

As I cast this bread upon the waters
lift my troubles off my shoulders.

Help me to know that last year is over,
washed away like crumbs in the current.

Open my heart to blessing and gratitude.
Renew my soul as the dew renews the grasses.

And we say together:
Amen.

(*Rabbi Rachel Barenblat*)

A prayer from Micah

Mi-el camocha no'esh avon v'over al pesha lisherit nachalato, lo hechezik la'ad apo ki chafetz chesed hu. Yashuv y'rachamenu yicbosh avonoteinu v'tashlich bim'tzulot yam col-chat tam. Titen emet l'Ya'akov, Rachel v'Leah, chesed l'Avraham v'Sarah, asher nishbata la'avoteinu mimei kedem.

מִי־אֵל כָּמוֹךָ נֹשֵׂא עָוֹן וְעֹבֵר
עַל־פֶּשַׁע לִשְׁאֵרִית נַחֲלָתוֹ
לֹא־הֶחֱזִיק לָעַד אַפּוֹ כִּי־חָפֵץ
חֶסֶד הוּא: יָשׁוּב יְרַחֲמֵנוּ
יִכְבֹּשׁ עֲוֺנֹתֵינוּ וְתַשְׁלִיךְ
בִּמְצֻלוֹת יָם כָּל־חַטֹּאתָם:
תִּתֵּן אֱמֶת לְיַעֲקֹב חֶסֶד
לְאַבְרָהָם אֲשֶׁר־נִשְׁבַּעְתָּ
לַאֲבֹתֵינוּ מִימֵי קֶדֶם:

Who is like You, Adonai,
forgiving iniquity and pardoning transgression?
You do not maintain anger, but delight in lovingkindness.
You will again have compassion upon us, subduing our sins,
casting our sins into the depths of the sea.
You will show faithfulness and enduring love to us
as You promised to our ancestors in days of old.

Tashlich Meditation

Think of a practice or attitude that you wish to change.
In the world of action: what is it that you do?
In the world of emotion: how does it make you feel?
In the world of knowledge: can you plan to do otherwise?
In the world of being: imagine God within, helping you change.
Sum all of this up for yourself in one word or concept.
Holding your bread in hand, focus on that word...
And then throw it in the water and watch it wash away.
Spend the year working on your plan to change.
Let each sighting of moving water be your reminder.

(Adapted from Avi Dolgin)

Ana BaKoach

Source of Mercy,
With loving strength
Untie our tangles.

Cleanse and bless us
Infuse us ever
With loving care.

Receive our prayer
Do hear our cry
Who secrets knows.

Your chanting folk
Raise high, make pure
Accept our song.

Gracious source
Of holy power!
Do guide Your folk.

Through time & space
Your glory shines,
Majestic One.

Ana bakoach gedulat yemincha tatir tzrurah.	אָנָּא בְּכֹחַ גְּדֻלַּת יְמִינְךָ תַּתִּיר צְרוּרָה.
Baruch sheim kavod malchuto le'olam va'ed.	בָּרוּךְ שֵׁם כְּבוֹד מַלְכוּתוֹ לְעוֹלָם וָעֶד.

(English translation by Rabbi Zalman Schachter-Shalomi z"l / of blessed memory.)

Take time for silent reflection; cast bread (or small stones) upon the waters.

TEKIAH GEDOLAH תקיעה גדולה!

Prayer Before Yom Kippur

I now prepare
to unify my whole self—

heart
mind
consciousness
body
passions

with this holy community
with the Jewish people everywhere
with all people everywhere
with all life and being
to commune with the Source of all being.

May I find the words,
the music, the movements
that will put me in touch
with the great light of God.

May the rungs of insight and joy
that I reach in my devotion
flow from me to others
and fill all my actions in the world.

May the beauty of God rest upon us.
May God establish the works of our hands.
And may the works of our hands establish God.

(Rabbi Burt Jacobson)

Before Kol Nidre

This is the one evening service of the year when we don don tallitot.

Baruch atah, Adonai, eloheinu melech ha'olam, asher kidshanu b'mitzvotav v'tzivanu l'hit'atef ba-tzitzit.	בָּרוּךְ אַתָּה יְיָ אֱלֹהֵינוּ מֶלֶךְ הָעוֹלָם אֲשֶׁר קִדְּשָׁנוּ בְּמִצְוֹתָיו, וְצִוָּנוּ לְהִתְעַטֵּף בַּצִּיצִת.

Blessed are You, Adonai our God, source of all being, Who makes us holy with mitzvot and commands us concerning the wearing of *tzitzit*.

□ Or zarua la-tzaddik U'l'yishrei-lev simcha.	□ אוֹר זָרֻעַ לַצַּדִּיק וּלְיִשְׁרֵי לֵב שִׂמְחָה.

Light is sown for the righteous
And for the upright of heart, joy!

Biy'shivah shel malah u-vishiva shel matah, al da'at hamakom v'al da'at hakahal anu matirin l'hitpallel im ha-avaryonim.	בִּישִׁיבָה שֶׁל מַעְלָה וּבִישִׁיבָה שֶׁל מַטָּה, עַל דַּעַת הַמָּקוֹם וְעַל דַּעַת הַקָּהָל, אָנוּ מַתִּירִין לְהִתְפַּלֵּל עִם הָעֲבַרְיָנִים.

As in heaven, so is it here; as God permits, so do we. No matter what our sins, no matter how we have strayed, we pray together tonight as one community.

Kol Nidre

כָּל נִדְרֵי וֶאֱסָרֵי וַחֲרָמֵי, וְקוֹנָמֵי וְכִנּוּיֵי, וְקִנּוּסֵי וּשְׁבוּעוֹת, דִּנְדַרְנָא וּדְאִשְׁתַּבַּעְנָא, וּדְאַחֲרִמְנָא וְדַאֲסַרְנָא עַל נַפְשָׁתָנָא, מִיּוֹם כִּפֻּרִים זֶה עַד יוֹם כִּפֻּרִים הַבָּא עָלֵינוּ לְטוֹבָה, כֻּלְּהוֹן אִחֲרַטְנָא בְהוֹן. כֻּלְּהוֹן יְהוֹן שָׁרָן, שְׁבִיקִין שְׁבִיתִין, בְּטֵלִין וּמְבֻטָּלִין, לָא שְׁרִירִין וְלָא קַיָּמִין. נִדְרָנָא לָא נִדְרֵי, וֶאֱסָרָנָא לָא אֱסָרֵי, וּשְׁבוּעָתָנָא לָא שְׁבוּעוֹת.

Kol nidrei ve'esarei vacharamei vekonamei vechinuyei vekinusei ushvu'ot. Dindarna udishtabana udacharimna veda'asarna al nafshatana, miyom kipurim zeh ad yom kipurim haba aleinu letovah, kulehon icharatna v'hon, kulehon yehon sheran, shevikin shevitin beteilin umvutalin la sharirin vela kayamin. Nidrana la nidrei ve'esarana la esarei ushv atana la shevuot.

All the vows, promises, and oaths we make with God,
all the obligations and restrictions we place on ourselves
in God's name, all the harsh things we say only to regret them,
the things we promise and forget, the punishments we call down
on ourselves from heaven, the deals we bargain with God
in a moment of duress, the good-hearted resolutions
we cannot fulfill after honest effort—for all of these,
from this Yom Kippur to the next, we request release.
May they be dissolved and annulled.
These vows shall not be binding vows,
these prohibitions shall not be binding prohibitions,
these oaths shall not be binding oaths.

V'nislach l'chol edat b'nei Yisrael v'lager hager b'tocham, ki l'chol ha'am bishgaga.

וְנִסְלַח לְכָל עֲדַת בְּנֵי יִשְׂרָאֵל וְלַגֵּר הַגָּר בְּתוֹכָם, כִּי לְכָל הָעָם בִּשְׁגָגָה.

May there be forgiveness for the entire congregation of Israel and all who live among them, for all the people have sinned. Please forgive the sin of this people in the greatness of Your love, as You have forgiven them since You brought them out of Egypt and to this very day. As it is said in Your Torah:

Vayomer Adonai: salachti kidvarecha.

וַיֹּאמֶר יְיָ סָלַחְתִּי כִּדְבָרֶךָ.

And God said: I forgive you, as you have asked.

☐ Baruch atah, Adonai, eloheinu melech ha'olam, shehecheyanu v'kiy'manu v'higianu lazman hazeh!

☐ בָּרוּךְ אַתָּה, יְיָ אֱלֹהֵינוּ, מֶלֶךְ הָעוֹלָם, שֶׁהֶחֱיָנוּ וְקִיְּמָנוּ וְהִגִּיעָנוּ לַזְּמַן הַזֶּה.

Blessed are You, Adonai our God, source of all being, Who has kept us alive, sustained us, and enabled us to reach this time!

Return Again

Return again, return again,
return to the land of your soul. (2x)
Return to who you are,
return to what you are,
return to where you are
born and reborn again—
Return again, return again
Return to the land of your soul.

(Rabbi Shlomo Carlebach)

Candle Lighting

May the candles we kindle tonight awaken us to love, to light, and to our deepest hopes for *teshuvah* (repentance and return).

בָּרוּךְ אַתָּה יְיָ אֱלֹהֵינוּ מֶלֶךְ
הָעוֹלָם, אֲשֶׁר קִדְּשָׁנוּ
בְּמִצְוֹתָיו, וְצִוָּנוּ לְהַדְלִיק נֵר
שֶׁל (שַׁבָּת וְשֶׁל) יוֹם
הַכִּפּוּרִים.

Baruch atah Adonai Eloheinu melech ha'olam, asher kideshanu bemitsvotav vitsivanu lehadlik neir shel (Shabbat veshel) yom ha-kippurim.

Blessed are You, Adonai our God, source of all being, who makes us holy with mitzvot and enjoins us to light the (Shabbat and) Yom Kippur candles.

On Shabbat (from) Psalm 92

Mizmor shir l'yom ha-Shabbat.

מִזְמוֹר שִׁיר לְיוֹם הַשַּׁבָּת׃

Tov l'hodot l'Adonai
u-l'zamer l'shimcha elyon.
L'hagid baboker chasdecha,
v'emunatecha baleilot.

טוֹב לְהֹדוֹת לַיְיָ
וּלְזַמֵּר לְשִׁמְךָ עֶלְיוֹן׃
לְהַגִּיד בַּבֹּקֶר חַסְדֶּךָ
וֶאֱמוּנָתְךָ בַּלֵּילוֹת׃

A psalm. A song of the day Shabbat.

How good it is to praise Adonai
and to sing to God on high,
To tell of Your love in the morning
and of Your faithfulness at night!

Alei asor va'alei navel
alei higayon b'chinor.
Ki samachtani Adonai
b'fo'alecha
B'ma'aseh yadecha aranen:

עֲלֵי עָשׂוֹר וַעֲלֵי נָבֶל
עֲלֵי הִגָּיוֹן בְּכִנּוֹר׃
כִּי שִׂמַּחְתַּנִי יְיָ בְּפָעֳלֶךָ
בְּמַעֲשֵׂי יָדֶיךָ אֲרַנֵּן׃

□ Mah gadlu ma'asecha Yah
M'od amku machshevotecha.

□ מַה גָּדְלוּ מַעֲשֶׂיךָ יְיָ
מְאֹד עָמְקוּ מַחְשְׁבֹתֶיךָ׃

I sing to the music of the harp,
to the sound of string and voice
for You have made me rejoice, Adonai.
I thrill at the beauty of Your world.

How great is Your work, Adonai:
How profound is the world's design!

Psalm 93

Adonai possesses us.
In sublimity is God robed,
robed in wonder.
God is the strength
of a world secure
and unshakable.

יְיָ מָלָךְ
גֵּאוּת לָבֵשׁ
לָבֵשׁ יְיָ
עֹז הִתְאַזָּר
אַף תִּכּוֹן תֵּבֵל
בַּל תִּמּוֹט:

From ancient time
we have sought You.
You are from eternity.
The ancient ocean sounds,
Adonai,
The serene ocean
sounds its voice,
The mysterious ocean
sounds its pounding.
Above the thunder
of the mighty waters,
Truer than the breakers
of the sea,
Is Adonai, the most sublime.

נָכוֹן כִּסְאֲךָ מֵאָז
מֵעוֹלָם אָתָּה:
נָשְׂאוּ נְהָרוֹת יְיָ
נָשְׂאוּ נְהָרוֹת
קוֹלָם יִשְׂאוּ נְהָרוֹת דָּכְיָם:
מִקֹּלוֹת מַיִם רַבִּים אַדִּירִים
מִשְׁבְּרֵי יָם
אַדִּיר בַּמָּרוֹם יְיָ:

Your wisdom is truer than truth.
Holiness is Your presence in the
world, Adonai,
for time without measure.

עֵדֹתֶיךָ נֶאֶמְנוּ מְאֹד לְבֵיתְךָ
נַאֲוָה קֹדֶשׁ
יְיָ לְאֹרֶךְ יָמִים:

The Shema and Her Blessings

Barchu: Call to Prayer

Bar'chu, dear One
Shekhinah, holy Name
As I call on the light of my soul
I come home.

(Lev Friedman)

Barchu et Adonai ha-mevorach.	בָּרְכוּ אֶת יְיָ הַמְבֹרָךְ:
☐ Baruch Adonai ha-mevorach l'olam va-ed.	☐ בָּרוּךְ יְיָ הַמְבֹרָךְ לְעוֹלָם וָעֶד:

Blessed is Adonai, the blessed One.

Blessed is Adonai, the blessed One,
now and forever!

Ma'ariv Aravim: God of Day and Night

Baruch atah Adonai
Eloheinu melech ha'olam
asher bidvaro ma'ariv
aravim bechochmah
poteach she'arim uvitvunah
meshaneh itim umachalif et
hazemanim umsadeir et
hakochavim b'mish
meroteihem baraki'ah
kirtsono. Borei yom valaila
goleil or mipnei choshech
vechoshech mipnei or
uma'avir yom umeivi lailah
umavdil bein yom uvein
lailah Adonai tzeva'ot
shemo.

בָּרוּךְ אַתָּה יְיָ,
אֱלֹהֵינוּ מֶלֶךְ הָעוֹלָם,
אֲשֶׁר בִּדְבָרוֹ מַעֲרִיב עֲרָבִים,
בְּחָכְמָה פּוֹתֵחַ שְׁעָרִים וּבִתְבוּנָה
מְשַׁנֶּה עִתִּים, וּמַחֲלִיף אֶת
הַזְּמַנִּים, וּמְסַדֵּר אֶת הַכּוֹכָבִים,
בְּמִשְׁמְרוֹתֵיהֶם בָּרָקִיעַ כִּרְצוֹנוֹ.
בּוֹרֵא יוֹם וָלָיְלָה, גּוֹלֵל אוֹר מִפְּנֵי
חֹשֶׁךְ, וְחֹשֶׁךְ מִפְּנֵי אוֹר. וּמַעֲבִיר
יוֹם וּמֵבִיא לָיְלָה, וּמַבְדִּיל בֵּין יוֹם
וּבֵין לָיְלָה,
יְיָ צְבָאוֹת שְׁמוֹ.

Blessed are You, Source of all being,
by whose word the evening falls.
In wisdom You open heaven's gates.
With understanding You make seasons change,
causing the times to come and go,
and ordering the stars on their appointed paths
through heaven's dome, all according to Your will.
Creator of day and night, who rolls back light before dark,
and dark before light, who makes day pass away
and brings on the night,
dividing between day and night:
the Leader of Heaven's Multitudes is Your name!

□ אֵל חַי וְקַיָּם, תָּמִיד יִמְלוֹךְ עָלֵינוּ לְעוֹלָם וָעֶד. בָּרוּךְ אַתָּה יְיָ, הַמַּעֲרִיב עֲרָבִים:

□ Eil chai vekayam tamid yimloch aleinu le'olam va'ed. Baruch atah Adonai hama'ariv aravim.

Living and enduring God, be our guide
Now and always.
Blessed are You, Adonai,
who makes evening fall.

Ahavat Olam: Eternal Love

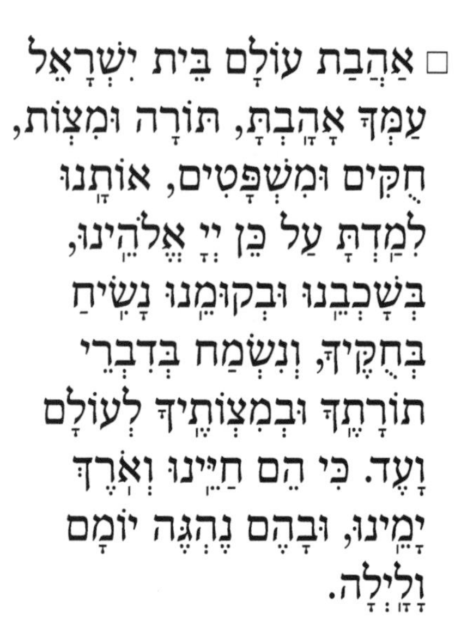
□ אַהֲבַת עוֹלָם בֵּית יִשְׂרָאֵל
עַמְּךָ אָהָבְתָּ, תּוֹרָה וּמִצְוֹת,
חֻקִּים וּמִשְׁפָּטִים, אוֹתָנוּ
לִמַּדְתָּ עַל כֵּן יְיָ אֱלֹהֵינוּ,
בְּשָׁכְבֵנוּ וּבְקוּמֵנוּ נָשִׂיחַ
בְּחֻקֶּיךָ, וְנִשְׂמַח בְּדִבְרֵי
תוֹרָתֶךָ וּבְמִצְוֹתֶיךָ לְעוֹלָם
וָעֶד. כִּי הֵם חַיֵּינוּ וְאֹרֶךְ
יָמֵינוּ, וּבָהֶם נֶהְגֶּה יוֹמָם
וָלָיְלָה.

□ Ahavat olam beit Yisrael
amecha ahavta
Torah umitsvot chukim
umishpatim otanu limadeta. Al
kein Adonai Eloheinu
beshochveinu uvkumeinu
nasiach bechukecha.
Venismach bedivrei Toratecha
Uvmitsvotecha le'olam va'ed.
Kee heim chayeinu ve'orech
yameinu uvahem negeh
yomam valailah.

□ וְאַהֲבָתְךָ אַל תָּסִיר מִמֶּנּוּ
לְעוֹלָמִים. בָּרוּךְ אַתָּה יְיָ,
אוֹהֵב עַמּוֹ יִשְׂרָאֵל:

□ Ve'ahavatcha al tasir
Mimenu le'olamim.
Baruch atah Adonai
oheiv amo Yisrael.

With eternal love, You love the house of Israel. Torah and mitzvot, laws and justice You have taught us. And so, Adonai, our God, when we lie down and when we rise, we reflect upon Your laws; we take pleasure in Your Torah's words and your mitzvot, now and always. Truly, they are our life, our length of days. On them we meditate by day and night.

Your love will never depart from us as long as worlds endure. Blessed are You, Adonai, who loves Your people Israel.

An Unending Love

We are loved by unending love.

We are embraced by arms that find us
even when we are hidden from ourselves.
We are touched by fingers that soothe us
even when we are too proud for soothing.
We are counseled by voices that guide us
even when we are too embittered to hear.

We are loved by unending love.

We are supported by hands that uplift us
even in the midst of a fall.
We are urged on by eyes that meet us
even when we are too weak for meeting.

We are loved by unending love.

Embraced, touched, soothed, and counseled,
ours are the arms, the fingers, the voices;
ours are the hands, the eyes, the smiles;

We are loved by unending love.

(Rabbi Rami Shapiro)

Shema

☐ שְׁמַע יִשְׂרָאֵל, יְיָ אֱלֹהֵינוּ, יְיָ אֶחָד:

בָּרוּךְ שֵׁם כְּבוֹד מַלְכוּתוֹ לְעוֹלָם וָעֶד.

☐ Shema Yisrael:
Adonai Eloheinu
Adonai echad!
Baruch sheim kevod
malchuto le'olam
va'ed!

Hear, O Israel: Adonai is our God, Adonai is One!
Through time and space Your glory shines, Majestic One!

☐וְאָהַבְתָּ אֵת יְיָ אֱלֹהֶיךָ,
בְּכָל-לְבָבְךָ, וּבְכָל-נַפְשְׁךָ,
וּבְכָל-מְאֹדֶךָ. וְהָיוּ הַדְּבָרִים
הָאֵלֶּה, אֲשֶׁר אָנֹכִי מְצַוְּךָ
הַיּוֹם, עַל-לְבָבֶךָ: וְשִׁנַּנְתָּם
לְבָנֶיךָ, וְדִבַּרְתָּ בָּם בְּשִׁבְתְּךָ
בְּבֵיתֶךָ, וּבְלֶכְתְּךָ בַדֶּרֶךְ
וְּבְשָׁכְבְּךָ, וּבְקוּמֶךָ.
וּקְשַׁרְתָּם לְאוֹת עַל-יָדֶךָ,
וְהָיוּ לְטֹטָפֹת בֵּין עֵינֶיךָ,
וּכְתַבְתָּם עַל מְזֻזוֹת בֵּיתֶךָ
וּבִשְׁעָרֶיךָ:

☐ V'ahavta et Adonai
elohecha, b'chol l'vavcha,
uv'chol nafshecha, uv'chol
me'odecha. V'hayu ha-
d'varim ha-eileh, asher
anochi m'tzv'cha hayom, al-
levavecha. V'shinantam
l'vanecha, v'dibarta bam
b'shiv't'cha b'veitecha,
uv'lech't'cha vaderech
uv'shochb'cha uv'kumecha.
Ukshartam l'ot al yadecha,
v'hayu l'totafor bein enecha,
uchtavtam al mezuzot
beitecha uvisharecha.

Love the One, your God, with every heartbeat, with every breath,
with every conscious act. Keep in mind the words
I command you today.
Teach them to your children, talk about them at work;
whether you are tired or you are rested.
Let them guide the work of your hands;
keep them in the forefront of your vision.
Do not leave them at the doorway, or outside your gate.

וְהָיָה אִם-שָׁמֹעַ תִּשְׁמְעוּ אֶל-מִצְוֹתַי, אֲשֶׁר אָנֹכִי מְצַוֶּה אֶתְכֶם
הַיּוֹם, לְאַהֲבָה אֶת יְיָ אֱלֹהֵיכֶם, וּלְעָבְדוֹ בְּכָל-לְבַבְכֶם וּבְכָל
נַפְשְׁכֶם. וְנָתַתִּי מְטַר-אַרְצְכֶם בְּעִתּוֹ, יוֹרֶה וּמַלְקוֹשׁ, וְאָסַפְתָּ
דְגָנֶךָ וְתִירֹשְׁךָ וְיִצְהָרֶךָ. וְנָתַתִּי עֵשֶׂב בְּשָׂדְךָ לִבְהֶמְתֶּךָ, וְאָכַלְתָּ
וְשָׂבָעְתָּ. הִשָּׁמְרוּ לָכֶם פֶּן-יִפְתֶּה לְבַבְכֶם, וְסַרְתֶּם וַעֲבַדְתֶּם
אֱלֹהִים אֲחֵרִים וְהִשְׁתַּחֲוִיתֶם לָהֶם. וְחָרָה אַף-יְיָ בָּכֶם, וְעָצַר
אֶת-הַשָּׁמַיִם וְלֹא-יִהְיֶה מָטָר, וְהָאֲדָמָה לֹא תִתֵּן אֶת-יְבוּלָהּ
וַאֲבַדְתֶּם מְהֵרָה מֵעַל הָאָרֶץ הַטֹּבָה אֲשֶׁ יְיָ נֹתֵן לָכֶם: וְשַׂמְתֶּם
אֶת דְּבָרַי אֵלֶּה עַל-לְבַבְכֶם וְעַל-נַפְשְׁכֶם וּקְשַׁרְתֶּם אֹתָם לְאוֹת
עַל-יֶדְכֶם, וְהָיוּ לְטוֹטָפֹת בֵּין עֵינֵיכֶם: וְלִמַּדְתֶּם אֹתָם אֶת-בְּנֵיכֶם,
לְדַבֵּר בָּם, בְּשִׁבְתְּךָ בְּבֵיתֶךָ, וּבְלֶכְתְּךָ בַדֶּרֶךְ, וּבְשָׁכְבְּךָ וּבְקוּמֶךָ:
וּכְתַבְתָּם עַל-מְזוּזוֹת בֵּיתֶךָ וּבִשְׁעָרֶיךָ: לְמַעַן יִרְבּוּ יְמֵיכֶם וִימֵי
בְנֵיכֶם עַל הָאֲדָמָה אֲשֶׁר נִשְׁבַּע יְיָ לַאֲבֹתֵיכֶם לָתֵת לָהֶם, כִּימֵי
הַשָּׁמַיִם עַל-הָאָרֶץ:

How good it will be when you really listen and hear My directions which I give you today, to love Yah who is your God and to act godly with feeling and inspiration. Your earthly needs will be met at the right time, appropriate to the season. You will reap what you have planted for your delight and health. Also your animals will have ample feed. All of you will eat and be content.

Be careful—watch out! Don't let your cravings delude you; don't become alienated; don't let your cravings become your gods; don't debase yourself to them because the God-sense within you will become distorted. Heaven will be shut to you, grace will not descend, Earth will not yield her produce. Your rushing will destroy you! And Earth will not be able to recover her good balance in which God's gifts manifest.

These are interpretive translations of the first and second paragraphs of the Shema; a literal translation appears on p. 94.

וַיֹּאמֶר יְיָ אֶל-מֹשֶׁה לֵּאמֹר:
דַּבֵּר אֶל-בְּנֵי יִשְׂרָאֵל וְאָמַרְתָּ
אֲלֵהֶם: וְעָשׂוּ לָהֶם צִיצִת עַל-
כַּנְפֵי בִגְדֵיהֶם לְדֹרֹתָם, וְנָתְנוּ
עַל-צִיצִת הַכָּנָף פְּתִיל תְּכֵלֶת.
וְהָיָה לָכֶם לְצִיצִת, וּרְאִיתֶם
אֹתוֹ וּזְכַרְתֶּם אֶת-כָּל-מִצְוֹת
יְיָ, וַעֲשִׂיתֶם אֹתָם, וְלֹא תָתוּרוּ
אַחֲרֵי לְבַבְכֶם וְאַחֲרֵי עֵינֵיכֶם,
אֲשֶׁר-אַתֶּם זֹנִים אַחֲרֵיהֶם:

Vayomer Adonai el Moshe lemor: daber el-bnei Yisrael v'amarta aleihem v'asu lahem tzitzit al kanfei bigdeihem l'dorotam, v'natnu al tzitzit ha-kanaf p'til tchelet. V'yaha lachem l'tzitzit, u'ritem oto, u'zchartem et-kol-mitzvot Adonai v'asitem otam. V'lo taturu acharei l'vavchem v'acharei eineihem asher-atem zonim achareihem.

And God spoke to Moses saying: speak to the children of Israel and say to them that they should make *tzitzit* on the corners of their garments for all time, and they shall place on the *tzitzit* a little thread of blue. And these shall be for you as *tzitzit*, that you may look upon them, that you will remember all of the mitzvot of Adonai and you shall do them, so that you will not go running after the cravings of your heart or the turnings of your eyes which might take you into places where you should not be!

Kol Nidre evening is the only time in the Jewish year when a tallit is worn at night. Ordinarily a tallit is only worn when it is light out and we can see the fringes.

Perhaps we wear tallitot at Kol Nidre because on this night, the "light" of our prayers and our connection with God burns so brightly that it illuminates us from within, and we can see our *tzitzit* gleaming in that holy light.

□ לְמַעַן תִּזְכְּרוּ וַעֲשִׂיתֶם אֶת-כָּל-מִצְוֹתָי, וִהְיִיתֶם קְדֹשִׁים לֵאלֹהֵיכֶם: אֲנִי יְיָ אֱלֹהֵיכֶם, אֲשֶׁר הוֹצֵאתִי אֶתְכֶם מֵאֶרֶץ מִצְרַיִם, לִהְיוֹת לָכֶם לֵאלֹהִים, אֲנִי יְיָ אֱלֹהֵיכֶם:

□ Lema'an tizkeru va'asitem et kol mitzvotai viheyitem kedoshim l'Eloheichem. Ani Adonai Eloheichem asher hotzeiti etcham me'eretz Mitzrayim lihiyot lachem l'Elohim. Ani Adonai Aloheichem.

Remember to do My mitzvot and be holy with your God. I am Adonai your God, who brought you out of the land of Egypt to be your God. I am Adonai your God.

Rabban Shimon ben Gamliel said, "[in the old days] there was no holiday in Israel like Yom Kippur... The unmarried girls of Jerusalem would go out to the vineyards dressed in white to dance, and invite the unmarried boys to join them."

Why was this a day of dancing and courtship and joy? Because on this day we received a clear sign that God had accepted our *teshuvah*. Yom Kippur is the anniversary of the day when Moshe returned from atop Mount Sinai with the second set of tablets, a sign that God had forgiven the idolatry which had caused the first set to be shattered. On Yom Kippur, we experience our bond with God anew.

Geulah: Redemption

אֱמֶת וֶאֱמוּנָה כָּל זֹאת, וְקַיָּם עָלֵינוּ, כִּי הוּא יְיָ אֱלֹהֵינוּ וְאֵין זוּלָתוֹ, וַאֲנַחְנוּ יִשְׂרָאֵל עַמּוֹ. הַפּוֹדֵנוּ מִיַּד מְלָכִים, מַלְכֵּנוּ הַגּוֹאֲלֵנוּ מִכַּף כָּל הֶעָרִיצִים. הָאֵל הַנִּפְרָע לָנוּ מִצָּרֵינוּ, וְהַמְשַׁלֵּם גְּמוּל לְכָל אֹיְבֵי נַפְשֵׁנוּ. הָעֹשֶׂה גְדֹלוֹת עַד אֵין חֵקֶר, וְנִפְלָאוֹת עַד אֵין מִסְפָּר. הַשָּׂם נַפְשֵׁנוּ בַּחַיִּים, וְלֹא נָתַן לַמּוֹט רַגְלֵנוּ, הַמַּדְרִיכֵנוּ עַל בָּמוֹת אוֹיְבֵינוּ, וַיָּרֶם קַרְנֵנוּ, עַל כָּל שׂוֹנְאֵנוּ. הָעֹשֶׂה לָנוּ נִסִּים וּנְקָמָה בְּפַרְעֹה, אוֹתוֹת וּמוֹפְתִים בְּאַדְמַת בְּנֵי חָם. הַמַּכֶּה בְעֶבְרָתוֹ כָּל בְּכוֹרֵי מִצְרָיִם, וַיּוֹצֵא אֶת עַמּוֹ יִשְׂרָאֵל מִתּוֹכָם, לְחֵרוּת עוֹלָם. הַמַּעֲבִיר בָּנָיו בֵּין גִּזְרֵי יַם סוּף, אֶת רוֹדְפֵיהֶם וְאֶת שׂוֹנְאֵיהֶם, בִּתְהוֹמוֹת טִבַּע, וְרָאוּ בָנָיו גְּבוּרָתוֹ. שִׁבְּחוּ וְהוֹדוּ לִשְׁמוֹ. וּמַלְכוּתוֹ בְּרָצוֹן קִבְּלוּ עֲלֵיהֶם, מֹשֶׁה וּבְנֵי יִשְׂרָאֵל לְךָ עָנוּ שִׁירָה בְּשִׂמְחָה רַבָּה, וְאָמְרוּ כֻלָּם:

All this is true and real and it is up to us:
Adonai is our only God, and we, Israel, are Your people.

You save us from oppression
and make our transformation possible.

You do great deeds beyond measure, wonders beyond counting.
You give our souls life and direct us from death.

You made miracles for us before Pharaoh,
Signs and wonders in the land of Egypt.

You led Your people Israel into freedom.
You led us through the Sea of Reeds.

When we saw Your power,
we thanked You and praised Your name.

Full of joy, Moses, Miriam, and all Israel sang:

☐ Mi chamocha ba'eilim Adonai, mi camocha nedar bakodesh, nora tehilot oseh feleh.

☐מִי כָמֹכָה בָּאֵלִים יְיָ,
מִי כָּמֹכָה נֶאְדָּר בַּקֹּדֶשׁ,
נוֹרָא תְהִלֹּת, עֹשֵׂה פֶלֶא:

Malchut'cha ra'u vanecha, bokea yam lifnei Moshe u Miriam. "Zeh eli," anu v'amru; "Adonai yimloch l'olam va'ed!"

מַלְכוּתְךָ רָאוּ בָנֶיךָ,
בּוֹקֵעַ יָם לִפְנֵי מֹשֶׁה וּמִרְיָם,
זֶה אֵלִי עָנוּ וְאָמְרוּ:
יְיָ יִמְלוֹךְ לְעוֹלָם וָעֶד.

V'ne'emar: ki fadah Adonai et Ya'akov, u'g'alo miyad chazak mimenu. Baruch atah, Adonai, ga'al Yisrael.

וְנֶאֱמַר: כִּי פָדָה יְיָ אֶת יַעֲקֹב,
וּגְאָלוֹ מִיַּד חָזָק מִמֶּנּוּ. בָּרוּךְ
אַתָּה יְיָ גָּאַל יִשְׂרָאֵל:

Who is like You, among the gods, Adonai? Who is like You, awesome and doing wonders?

Your children saw Your majesty, splitting the sea before Moses and Miriam.

"This is our God," they cried, "Adonai will reign through all space and time!"

And it is said: Adonai has saved the people of Jacob, and redeems the weak from the mighty. Blessed are You, Adonai, who redeems Israel.

Hashkivenu: Shelter of Peace

Hashkivenu Adonai eloheinu l'shalom, v'hamideinu malkeinu l'chayyim, ufros aleinu sukat shlomecha, v'taknenu b'etza tovah milfanecha, v'hoshienu l'ma'an shmecha, v'hagen b'adeinu, v'haser me'aleinu oyev, dever, v'cherev, v'raav v'yagon, v'haser satan milfaneinu u-me'achareinu, u'vtzel canfecha tastireinu. Ki el shomreinu u-matzilenu atah, ki el melech chanun v'rachum atah, ushmor tzeiteinu u-voeinu, l'chayyim u'l'shalom, me'atah v'ad olam.

הַשְׁכִּיבֵנוּ יְיָ אֱלֹהֵינוּ לְשָׁלוֹם,
וְהַעֲמִידֵנוּ מַלְכֵּנוּ לְחַיִּים וּפְרוֹשׂ
עָלֵינוּ סֻכַּת שְׁלוֹמֶךָ, וְתַקְּנֵנוּ
בְּעֵצָה טוֹבָה מִלְּפָנֶיךָ,
וְהוֹשִׁיעֵנוּ לְמַעַן שְׁמֶךָ, וְהָגֵן
בַּעֲדֵנוּ, וְהָסֵר מֵעָלֵינוּ אוֹיֵב,
דֶּבֶר, וְחֶרֶב, וְרָעָב וְיָגוֹן, וְהָסֵר
שָׂטָן מִלְּפָנֵינוּ וּמֵאַחֲרֵנוּ, וּבְצֵל
כְּנָפֶיךָ תַּסְתִּירֵנוּ. כִּי אֵל
שׁוֹמְרֵנוּ וּמַצִּילֵנוּ אָתָּה, כִּי אֵל
מֶלֶךְ חַנּוּן וְרַחוּם אָתָּה, וּשְׁמוֹר
צֵאתֵנוּ וּבוֹאֵנוּ, לְחַיִּים
וּלְשָׁלוֹם, מֵעַתָּה וְעַד עוֹלָם.

Help us to lie down in peace, Adonai our God, and to arise again to life. Spread over the world Your sheltering peace. Direct us with Your guidance and save us. Protect and keep us from enmity, illness, violence, want, and sorrow. Remove envy and recrimination from us. Shelter us in the shadow of Your wings, for You are a protecting, redeeming God. You are God, our source of grace and mercy. Guard our going out and our coming in, for life and for peace, now and forever.

□ U-fros aleinu sukkat shlomecha.
Baruch atah Adonai, shomer amo Yisrael la-ad.

□ וּפְרֹשׂ עָלֵינוּ סֻכַּת שְׁלוֹמֶךָ.
בָּרוּךְ אַתָּה יְיָ, שׁוֹמֵר עַמּוֹ יִשְׂרָאֵל לָעַד:

Spread your sheltering peace over us. Blessed are you, Adonai, who spreads a shelter of peace over all of your people.

Hashkivenu Chant

Hashkivenu Yah eloheinu l'shalom.
Ufros aleinu sukkat shlomecha.

הַשְׁכִּיבֵנוּ יָהּ אֱלֹהֵינוּ לְשָׁלוֹם.
וּפְרֹשׂ עָלֵינוּ סֻכַּת שְׁלוֹמֶךָ.

Help us to lie down in peace, Adonai our God.
Spread over us Your shelter of peace.

(Rabbi Hanna Tiferet Siegel)

The Zohar teaches
that Yom Kippur is the day
when the world we live in
—*malkhut*, the world of creation,
inevitably a world of brokenness
and disconnection—
unites with the world above
the world of the transcendent
where all is One.

Veshameru (on Shabbat)

□ Veshameru venei Yisrael et ha-Shabbat, la'asot et ha-Shabbat l'dorotam berit olam. Beini u-vein b'nei Yisrael ot hee l'olam. Ki sheshet yamim asah Adonai et ha-shamayim v'et ha-aretz, uvayom ha-shvi'i shavat vayinafash.	□וְשָׁמְרוּ בְנֵי יִשְׂרָאֵל אֶת הַשַּׁבָּת, לַעֲשׂוֹת אֶת הַשַּׁבָּת לְדֹרֹתָם בְּרִית עוֹלָם: בֵּינִי וּבֵין בְּנֵי יִשְׂרָאֵל אוֹת הִיא לְעוֹלָם, כִּי שֵׁשֶׁת יָמִים עָשָׂה יְיָ אֶת הַשָּׁמַיִם וְאֶת הָאָרֶץ, וּבַיּוֹם הַשְּׁבִיעִי שָׁבַת וַיִּנָּפַשׁ.

The children of Israel shall keep the day of Shabbat and make
Shabbat a perpetual covenant for all their generations.
It shall be a sign between Me and the children of Israel forever.
For in six days, Adonai made the heavens and earth
But on the seventh day, God rested and was refreshed.

"You Shall Be Cleansed"

כִּי בַיּוֹם הַזֶּה יְכַפֵּר עֲלֵיכֶם לְטַהֵר אֶתְכֶם,
מִכֹּל חַטֹּאתֵיכֶם לִפְנֵי יְיָ תִּטְהָרוּ.

On this day God atones and purifies you.
You shall be cleansed of all your sins before Adonai.

The Kaddish: A Door

In all of its forms, the Kaddish is a door in the service
between one part of the service and the next.

As we move through this door:
what is happening in your heart and mind?

Bring whatever you're feeling
into your prayer.

We'll move from the Kaddish
into the amidah

our chance to stand before God
as individuals within community.

Chatzi Kaddish

Yitgadal v'yitkadash sh'mei rabah. (Amen.) Be'alma div'ra chirutei v'yamlich malchutei. B'chayeichon uv'yomeichon uv'chayei d'chol beit Yisrael. Ba'agala uvizman kariv v'imru Amen.

יִתְגַּדַּל וְיִתְקַדַּשׁ שְׁמֵהּ רַבָּא.
בְּעָלְמָא דִּי בְרָא כִרְעוּתֵהּ,
וְיַמְלִיךְ מַלְכוּתֵהּ בְּחַיֵּיכוֹן
וּבְיוֹמֵיכוֹן וּבְחַיֵּי דְכָל בֵּית
יִשְׂרָאֵל. בַּעֲגָלָא וּבִזְמַן קָרִיב
וְאִמְרוּ אָמֵן:

□ Yehei shmei rabah m'vorach l'olam ul'almei almaya.

□יְהֵא שְׁמֵהּ רַבָּא מְבָרַךְ
לְעָלַם וּלְעָלְמֵי עָלְמַיָּא:

Yitbarach v'yishtabah v'yitpa'ar v'yitromam v'yitnaseh. V'yithadar v'yitaleh v'yithalal shmeh d'kudsha brich hu. L'eila u-l'eila min kol birchata v'shirata, tushb'chata v'nechemata, d'amiran b'alma, v'imru Amen.

יִתְבָּרַךְ וְיִשְׁתַּבַּח, וְיִתְפָּאַר
וְיִתְרוֹמַם וְיִתְנַשֵּׂא וְיִתְהַדָּר
וְיִתְעַלֶּה וְיִתְהַלָּל שְׁמֵהּ
דְּקֻדְשָׁא בְּרִיךְ הוּא לְעֵלָּא
וּלְעֵלָּא מִן כָּל בִּרְכָתָא
וְשִׁירָתָא, תֻּשְׁבְּחָתָא
וְנֶחֱמָתָא, דַּאֲמִירָן בְּעָלְמָא,
וְאִמְרוּ אָמֵן:

Magnified and sanctified! Magnified and sanctified! May God's Great Name fill the world God created. May God's splendor be seen in the world in your life, in your days, in the life of all Israel. Quickly and soon! And let us say, Amen.

Forever may the Great Name be blessed!

Blessed and praised! Splendid and supreme! May the holy name, Bless God, be praised, far beyond all the blessings and songs, comforts and consolations, that can be offered in this world. And let us say: Amen.

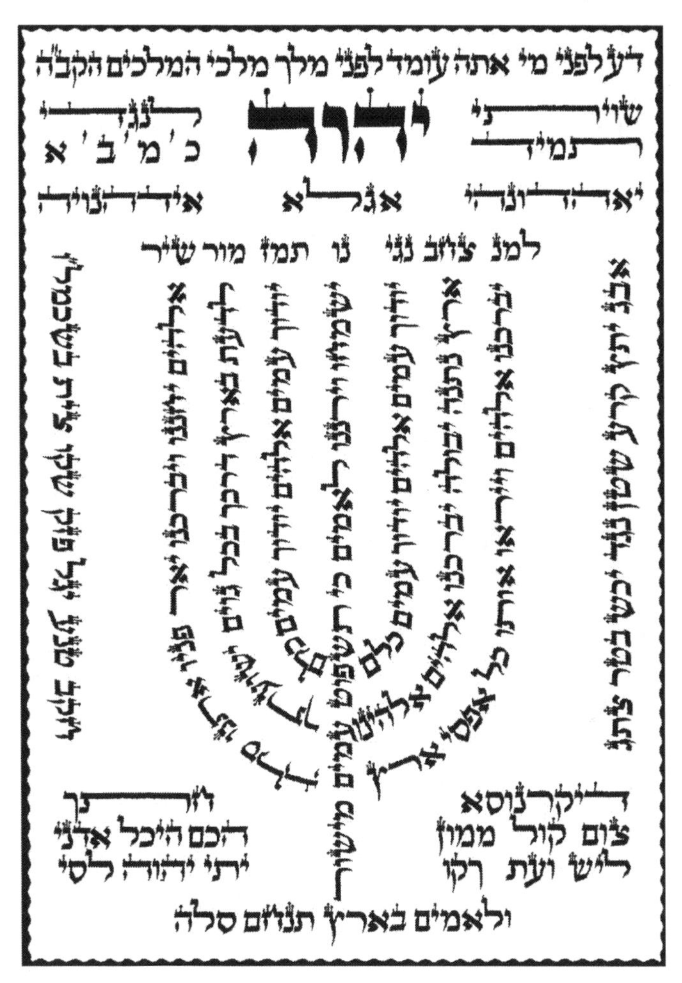

Shviti (Meditative Image of the Divine Name)

This is a shviti, *a calligraphy illustration of one of God's Names, drawn by anonymous sofer Ba'al Hakochav.*

The word "shviti" is Hebrew for "I have placed," and comes from Psalm 16:8: "I have placed God before me always."

As you gaze upon this shviti, imagine God's presence before you in this very piece of paper. Prepare yourself to encounter God during the Amidah.

Amidah

Adonai sefatai tiftach ufi yagid tehilatecha.	אֲדֹנָי שְׂפָתַי תִּפְתָּח וּפִי יַגִּיד תְּהִלָּתֶךָ:

Eternal God, open my lips
that my mouth may declare Your praise.

Avot v'Imahot: Our Ancestors

Baruch atah Adonai Eloheinu v'Elohei avoteinu v'imoteinu, elohei Avraham, elohei Yitzchak, elohei Ya'akov, elohei Sarah, elohei Rivkah, elohei Leah, v'elohei Rachel. Ha'el hagadol hagibor v'hanora Eil elyon, gomeil chasadim tovim v'koneh hakol v'zocheir chasei avot v'imahot, umeivi go'el livnei veneihem lema'an shemo b'ahavah.	בָּרוּךְ אַתָּה יְיָ אֱלֹהֵינוּ וֵאלֹהֵי אֲבוֹתֵינוּ, אֱלֹהֵי אַבְרָהָם, אֱלֹהֵי יִצְחָק, וֵאלֹהֵי יַעֲקֹב, אלֹהֵי שָׂרָה, אלֹהֵי רִבְקָה, אלֹהֵי לֵאָה, וֵאלֹהֵי רָחֵל. הָאֵל הַגָּדוֹל הַגִּבּוֹר וְהַנּוֹרָא, אֵל עֶלְיוֹן, גּוֹמֵל חֲסָדִים טוֹבִים, וְקוֹנֵה הַכֹּל, וְזוֹכֵר חַסְדֵי אָבוֹת ואמהות, וּמֵבִיא גוֹאֵל לִבְנֵי בְנֵיהֶם לְמַעַן שְׁמוֹ בְּאַהֲבָה:

Blessed are You, Adonai our God and God of our ancestors, God of Abraham, God of Isaac, God of Jacob; God of Sarah, God of Rebecca, God of Rachel and God of Leah; the great, mighty, and awesome God, God on high, who does deeds of loving kindness, who is the Source of all, and who remembers the steadfast love of our ancestors, who lovingly brings redemption to their children's children for Your name's sake.

Zochreinu lechayim melech chafeitz bachayim, vekotveinu beseifer ha-chayyim le ma'ancha Elohim chayyim.

זָכְרֵנוּ לְחַיִּים, מֶלֶךְ חָפֵץ בַּחַיִּים, וְכָתְבֵנוּ בְּסֵפֶר הַחַיִּים, לְמַעַנְךָ אֱלֹהִים חַיִּים.

Melech ozeir u-moshia u-magen. Baruch Atah Adonai, magein Avraham v'ezrat Sarah.

מֶלֶךְ עוֹזֵר וּמוֹשִׁיעַ וּמָגֵן: בָּרוּךְ אַתָּה יְיָ, מָגֵן אַבְרָהָם ואזרת שָׂרָה:

Remember us for life, creator Who delights in life, and inscribe us in the book of life for Your own sake, O God of life.

Ruler, helper, redeemer, and protector, blessed are You Adonai, Abraham’s shield and Sarah’s strength.

Gevurot: God's Strength

Atah gibor l'olam Adonai, mechayeh meitim atah rav l'hoshia. Morid ha-tal.

אַתָּה גִּבּוֹר לְעוֹלָם אֲדֹנָי, מְחַיֵּה מֵתִים אַתָּה, רַב לְהוֹשִׁיעַ: מוֹרִיד הַטָּל:

You are our eternal strength, Adonai. Your saving power gives life that transcends death. You bring the dew of the field.

מְכַלְכֵּל חַיִּים בְּחֶסֶד, מְחַיֵּה
מֵתִים בְּרַחֲמִים רַבִּים, סוֹמֵךְ
נוֹפְלִים, וְרוֹפֵא חוֹלִים, וּמַתִּיר
אֲסוּרִים, וּמְקַיֵּם אֱמוּנָתוֹ
לִישֵׁנֵי עָפָר, מִי כָמוֹךָ בַּעַל
גְּבוּרוֹת וּמִי דּוֹמֶה לָּךְ, מֶלֶךְ
מֵמִית וּמְחַיֶּה וּמַצְמִיחַ יְשׁוּעָה:

Mechalkel chayyim b'chesed, m'chayeh meitim b'rachamim rabim, somech noflim, v'rofeh cholim, umatir asurim, um'kayem emunato lishenei afar. Mi chamocha ba'al gevurot? U-mi domeh lach? Melech meimit u'm'chayeh, umatzmiach yeshuah.

מִי כָמוֹךָ אַב הָרַחֲמִים, זוֹכֵר
יְצוּרָיו לְחַיִּים בְּרַחֲמִים:

Mi chamocha av harachaman, zocheir yetzurav l'chayyim b'rachamim.

וְנֶאֱמָן אַתָּה לְהַחֲיוֹת מֵתִים.
בָּרוּךְ אַתָּה יְיָ, מְחַיֵּה הַמֵּתִים:

V'ne'eman atah le'ha-chayot meitim. Baruch atah Adonai, mechayeh hameitim.

You sustain the living with kindness, in Your great mercy You bestow eternal life. You support the fallen, heal the sick, and free the captive. You keep Your faith with us beyond life and death. There is none like You, our source of strength, the ruler of life and death, the source of our redemption.

Who is like You, source of mercy, Who mercifully remembers Your creatures for life?

Our faith is with You, the God Who brings eternal life.
Blessed are You, Adonai, Who gives life which transcends death.

Kidushat Hashem: Making the Name Holy

You are holy,
and Your name is holy,
and holy ones praise You
always, *selah*.

אַתָּה קָדוֹשׁ וְשִׁמְךָ קָדוֹשׁ
וּקְדוֹשִׁים בְּכָל יוֹם יְהַלְלוּךָ,
סֶּלָה.

And so
May fear and concern
be instilled in all living beings,
deep concern for all created.
All creation should be in awe,
all of life humbled before You.
May all of creation form
a single bond to do Your will.
We know that You alone rule
that Your strength is justice
and Your awesome being
transcends all which You
have created.

וּבְכֵן
תֵּן פַּחְדְּךָ יְיָ אֱלֹהֵינוּ, עַל כָּל
מַעֲשֶׂיךָ, וְאֵימָתְךָ עַל כָּל מַה
שֶּׁבָּרָאתָ, וְיִירָאוּךָ כָּל
הַמַּעֲשִׂים וְיִשְׁתַּחֲווּ לְפָנֶיךָ כָּל
הַבְּרוּאִים, וְיֵעָשׂוּ כֻלָּם אֲגֻדָּה
אַחַת לַעֲשׂוֹת רְצוֹנְךָ בְּלֵבָב
שָׁלֵם, כְּמוֹ שֶׁיָּדַעְנוּ יְיָ אֱלֹהֵינוּ,
שֶׁהַשָּׁלְטָן לְפָנֶיךָ, עֹז בְּיָדְךָ
וּגְבוּרָה בִּימִינֶךָ, וְשִׁמְךָ נוֹרָא
עַל כָּל מַה שֶּׁבָּרָאתָ.

And so
May honor be granted
to Your people,
Praise to those who feel awe,
hope to those who seek You
and voice sincere yearnings.
May there be joy
throughout the land
and joyfulness for the
inhabitants of Your city.
May the light of joy and justice
shine forth in our lifetime.

וּבְכֵן
תֵּן כָּבוֹד, יְיָ לְעַמֶּךָ, תְּהִלָּה
לִירֵאֶיךָ וְתִקְוָה טוֹבָה
לְדוֹרְשֶׁיךָ, וּפִתְחוֹן פֶּה
לַמְיַחֲלִים לָךְ, שִׂמְחָה לְאַרְצֶךָ
וְשָׂשׂוֹן לְעִירֶךָ, וּצְמִיחַת קֶרֶן
לְדָוִד עַבְדֶּךָ, וַעֲרִיכַת נֵר
לְבֶן־יִשַׁי מְשִׁיחֶךָ, בִּמְהֵרָה
בְיָמֵינוּ.

וּבְכֵן
צַדִּיקִים יִרְאוּ וְיִשְׂמָחוּ, וִישָׁרִים
יַעֲלֹזוּ, וַחֲסִידִים בְּרִנָּה יָגִילוּ,
וְעוֹלָתָה תִּקְפָּץ־פִּיהָ, וְכָל
הָרִשְׁעָה כֻּלָּהּ כְּעָשָׁן תִּכְלֶה, כִּי
תַעֲבִיר מֶמְשֶׁלֶת זָדוֹן מִן
הָאָרֶץ.

And so
When such a day arrives
those who struggled for justice
will be first to rejoice;
the upright will be glad,
the faithful will sing with joy,
injustice will close its mouth,
evil will vanish like smoke,
falsehoods will depart from the
earth.

וְתִמְלֹךְ, אַתָּה יְיָ לְבַדֶּךָ, עַל כָּל
מַעֲשֶׂיךָ, בְּהַר צִיּוֹן מִשְׁכַּן
כְּבוֹדֶךָ, וּבִירוּשָׁלַיִם עִיר
קָדְשֶׁךָ, כַּכָּתוּב בְּדִבְרֵי קָדְשֶׁךָ:
יִמְלֹךְ יְיָ לְעוֹלָם, אֱלֹהַיִךְ צִיּוֹן
לְדֹר וָדֹר: הַלְלוּיָהּ.

Sacred Oneness will govern
all things; Mount Zion
will be among Your resting-
places, as will Your holy city,
the city of Shalom, Jerusalem.
As it is written in these holy
words: "Adonai will reign
forever, Your God, O Zion, for
all generations, halleluyah."

קָדוֹשׁ אַתָּה וְנוֹרָא שְׁמֶךָ,
וְאֵין אֱלוֹהַּ מִבַּלְעָדֶיךָ, כַּכָּתוּב:
וַיִּגְבַּהּ יְיָ צְבָאוֹת בַּמִּשְׁפָּט,
וְהָאֵל הַקָּדוֹשׁ נִקְדַּשׁ בִּצְדָקָה.
בָּרוּךְ אַתָּה, יְיָ, הַמֶּלֶךְ הַקָּדוֹשׁ.

You are holy,
Your name is holy
And there is no God besides
You, as it is written:
"The Eternal, the power of all
creation, is elevated through
justice, God's holiness
sanctified through
acts of justice."
Blessed is the Ineffable One,
the sacred Power.

Kidushat Hayom: Sanctifying This Day

אַתָּה בְחַרְתָּֽנוּ עִם כָּל הָעַמִּים,
אָהַֽבְתָּ אוֹתָֽנוּ וְרָצִֽיתָ בָּֽנוּ,
וְרוֹמַמְתָּֽנוּ מִכָּל הַלְּשׁוֹנוֹת,
וְקִדַּשְׁתָּֽנוּ בְּמִצְוֹתֶֽיךָ, וְקֵרַבְתָּֽנוּ
מַלְכֵּֽנוּ לַעֲבוֹדָתֶֽךָ, וְשִׁמְךָ הַגָּדוֹל
וְהַקָּדוֹשׁ עָלֵֽינוּ קָרָֽאתָ.

You have delighted in us
among the people,
loving us, desiring us, elevating
us and sanctifying us
with mitzvot,
drawing us near to serve You,
that Your great holy Presence
might be known to us.

וַתִּתֶּן לָֽנוּ, יְיָ אֱלֹהֵֽינוּ, בְּאַהֲבָה
אֶת יוֹם
(הַשַּׁבָּת הַזֶּה וְאֶת יוֹם) הַזִּכָּרוֹן
הַזֶּה, (בְּאַהֲבָה) מִקְרָא קֹֽדֶשׁ,
זֵֽכֶר לִיצִיאַת מִצְרָֽיִם.

With love, we have been given
(on Shabbat: this Shabbat and)
this Day of Atonement
for renouncing our wrongs,
for asking for forgiveness,
for cleansing, for
reconciliation.

A day of holy gathering
reminding us of our liberation
from the straits of
enslavement.

On Yom Kippur, as on Shabbat, the light of the Shekhinah shines into our souls and removes the *tum'ah*, the soul-corruption or inner impurity, which is caused when we sin.
(Rabbi Shalom Noach Barzovsky)

When we miss the mark, our souls become clogged-up with plaque. Our misdeeds create a karmic build-up. On Yom Kippur, God's light shines into us and dissolves those places.

Ya'aleh v'yavo: May These Ascend

Our God
and God of our ancestors:
allow memory to ascend,
to come, to reach us.
May our memory
and our ancestors' memory
and the memory of the dream
of a messianic time,
and the memory of the vision
of Jerusalem as a city of peace,
and the memories of all of Your
people of the House of Israel,
be before You.
On this day
may these memories,
these dreams of redemption,
inspire graciousness,
lovingkindness,
and compassion in us,
for life and for peace,
on this Yom Kippur.

אֱלֹהֵינוּ
וֵאלֹהֵי אֲבוֹתֵינוּ וְאִמּוֹתֵינוּ,
יַעֲלֶה וְיָבֹא, וְיַגִּיעַ וְיֵרָאֶה,
וְיֵרָצֶה וְיִשָּׁמַע,
וְיִפָּקֵד וְיִזָּכֵר
זִכְרוֹנֵנוּ וּפִקְדוֹנֵנוּ,
וְזִכְרוֹן אֲבוֹתֵינוּ וְאִמּוֹתֵינוּ,
וְזִכְרוֹן מָשִׁיחַ בֶּן־דָּוִד עַבְדֶּךָ,
וְזִכְרוֹן יְרוּשָׁלַיִם עִיר קָדְשֶׁךָ,
וְזִכְרוֹן כָּל עַמְּךָ
בֵּית יִשְׂרָאֵל לְפָנֶיךָ
לִפְלֵיטָה וּלְטוֹבָה,
לְחֵן וּלְחֶסֶד וּלְרַחֲמִים, לְחַיִּים
וּלְשָׁלוֹם,
בְּיוֹם הַכִּפּוּרִים הַזֶּה.

זָכְרֵנוּ, יְיָ אֱלֹהֵינוּ בּוֹ לְטוֹבָה,
וּפָקְדֵנוּ בוֹ לִבְרָכָה, וְהוֹשִׁיעֵנוּ
בוֹ לְחַיִּים; וּבִדְבַר יְשׁוּעָה
וְרַחֲמִים חוּס וְחָנֵּנוּ, וְרַחֵם
עָלֵינוּ וְהוֹשִׁיעֵנוּ, כִּי אֵלֶיךָ
עֵינֵינוּ, כִּי אֵל מֶלֶךְ חַנּוּן וְרַחוּם
אָתָּה.

Remember us, Adonai our
God, for goodness. Count us in
for blessing. Save us with life.
Shower us with salvation
and with compassion;
be merciful to us; enfold us
in the compassion we knew
before we were born.
For You are our merciful
parent and sovereign.

אֱלֹהֵינוּ וֵאלֹהֵי אֲבוֹתֵינוּ, מְלוֹךְ
עַל כָּל הָעוֹלָם כֻּלּוֹ בִּכְבוֹדֶךָ,
וְהִנָּשֵׂא עַל כָּל הָאָרֶץ בִּיקָרֶךָ,
וְהוֹפַע בַּהֲדַר גְּאוֹן עֻזֶּךָ, עַל כָּל
יוֹשְׁבֵי תֵבֵל אַרְצֶךָ, וְיֵדַע כָּל
פָּעוּל כִּי אַתָּה פְּעַלְתּוֹ, וְיָבִין
כָּל יָצוּר כִּי אַתָּה יְצַרְתּוֹ,
וְיֹאמַר כֹּל אֲשֶׁר נְשָׁמָה בְּאַפּוֹ,
יְיָ אֱלֹהֵי יִשְׂרָאֵל מֶלֶךְ, וּמַלְכוּתוֹ
בַּכֹּל מָשָׁלָה.

Our God
and God of our generations:
shine Your glory
on all creation.
Remind us that You cherish
all who live on this earth,
here and everywhere.
You are our Creator;
You formed us; You breathe
life into us in every moment.
You are King/Queen
of all creation.

אֱלֹהֵינוּ וֵאלֹהֵי אֲבוֹתֵינוּ, (רְצֵה
בִמְנוּחָתֵנוּ) קַדְּשֵׁנוּ בְּמִצְוֹתֶיךָ
וְתֵן חֶלְקֵנוּ בְּתוֹרָתֶךָ, שַׂבְּעֵנוּ
מִטּוּבֶךָ וְשַׂמְּחֵנוּ בִּישׁוּעָתֶךָ
(וְהַנְחִילֵנוּ, יְיָ אֱלֹהֵינוּ, בְּאַהֲבָה
וּבְרָצוֹן שַׁבַּת קָדְשֶׁךָ, וְיָנוּחוּ
בָהּ יִשְׂרָאֵל מְקַדְּשֵׁי שְׁמֶךָ)

Our God
and God of our generations
(accept our rest with mercy)
help us make ourselves holy
with Your mitzvot; give us
a portion of Your Torah's
sweetness; grant us
Your goodness, help us rejoice
in Your salvation
(and on this Shabbat which is
also a holiday, help us be
mindful of both, and to wholly
rest as befits Your people
who yearn to sanctify Your
name).

וְטַהֵר לִבֵּנוּ לְעָבְדְּךָ בֶּאֱמֶת, כִּי אַתָּה אֱלֹהִים אֱמֶת, וּדְבָרְךָ אֱמֶת וְקַיָּם לָעַד. בָּרוּךְ אַתָּה, יְיָ, מֶלֶךְ עַל כָּל הָאָרֶץ, מְקַדֵּשׁ (הַשַּׁבָּת וְ) יִשְׂרָאֵל וְיוֹם הַזִּכָּרוֹן.

Purify our hearts to serve You in truth, for You are God of truth and Your truth endures forever.
Blessed are You, Adonai, ruler over all the earth, Who sanctifies (Shabbat and) Israel and this Day of Remembrance.

Avodah: Worship

רְצֵה, יְיָ אֱלֹהֵינוּ, בְּעַמְּךָ יִשְׂרָאֵל וּבִתְפִלָּתָם, בְּאַהֲבָה תְקַבֵּל וּתְהִי לְרָצוֹן תָּמִיד עֲבוֹדַת יִשְׂרָאֵל עַמֶּךָ.

May it be Your will, Adonai our God, that You accept our rest and take pleasure in our prayers. Accept the service of our hearts and our lips which we mean to offer in love. May the offerings of our hearts always bring You joy in Your people.

וְתֶחֱזֶינָה עֵינֵינוּ בְּשׁוּבְךָ לְצִיּוֹן בְּרַחֲמִים. בָּרוּךְ אַתָּה יְיָ, הַמַּחֲזִיר שְׁכִינָתוֹ לְצִיּוֹן.

May Your presence return to Zion speedily and with compassion. Blessed are You, Adonai, Whose presence returns to Zion and fills all creation.

Hoda'ah: Giving Thanks

We are grateful before You,
that You are our God and God
of our generations, for ever.
You are the rock of our lives,
the shield of our salvation;
You, only You, from generation
to generation we sing praises.
For our lives which are in Your
keeping; for our souls of which
You take daily account; for all
of the miracles which You
perform for us, and all of the
wonders and goodnesses which
You bring forth in every era
and in every day, evening and
morning and afternoon; for the
goodness of Your compassion;
for all of these things we could
never thank You enough.

מוֹדִים אֲנַֽחְנוּ לָךְ, שָׁאַתָּה
הוּא, יְיָ אֱלֹהֵֽינוּ וֵאלֹהֵי
אֲבוֹתֵֽינוּ, לְעוֹלָם וָעֶד, צוּר
חַיֵּֽינוּ, מָגֵן יִשְׁעֵֽנוּ, אַתָּה הוּא
לְדוֹר וָדוֹר נוֹדֶה לְּךָ וּנְסַפֵּר
תְּהִלָּתֶֽךָ. עַל חַיֵּֽינוּ הַמְּסוּרִים
בְּיָדֶֽךָ, וְעַל נִשְׁמוֹתֵֽינוּ הַפְּקוּדוֹת
לָךְ, וְעַל נִסֶּֽיךָ שֶׁבְּכָל יוֹם עִמָּֽנוּ,
וְעַל נִפְלְאוֹתֶֽיךָ וְטוֹבוֹתֶֽיךָ
שֶׁבְּכָל עֵת, עֶֽרֶב וָבֹֽקֶר
וְצָהֳרָֽיִם, הַטּוֹב כִּי לֹא כָלוּ
רַחֲמֶֽיךָ, וְהַמְרַחֵם כִּי לֹא תַֽמּוּ
חֲסָדֶֽיךָ מֵעוֹלָם קִוִּֽינוּ לָךְ.

For all of these we bless and
elevate Your name, our
Sovereign and Source, forever
and ever.

וְעַל כֻּלָּם יִתְבָּרַךְ וְיִתְרוֹמַם
שִׁמְךָ מַלְכֵּֽנוּ תָּמִיד לְעוֹלָם וָעֶד.

And we thank You for
inscribing us, the children of
Your covenant, into the book of
life.

וּכְתוֹב לְחַיִּים טוֹבִים כָּל בְּנֵי
בְרִיתֶֽךָ.

All that lives praises Your
name in truth, our God and our
help. Blessed are You, Adonai,
for Your goodness and for the
many wonders which merit our
thanks.

וְכֹל הַחַיִּים יוֹדֽוּךָ סֶּֽלָה, וִיהַלְלוּ
אֶת שִׁמְךָ בֶּאֱמֶת, הָאֵל
יְשׁוּעָתֵֽנוּ וְעֶזְרָתֵֽנוּ סֶֽלָה. בָּרוּךְ
אַתָּה יְיָ, הַטּוֹב שִׁמְךָ וּלְךָ נָאֶה
לְהוֹדוֹת.

Birkat Shalom: Peace

שָׁלוֹם רָב עַל יִשְׂרָאֵל עַמְּךָ
תָּשִׂים לְעוֹלָם, כִּי אַתָּה הוּא
מֶלֶךְ אָדוֹן לְכָל הַשָּׁלוֹם. וְטוֹב
בְּעֵינֶיךָ לְבָרֵךְ אֶת עַמְּךָ
יִשְׂרָאֵל, בְּכָל עֵת וּבְכָל שָׁעָה
בִּשְׁלוֹמֶךָ.

Shalom rav al Yisrael amcha
tasim le'olam, ki atah hu
melech adon l'chol hashalom.
V'tov b'einecha levarech et
amcha Yisrael, b'chol eit
u'vchol sha'ah bishlomecha.

בְּסֵפֶר חַיִּים, בְּרָכָה וְשָׁלוֹם
וּפַרְנָסָה טוֹבָה, נִזָּכֵר וְנִכָּתֵב
לְפָנֶיךָ, אֲנַחְנוּ וְכָל עַמְּךָ בֵּית
יִשְׂרָאֵל, לְחַיִּים טוֹבִים
וּלְשָׁלוֹם.

B'sefer chayyim, bracha
v'shalom, ufarnasah tovah,
n'zacher v'nikatev l'fanecha,
anachnu v'chol amcha beit
Yisrael, l'chayyim tovim
u'l'shalom.

בָּרוּךְ אַתָּה יְיָ, עוֹשֵׂה הַשָּׁלוֹם.

Baruch atah, Adonai, oseh ha-
shalom.

May there be abundant peace for Israel Your people, always; for You are the sovereign of peace. Let it be good in Your eyes to bless Your people Israel, in every time and in every hour, with Your peace.

In the book of life, blessing, peace, and making a good living may we be remembered and written before You: us, and all of Your people in our many communities, for a good life and for peace.

Blessed are You, Adonai, maker of peace.

The Soul of a Person is the Candle of God

Text: Mishlei / Proverbs 20:27

Meditations After Prayer

אֱלֹהַי, נְצוֹר לְשׁוֹנִי מֵרָע.
וּשְׂפָתַי מִדַּבֵּר מִרְמָה:
וְלִמְקַלְלַי נַפְשִׁי תִדּוֹם, וְנַפְשִׁי
כֶּעָפָר לַכֹּל תִּהְיֶה. פְּתַח לִבִּי
בְּתוֹרָתֶךָ, וּבְמִצְוֹתֶיךָ תִּרְדּוֹף
נַפְשִׁי.

Elohai n'tzor l'shoni mera
usfatai m'daber mirmah
v'limkallelai nafshi tidom
v'nafshi ke'afar l'kol tihiyeh.
Petach libi ba-Toratecha,
uv'mitzvotecha tirdof nafshi.

God, keep my tongue from evil
and my lips from speaking deceit.
Before those who slander me, I will hold my tongue;
I will practice humility.
Open my heart to Your Torah,
and connect my heart to Your mitzvot.

יִהְיוּ לְרָצוֹן אִמְרֵי פִי וְהֶגְיוֹן לִבִּי
לְפָנֶיךָ, יְיָ צוּרִי וְגוֹאֲלִי.

Yihiyu l'ratzon imrei fi
v'hegyon libi l'fanecha
Adonai tzuri v'goali.

עֹשֶׂה שָׁלוֹם בִּמְרוֹמָיו הוּא
יַעֲשֶׂה שָׁלוֹם עָלֵינוּ וְעַל כָּל
יִשְׂרָאֵל, וְעַל כָּל יוֹשְׁבֵי תֵבֵל,
וְאִמְרוּ אָמֵן:

Oseh shalom bimromav,
hu ya'aseh shalom, aleinu
v'al kol yisrael, v'al kol yoshvei
tevel, v'imru Amen.

May the words of my mouth
and the meditations of my heart
be acceptable to You, O God,
my rock and my redeemer.

May the one Who makes peace in the heavens
make peace for us and for all Israel
and for all who dwell on earth,
and let us say: Amen.

Three Kinds of Forgiveness

In the *Al Chet* prayer, we plead with God:

סְלַח לָנוּ, מְחַל לָנוּ, כַּפֶּר-לָנוּ!
S'lach lanu, m'chal lanu, kaper–lanu!
Forgive us, pardon us, grant us atonement!

Is this a list of synonyms?

Reb Zalman z"l (of blessed memory) offers a computer metaphor:

The first one means, "delete the files."

The second one means, "empty the trash on the desktop of our hearts."

And the third one means, "wipe the disk clean to make room for something new."

Selichot: Prayers for Forgiveness

Ya'aleh Tachanuneinu—May Prayers Rise

Ya'aleh tachanuneinu me'erev
v'yavo shavateinu miboker,
v'y'raeh rinoneinu ad arev.

יַעֲלֶה · תַּחֲנוּנֵנוּ מֵעֶרֶב,
וְיָבֹא ˙ שַׁוְעָתֵנוּ מִבֹּקֶר,
וְיֵרָאֶה . רִנּוּנֵנוּ עַד עָרֶב.

May our prayer arise this evening,
May our cry come before You by tomorrow morning,
May our song be heard by next nightfall.

Ya'aleh koleinu me'erev
v'yavo tz'dakteinu miboker,
v'y'raeh p'dyoneinu ad arev.

יַעֲלֶה קוֹלֵנוּ מֵעֶרֶב,
וְיָבֹא צְדָקָתֵנוּ מִבֹּקֶר,
וְיֵרָאֶה · פִּדְיוֹנֵנוּ עַד עָרֶב.

May our voices arise this evening,
May our righteousness be found by tomorrow morning,
May our redemption be fulfilled by next nightfall.

Ya'aleh inoneinu me'erev
v'yavo s'lichateinu miboker,
v'y'raeh na'aketeinu ad arev.

יַעֲלֶה עִנּוּיֵנוּ מֵעֶרֶב,
וְיָבֹא סְלִיחָתֵנוּ מִבֹּקֶר,
וְיֵרָאֶה נַאֲקָתֵנוּ עַד עָרֶב.

May our fast arise this evening,
May our plea for pardon come by tomorrow morning,
May our sighs be answered by next nightfall.

Ya'aleh m'nosenu me'erev
v'yavo l'maanenu miboker,
v'y'raeh p'dyoneinu ad arev.

יַעֲלֶה מְנוּסֵנוּ מֵעֶרֶב,
וְיָבֹא לְמַעֲנוֹ מִבֹּקֶר,
וְיֵרָאֶה · כִּפּוּרֵנוּ עַד עָרֶב.

May our search for refuge arise this evening,
May we submit to You by tomorrow morning,
May our atonement be granted by next nightfall.

יַעֲלֶה יִשְׁעֵנוּ מֵעֶרֶב,
וְיָבֹא טָהֳרֵנוּ מִבֹּקֶר,
וְיֵרָאֶה חִנּוּנֵנוּ עַד עָרֶב.

Ya'aleh y'sha'enu me'erev
v'yavo taharenu miboker,
v'y'raeh chinonenu ad arev.

May our journey to salvation arise this evening,
May our purest selves come by tomorrow morning,
May our grace arise within us by next nightfall.

יַעֲלֶה זִכְרוֹנֵנוּ מֵעֶרֶב,
וְיָבֹא וִעוּדֵנוּ מִבֹּקֶר,
וְיֵרָאֶה הֲדָרָתֵנוּ עַד עָרֶב.

Ya'aleh zichroneinu me'erev
v'yavo vivedenu miboker,
v'y'raeh hadarateinu ad arev.

May our memory arise this evening,
May our community unite by tomorrow morning,
May we see Your splendor by next nightfall.

יַעֲלֶה דְּפָקֵנוּ מֵעֶרֶב,
וְיָבֹא גִּילֵנוּ מִבֹּקֶר,
וְיֵרָאֶה בָּקָשָׁתֵנוּ עַד עָרֶב.

Ya'aleh d'fakenu me'erev
v'yavo gilenu miboker,
v'y'raeh bakishateinu ad arev.

May our knocking upon Your gates arise this evening, May our joyfulness come by tomorrow morning,
May our search for You be crowned by next nightfall.

יַעֲלֶה אֶנְקָתֵנוּ מֵעֶרֶב,
וְיָבֹא אֵלֶיךָ מִבֹּקֶר,
וְיֵרָאֶה אֵלֵינוּ עַד עָרֶב.

Ya'aleh anaktenu me'erev
v'yavo eilecha miboker,
v'y'raeh eileinu ad arev.

May our weeping arise this evening,
May it reach You by tomorrow morning.
May You answer us by next nightfall.

Adon HaSelichot: Master of Repentance

Master of forgiveness, examiner of hearts, Revealer of depths, declarer of righteousness, we have sinned before You. Have mercy on us!

Adon haselichot,
Bochen levavot,
Golah amukot,
Doveir tzedakot,
Chatanu lefanecha.
Rachem aleinu!

אֲדוֹן הַסְלִיחוֹת,
בּוֹחֵן לְבָבוֹת,
גֹּלֶה עֲמֻקוֹת,
דּוֹבֵר צְדָקוֹת.
חָטָאנוּ לְפָנֶךָ. רַחֵם עָלֵינוּ!

The One who dwells in wonders, Ancient One of mercy, Who remembers our ancestors' covenant and examines inward parts, we have sinned before You. Have mercy on us!

Hadur baniflaot,
Vatik benachamot,
Zocheir berit avot,
Chokeir kelayot,
Chatanu lefanecha.
Rachem aleinu!

הָדוּר בְּנִפְלָאוֹת,
וָתִיק בְּנֶחָמוֹת,
זוֹכֵר בְּרִית אָבוֹת,
חוֹקֵר כְּלָיוֹת.
חָטָאנוּ לְפָנֶךָ. רַחֵם עָלֵינוּ!

The One who is good and benefits all life, who knows all that is hidden, Subduer of transgressions, wrapped in righteousness, we have sinned before You. Have mercy on us!

Tov umeitiv labriot,
Yodei'a kol nistarot,
Koveish avonot,
Loveish tzedakot,
Chatanu lefanecha.
Rachem aleinu!

טוֹב וּמֵטִיב לַבְּרִיּוֹת,
יוֹדֵעַ כָּל נִסְתָּרוֹת,
כּוֹבֵשׁ עֲווֹנוֹת,
לוֹבֵשׁ צְדָקוֹת.
חָטָאנוּ לְפָנֶךָ. רַחֵם עָלֵינוּ!

The Thirteen Attributes

□ יְיָ, יְיָ, אֵל רַחוּם וְחַנּוּן, אֶֽרֶךְ אַפַּֽיִם, וְרַב חֶֽסֶד וֶאֱמֶת: נֹצֵר חֶֽסֶד לָאֲלָפִים, נֹשֵׂא עָוֹן וָפֶֽשַׁע וְחַטָּאָה, וְנַקֵּה:

□ Adonai, Adonai, El rachum vechanun, erech apayim, verav chesed ve'emet, notseir chesed la'alafim, nosei avon, vafesha, vechata'ah, venakeih.

Adonai, Adonai, God of mercy and grace, patient, loving and faithful. Who extends love to the thousandth generation, forgiving transgression, rebellion and sin, and granting pardon.

Singable English:

□ Yod Hay, Vav Hay, Compassion and Tenderness,
Patience, Forebearance, Kindness, Awareness.
Bearing love from age to age,
Lifting guilt and mistakes and making us free.

Sh'ma Koleinu: Hear Our Voice

שְׁמַע קוֹלֵֽנוּ, יְיָ אֱלֹהֵֽינוּ, חוּס וְרַחֵם עָלֵֽינוּ, וְקַבֵּל בְּרַחֲמִים וּבְרָצוֹן אֶת תְּפִלָּתֵֽנוּ.
הֲשִׁיבֵֽנוּ יְיָ אֵלֶֽיךָ וְנָשֽׁוּבָה, חַדֵּשׁ יָמֵֽינוּ כְּקֶֽדֶם.

Sh'ma koleinu, Adonai eloheinu, chus v'rachem aleinu, v'kabel b'rachamim u'v'ratzon et t'filateinu.
Hashiveinu Adonai elecha v'nashuva, chadesh yameinu k'kedem.

Hear our voice, Adonai our God. Be merciful with us and accept our prayer. Return us, Adonai, to You and we will be returned. Renew our days, as in days of old.

Find the full Sh'ma Koleinu on p. 327.

Ki Anu Amecha: We Are Your People

Ki anu amecha ve'atah Eloheinu. Anu vanecha ve'atah avinu. Anu avdecha, ve'atah adoneinu. Anu kehalecha, ve'atah chelkeinu. Anu nachalatecha, ve'atah goraleinu. Anu tzonecha, ve'atah ro'einu. Anu charmecha, ve'atah notreinu. Anu fe'ulatecha, ve'atah yotzreinu. Anu rayatecha, ve'atah dodeinu. Anu segulatecha, ve'atah keroveinu. Anu amecha, ve'atah malkeinu. Anu ma'amirecha, ve'ata ma'amireinu.

כִּי אָנוּ עַמֶּךָ, וְאַתָּה אֱלֹהֵינוּ.
אָנוּ בָנֶיךָ וְאַתָּה אָבִינוּ.
אָנוּ עֲבָדֶיךָ, וְאַתָּה אֲדוֹנֵינוּ.
אָנוּ קְהָלֶךָ, וְאַתָּה חֶלְקֵנוּ.
אָנוּ נַחֲלָתֶךָ, וְאַתָּה גוֹרָלֵנוּ.
אָנוּ צֹאנֶךָ, וְאַתָּה רוֹעֵנוּ.
אָנוּ כַרְמֶךָ, וְאַתָּה נוֹטְרֵנוּ.
אָנוּ פְעֻלָּתֶךָ וְאַתָּה יוֹצְרֵנוּ.
אָנוּ רַעְיָתֶךָ, וְאַתָּה דוֹדֵנוּ.
אָנוּ סְגֻלָּתֶךָ, וְאַתָּה קְרוֹבֵנוּ.
אָנוּ עַמֶּךָ, וְאַתָּה מַלְכֵּנוּ.
אָנוּ מַאֲמִירֶיךָ, וְאַתָּה מַאֲמִירֵנוּ.

We are Your people,
and You our holy source.
We are Your children, and You our parent.
We are Your helpers,
and You our guiding spirit.
We are Your body,
and You our designer.
We are Your images,
and You our true essence.
We are Your flock,
and You our shepherd.

We are Your plantings, and
You our gardener.
We are Your creation,
and You our origin.
We are Your companions,
and You our beloved.
We are Your treasure,
and You delight in us.
We are Your people,
and You are our sovereign.
We solely favor You,
and You recognize us.

Vidui: Confessional Prayers

Many people have the custom of beating the breast during the recitation of this alphabetical list of places where we've missed the mark. Another way to understand that act is: we're knocking on our hearts, imploring them to open.

Our God and God of our ancestors, accept our prayer and do not hide from us. We are not so hard-hearted and stiff-necked to say before You, Adonai, that we are righteous and pure. Rather, we confess that we have sinned.

אֱלֹהֵינוּ וֵאלֹהֵי אֲבוֹתֵינוּ, תָּבֹא
לְפָנֶיךָ תְּפִלָּתֵנוּ, וְאַל תִּתְעַלַּם
מִתְּחִנָּתֵנוּ, שֶׁאֵין אָנוּ עַזֵּי פָנִים
וּקְשֵׁי עֹרֶף, לוֹמַר לְפָנֶיךָ יְיָ
אֱלֹהֵינוּ וֵאלֹהֵי אֲבוֹתֵינוּ,
צַדִּיקִים אֲנַחְנוּ וְלֹא חָטָאנוּ,
אֲבָל אֲנַחְנוּ וַאֲבוֹתֵינוּ חָטָאנוּ.

□ Ashamnu, bagadnu, gazal nu, dibarnu dofi. He'evinu, ve hirshanu, zadnu, chamasnu, tafalnu shaker. Ya'atsnu ra, kizavnu, latsnu, maradnu, ni'atsnu, sararnu, avinu, pashanu, tzararnu, kishinu oref. Rashanu, shichatnu, ti'avnu, ta'inu, titanu.

□ אָשַׁמְנוּ, בָּגַדְנוּ, גָּזַלְנוּ,
דִּבַּרְנוּ דֹפִי. הֶעֱוִינוּ,
וְהִרְשַׁעְנוּ, זַדְנוּ, חָמַסְנוּ,
טָפַלְנוּ שֶׁקֶר. יָעַצְנוּ רָע,
כִּזַּבְנוּ, לַצְנוּ, מָרַדְנוּ, נִאַצְנוּ,
סָרַרְנוּ, עָוִינוּ, פָּשַׁעְנוּ, צָרַרְנוּ,
קִשִּׁינוּ עֹרֶף. רָשַׁעְנוּ, שִׁחַתְנוּ,
תִּעַבְנוּ, תָּעִינוּ, תִּעְתָּעְנוּ.

We have abused, betrayed, conspired, deceived, endangered, flattered, gossiped, hated, insulted, jeered, kept grudges, lied, mocked, neglected, oppressed, perverted, quarreled, rebelled, stolen, threatened, undermined, vilified, wasted, and yielded to temptation.

Ashamnu (Singable English)

Who are we? We're light and truth and infinite wisdom, eternal goodness. Yet we've **A**bused, we've **B**etrayed, we've been **C**ruel, we've **D**estroyed. We've **E**mbittered, we have **F**alsified, we have **G**ossiped, we have **H**ated. We've **I**nsulted, we have **J**eered, we have **K**illed, we have **L**ied.

Sweep it out! Throw it out! Wipe it out! Clean it all out!

At our core, we're light and truth and infinite wisdom, eternal goodness. Yet we have **M**ocked, we've **N**eglected, we've **O**ppressed, we have **P**erverted. We have **Q**uarreled, we've been **R**acist, we have **S**tolen, we've Transgressed. We've been **U**nkind, we've been **V**iolent, we've been **W**icked, we've been **X**enophobic.

Sweep it out! Throw it out! Wipe it out! Clean it all out!

Ki Hineh Kachomer: We are as clay

We are as clay in potter's hand,
She does contract, she does expand.
So we are Yours to shape at will,
We yield to You, our passions still.

Like masons shaping rough hewn stone,
We are Your stuff in flesh and bone.
You deal with us in death, in life,
We yield to You—please heal our strife!

Ken anachnu b'yadcha chesed notzer	כֵּן אֲנַחְנוּ בְּיָדְךָ חֶסֶד נוֹצֵר
Labrit habeit v'al tefen layetzer.	לַבְּרִית הַבֵּט וְאַל תֵּפֶן לַיֵּצֶר.

(We are in Your hands, God of love;
Remember the covenant, and don't destroy Your creation!)

The smith can shape a blade of steel,
Shape the edge and bend the heel,
So through life's fires You temper us,
We yield to You—surrender us!

As jewelry is wrought from gold,
And silver, too, is poured in mold,
So You our souls created, built,
We yield to You—erase our guilt!

Ken anachnu b'yadcha m'mavet um'motet	כֵּן אֲנַחְנוּ בְּיָדְךָ מְחַיֶּה וּמְמוֹתֵת
Labrit habeit v'al tefen layetzer.	לַבְּרִית הַבֵּט וְאַל תֵּפֶן לַיֵּצֶר.

(We are in Your hands, God of life;
Remember the covenant, and don't destroy Your creation!)

(Transl. R' Zalman Schachter-Shalomi z"l)

Al Chet: for the sins we have sinned

For the sin we have sinned against You under duress and by choice, and for the sin we have sinned against You by hardness of heart.

עַל חֵטְא שֶׁחָטָאנוּ לְפָנֶיךָ
בְּאֹנֶס וּבְרָצוֹן,
וְעַל חֵטְא שֶׁחָטָאנוּ לְפָנֶיךָ
בְּאִמּוּץ הַלֵּב.

For the sin we have sinned against You without knowing, and for the sin we have sinned against You in our speech.

עַל חֵטְא שֶׁחָטָאנוּ לְפָנֶיךָ
בִּבְלִי דָעַת,
וְעַל חֵטְא שֶׁחָטָאנוּ לְפָנֶיךָ
בְּבִטּוּי שְׂפָתָיִם.

For the sin we have sinned against You by public immorality, and for the sin we have sinned against You openly and privately.

עַל חֵטְא שֶׁחָטָאנוּ לְפָנֶיךָ
בְּגִלּוּי עֲרָיוֹת,
וְעַל חֵטְא שֶׁחָטָאנוּ לְפָנֶיךָ
בַּגָּלוּי וּבַסָּתֶר.

For the sin we have sinned against You with knowledge and with deceit, and for the sin we have sinned against You by speaking harshly.

עַל חֵטְא שֶׁחָטָאנוּ לְפָנֶיךָ
בְּדַעַת וּבְמִרְמָה,
וְעַל חֵטְא שֶׁחָטָאנוּ לְפָנֶיךָ
בְּדִבּוּר פֶּה.

For the sin we have sinned against You by wronging a friend, and the sin we have sinned against You in our deepest thoughts.

עַל חֵטְא שֶׁחָטָאנוּ לְפָנֶיךָ
בְּהוֹנָאַת רֵעַ,
וְעַל חֵטְא שֶׁחָטָאנוּ לְפָנֶיךָ
בְּהַרְהוֹר הַלֵּב.

For the sin we have sinned against You through immodesty, and the sin we have sinned against You through insincerity.

עַל חֵטְא שֶׁחָטָאנוּ לְפָנֶיךָ
בִּוְעִידַת זְנוּת, וְעַל חֵטְא
שֶׁחָטָאנוּ לְפָנֶיךָ בְּוִדּוּי פֶּה.

עַל חֵטְא שֶׁחָטָאנוּ לְפָנֶיךָ
בְּזִלְזוּל הוֹרִים וּמוֹרִים,
וְעַל חֵטְא שֶׁחָטָאנוּ לְפָנֶיךָ
בְּזָדוֹן וּבִשְׁגָגָה.

For the sin we have sinned against You by contempt for teachers and parents, and the sin we have sinned against You willfully or unintentionally.

עַל חֵטְא שֶׁחָטָאנוּ לְפָנֶיךָ
בְּחֹזֶק יָד,
וְעַל חֵטְא שֶׁחָטָאנוּ לְפָנֶיךָ
בְּחִלּוּל הַשֵּׁם.

For the sin we have sinned against You in the abuse of power and for the sin we have sinned against You in failing to live up to Your name.

עַל חֵטְא שֶׁחָטָאנוּ לְפָנֶיךָ
בְּטֻמְאַת שְׂפָתָיִם,
וְעַל חֵטְא שֶׁחָטָאנוּ לְפָנֶיךָ
בְּטִפְשׁוּת פֶּה.

For the sin we have sinned against You with defiling speech, and for the sin we have sinned against You with foolish talk.

עַל חֵטְא שֶׁחָטָאנוּ לְפָנֶיךָ
בְּיֵצֶר הָרָע,
וְעַל חֵטְא שֶׁחָטָאנוּ לְפָנֶיךָ
בְּיוֹדְעִים וּבְלֹא יוֹדְעִים.

For the sin we have sinned against You by giving in to evil impulses, and the sin we have sinned against You by harming both strangers and friends.

□ וְעַל כֻּלָּם, אֱלוֹהַּ סְלִיחוֹת,סְלַח לָנוּ, מְחַל לָנוּ, כַּפֶּר-לָנוּ.

□ Ve'al kulam, Elo'ah selichot,
selach lanu, mechal lanu, kaper lanu.

For all of these—God of forgiveness— forgive us, pardon us, grant us atonement.

For the sin we have sinned against You with lies and broken promises, and for the sin we have sinned against You through bribery.

עַל חֵטְא שֶׁחָטָאנוּ לְפָנֶיךָ
בְּכַחַשׁ וּבְכָזָב,
וְעַל חֵטְא שֶׁחָטָאנוּ לְפָנֶיךָ
בְּכַפַּת שֹׁחַד.

For the sin we have sinned against You with scorn, and for the sin we have sinned against You with slander.

עַל חֵטְא שֶׁחָטָאנוּ לְפָנֶיךָ
בְּלָצוֹן, וְעַל חֵטְא שֶׁחָטָאנוּ
לְפָנֶיךָ בְּלָשׁוֹן הָרָע.

For the sin we have sinned against You in business, and for the sin we have sinned against You with food and drink.

עַל חֵטְא שֶׁחָטָאנוּ לְפָנֶיךָ
בְּמַשָּׂא וּבְמַתָּן, וְעַל חֵטְא
שֶׁחָטָאנוּ לְפָנֶיךָ בְּמַאֲכָל
וּבְמִשְׁתֶּה.

For the sin we have sinned against You through greed, and for the sin we have sinned against You through arrogance.

עַל חֵטְא שֶׁחָטָאנוּ לְפָנֶיךָ
בְּנֶשֶׁךְ וּבְמַרְבִּית, וְעַל חֵטְא
שֶׁחָטָאנוּ לְפָנֶיךָ בִּנְטִיַּת גָּרוֹן.

For the sin we have sinned against You by conspiring, and for the sin we have sinned against You by spying.

עַל חֵטְא שֶׁחָטָאנוּ לְפָנֶיךָ
בְּשִׂיחַ שִׂפְתוֹתֵינוּ,
וְעַל חֵטְא שֶׁחָטָאנוּ לְפָנֶיךָ
בְּשִׂקּוּר עָיִן.

For the sin we have sinned against You by looking down on others and the sin we have sinned against You by ignoring others.

עַל חֵטְא שֶׁחָטָאנוּ לְפָנֶיךָ
בְּעֵינַיִם רָמוֹת,
וְעַל חֵטְא שֶׁחָטָאנוּ לְפָנֶיךָ
בְּעַזּוּת מֵצַח.

□ וְעַל כֻּלָּם, אֱלוֹהַ סְלִיחוֹת, סְלַח לָנוּ, מְחַל לָנוּ, כַּפֶּר-לָנוּ.

□ Ve'al kulam, Elo'ah selichot,
selach lanu, mechal lanu, kaper lanu.

For all of these—God of forgiveness— forgive us, pardon us, grant us atonement.

עַל חֵטְא שֶׁחָטָאנוּ לְפָנֶיךָ
· בִּפְרִיקַת עֹל, וְעַל חֵטְא
· שֶׁחָטָאנוּ לְפָנֶיךָ · בִּפְלִילוּת.

For the sin we have sinned against You by defying You, and for the sin we have sinned against You by judging others.

עַל חֵטְא שֶׁחָטָאנוּ לְפָנֶיךָ
· בִּצְדִיַּת רֵעַ, וְעַל חֵטְא
· שֶׁחָטָאנוּ לְפָנֶיךָ · בְּצָרוּת עָיִן.

For the sin we have sinned against You by forcing our will on others, and the sin we have sinned against You by giving in to our desires.

עַל חֵטְא שֶׁחָטָאנוּ לְפָנֶיךָ
· בְּקַלּוּת רֹאשׁ, וְעַל חֵטְא
· שֶׁחָטָאנוּ לְפָנֶיךָ · בְּקַשְׁיוּת עֹרֶף.

For the sin we have sinned against You through our thoughtlessness, and the sin we have sinned against You through our stubbornness.

עַל חֵטְא שֶׁחָטָאנוּ לְפָנֶיךָ
· בְּרִיצַת רַגְלַיִם לְהָרַע, וְעַל
חֵטְא שֶׁחָטָאנוּ לְפָנֶיךָ
· בִּרְכִילוּת.

For the sin we have sinned against You by rushing to do evil and the sin we have sinned against You by gossiping.

For the sin we have sinned against You with insincere promises, and for the sin we have sinned against You with baseless hatred.

עַל חֵטְא שֶׁחָטָאנוּ לְפָנֶיךָ · בִּשְׁבוּעַת שָׁוְא, וְעַל חֵטְא שֶׁחָטָאנוּ לְפָנֶיךָ · בְּשִׂנְאַת חִנָּם.

For the sin we have sinned against You by failing to lend a hand, and for the sin we have sinned against You by failing to give our hearts.

עַל חֵטְא שֶׁחָטָאנוּ לְפָנֶיךָ · בִּתְשׂוּמֶת יָד, וְעַל חֵטְא שֶׁחָטָאנוּ לְפָנֶיךָ · בְּתִמְהוֹן לֵבָב.

□ וְעַל כֻּלָּם, אֱלוֹהַּ סְלִיחוֹת, סְלַח לָנוּ, מְחַל לָנוּ, כַּפֶּר-לָנוּ

□ Ve'al kulam, Elo'ah selichot,
selach lanu, mechal lanu, kaper lanu.

For all of these—God of forgiveness— forgive us, pardon us, grant us atonement.

On Yom Kippur, we download a year's worth of blessing for the entire world. The blessings come down tightly-condensed, a spiritual package which we can "unstuff" once the download work is through.

(Rabbi Zalman Schachter-Shalomi z"l / of blessed memory)

Rachamana / Merciful One!

Rachamana d'anei l'ani-yei aneina!
Rachamana d'ani litbirei liba, aneina, aneina!

רַחֲמָנָא דְעָנִי לַעֲנִיֵּי עֲנֵינָא!
רַחֲמָנָא דְעָנִי לִתְבִירֵי לִבָּא
עֲנֵינָא, עֲנֵינָא!

O Merciful One who answers those in need, answer us!
O Merciful One who answers the broken-hearted, answer us!

Avinu Malkeinu / Imeinu Malkateinu

Optionally: begin with this interpretive reading.

Our Father, our King, help us make this year a new beginning.
Our Mother, our Queen, help us to grow when life is hard.

Our Source and our Destiny, teach us to accept what we must.
Our Guide and our Truth, teach us to change what we must.

Our Father, our King, teach us how to face disease and death.
Our Mother, our Queen, teach us how to enjoy the gifts of life.

Our Source and our Destiny, teach us how to make peace.
Our Guide and our Truth, teach us how to help our people.

Our Father, our King, teach us how to help all humanity.
Our Mother, our Queen, let us find pardon for our wrongdoings.

Our Source and our Destiny, let us return to You, completely.
Our Guide and our Truth, teach us to help those who are ill.

Our Father, our King, let us write our names in the Book of Life.
Our Mother, our Queen, help us to find meaningful work.

Our Source and our Destiny, help us to find inner freedom.
Our Guide and our Truth, help us to learn how to love.

Our Father, our King, receive our prayers.
Our Mother, our Queen, teach us how to be good partners.

Our Source and our Destiny, teach us how to be good parents.
Our Guide and our Truth, teach us how to be good children.

Our Father, our King, teach us how to be good friends.
Our Mother, our Queen, teach us how to be good Jews.

Our Source and our Destiny, teach us how to be good people.
Our Guide and our Truth, teach us to be one with You.

Avinu Malkeinu, grant us justice and bring us salvation,
Grant us justice and loving kindness and bring us salvation!

Singable refrain

Our center, Whole Being that we are
Please help us to open our hearts
Our deep inner self, oh now open our hearts
That we may grace this world with our deeds.

Let us bring forth all that we are
Through lives of justice and love
Let us become more loving and just
To set free the God that we are.

This is abridged to fit the Max Janowski melody.
If you prefer to daven the full text, find it on p. 336.

אָבִינוּ מַלְכֵּנוּ, שְׁמַע קוֹלֵנוּ.
אָבִינוּ מַלְכֵּנוּ, חָטָאנוּ לְפָנֶיךָ.
אָבִינוּ מַלְכֵּנוּ, חֲמוֹל עָלֵינוּ
וְעַל עוֹלָלֵינוּ וְטַפֵּנוּ.

Avinu malkeinu, sh'ma koleinu.
Avinu malkeinu,
chatanu l'fanecha.
Avinu malkeinu, chamol aleinu
v'al olaleinu v'tapeinu.

אָבִינוּ מַלְכֵּנוּ, כַּלֵּה דֶּבֶר
וְחֶרֶב וְרָעָב מֵעָלֵינוּ.
אָבִינוּ מַלְכֵּנוּ, כַּלֵּה כָּל–צַר
וּמַשְׂטִין מֵעָלֵינוּ.

Avinu malkeinu, chaleh dever
v'cherev v'ra'av me'aleinu.
Avinu malkeinu, chaleh
kol-tzar u-masteen me'aleinu.

אָבִינוּ מַלְכֵּנוּ, אָבִינוּ מַלְכֵּנוּ
כָּתְבֵנוּ בְּסֵפֶר חַיִּים טוֹבִים.
אָבִינוּ מַלְכֵּנוּ, חַדֵּשׁ עָלֵינוּ,
חַדֵּשׁ עָלֵינוּ שָׁנָה טוֹבָה.

Avinu malkeinu!
Cotveinu b'sefer
chayyim tovim.
Avinu malkeinu,
chadesh aleinu shanah tovah.

Avinu malkeinu, hear our prayer.
Avinu malkeinu, we have sinned before You.
Avinu malkeinu, have mercy on us and on our children.
Avinu Malkeinu, rid us of sickness, sword, hunger, destruction.
Avinu Malkeinu, rid us of persecution. *Avinu Malkeinu,*
inscribe us in the book of a good life.
Avinu Malkeinu, renew us; renew us for a good year.

Avinu Malkeinu continues on the next page.

□ Avinu malkeinu, chanenu va'anenu, ki ein banu ma'asim, aseh imanu tzedakah vachesed v'hoshienu.	□אָבִינוּ מַלְכֵּנוּ, חָנֵּנוּ וַעֲנֵנוּ, כִּי אֵין בָּנוּ מַעֲשִׂים, עֲשֵׂה עִמָּנוּ צְדָקָה וָחֶסֶד וְהוֹשִׁיעֵנוּ.

Avinu malkeinu, be gracious and answer us,

for we have no deeds within us.

Treat us generously and with kindness, and be our help.

"For we have no deeds within us..."

What we do is not "within us", not who we are. We are vessels; our past is not etched into us, we stand naked and open, receiving, being shaped and used by Spirit. This is what it means to be fully present. We can't be there always. But we invite ourselves, again and again, to be there during the *Yamim Nora'im*. To get there is what it means to be shown grace. This is the answer to prayer, once we recognize that *ein banu ma'asim*, we have nothing of our own. So we ask You, source of holiness, justice, love, to fill us with acts of love, *v'hoshi'einu!*

(Rabbi David Seidenberg)

On Kol Nidre night: *continue on the next page.*

On ***Yom Kippur morning****: continue on p.120 (removing the scroll from the ark), then p. 249 (Yom Kippur Torah reading)*

If you've flipped back here to daven the Amidah and Selichot one more time ***on Yom Kippur afternoon:*** *continue with Ne'ilah on p. 306.*

The Kaddish: A Doorway in Prayer

The Kaddish which follows
—known as *Kaddish shalem*
(whole Kaddish)—

is the doorway
between Avinu Malkeinu
and our concluding prayers.

Where have our prayers taken you?
Whatever you're feeling in this moment,
bring that into your prayer.

Kaddish Shalem

Yitgadal v'yitkadash, shmeh rabah. B'alma divra chiruteh, v'yamlich malchuteh b'chayyeichon u'v'yomeichon u'vchayyei d'chol beit Yisrael. Ba'agala u-vizman kariv v'imru amen.

יִתְגַּדַּל וְיִתְקַדַּשׁ שְׁמֵהּ רַבָּא.
בְּעָלְמָא דִּי בְרָא כִרְעוּתֵהּ,
וְיַמְלִיךְ מַלְכוּתֵהּ בְּחַיֵּיכוֹן
וּבְיוֹמֵיכוֹן וּבְחַיֵּי דְכָל בֵּית
יִשְׂרָאֵל. בַּעֲגָלָא וּבִזְמַן קָרִיב
וְאִמְרוּ אָמֵן:

□ Y'hei sh'mei raba m'varakh l'olam ol'almey almaya.

□ יְהֵא שְׁמֵהּ רַבָּא מְבָרַךְ
לְעָלַם וּלְעָלְמֵי עָלְמַיָּא:

Magnified and sanctified! Magnified and sanctified! May God's Great Name fill the world God created. May God's splendor be seen in the world in your life, in your days, in the life of all Israel. Quickly and soon! And let us say, Amen.

Forever may the Great Name be blessed!

Yitbarach v'yishtabach, v'yitpa'ar v'yit-romam v'yit-naseh. V'yithadar v'yitaleh v'yithallal shmeh d'kud'sha b'rich hu. L'eyla u'leyla min kol birchata v'shirata, tushbechata v'nechemata, damiran b'alma, v'imru amen.

יִתְבָּרַךְ וְיִשְׁתַּבַּח, וְיִתְפָּאַר
וְיִתְרוֹמַם וְיִתְנַשֵּׂא וְיִתְהַדָּר
וְיִתְעַלֶּה וְיִתְהַלָּל שְׁמֵהּ
דְּקֻדְשָׁא בְּרִיךְ הוּא לְעֵלָּא
וּלְעֵלָּא מִכָּל בִּרְכָתָא
וְשִׁירָתָא, תֻּשְׁבְּחָתָא
וְנֶחֱמָתָא, דַּאֲמִירָן בְּעָלְמָא,
וְאִמְרוּ אָמֵן:

Blessed and praised! Splendid and supreme! May the holy name, Bless God, be praised, beyond all the blessings and songs, comforts and consolations, that can be offered in this world. And let us say: Amen.

תִּתְקַבֵּל צְלוֹתְהוֹן וּבָעוּתְהוֹן דְּכָל (בֵּית) יִשְׂרָאֵל קֳדָם אֲבוּהוֹן דִּי בִשְׁמַיָּא וְאִמְרוּ אָמֵן:

Titkabel tzlo'uthon uva-ut'hon d'chol beit Yisrael kadam avuhon di vishmaia v'imru Amen.

יְהֵא שְׁלָמָא רַבָּא מִן שְׁמַיָּא וְחַיִּים עָלֵינוּ וְעַל כָּל יִשְׂרָאֵל, וְאִמְרוּ אָמֵן:

Y'hei shlama raba min shemaya v'chayyim tovim aleinu v'al kol Yisrael, v'imru amen.

עֹשֶׂה שָׁלוֹם בִּמְרוֹמָיו הוּא יַעֲשֶׂה שָׁלוֹם עָלֵינוּ וְעַל כָּל יִשְׂרָאֵל, וְעַל כָּל יוֹשְׁבֵי תֵבֵל, וְאִמְרוּ אָמֵן:

Oseh shalom bimromav, hu ya'aseh shalom, aleinu v'al kol yisrael, v'al kol yoshvei tevel, v'imru Amen.

May our prayers, and the prayers of the entire community, be accepted before You, our Parent.

May there be peace and life, great peace and life from heaven above for us and all Israel. And let us say, Amen!

May the One who makes peace in the high heavens make peace for us, for our whole community, and for all the peoples of the world. And let us say: Amen.

Aleinu (option 1)

This Aleinu is abbreviated; the full text can be found on p. 53.

□ Aleinu l'shabe'ach la'adon hakol, latet gedulah l'yotzer breshit. Shelo asanu k'goyei ha'aratzot, v'lo samanu k'mishpachot ha-adamah. Shelo sam chelkeinu kahem, v'goralenu k'chol hamonam.

□ עָלֵינוּ לְשַׁבֵּחַ לַאֲדוֹן הַכֹּל,
לָתֵת גְּדֻלָּה לְיוֹצֵרבְּרֵאשִׁית,
שֶׁלֹּא/שֶׁלוֹ* עָשָׂנוּ כְּגוֹיֵי
הָאֲרָצוֹת, וְלֹא/וְלוֹ* שָׂמָנוּ
כְּמִשְׁפְּחוֹת הָאֲדָמָה, שֶׁלֹּא/
שֶׁלוֹ* שָׂם חֶלְקֵנוּ כָּהֶם,
וְגֹרָלֵנוּ כְּכָל הֲמוֹנָם.

It is up to us to praise the Source of all, to exalt the Molder of creation.
We are:

	made for God like all nations.	not made like other nations.
We are:		
	placed here for God like all humanity.	unlike other peoples.
Our portion and our fate are:		
	for God's own sake.	not like those of other peoples.

□ Va-anachnu korim, u-mishtachavim u-modim, lifnei melech malchei ham'lachim, hakadosh baruch hu.

□ וַאֲנַחְנוּ כּוֹרְעִים וּמִשְׁתַּחֲוִים
וּמוֹדִים, לִפְנֵי מֶלֶךְ, מַלְכֵי
הַמְּלָכִים, הַקָּדוֹשׁ בָּרוּךְ הוּא.

We bow low and prostrate in thanks before the Source of all sources, the Holy One, blessed is God.

**Daven either* לא*, pronounced lo ("not"), or* לו*, also pronounced lo ("for God"). The first articulates Jewish chosenness; the second, a post-triumphalism in which all peoples are chosen for their own unique roles. For more on this, see p. 53.*

□ שֶׁהוּא נוֹטֶה שָׁמַיִם וְיֹסֵד
אָרֶץ, וּמוֹשַׁב יְקָרוֹ בַּשָּׁמַיִם
מִמַּעַל, וּשְׁכִינַת עֻזּוֹ בְּגָבְהֵי
מְרוֹמִים, הוּא אֱלֹהֵינוּ אֵין
עוֹד. אֱמֶת מַלְכֵּנוּ אֶפֶס
זוּלָתוֹ, כַּכָּתוּב בְּתוֹרָתוֹ:
וְיָדַעְתָּ הַיּוֹם וַהֲשֵׁבֹתָ אֶל
לְבָבֶךָ, כִּי יְיָ הוּא הָאֱלֹהִים
בַּשָּׁמַיִם מִמַּעַל, וְעַל הָאָרֶץ
מִתָּחַת, אֵין עוֹד:

□ Shehu noteh shamayim v'yosed aretz, u-moshav yekaro bashamayim mima'al, uschinat uzo b'gavheh meromim. Hu eloheinu, ein od. Emet malkenu efes zulato. Kakatuv b'torato: v'yadata hayom vahashevota el levavecha. Ki adonai, hu ha-elohim, bashamayim mima'al, v'al ha-aretz mitachat ein od.

God sets out the heavens and establishes the earth. God's honored place is in the heights of our aspirations; God's powerful presence is in the heavens of our hopes. This is our God, there is none else. God is the world's truth; there is nothing that God is not.

□ כַּכָּתוּב בְּתוֹרָתֶךָ, יְיָ יִמְלֹךְ
לְעוֹלָם וָעֶד: וְנֶאֱמַר, וְהָיָה יְיָ
לְמֶלֶךְ עַל כָּל הָאָרֶץ, בַּיּוֹם
הַהוּא יִהְיֶה יְיָ אֶחָד, וּשְׁמוֹ אֶחָד.

□ Kakatuv b'toratecha, Adonai yimloch leolam vaed. V'ne-emar, v'haya Adonai l'melech al kol ha-aretz. Bayom hahu yiheh Adonai echad, ushmo echad!

As it is written in God's sacred teaching: "You shall know this day and place upon your heart that Adonai is God in heaven above and earth below; there is none else."

Then shall your realm be established on earth, and the word of Your prophet fulfilled: "Adonai will reign forever and ever. On that day, Adonai shall be One, and God's name shall be One."

Aleinu (2): It's Upon Us

May we feel Your holy power
May we feel Your holy strength
May we feel Your holy presence
Surround us in this holy place!

May we feel the earth beneath our feet
As we bend and bow to You
May our bodies rise to greet You
As we feel Your presence pouring through!

1) It's upon us, it's upon us
To feel Your holy ground
It's upon us, it's upon us
To hear Your holy sound

2) It's upon us, it's upon us
To feel the love inside
It's upon us, it's upon us
To face You and not hide

3) It's upon us, it's upon us
To think, to act, to do
It's upon us, it's upon us
To do what's right and true

4) It's upon us, it's upon us
To reach up to the sky
It's upon us, it's upon us
To take our wings and fly!

Aleinu l'shabe'ach la-adon hakol! (4 times)

May we feel Your holy power
May we feel Your holy strength
May we feel Your holy presence
Surround us in this holy place!

(Rabbinic Pastor Shayndel Kahn)

Aleinu (3)

Hareinu M'kabel Aleinu / V'Ne'emar

הֲרֵינוּ מְקַבֵּל עָלֵינוּ
אֶת מִצְוַת הַבֹּרֵא
וְאָהַבְתָּ לְרֵעֲךָ כָּמוֹךָ
לְרֵעֲךָ כָּמוֹךָ!

Hareinu m'kabel aleinu
Et mitzvat ha-borei
V'ahavta l'reakha camokha,
l'reakha camokha!

Behold: we take upon ourselves
the mitzvah of the Creator:
to love our neighbor as ourselves!

וְנֶאֱמַר, וְהָיָה יְיָ
לְמֶלֶךְ עַל כָּל הָאָרֶץ,
בַּיּוֹם הַהוּא יִהְיֶה יְיָ אֶחָד,
וּשְׁמוֹ אֶחָד:

V'ne'emar v'haya Adonai
l'melech al kol ha-aretz,
bayom hahu yihyeh Adonai
echad ushmo echad.

And it is said: on that day
[when we take on that obligation of loving our neighbor wholly]
Adonai will be God over all the earth,
and on that day God will be One and God's Name will be One.

Mourner's *Kaddish*

יִתְגַּדַּל וְיִתְקַדַּשׁ שְׁמֵהּ רַבָּא.
בְּעָלְמָא דִּי בְרָא כִרְעוּתֵהּ,
וְיַמְלִיךְ מַלְכוּתֵהּ בְּחַיֵּיכוֹן
וּבְיוֹמֵיכוֹן וּבְחַיֵּי דְכָל בֵּית
יִשְׂרָאֵל.
בַּעֲגָלָא וּבִזְמַן קָרִיב וְאִמְרוּ אָמֵן:

Yitgadal v'yitkadash,
shmeh rabah. B'alma divra
chiruteh, v'yamlich
malchuteh b'chayyeichon
u'v'yomeichon u'vchayyei
d'chol beit Yisrael.
Ba'agala u-vizman kariv
v'imru amen.

□ יְהֵא שְׁמֵהּ רַבָּא מְבָרַךְ לְעָלַם
וּלְעָלְמֵי עָלְמַיָּא:

□ Y'hei sh'mei raba
m'varakh l'olam ol'almey
almaya.

יִתְבָּרַךְ וְיִשְׁתַּבַּח, וְיִתְפָּאַר
וְיִתְרוֹמַם וְיִתְנַשֵּׂא וְיִתְהַדָּר
וְיִתְעַלֶּה וְיִתְהַלָּל שְׁמֵהּ דְּקֻדְשָׁא
בְּרִיךְ הוּא לְעֵלָּא וּלְעֵלָּא מִן כָּל
בִּרְכָתָא וְשִׁירָתָא, תֻּשְׁבְּחָתָא
וְנֶחֱמָתָא, דַּאֲמִירָן בְּעָלְמָא,
וְאִמְרוּ אָמֵן:

Yitbarach v'yishtabach,
v'yitpa'ar v'yit-romam
v'yit-naseh. V'yithadar
v'yitaleh v'yithallal shmeh
d'kudh'sha b'rich hu. L'eyla
u l'eyla min kol birchata
v'shirata, tushbechata
v'nechemata, damiran
b'alma, v'imru amen.

יְהֵא שְׁלָמָא רַבָּא מִן שְׁמַיָּא
וְחַיִּים עָלֵינוּ וְעַל כָּל יִשְׂרָאֵל,
וְאִמְרוּ אָמֵן:

Y'hei shlama raba min
shemaya v'chayyim tovim
aleinu v'al kol Yisrael,
v'imru amen.

עֹשֶׂה שָׁלוֹם בִּמְרוֹמָיו הוּא יַעֲשֶׂה
שָׁלוֹם עָלֵינוּ וְעַל כָּל יִשְׂרָאֵל,
וְעַל כָּל יוֹשְׁבֵי תֵבֵל, וְאִמְרוּ אָמֵן:

Oseh shalom bimromav,
hu ya'aseh shalom, aleinu
v'al kol yisrael, v'al kol
yoshvei tevel, v'imru
Amen.

I pray to You God,
that the power residing in Your Great Name
be increased and made sacred
in this world which God created freely
in order to preside in it, and grow its freeing power
and bring about the messianic era.
May this happen during our lifetime
and during the lifetime of all of us
living now, the house of Israel.
May this happen soon, without delay
and by saying AMEN we express agreement and hope, **AMEN**.

May the immense power residing in God's great name
flow freely into our world and worlds beyond.

May that Great Name, that sacred energy,
be shaped and made effective
and be acknowledged and be given the right honor
and be seen as beautiful and uplifting and bring jubilation.
Way beyond our input of worshipful song and praise
which we express in this world
as our agreement and hope, **AMEN**.

May that endless peace that heaven can release for us
bring about the good life for us and for all Israel
as we express our agreement and hope, **AMEN**.

You, who harmonize it all on the highest planes:
bring harmony and peace to us,
to all Israel and all sentient beings
as we express our agreement and hope, **AMEN.**

(Translation: R' Zalman Shachter-Shalomi z"l.)

Psalm 27

Yah! You are my light. You are my savior. Whom need I dread?	לְדָוִד: יְיָ אוֹרִי וְיִשְׁעִי מִמִּי אִירָא;
Yah, with You as my strong protector who can make me panic?	יְיָ מָעוֹז-חַיַּי מִמִּי אֶפְחָד.
When hateful bullies gang up on me, wanting to harass me,	בִּקְרֹב עָלַי, מְרֵעִים לֶאֱכֹל אֶת-בְּשָׂרִי:
To oppress and terrorize me, they are the ones who stumble and fall.	צָרַי וְאֹיְבַי לִי הֵמָּה כָּשְׁלוּ וְנָפָלוּ.
Even if a gang surrounds me my heart is not weakened.	אִם-תַּחֲנֶה עָלַי, מַחֲנֶה לֹא-יִירָא לִבִּי:
If a battle is joined around me my trust in You is firm.	אִם-תָּקוּם עָלַי, מִלְחָמָה בְּזֹאת, אֲנִי בוֹטֵחַ.
Only one thing do I ask of You, Yah: Just this alone do I seek,	אַחַת שָׁאַלְתִּי מֵאֵת-יְיָ אוֹתָהּ אֲבַקֵּשׁ:
I want to be at home with you, Yah, all the days of my life.	שִׁבְתִּי בְּבֵית-יְיָ כָּל-יְמֵי חַיַּי;
I want to delight in seeing You when I come to visit You in Your temple.	לַחֲזוֹת בְּנֹעַם-יְיָ וּלְבַקֵּר בְּהֵיכָלוֹ.
You hide me in your sukkah on a foul day.	כִּי יִצְפְּנֵנִי בְּסֻכֹּה בְּיוֹם רָעָה:
You conceal me unseen in Your tent; You raise me beyond anyone's reach.	יַסְתִּרֵנִי בְּסֵתֶר אָהֳלוֹ; בְּצוּר, יְרוֹמְמֵנִי.
And now, as You have held my head high despite the presence of my powerful foes	וְעַתָּה יָרוּם רֹאשִׁי, עַל אֹיְבַי סְבִיבוֹתַי
I prepare to celebrate and thrill, singing and making music to You, Yah!	וְאֶזְבְּחָה בְאָהֳלוֹ, זִבְחֵי תְרוּעָה; אָשִׁירָה וַאֲזַמְּרָה לַיְיָ.

שְׁמַע-יְיָ קוֹלִי אֶקְרָא וְחָנֵּנִי וַעֲנֵנִי.

Listen, Yah, to the sound of my cry, and, being kind, answer me!

לְךָ, אָמַר לִבִּי בַּקְּשׁוּ פָנָי; אֶת-פָּנֶיךָ יְיָ אֲבַקֵּשׁ.

My heart has said, I seek Your face. Your presence is what I beg for.

אַל-תַּסְתֵּר פָּנֶיךָ, מִמֶּנִּי אַל תַּט-בְּאַף, עַבְדֶּךָ:

Don't hide Your face from me. Don't just put me down.

עֶזְרָתִי הָיִיתָ, אַל-תִּטְּשֵׁנִי וְאַל-תַּעַזְבֵנִי, אֱלֹהֵי יִשְׁעִי.

You who have been my helper, don't abandon me, don't forsake me, God my support.

כִּי-אָבִי וְאִמִּי עֲזָבוּנִי; וַיְיָ יַאַסְפֵנִי.

Though my father and my mother have left me, You, Yah, will hold me securely.

הוֹרֵנִי יְיָ, דַּרְכֶּךָ:

Please teach me Your way.

וּנְחֵנִי, בְּאֹרַח מִישׁוֹר לְמַעַן, שׁוֹרְרָי.

Teach me Your way and guide me on the straight path.

אַל-תִּתְּנֵנִי בְּנֶפֶשׁ צָרָי: כִּי קָמוּ-בִי עֵדֵי-שֶׁקֶר, וִיפֵחַ חָמָס.

Discourage those who defame me
Because false witnesses stood up against me belching out violence.

Don't let me become the victim of my foes.

לוּלֵא הֶאֱמַנְתִּי, לִרְאוֹת בְּטוּב-יְיָ: בְּאֶרֶץ חַיִּים.

I wouldn't have survived
If I hadn't hoped that I would yet see Your goodness, God, fully alive on earth.

קַוֵּה, אֶל-יְיָ: חֲזַק, וְיַאֲמֵץ לִבֶּךָ; וְקַוֵּה אֶל-יְיָ.

So I tell you, my friends: you too hope to Yah! Be sturdy!

And make strong your heart. And most of all, keep hoping to Yah.

(translated by

Rabbi Zalman Schachter-Shalomi z"l / of blessed memory)

from Psalm 27

□ אַחַת שָׁאַלְתִּי מֵאֵת-יְיָ
אוֹתָהּ אֲבַקֵּשׁ:
שִׁבְתִּי בְּבֵית-יְיָ, כָּל-יְמֵי חַיַּי;
לַחֲזוֹת בְּנֹעַם-יְיָ,
וּלְבַקֵּר בְּהֵיכָלוֹ.

□ Achat sha'alti me'eit Adonai,
otah avakesh
Shivti b'veit Adonai,
kol y'mei chayyay
Lachazot b'noam, b'noam
Adonai, u'l'vaker b'heikhalo

□ One thing I ask, I ask of You, I earnestly pray for:
That I might dwell in Your house all the days of my life
Knowing the beauty, the beauty of You
and to dwell in Your holy place!

□ לַךְ אָמַר לִבִּי בַּקְּשׁוּ פָנָי;
אֶת-פָּנַיִךְ הויה
אֲבַקֵּשׁ.

□ Lach amar libi bakshu panai;
Et panayich, Havayah,
avakesh.

To You, my heart says: God, I seek Your face!

May our night of fasting and prayer be meaningful and sweet.

Yom Kippur Morning

The first part of Yom Kippur morning worship uses the same liturgy as Rosh Hashanah morning, starting on ***p. 68.***

Sanctuary

V'asu li mikdash	וְעָשׂוּ לִי מִקְדָּשׁ
V'shachanti b'tocham	וְשָׁכַנְתִּי בְּתוֹכָם
Va-anachnu n'varech Yah	וַאֲנַחְנוּ נְבָרֵךְ יָהּ
Me-ata v'ad olam!	מֵעַתָּה וְעַד עוֹלָם!

O Lord, prepare me to be a sanctuary
Pure and holy, tried and true
And in thanksgiving I'll be a living
Sanctuary for You!

The ***blessings before the Torah reading*** *can be found on* ***p. 124****.*

Torah Reading

Yom Kippur Morning: Deut. 29:9-14; 30:1-14

First Aliyah

You stand today, all of you, before Adonai your God. Every Israelite — your tribal chiefs, your elders, your officials, your little ones, your women, the	אַתֶּם נִצָּבִים הַיּוֹם כֻּלְּכֶם לִפְנֵי יְיָ אֱלֹהֵיכֶם רָאשֵׁיכֶם שִׁבְטֵיכֶם זִקְנֵיכֶם וְשֹׁטְרֵיכֶם כֹּל אִישׁ יִשְׂרָאֵל: טַפְּכֶם נְשֵׁיכֶם

foreigners within your camp, from the one who chops your wood to the one who draws your water — all of you enter into the covenant with Adonai your God, which God is making with you today. This is to establish you today as God's people, and God will be your God, as God swore to you and to your ancestors, Abraham, Isaac, and Jacob. But it is not with you alone that I make this covenant. It is with both those who are standing here with us today before Adonai our God, and with those who are not here with us today.

וְגֵרְךָ אֲשֶׁר בְּקֶרֶב מַחֲנֶיךָ
מֵחֹטֵב עֵצֶיךָ עַד שֹׁאֵב
מֵימֶיךָ׃ לְעָבְרְךָ בִּבְרִית יְיָ
אֱלֹהֶיךָ וּבְאָלָתוֹ אֲשֶׁר יְיָ אֱלֹהֶיךָ
כֹּרֵת עִמְּךָ הַיּוֹם׃ לְמַעַן
הָקִים־אֹתְךָ הַיּוֹם | לוֹ לְעָם
וְהוּא יִהְיֶה־לְּךָ לֵאלֹהִים כַּאֲשֶׁר
דִּבֶּר־לָךְ וְכַאֲשֶׁר נִשְׁבַּע
לַאֲבֹתֶיךָ לְאַבְרָהָם לְיִצְחָק
וּלְיַעֲקֹב׃ וְלֹא אִתְּכֶם לְבַדְּכֶם
אָנֹכִי כֹּרֵת אֶת־הַבְּרִית הַזֹּאת
וְאֶת־הָאָלָה הַזֹּאת׃ כִּי אֶת־אֲשֶׁר
יֶשְׁנוֹ פֹּה עִמָּנוּ עֹמֵד הַיּוֹם לִפְנֵי
יְיָ אֱלֹהֵינוּ וְאֵת אֲשֶׁר אֵינֶנּוּ פֹּה
עִמָּנוּ הַיּוֹם׃

Second aliyah

When all of the things that I have set before you come about — the rewards and the punishments — and you take them to heart, and you are scattered among the nations where Adonai your God banishes you, and you and your children then return to Adonai and hear God's voice — all that I have taught you today — with all your heart and all your soul,

וְהָיָה כִי־יָבֹאוּ עָלֶיךָ
כָּל־הַדְּבָרִים הָאֵלֶּה הַבְּרָכָה
וְהַקְּלָלָה אֲשֶׁר נָתַתִּי לְפָנֶיךָ
וַהֲשֵׁבֹתָ אֶל־לְבָבֶךָ בְּכָל־הַגּוֹיִם
אֲשֶׁר הִדִּיחֲךָ יְיָ אֱלֹהֶיךָ שָׁמָּה׃
וְשַׁבְתָּ עַד־יְיָ אֱלֹהֶיךָ וְשָׁמַעְתָּ
בְקֹלוֹ כְּכֹל אֲשֶׁר־אָנֹכִי מְצַוְּךָ
הַיּוֹם אַתָּה וּבָנֶיךָ בְּכָל־לְבָבְךָ
וּבְכָל־נַפְשֶׁךָ׃

וְשָׁב יְיָ אֱלֹהֶיךָ אֶת־שְׁבוּתְךָ
וְרִחֲמֶךָ וְשָׁב וְקִבֶּצְךָ
מִכָּל־הָֽעַמִּים אֲשֶׁר הֱפִיצְךָ יְיָ
אֱלֹהֶיךָ שָׁמָּה׃ אִם־יִהְיֶה נִדַּחֲךָ
בִּקְצֵה הַשָּׁמָיִם מִשָּׁם יְקַבֶּצְךָ יְיָ
אֱלֹהֶיךָ וּמִשָּׁם יִקָּחֶךָ׃ וֶהֱבִיאֲךָ
יְיָ אֱלֹהֶיךָ אֶל־הָאָרֶץ
אֲשֶׁר־יָרְשׁוּ אֲבֹתֶיךָ וִירִשְׁתָּהּ
וְהֵיטִבְךָ וְהִרְבְּךָ מֵאֲבֹתֶיךָ׃ וּמָל
יְיָ אֱלֹהֶיךָ אֶת־לְבָבְךָ וְאֶת־לְבַב
זַרְעֶךָ לְאַהֲבָה אֶת־יְיָ אֱלֹהֶיךָ
בְּכָל־לְבָבְךָ וּבְכָל־נַפְשְׁךָ לְמַעַן
חַיֶּיךָ׃ וְנָתַן יְיָ אֱלֹהֶיךָ אֵת
כָּל־הָאָלוֹת הָאֵלֶּה עַל־אֹיְבֶיךָ
וְעַל־שֹׂנְאֶיךָ אֲשֶׁר רְדָפוּךָ׃

then Adonai will return to you. God will have compassion for you and gather you back from the nations where Adonai has scattered you. Even if you have been driven to the far ends of the heavens, Adonai will gather you from there and take you back. Adonai will bring you to the land that your ancestors inherited and you shall inherit it. God will be good to you and increase you, even more than your ancestors. Adonai your God will circumcise your heart and the hearts of your descendants to love Adonai with all your heart and all your soul, for the sake of your life. Adonai your God will place all strength against the enmity and hatred that pursue you.

Third aliyah

וְאַתָּה תָשׁוּב וְשָׁמַעְתָּ בְּקוֹל יְיָ
וְעָשִׂיתָ אֶת־כָּל־מִצְוֹתָיו אֲשֶׁר
אָנֹכִי מְצַוְּךָ הַיּוֹם׃ וְהוֹתִירְךָ יְיָ
אֱלֹהֶיךָ בְּכֹל | מַעֲשֵׂה יָדֶךָ
בִּפְרִי בִטְנְךָ וּבִפְרִי בְהֶמְתְּךָ
וּבִפְרִי אַדְמָתְךָ לְטֹבָה כִּי |
יָשׁוּב יְיָ

You will return and hear the voice of Adonai and do all of God's mitzvot that I enjoin upon you today. Adonai will allow you to prosper well in all the work of your hands, in the fruit of your womb, the offspring of your cattle, and the produce of your land. Adonai

לָשׂוּשׂ עָלֶיךָ לְטוֹב כַּאֲשֶׁר־שָׂשׂ
עַל־אֲבֹתֶיךָ כִּי תִשְׁמַע בְּקוֹל יְיָ
אֱלֹהֶיךָ לִשְׁמֹר מִצְוֹתָיו וְחֻקֹּתָיו
הַכְּתוּבָה בְּסֵפֶר הַתּוֹרָה הַזֶּה
כִּי תָשׁוּב אֶל־יְיָ אֱלֹהֶיךָ
בְּכָל־לְבָבְךָ וּבְכָל־נַפְשֶׁךָ: כִּי
הַמִּצְוָה הַזֹּאת אֲשֶׁר אָנֹכִי
מְצַוְּךָ הַיּוֹם לֹא־נִפְלֵאת הִוא
מִמְּךָ וְלֹא־רְחֹקָה הִוא: לֹא
בַשָּׁמַיִם הִוא לֵאמֹר מִי
יַעֲלֶה־לָּנוּ הַשָּׁמַיְמָה וְיִקָּחֶהָ לָּנוּ
וְיַשְׁמִעֵנוּ אֹתָהּ
וְנַעֲשֶׂנָּה: וְלֹא־מֵעֵבֶר לַיָּם הִוא
לֵאמֹר מִי יַעֲבָר־לָנוּ אֶל־עֵבֶר
הַיָּם וְיִקָּחֶהָ לָּנוּ וְיַשְׁמִעֵנוּ אֹתָהּ
וְנַעֲשֶׂנָּה: כִּי־קָרוֹב אֵלֶיךָ הַדָּבָר
מְאֹד בְּפִיךָ וּבִלְבָבְךָ לַעֲשֹׂתוֹ:

will return in delight to you for your well-being, as God delighted in your ancestors. For when you hear the voice of Adonai your God and observe what God has enjoined—God's laws written in this Torah scroll—you will return to Adonai your God with all your heart and soul. Surely, this mitzvah that I enjoin upon you today is not so wondrous for you, and it is not so far. It is not in the heavens that one should say, "Who shall go up into the heavens for us and get it for us that we will hear it and do it?" It is not over the sea that one should say, "Who will cross over to the other side of the sea for us to get it for us that we will hear it and do it?" The word is very close to you, in your own mouth and in your heart to do it.

Blessing After Torah

בָּרוּךְ אַתָּה יְיָ אֱלֹהֵינוּ מֶלֶךְ
הָעוֹלָם, אֲשֶׁר נָתַן לָנוּ תּוֹרַת
אֱמֶת, וְחַיֵּי עוֹלָם נָטַע בְּתוֹכֵנוּ:
בָּרוּךְ אַתָּה יְיָ, נוֹתֵן הַתּוֹרָה:

Baruch atah, Adonai, eloheinu melech haolam. Asher natan lanu Torat emet, v'chayyei olam nata b'tocheinu. Baruch atah, Adonai, noten haTorah.

Holy One of Blessing, Your Presence fills creation. This Torah is a teaching of truth, whole and balanced, and from it comes eternal life for the people who embrace it. Blessed are You, Merciful One, giver of the Torah.

Fasting

There is an unseen sweetness in the stomach's emptiness.

We are lutes. When the soundbox is filled, no music can come forth.

When the brain and the belly burn from fasting, every moment a new song rises out of the fire. The mists clear, and a new vitality makes you spring up the steps before you.

Be empty and cry as a reed instrument.

Be empty and write secrets with a reed pen.

When satiated by food and drink, an unsightly metal statue is seated where your spirit should be.

When fasting, good habits gather like helpful friends. Fasting is Solomon's ring.

Don't give in to illusion and lose your power. But even when will and control have been lost, they will return when you fast, like soldiers appearing out of the ground, or pennants flying in the breeze.

(*Rumi, translated by Coleman Barks*)

"We are lutes..."

Haftarah Reading

Blessing Before the Reading

Blessed are You, Adonai our God, source of all, who has chosen good prophets and has delighted in the faithful words they have spoken. Blessed are You Adonai, who continues to choose Torah, Moses, the people Israel, and prophets of truth and justice.

בָּרוּךְ אַתָּה יְיָ אֱלֹהֵינוּ מֶלֶךְ
הָעוֹלָם, אֲשֶׁר בָּחַר בִּנְבִיאִים
טוֹבִים, וְרָצָה בְדִבְרֵיהֶם
הַנֶּאֱמָרִים בֶּאֱמֶת, בָּרוּךְ
אַתָּה יְיָ, הַבּוֹחֵר בַּתּוֹרָה
וּבְמֹשֶׁה עַבְדּוֹ, וּבְיִשְׂרָאֵל
עַמּוֹ, וּבִנְבִיאֵי הָאֱמֶת וָצֶדֶק.

For Yom Kippur Morning Isaiah 57:14 - 58:14

The English setting is meant for two voices.

VOICE ONE: "Build a highway! Clear a road! Remove all obstacles from My people's path!"

VOICE TWO: So says the One who dwells on high, whose name is holy: "I dwell in high holiness—but also with the oppressed and those whose spirits are low. I breathe new life into the low-spirited, I restore the hearts of the oppressed. I will not be angry forever. No: I who make spirits flag also create the breath of life."

VOICE ONE: "Your sinful greed made Me angry. I lashed out; I hid My face. The people are stubborn, they walk on a path of their own devising, but I take note of them and I will heal them.

וְאָמַר סֹלּוּ־סֹלּוּ פַּנּוּ־דָרֶךְ הָרִימוּ
מִכְשׁוֹל מִדֶּרֶךְ עַמִּי׃ כִּי כֹה אָמַר
רָם וְנִשָּׂא שֹׁכֵן עַד וְקָדוֹשׁ שְׁמוֹ
מָרוֹם וְקָדוֹשׁ אֶשְׁכּוֹן וְאֶת־דַּכָּא
וּשְׁפַל־רוּחַ לְהַחֲיוֹת רוּחַ שְׁפָלִים
וּלְהַחֲיוֹת לֵב נִדְכָּאִים׃ כִּי לֹא
לְעוֹלָם אָרִיב וְלֹא לָנֶצַח אֶקְצוֹף
כִּי־רוּחַ מִלְּפָנַי יַעֲטוֹף וּנְשָׁמוֹת אֲנִי
עָשִׂיתִי׃ בַּעֲוֺן בִּצְעוֹ קָצַפְתִּי וְאַכֵּהוּ
הַסְתֵּר וְאֶקְצֹף וַיֵּלֶךְ שׁוֹבָב בְּדֶרֶךְ
לִבּוֹ׃ דְּרָכָיו רָאִיתִי וְאֶרְפָּאֵהוּ
וְאַנְחֵהוּ וַאֲשַׁלֵּם נִחֻמִים לוֹ
וְלַאֲבֵלָיו׃ בּוֹרֵא נִוב] שְׂפָתָיִם שָׁלוֹם
| שָׁלוֹם לָרָחוֹק וְלַקָּרוֹב אָמַר יְהוָה
וּרְפָאתִיו׃

I will guide them. I will bring solace. To mourners I bring comforting words: peace, peace to the far and the near," says Adonai, "And I will heal them."

VOICE TWO: "The wicked are like a choppy sea, never at rest, whose waters are dark with mud. There is no rest," said my God, "for the wicked."

VOICE ONE: "Cry out, don't hold back. Raise your voice like a shofar! Remind My people that they've transgressed; remind the house of Jacob of their misdeeds. Every day they seek me, eager to learn My ways. As if they were a righteous nation which has not abandoned justice, they ask Me for the right way. They are eager to be near Me. They ask, 'Why, when we fasted, did You not see us? When we starved our bodies, You paid no heed!'"

VOICE TWO: "Do you think that this is this the kind of fast that I want? A day for people to starve their bodies? Do I want you to bow your heads like the reeds, to mortify your bodies with coarse cloth and ashes? You call that a fast, a day when Adonai will look upon you with favor?"

VOICE ONE: "No! This is the fast I want: unlock the chains of wickedness, untie the knots of servitude. Let the oppressed go free, their bonds broken. Share your bread with the hungry, and welcome the homeless into your home.

וְהָרְשָׁעִים כַּיָּם נִגְרָשׁ כִּי הַשְׁקֵט לֹא
יוּכָל וַיִּגְרְשׁוּ מֵימָיו רֶפֶשׁ וָטִיט׃ אֵין
שָׁלוֹם אָמַר אֱלֹהַי לָרְשָׁעִים׃ קְרָא
בְגָרוֹן אַל־תַּחְשֹׂךְ כַּשּׁוֹפָר הָרֵם
קוֹלֶךָ וְהַגֵּד לְעַמִּי פִּשְׁעָם וּלְבֵית
יַעֲקֹב חַטֹּאתָם׃ וְאוֹתִי יוֹם יוֹם
יִדְרֹשׁוּן וְדַעַת דְּרָכַי יֶחְפָּצוּן כְּגוֹי
אֲשֶׁר־צְדָקָה עָשָׂה וּמִשְׁפַּט אֱלֹהָיו
לֹא עָזָב יִשְׁאָלוּנִי מִשְׁפְּטֵי־צֶדֶק
קִרְבַת אֱלֹהִים יֶחְפָּצוּן׃ לָמָּה צַּמְנוּ
וְלֹא רָאִיתָ עִנִּינוּ נַפְשֵׁנוּ וְלֹא תֵדָע
הֵן בְּיוֹם צֹמְכֶם תִּמְצְאוּ־חֵפֶץ
וְכָל־עַצְּבֵיכֶם תִּנְגֹּשׂוּ׃ הֵן לְרִיב
וּמַצָּה תָּצוּמוּ וּלְהַכּוֹת בְּאֶגְרֹף רֶשַׁע
לֹא־תָצוּמוּ כַיּוֹם לְהַשְׁמִיעַ בַּמָּרוֹם
קוֹלְכֶם׃ הֲכָזֶה יִהְיֶה צוֹם אֶבְחָרֵהוּ
יוֹם עַנּוֹת אָדָם נַפְשׁוֹ הֲלָכֹף כְּאַגְמֹן
רֹאשׁוֹ וְשַׂק וָאֵפֶר יַצִּיעַ הֲלָזֶה
תִּקְרָא־צוֹם וְיוֹם רָצוֹן לַיהוָה׃ הֲלוֹא
זֶה צוֹם אֶבְחָרֵהוּ פַּתֵּחַ חַרְצֻבּוֹת
רֶשַׁע הַתֵּר אֲגֻדּוֹת מוֹטָה וְשַׁלַּח
רְצוּצִים חָפְשִׁים וְכָל־מוֹטָה
תְּנַתֵּקוּ׃ הֲלוֹא פָרֹס לָרָעֵב לַחְמֶךָ
וַעֲנִיִּים מְרוּדִים תָּבִיא בָיִת
כִּי־תִרְאֶה עָרֹם וְכִסִּיתוֹ וּמִבְּשָׂרְךָ
לֹא תִתְעַלָּם׃ אָז יִבָּקַע כַּשַּׁחַר
אוֹרֶךָ וַאֲרֻכָתְךָ מְהֵרָה תִצְמָח וְהָלַךְ
לְפָנֶיךָ צִדְקֶךָ כְּבוֹד יְהוָה
יַאַסְפֶךָ׃ אָז תִּקְרָא וַיהוָה יַעֲנֶה
תְּשַׁוַּע וְיֹאמַר הִנֵּנִי אִם־תָּסִיר
מִתּוֹכְךָ מוֹטָה שְׁלַח אֶצְבַּע
וְדַבֶּר־אָוֶן׃

When you see the naked, clothe them. All people are your kin: do not ignore them."

VOICE TWO:"Then you will shine like the dawn, and healing will rise up. Your own righteousness will vindicate you, and the presence of God will guard your safety. Then, when you call, Adonai will answer. When you cry out, God will say, 'Here I am.'"

VOICE ONE: "If you banish oppression, scornful finger-pointing and hateful speech; if you offer compassion to the hungry and sustenance to those who are famished; then your light will shine in the darkness, your gloom will disappear like fog at noon. Adonai will guide you. God will slake your thirst when you are parched; God will give you strength deep in your bones. You will be like a watered garden, an unfailing spring. You will rebuild yourselves, you will restore foundations laid long ago. You will be known as one who restores what has fallen."

VOICE TWO: "If you refrain from trampling Shabbat, from pursuing work on My holy day, if you find the delight in Shabbat and you honor sacred time, if you honor Shabbat by pausing from work, from bargaining, from your weekday way of being— then you can seek My favor. I will lift you up to the heights. I will let you enjoy the heritage of your ancestors. God has spoken."

וְתָפֵק לָרָעֵב נַפְשֶׁךָ וְנֶפֶשׁ נַעֲנָה
תַּשְׂבִּיעַ וְזָרַח בַּחֹשֶׁךְ אוֹרֶךָ
וַאֲפֵלָתְךָ כַּצָּהֳרָיִם׃ וְנָחֲךָ יְהֹוָה
תָּמִיד וְהִשְׂבִּיעַ בְּצַחְצָחוֹת נַפְשֶׁךָ
וְעַצְמֹתֶיךָ יַחֲלִיץ וְהָיִיתָ כְּגַן רָוֶה
וּכְמוֹצָא מַיִם אֲשֶׁר לֹא־יְכַזְּבוּ
מֵימָיו׃ וּבָנוּ מִמְּךָ חָרְבוֹת עוֹלָם
מוֹסְדֵי דוֹר־וָדוֹר תְּקוֹמֵם וְקֹרָא לְךָ
גֹּדֵר פֶּרֶץ מְשׁוֹבֵב נְתִיבוֹת
לָשָׁבֶת׃ אִם־תָּשִׁיב מִשַּׁבָּת רַגְלֶךָ
עֲשׂוֹת חֲפָצֶיךָ בְּיוֹם קָדְשִׁי וְקָרָאתָ
לַשַּׁבָּת עֹנֶג לִקְדוֹשׁ יְהֹוָה מְכֻבָּד
וְכִבַּדְתּוֹ מֵעֲשׂוֹת דְּרָכֶיךָ מִמְּצוֹא
חֶפְצְךָ וְדַבֵּר דָּבָר׃ אָז תִּתְעַנַּג
עַל־יְהֹוָה וְהִרְכַּבְתִּיךָ עַל־בָּמֳותֵי
[בָּמֳתֵי] אָרֶץ וְהַאֲכַלְתִּיךָ נַחֲלַת
יַעֲקֹב אָבִיךָ כִּי פִּי יְהֹוָה דִּבֵּר׃

Blessings After the Haftarah

Blessed are You, Adonai our God, source of all, rock of all time and space, righteous in every generation, the faithful God whose word is deed, who speaks and establishes, whose every word is truth and justice.

בָּרוּךְ אַתָּה יְיָ אֱלֹהֵינוּ מֶלֶךְ הָעוֹלָם, צוּר כָּל הָעוֹלָמִים, צַדִּיק בְּכָל הַדּוֹרוֹת, הָאֵל הַנֶּאֱמָן הָאוֹמֵר וְעֹשֶׂה, הַמְדַבֵּר וּמְקַיֵּם, שֶׁכָּל דְּבָרָיו אֱמֶת וָצֶדֶק.

You are faithful, Adonai our God, and faithful is Your word. Not a single word You have spoken goes unfulfilled, for You are God, faithful, just (and merciful). Blessed are You, Adonai our God, faithful in all ways.

נֶאֱמָן אַתָּה הוּא יְיָ אֱלֹהֵינוּ, וְנֶאֱמָנִים דְּבָרֶיךָ, וְדָבָר אֶחָד מִדְּבָרֶיךָ אָחוֹר לֹא יָשׁוּב רֵיקָם, כִּי אֵל מֶלֶךְ נֶאֱמָן (וְרַחֲמָן) אָתָּה. בָּרוּךְ אַתָּה יְיָ, הָאֵל הַנֶּאֱמָן בְּכָל דְּבָרָיו.

Be compassionate upon Zion, for it is a life-giving home for our people. Restore her soon. Blessed are You, Adonai, who brings rejoicing to Zion and her children.

רַחֵם עַל צִיּוֹן כִּי הִיא בֵּית חַיֵּינוּ, וְלַעֲלוּבַת נֶפֶשׁ תּוֹשִׁיעַ בִּמְהֵרָה בְיָמֵינוּ. בָּרוּךְ אַתָּה יְיָ, מְשַׂמֵּחַ צִיּוֹן בְּבָנֶיהָ.

Adonai our God, let us rejoice in the fulfillment of our dream of Elijah and David. Let messianic redemption come soon and bring joy to our hearts. Let us not be misled by false prophets, for You have promised that redemption's light shall never be extinguished. Blessed are You, Adonai, shield of David.

שַׂמְּחֵנוּ יְיָ אֱלֹהֵינוּ בְּאֵלִיָּהוּ הַנָּבִיא עַבְדֶּךָ, וּבְמַלְכוּת בֵּית דָּוִד מְשִׁיחֶךָ, בִּמְהֵרָה יָבֹא וְיָגֵל לִבֵּנוּ, עַל כִּסְאוֹ לֹא יֵשֵׁב זָר וְלֹא יִנְחֲלוּ עוֹד אֲחֵרִים אֶת כְּבוֹדוֹ, כִּי בְשֵׁם קָדְשְׁךָ נִשְׁבַּעְתָּ לּוֹ, שֶׁלֹּא יִכְבֶּה נֵרוֹ לְעוֹלָם וָעֶד. בָּרוּךְ אַתָּה יְיָ, מָגֵן דָּוִד.

We thank You for the Torah and worship, for the prophets, (for this Shabbat,) and for this Yom Kippur that You have given us, Adonai our God (for holiness and rest), for honor and splendor. We thank You for everything, Adonai our God. Let Your name ever be blessed by all that lives. Your word is true forever. Blessed are You, Adonai, source of all the earth, who sanctifies (Shabbat,) the people Israel and the Day of Atonement.

עַל הַתּוֹרָה, וְעַל הָעֲבוֹדָה, וְעַל
הַנְּבִיאִים, (וְעַל יוֹם הַשַּׁבָּת הַזֶּה,)
וְעַל יוֹם הַכִּפּוּרִים הַזֶּה, שֶׁנָּתַתָּ לָּנוּ
יְיָ אֱלֹהֵינוּ, (לִקְדֻשָּׁה וְלִמְנוּחָה,)
לְכָבוֹד וּלְתִפְאָרֶת. עַל הַכֹּל יְיָ
אֱלֹהֵינוּ, אֲנַחְנוּ מוֹדִים לָךְ,
וּמְבָרְכִים אוֹתָךְ, יִתְבָּרַךְ שִׁמְךָ בְּפִי
כָּל חַי תָּמִיד לְעוֹלָם וָעֶד וּדְבָרְךָ
אֱמֶת וְקַיָּם לָעַד. בָּרוּךְ אַתָּה יְיָ,
מְקַדֵּשׁ (הַשַּׁבָּת וְ) יִשְׂרָאֵל וְיוֹם
הַכִּפּוּרִים.

The Mi Sheberach prayer for healing is on p. 125.

Before Yizkor, you may wish to read or chant some version of Hineni (p. 30 or p. 32.)

We continue with Yizkor, the memorial service recited four times a year: Yom Kippur, Shemini Atzeret, Pesach, and Shavuot. These correspond to the four seasons: in each season of our lives, an opportunity to connect with, or at least to remember, our beloveds who have left this life.

Yizkor: Memorial Service

We Remember

We remember those who lived, learned,
prayed, celebrated and mourned with us in times gone by.
We remember mothers and fathers
who built a foundation for our lives.
We remember the partnership of spouses.
We remember the love that made those relationships holy.
We remember brothers and sisters.
We remember children, taken before we were ready.
We remember friends who touched our lives.
May this sanctuary be a safe container
for our memory and our grief.
O God, on this holy day, help us to remember.

And we say together:

Let their memories be a blessing.

In recalling their struggles, we become able to face our own.

Let their memories be a blessing.

In reflecting on their joy, we become able to savor our own.

Let their memories be a blessing.

Give us the courage to transform loss into hope for the future.

Let their memories be a blessing.

And we say: Amen.

To Every Thing There Is A Season
Ecclesiastes 3:1-8

To every thing there is a season,
and a time to every purpose under heaven.
A time to be born, and a time to die,
A time to plant, and a time to uproot.
A time to kill, and a time to heal,
A time to break down, and a time to build up.
A time to weep, and a time to laugh,
A time to mourn, and a time to dance.
A time to cast away stones, and a time to gather them together,
A time to embrace, and a time to refrain from embracing.
A time to seek, and a time to lose,
A time to keep, and a time to cast away.
A time to rend, and a time to sew,
A time to keep silence, and a time to speak.

Life After Death

These things I know
    how the living go on living
    and how the dead go on living with them
so that in a forest
    even a dead tree casts a shadow
    and the leaves fall one by one
and the branches break in the wind
and the bark peels off slowly
and the trunk cracks
    and the rain seeps in through the cracks

and the trunk falls to the ground
and the moss covers it
    and in the spring the rabbits find it
and build their nest
inside the dead tree
so that nothing is wasted in nature
    or in love.

(Laura Gilpin)

from What the Living Do

...For weeks now, driving, or dropping a bag of groceries in the street, the bag breaking,

I've been thinking: This is what the living do. And yesterday, hurrying along those /wobbly bricks in the Cambridge sidewalk, spilling my coffee down my wrist and sleeve,

I thought it again, and again later, when buying a hairbrush: This is it. / Parking. Slamming the car door shut in the cold. What you called that yearning.

What you finally gave up. We want the spring to come and the winter to pass. We want / whoever to call or not call, a letter, a kiss—we want more and more and then more of it.

But there are moments, walking, when I catch a glimpse of myself in the window glass, / say, the window of the corner video store, and I'm gripped by a cherishing so deep

for my own blowing hair, chapped face, and unbuttoned coat that I'm speechless: / I am living. I remember you.

(Marie Howe)

We enter the world...

Ecclesiastes Rabbah 5:14

We enter the world in the same way we depart.
We enter with a cry and go with a cry.
We enter with weeping and go with weeping.
We enter with love and go with love.
We enter with a sigh and go with a sigh.
We enter without knowing and go without knowing.
It has been taught in the name of Rabbi Meir:
When we enter the world our hands are clenched, as if to say, "The whole world is mine. I shall inherit it."
But when we take leave of it, our hands are spread open,
as if to say, "I have taken nothing from the world."

from Kaddish

May His Great Name be sanctified
by the sweet cheap sodas
you bought me and my brothers
from the laundromat vending machine
along with forbidden diner BLTs
created according to His will. *Omein*

Blessed, praised, glorified, exalted, extolled, honored, elevated,
lauded—
His Name and your name,
and the one name you called us—
"Sweetie" this, "sweetie" that—
for you could never remember
your grandchildren's names.

Blessings, hymns, praise, consolation
for the grease monkeys half your age
who flirted with you at the Olds dealership
where you kept the books upon which
all of them suckled. *Omein...*

Now that you rest in your House of Israel
made of pine, we stand with a sweating rabbi
and his minion of flies in the crux of summer
dust in our collages, rivers in our palms,
the dry taste of prayer on our lips.

Yis'ga'dal v'yis'kadash
The least we can do
is stand for you, stand
forever and ever. *Omein*

(*Alan Elyshevitz*)

Silent Prayers of Remembrance

In memory of a father:

May God remember the soul of my father who has gone to his eternal reward. I pledge acts of justice and charity in his memory. May his soul be bound in the bonds of eternal life. May he rest in the perfect joy of Your presence. Amen.

יִזְכֹּר אֱלֹהִים נִשְׁמַת אָבִי מוֹרִי...
שֶׁהָלַךְ לְעוֹלָמוֹ, בַּעֲבוּר שֶׁבְּלִי נֶֽדֶר
אֶתֵּן צְדָקָה בַּעֲדוֹ. בִּשְׂכַר זֶה, תְּהֵא
נַפְשׁוֹ צְרוּרָה בִּצְרוֹר הַחַיִּים עִם
נִשְׁמוֹת אַבְרָהָם יִצְחָק וְיַעֲקֹב, שָׂרָה
רִבְקָה רָחֵל וְלֵאָה, וְעִם שְׁאָר צַדִּיקִים
וְצִדְקָנִיּוֹת שֶׁבְּגַן עֵֽדֶן, וְנֹאמַר אָמֵן.

In memory of a mother:

May God remember the soul of my mother who has gone to her eternal reward. I pledge acts of justice and charity in her memory. May her soul be bound in the bonds of eternal life. May she rest in the perfect joy of Your presence. Amen.

יִזְכֹּר אֱלֹהִים נִשְׁמַת אִמִּי מוֹרָתִי...
שֶׁהָלְכָה לְעוֹלָמָהּ, בַּעֲבוּר שֶׁבְּלִי נֶֽדֶר
אֶתֵּן צְדָקָה בַּעֲדוֹ. בִּשְׂכַר זֶה, תְּהֵא
נַפְשָׁהּ צְרוּרָה בִּצְרוֹר הַחַיִּים עִם
נִשְׁמוֹת אַבְרָהָם יִצְחָק וְיַעֲקֹב, שָׂרָה
רִבְקָה רָחֵל וְלֵאָה, וְעִם שְׁאָר צַדִּיקִים
וְצִדְקָנִיּוֹת שֶׁבְּגַן עֵֽדֶן, וְנֹאמַר אָמֵן.

In memory of a husband:

May God remember the soul of my husband who has gone to his eternal reward. May his soul be bound in the bonds of eternal life. May he rest in the perfect joy of Your presence. Amen.

יִזְכּוֹר אֱלֹהִים נִשְׁמַת בַּעְלִי הַיָּקָר...
שֶׁהָלַךְ לְעוֹלָמוֹ. בַּעֲבוּר שֶׁאֲנִי נוֹדֵר
צְדָקָה בַּעֲדוֹ, בִּשְׂכַר זֶה, תְּהֵא נַפְשׁוֹ
צְרוּרָה בִּצְרוֹר הַחַיִּים עִם נִשְׁמוֹת
אַבְרָהָם יִצְחָק וְיַעֲקֹב, שָׂרָה רִבְקָה
רָחֵל וְלֵאָה, וְעִם שְׁאָר צַדִּיקִים
וְצִדְקָנִיּוֹת שֶׁבְּגַן עֵֽדֶן. אָמֵן.

In memory of a wife:

May God remember the soul of my wife who has gone to her eternal reward. May her soul be bound in the bonds of eternal life. May she rest satisfied in the perfect joy of Your presence. Amen.

יִזְכּוֹר אֱלֹהִים נִשְׁמַת אִשְׁתִּי הַיְקָרָה...
שֶׁהָלְכָה לְעוֹלָמָהּ. בַּעֲבוּר שֶׁאֲנִי נוֹדֵר
צְדָקָה בַּעֲדָהּ, בִּשְׂכַר זֶה, תְּהֵא נַפְשָׁהּ
צְרוּרָה בִּצְרוֹר הַחַיִּים עִם נִשְׁמוֹת
אַבְרָהָם יִצְחָק וְיַעֲקֹב, שָׂרָה רִבְקָה
רָחֵל וְלֵאָה, וְעִם שְׁאָר צַדִּיקִים
וְצִדְקָנִיּוֹת שֶׁבְּגַן עֵדֶן. אָמֵן.

In memory of a son:

May God remember the soul of my beloved son who has gone to his eternal reward. May his soul be bound in the bonds of eternal life. May he rest in the perfect joy of Your presence. Amen.

יִזְכֹּר אֱלֹהִים נִשְׁמַת בְּנִי הָאָהוּב...
מַחְמַד עֵינַי שֶׁהָלַךְ לְעוֹלָמוֹ. אָנָּא
תְּהִי נַפְשׁוֹ צְרוּרָה בִּצְרוֹר הַחַיִּים
וּתְהִי מְנוּחָתוֹ כָּבוֹד, שֹׂבַע שְׂמָחוֹת
אֶת–פָּנֶיךָ, נְעִימוֹת בִּימִינְךָ נֶצַח. אָמֵן.

In memory of a daughter:

May God remember the soul of my beloved daughter who has gone to her eternal reward. May her soul be bound in the bonds of eternal life. May she rest in the perfect joy of Your presence. Amen.

יִזְכֹּר אֱלֹהִים נִשְׁמַת בִּתִּי הָאֲהוּבָה...
מַחְמַד עֵינַי שֶׁהָלְכָה לְעוֹלָמָהּ. אָנָּא
תְּהִי נַפְשָׁהּ צְרוּרָה בִּצְרוֹר הַחַיִּים
וּתְהִי מְנוּחָתָהּ כָּבוֹד, שֹׂבַע שְׂמָחוֹת
אֶת–פָּנֶיךָ, נְעִימוֹת בִּימִינְךָ נֶצַח.
אָמֵן.

In memory of other relatives and friends:

יִזְכֹּר אֱלֹהִים נִשְׁמוֹת · קְרוֹבַי
וְרֵעַי שֶׁהָלְכוּ לְעוֹלָמָם. הִנְנִי
נודר/ת* צְדָקָה · בַּעַד הַזְכָּרַת
נִשְׁמוֹתֵיהֶם. אָנָּא · תִּהְיֶינָה
נַפְשׁוֹתֵיהֶם צְרוּרוֹת · בִּצְרוֹר
הַחַיִּים · וּתְהִי מְנוּחָתָם · כָּבוֹד,
שֹׂבַע שְׂמָחוֹת אֶת-פָּנֶיךָ,
נְעִימוֹת · בִּימִינְךָ נֶצַח. אָמֵן.

May God remember the soul of my relatives and friends who have gone to their eternal reward. I pledge acts of justice and charity in their memories. May their souls be bound in the bonds of eternal life. May they rest in the perfect joy of Your presence. Amen.

In memory of those who died to sanctify God's Name:

יִזְכֹּר אֱלֹהִים נִשְׁמוֹת · כָּל-אַחֵינוּ
וְכָל-אַחְיוֹתֵינוּ, · בְּנֵי יִשְׂרָאֵל
שֶׁמָּסְרוּ אֶת-נַפְשָׁם עַל · קִדּוּשׁ
הַשֵּׁם. הִנְנִי נודר/ת* צְדָקָה
בַּעַד הַזְכָּרַת נִשְׁמוֹתֵיהֶם. אָנָּא
יִשָּׁמַע · בְּחַיֵּינוּ הֵד · גְּבוּרָתָם
וּמְסִירוּתָם וְיֵרָאֶה · בְּמַעֲשֵׂינוּ
טֹהַר לִבָּם וְתִהְיֶינָה נַפְשׁוֹתֵיהֶם
צְרוּרוֹת · בִּצְרוֹר הַחַיִּים · וּתְהִי
מְנוּחָתָם · כָּבוֹד, שֹׂבַע שְׂמָחוֹת
אֶת-פָּנֶיךָ, נְעִימוֹת · בִּימִינְךָ
נֶצַח. אָמֵן.

May God remember the soul of our brothers and sisters, martyrs of our people, who gave their lives for the sanctification of God's name. I pledge acts of justice and charity in their memories. May echoes of their bravery and devotion be heard in our lives and may the purity of their hearts be seen in our actions. May their souls be bound in the bonds of eternal life. May they rest in the perfect joy of Your presence. Amen.

* *Hebrew is a gendered language. Men say* נודר *(noder) and women say* נודרת *(noderet)*

Eil Maleh Rachamim: God of Compassion

Eil maleh rachamim,
shochen ba-m'romim.
Hamtze m'nucha n'chonah
tachat canfei ha-shekhinah,
im k'doshim u-t'horim
k'zohar harakia mazhirim,
l'neshamot y'kareinu
shehalko l'olama,
b'gan Eden t'hei menuchatam.
Ba'al harachamim yastirem
b'seter k'nafav l'olamim,
v'yitzror bitzror ha-chayyim
et-nishmoteihem,
Adonai hu n'chalatam.
V'yanuchu bashalom al
mish-k'voteiheim, v'nomar:
Amen.

אֵל מָלֵא רַחֲמִים,
שׁוֹכֵן בַּמְּרוֹמִים,
הַמְצֵא מְנוּחָה נְכוֹנָה
תַּחַת כַּנְפֵי הַשְּׁכִינָה,
עִם קְדוֹשִׁים וּטְהוֹרִים
כְּזֹהַר הָרָקִיעַ מַזְהִירִים,
לְנִשְׁמוֹת יַקִּירֵינוּ
שֶׁהָלְכוּ לְעוֹלָמָם,
בְּגַן עֵדֶן · תְּהֵא מְנוּחָתָם.
בַּעַל הָרַחֲמִים יַסְתִּירֵם בְּסֵתֶר
כְּנָפָיו לְעוֹלָמִים, וְיִצְרוֹר
בִּצְרוֹר הַחַיִּים
אֶת–נִשְׁמוֹתֵיהֶם,
יְיָ הוּא נַחֲלָתָם.
וְיָנוּחוּ · בְשָׁלוֹם עַל
מִשְׁכְּבוֹתֵיהֶם, וְנֹאמַר: אָמֵן.

Compassionate God, Spirit of the universe,
grant perfect peace
in Your sheltering Presence,
among the holy and the pure
who shine with the splendor
of the heavens,
to the souls of our dear ones
who have gone to their reward,
may the Garden of Eden
be their rest. O God of mercy,
guard them forever in the shadow of Your wings.
May their souls be bound up
in the bond of life.
May they rest in peace.
And let us say: Amen.

Psalm 23

A psalm of David:
God is my shepherd;
I shall not want.
God makes me lie down in
green pastures, and leads me
beside still waters
to restore my soul;
God leads me in paths
of righteousness
for the sake of God's name.
Though I walk through the
valley of the shadow of death,
I shall fear no evil,
for You are with me;
Your rod and Your staff,
they comfort me.
You set a table before me
in the presence of my enemies
You anoint my head with oil;
my cup overflows.
Truly goodness and mercy
will follow me
all the days of my life
And I will dwell
in the house of Adonai forever.

מִזְמוֹר לְדָוִד:
יְיָ רֹעִי, לֹא אֶחְסָר.
בִּנְאוֹת דֶּשֶׁא, יַרְבִּיצֵנִי;
עַל-מֵי מְנֻחוֹת יְנַהֲלֵנִי.
נַפְשִׁי יְשׁוֹבֵב;
יַנְחֵנִי בְמַעְגְּלֵי-צֶדֶק,
לְמַעַן שְׁמוֹ.
גַּם כִּי-אֵלֵךְ בְּגֵיא צַלְמָוֶת,
לֹא-אִירָא רָע כִּי-אַתָּה עִמָּדִי
שִׁבְטְךָ וּמִשְׁעַנְתֶּךָ,
הֵמָּה יְנַחֲמֻנִי.
תַּעֲרֹךְ לְפָנַי, שֻׁלְחָן נֶגֶד צֹרְרָי;
דִּשַּׁנְתָּ בַשֶּׁמֶן רֹאשִׁי,
כּוֹסִי רְוָיָה.
אַךְ טוֹב וָחֶסֶד יִרְדְּפוּנִי
כָּל-יְמֵי חַיָּי;
וְשַׁבְתִּי בְּבֵית-יְיָ לְאֹרֶךְ יָמִים.

Eli, Eli

Eli, Eli shelo yigameir le'olam
Hachol vechayam
Rishrush shel hamayim
Berak hashamayim
Tefilat ha'adam.

אֵלִי, אֵלִי שֶׁלֹּא יִגָּמֵר לְעוֹלָם
הַחוֹל וְהַיָּם
רִשְׁרוּשׁ שֶׁל הַמַּיִם
בְּרַק הַשָּׁמַיִם, תְּפִלַּת הָאָדָם.

My God, my God, I pray that these things never end: the sand and the sea, the rush of the waters, the crash of the heavens, the prayer of the heart. *(Hannah Szenes)*

Mourner's *Kaddish*

Yitgadal v'yitkadash, shmeh rabah.B'alma di vra chiruteh, v'yamlich malchuteh b'chayyeichon u'v'yomeichon u'vchayyei d'chol beit Yisrael. Ba'agala u-vizman kariv v'imru amen.

יִתְגַּדַּל וְיִתְקַדַּשׁ שְׁמֵהּ רַבָּא.
בְּעָלְמָא דִּי בְרָא כִרְעוּתֵהּ,
וְיַמְלִיךְ מַלְכוּתֵהּ בְּחַיֵּיכוֹן
וּבְיוֹמֵיכוֹן וּבְחַיֵּי דְכָל בֵּית
יִשְׂרָאֵל.
בַּעֲגָלָא וּבִזְמַן קָרִיב וְאִמְרוּ אָמֵן:

□ Y'hei sh'mei raba m'varakh l'olam ol'almey almaya.

□יְהֵא שְׁמֵהּ רַבָּא מְבָרַךְ לְעָלַם
וּלְעָלְמֵי עָלְמַיָּא:

Yitbarach v'yishtabach, v'yitpa'ar v'yit-romam v'yit-naseh. V'yithadar v'yitaleh v'yithallal shmeh d'kudh'sha b'rich hu. L'eyla u l'eyla min kol birchata v'shirata, tushbechata v'nechemata, damiran b'alma, v'imru amen.

יִתְבָּרַךְ וְיִשְׁתַּבַּח, וְיִתְפָּאַר
וְיִתְרוֹמַם וְיִתְנַשֵּׂא וְיִתְהַדָּר
וְיִתְעַלֶּה וְיִתְהַלָּל שְׁמֵהּ דְּקֻדְשָׁא
בְּרִיךְ הוּא לְעֵלָּא וּלְעֵלָּא מִן כָּל
בִּרְכָתָא וְשִׁירָתָא, תֻּשְׁבְּחָתָא
וְנֶחֱמָתָא, דַּאֲמִירָן בְּעָלְמָא,
וְאִמְרוּ אָמֵן:

Y'hei shlama raba min shemaya v'chayyim tovim aleinu v'al kol Yisrael, v'imru amen.

יְהֵא שְׁלָמָא רַבָּא מִן שְׁמַיָּא
וְחַיִּים עָלֵינוּ וְעַל כָּל יִשְׂרָאֵל,
וְאִמְרוּ אָמֵן:

Oseh shalom bimromav, hu ya'aseh shalom, aleinu v'al kol yisrael, v'al kol yoshvei tevel, v'imru Amen.

עֹשֶׂה שָׁלוֹם בִּמְרוֹמָיו הוּא יַעֲשֶׂה
שָׁלוֹם עָלֵינוּ וְעַל כָּל יִשְׂרָאֵל,
וְעַל כָּל יוֹשְׁבֵי תֵבֵל, וְאִמְרוּ אָמֵן:

I pray to You God,
that the power residing in Your Great Name
be increased and made sacred
in this world which God created freely
in order to preside in it, and grow its freeing power
and bring about the messianic era.
May this happen during our lifetime
and during the lifetime of all of us
living now, the house of Israel.
May this happen soon, without delay
and by saying AMEN we express agreement and hope, **AMEN**.

**May the immense power residing in God's great name
flow freely into our world and worlds beyond.**

May that Great Name, that sacred energy,
be shaped and made effective
and be acknowledged and be given the right honor
and be seen as beautiful and uplifting and bring jubilation.
Way beyond our input of worshipful song and praise
which we express in this world
as our agreement and hope, **AMEN**.

May that endless peace that heaven can release for us
bring about the good life for us and for all Israel
as we express our agreement and hope, **AMEN**.

You, who harmonize it all on the highest planes:
bring harmony and peace to us,
to all Israel and all sentient beings
as we express our agreement and hope, **AMEN.**

(Translation: R' Zalman Shachter-Shalomi z"l.)

We move now into Unetaneh Tokef. During Yizkor, we remembered our loved ones, inscribed on our hearts; during the prayer to come, we acknowledge that we inscribe the stories of our own lives with our choices in each day.

Unetaneh Tokef

Unetaneh tokef kedushat hayom, kee hu nora ve'ayom; uvo tinasei malchutecha, veyikon bechesed kisecha, veteisheiv alav be'emet. Emet kee atah hu dayan umochi'ach, veyodei'a va'eid, vechoteiv vechoteim, vesofeir umoneh, vetizkor kol hanishkachot; vetiftach et sefer hazichronot, umei'eilav yikarei, vechotam yad kol adam bo.

וּנְתַנֶּה תֹּקֶף קְדֻשַּׁת הַיּוֹם, כִּי הוּא נוֹרָא וְאָיוֹם: וּבוֹ תִנָּשֵׂא מַלְכוּתֶךָ, וְיִכּוֹן בְּחֶסֶד כִּסְאֶךָ, וְתֵשֵׁב עָלָיו בֶּאֱמֶת. אֱמֶת כִּי אַתָּה הוּא דַיָּן וּמוֹכִיחַ, וְיוֹדֵעַ וָעֵד, וְכוֹתֵב וְחוֹתֵם, וְסוֹפֵר וּמוֹנֶה, וְתִזְכּוֹר כָּל הַנִּשְׁכָּחוֹת: וְתִפְתַּח אֶת סֵפֶר הַזִּכְרוֹנוֹת, וּמֵאֵלָיו יִקָּרֵא, וְחוֹתַם יַד כָּל אָדָם בּוֹ.

Let us declare the sacred power of this day, for it is awesome and dreadful. On this day, Your rule is exalted, Your throne is established with love, and You sit upon it in truth. For it is truth that You judge and determine, know and witness, write and seal, count and account. You remember all that was forgotten. You open the Book of Memory. It reads from itself and the signature of every human being is in it.

The great shofar sounds—the still, small voice is heard. Even the angels are seized by trembling and fear as they declare, “This is the day of judgment when even the hosts of heaven are judged.” Nothing can evade Your eyes in judgment. All who live must pass before You like flocks before the shepherd. Just as a shepherd inspects the sheep and makes them pass under the staff, so do You account for the souls of all who live. You weigh the measure of each life and inscribe the verdict of their judgment.

וּבְשׁוֹפָר גָּדוֹל יִתָּקַע, וְקוֹל דְּמָמָה דַקָּה יִשָּׁמַע: וּמַלְאָכִים יֵחָפֵזוּן, וְחִיל וּרְעָדָה יֹאחֵזוּן, וְיֹאמְרוּ הִנֵּה יוֹם הַדִּין, לִפְקוֹד עַל צְבָא מָרוֹם בַּדִּין, כִּי לֹא יִזְכּוּ בְעֵינֶיךָ בַּדִּין. וְכָל בָּאֵי עוֹלָם יַעַבְרוּן לְפָנֶיךָ כִּבְנֵי מָרוֹן. כְּבַקָּרַת רוֹעֶה עֶדְרוֹ, מַעֲבִיר צֹאנוֹ תַּחַת שִׁבְטוֹ, כֵּן תַּעֲבִיר וְתִסְפּוֹר וְתִמְנֶה, וְתִפְקוֹד נֶפֶשׁ כָּל חָי, וְתַחְתּוֹךְ קִצְבָה לְכָל בְּרִיָּה, וְתִכְתּוֹב אֶת גְּזַר דִּינָם.

□ B’Rosh Hashanah yikateivun, uv’Yom tzom Kippur yeichateimun.

□ בְּרֹאשׁ הַשָּׁנָה יִכָּתֵבוּן, וּבְיוֹם צוֹם כִּפּוּר יֵחָתֵמוּן.

For on Rosh Hashanah it is written,
and on Yom Kippur it is sealed:

כַּמָּה יַעַבְרוּן, וְכַמָּה יִבָּרֵאוּן:
מִי יִחְיֶה, וּמִי יָמוּת: מִי בְקִצּוֹ,
וּמִי לֹא בְקִצּוֹ: מִי בָאֵשׁ, וּמִי
בַמַּֽיִם: מִי בַחֶֽרֶב, וּמִי בַחַיָּה:
מִי בָרָעָב, וּמִי בַצָּמָא: מִי
בָרַֽעַשׁ, וּמִי בַמַּגֵּפָה: מִי
בַחֲנִיקָה, וּמִי בִסְקִילָה: מִי
יָנֽוּחַ, וּמִי יָנֽוּעַ: מִי יִשָּׁקֵט, וּמִי
יִטָּרֵף: מִי יִשָּׁלֵו, וּמִי יִתְיַסָּר: מִי
יֵעָנִי, וּמִי יֵעָשֵׁר: מִי יִשָּׁפֵל, וּמִי
יָרוּם.

Kamah ya'avrun, vechamah yibarei'un; mi yichyeh, umi yamut; mi vekitso, umi lo vekitso; mi va'eish, umi vamayim; mi vacherev umi vachayah; mi vara'av, umi vatsama; mi varei'ash, umi vamageifah; mi vachanikah, umi viskilah; mi yanu'ach, umi yanu'a; mi yishakeit umi yitareif; mi yishaleiv, umi yityasar; mi yei'ani, umi yei'asheir; mi yishafeil, umi yarum.

How many will pass from this life and how many will be created; who shall live and who shall die; who in old age, and who in youth; who by fire and who by water; who by sword and who by beast; who by famine and who by stoning; who shall find rest and who shall wander; who shall be torn and who shall be whole; who shall be tranquil and who shall be driven; who shall be impoverished and who shall be enriched; who shall be laid low and who shall be exalted.

☐ וּתְשׁוּבָה וּתְפִלָּה וּצְדָקָה
מַעֲבִירִין אֶת רֹֽעַ הַגְּזֵרָה.

☐ Utshuvah utfilah utzedakah ma'avirin et ro'a hagezeirah.

But *teshuvah*, *tefilah*, and *tzedakah*
(repentance, prayer, and righteous giving)
temper the harshness of the decree.

כִּי כְּשִׁמְךָ כֵּן תְּהִלָּתֶךָ, קָשֶׁה לִכְעוֹס וְנוֹחַ לִרְצוֹת: כִּי לֹא תַחְפּוֹץ בְּמוֹת הַמֵּת, כִּי אִם בְּשׁוּבוֹ מִדַּרְכּוֹ וְחָיָה. וְעַד יוֹם מוֹתוֹ תְּחַכֶּה לוֹ, אִם יָשׁוּב מִיַּד תְּקַבְּלוֹ.

For as Your name is mercy, so is Your mercy praised. You are slow to anger and ready to forgive. You do not seek our death, rather that we turn from our ways and live. Even until the day of our death You wait for us, to take us back the moment we turn to You.

אֱמֶת כִּי אַתָּה הוּא יוֹצְרָם, וְאַתָּה יוֹדֵעַ יִצְרָם, כִּי הֵם בָּשָׂר וָדָם. אָדָם יְסוֹדוֹ מֵעָפָר וְסוֹפוֹ לֶעָפָר: בְּנַפְשׁוֹ יָבִיא לַחְמוֹ: מָשׁוּל כְּחֶרֶס הַנִּשְׁבָּר, כְּחָצִיר יָבֵשׁ, וּכְצִיץ נוֹבֵל, כְּצֵל עוֹבֵר, וּכְעָנָן כָּלָה, וּכְרוּחַ נוֹשָׁבֶת, וּכְאָבָק פּוֹרֵחַ, וְכַחֲלוֹם יָעוּף.

Truly, You are our creator and You know our ways—good and bad—for we are but flesh and blood. Our origin is dust and to dust is our end. Our sustenance is bought with peril. We are a broken urn, withering grass, a fading flower, a passing shadow, a vanishing cloud, a blowing wind, settling dust, a fleeting dream.

וְאַתָּה הוּא מֶלֶךְ אֵל חַי וְקַיָּם.

Ve'atah hu melech Eil chai vekayam.

But You are the ruler,
the God of life and all that exists.

A word about prostration

The prayer we know as the *Aleinu,* which closes every service, originated in the high holiday liturgy. The Aleinu we're about to recite is also known as the Great Aleinu. There is a custom of praying this prayer with our whole bodies.

When we recite the words *va-anachnu kor'im,* "We bow low and prostrate ourselves in thanks," some of us will drop to our knees and place our foreheads on the earth. This is done only at this time of year.

For some, this position evokes the comfort and surrender of "child's pose" in yoga. For others it evokes the posture assumed by our spiritual cousins, the descendants of Ishmael, five times a day in prayer. And for others, it is an opportunity to "let go and let God."

Of course, if this is not comfortable for you—either physically or emotionally—you are welcome to remain standing.

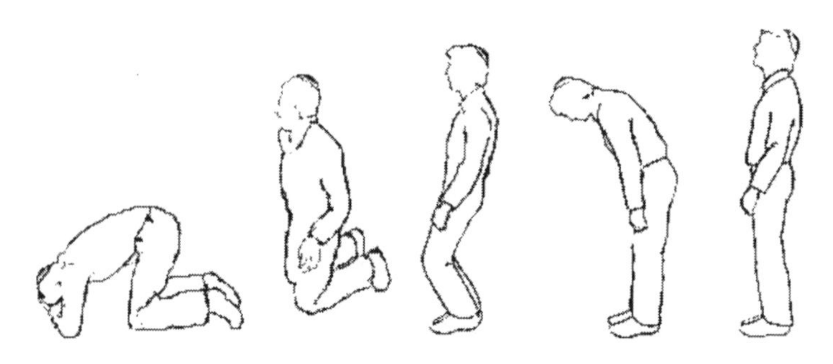

Illustration of classical Jewish prostration

The Great Aleinu

□ עָלֵינוּ לְשַׁבֵּחַ לַאֲדוֹן הַכֹּל,
לָתֵת גְּדֻלָּה לְיוֹצֵר בְּרֵאשִׁית,
שֶׁלֹּא עָשָׂנוּ כְּגוֹיֵי הָאֲרָצוֹת,
וְלֹא שָׂמָנוּ כְּמִשְׁפְּחוֹת
הָאֲדָמָה, שֶׁלֹּא שָׂם חֶלְקֵנוּ
כָּהֶם, וְגֹרָלֵנוּ כְּכָל הֲמוֹנָם.

□ Aleinu l'shabe'ach la'adon hakol, latet gedulah l'yotzer breshit. Shelo asanu k'goyei ha'aratzot, v'lo samanu k'mishpachot ha-adamah. Shelo sam chelkenu kahem, v'goralenu k'chol hamonam.

It is up to us to praise the Source of all, to exalt the Molder of creation. We are made for God, like the nations of the earth; we are placed here for God, like the families of humanity. For God's own sake is our portion here and our fate here.

□ וַאֲנַחְנוּ* כּוֹרְעִים*
וּמִשְׁתַּחֲוִים וּמוֹדִים*, לִפְנֵי
מֶלֶךְ, מַלְכֵי הַמְּלָכִים, הַקָּדוֹשׁ
בָּרוּךְ הוּא.

□ Va-anachnu* korim*, u-mishtachavim u-modim*, lifnei melech malchei ham'lachim, hakadosh baruch hu.

We bow low and prostrate in thanks before the Source of all sources, the Holy One, blessed is God.

** On these three words, many people 1) drop down to their knees, 2) place their hands on the floor, and 3) touch their foreheads to the ground. See more about this custom on the note on p. 157.*

□ שֶׁהוּא נוֹטֶה שָׁמַיִם וְיֹסֵד אָרֶץ, וּמוֹשַׁב יְקָרוֹ בַּשָּׁמַיִם מִמַּעַל, וּשְׁכִינַת עֻזּוֹ בְּגָבְהֵי מְרוֹמִים, הוּא אֱלֹהֵינוּ אֵין עוֹד. אֱמֶת מַלְכֵּנוּ אֶפֶס זוּלָתוֹ, כַּכָּתוּב בְּתוֹרָתוֹ: וְיָדַעְתָּ הַיּוֹם וַהֲשֵׁבֹתָ אֶל לְבָבֶךָ, כִּי יְיָ הוּא הָאֱלֹהִים בַּשָּׁמַיִם מִמַּעַל, וְעַל הָאָרֶץ מִתָּחַת, אֵין עוֹד:

□ Shehu noteh shamayim v'yosed aretz, u-moshav yekaro bashamayim mima'al, uschinat uzo b'gavheh meromim. Hu eloheinu, ein od. Emet malkenu efes zulato. Kakatuv b'torato: v'yadata hayom vahashevota el levavecha. Ki adonai, hu ha-elohim, bashamayim mima'al, v'al ha-aretz mitachat ein od.

God sets out the heavens and establishes the earth. God's honored place is in the heights of our aspirations; God's powerful presence is in the heavens of our hopes. This is our God, there is none else. God is the world's truth; there is nothing that God is not.

"There is nothing that God is not..."

The Kaddish: A Doorway in Prayer

The Kaddish which follows—known
as *Kaddish shalem* (whole Kaddish) —is the doorway
out of this morning's services.

Where have today's prayers taken you?
Whatever you're feeling in this moment,
bring that into your prayer.

Kaddish Shalem

Yitgadal v'yitkadash, shmeh rabah. B'alma divra chiruteh, v'yamlich malchuteh b'chayyeichon u'v'yomeichon u'vchayyei d'chol beit Yisrael. Ba'agala u-vizman kariv v'imru amen.

יִתְגַּדַּל וְיִתְקַדַּשׁ שְׁמֵהּ רַבָּא.
בְּעָלְמָא דִּי בְרָא כִרְעוּתֵהּ,
וְיַמְלִיךְ מַלְכוּתֵהּ בְּחַיֵּיכוֹן
וּבְיוֹמֵיכוֹן וּבְחַיֵּי דְכָל בֵּית
יִשְׂרָאֵל. בַּעֲגָלָא וּבִזְמַן קָרִיב
וְאִמְרוּ אָמֵן:

□ Y'hei sh'mei raba m'varakh l'olam ol'almey almaya.

□ יְהֵא שְׁמֵהּ רַבָּא מְבָרַךְ
לְעָלַם וּלְעָלְמֵי עָלְמַיָּא:

Magnified and sanctified! Magnified and sanctified! May God's Great Name fill the world God created. May God's splendor be seen in the world in your life, in your days, in the life of all Israel. Quickly and soon! And let us say, Amen.

Forever may the Great Name be blessed!

Yitbarach v'yishtabach, v'yitpa'ar v'yit-romam v'yit-naseh. V'yithadar v'yitaleh v'yithallal shmeh d'kud'sha b'rich hu. L'eyla u'leyla min kol birchata v'shirata, tushbechata v'nechemata, damiran b'alma, v'imru amen.

יִתְבָּרַךְ וְיִשְׁתַּבַּח, וְיִתְפָּאַר
וְיִתְרוֹמַם וְיִתְנַשֵּׂא וְיִתְהַדָּר
וְיִתְעַלֶּה וְיִתְהַלָּל שְׁמֵהּ
דְּקֻדְשָׁא בְּרִיךְ הוּא לְעֵלָּא
וּלְעֵלָּא מִכָּל בִּרְכָתָא
וְשִׁירָתָא, תֻּשְׁבְּחָתָא
וְנֶחֱמָתָא, דַּאֲמִירָן בְּעָלְמָא,
וְאִמְרוּ אָמֵן:

Blessed and praised! Splendid and supreme! May the holy name, Bless God, be praised, beyond all the blessings and songs, comforts and consolations, that can be offered in this world. And let us say: Amen.

Titkabel tzlo'uthon uva-ut'hon d'chol beit Yisrael kadam avuhon di vishmaia v'imru Amen.

תִּתְקַבֵּל צְלוֹתְהוֹן וּבָעוּתְהוֹן דְּכָל (בֵּית) יִשְׂרָאֵל קֳדָם אֲבוּהוֹן דִּי בִשְׁמַיָּא וְאִמְרוּ אָמֵן:

Y'hei shlama raba min shemaya v'chayyim tovim aleinu v'al kol Yisrael, v'imru amen.

יְהֵא שְׁלָמָא רַבָּא מִן שְׁמַיָּא וְחַיִּים עָלֵינוּ וְעַל כָּל יִשְׂרָאֵל, וְאִמְרוּ אָמֵן:

Oseh shalom bimromav, hu ya'aseh shalom, aleinu v'al kol yisrael, v'al kol yoshvei tevel, v'imru Amen.

עֹשֶׂה שָׁלוֹם בִּמְרוֹמָיו הוּא יַעֲשֶׂה שָׁלוֹם עָלֵינוּ וְעַל כָּל יִשְׂרָאֵל, וְעַל כָּל יוֹשְׁבֵי תֵבֵל, וְאִמְרוּ אָמֵן:

Accept them! Accept them! May our words of prayer and pleading from all the people of Israel be accepted before God in heaven. And let us say, Amen!

May there be peace and life, great peace and life from heaven above for us and all Israel. And let us say, Amen!

May the One who makes peace in the high heavens make peace for us, for our whole community, and for all the peoples of the world. And let us say: Amen.

Adon Olam

Adon olam asher malach,
beterem kol yetsir nivra.
Le'eit na'asah vecheftso kol,
azai melech shemo nikra.

אֲדוֹן עוֹלָם אֲשֶׁר מָלַךְ,
בְּטֶרֶם · כָּל יְצִיר נִבְרָא.
לְעֵת נַעֲשָׂה בְחֶפְצוֹ · כֹּל,
אֲזַי מֶלֶךְ שְׁמוֹ נִקְרָא.

You are the source of all, who reigned before any being was created; When all was done according to Your will, Your rule already had been proclaimed.

Ve'acharei kichlot hakol,
levado yimloch nora.
Vehu haya vehu hoveh,
vehu yiheyeh betifarah.

וְאַחֲרֵי · כִּכְלוֹת הַכֹּל,
לְבַדּוֹ יִמְלוֹךְ נוֹרָא.
וְהוּא הָיָה, וְהוּא הֹוֶה,
וְהוּא יִהְיֶה, · בְּתִפְאָרָה.

And after all has ended, still, You alone will rule in majesty; You were, You are, You will be in glory.

Vehu echad ve'ein sheini,
lehamshil lo lehachbirah.
Beli reishit beli tachlit,
velo ha'oz vehamisrah.

וְהוּא אֶחָד וְאֵין שֵׁנִי,
לְהַמְשִׁיל לוֹ לְהַחְבִּירָה. ·
בְּלִי רֵאשִׁית · בְּלִי תַכְלִית,
ולוֹ הָעֹז וְהַמִּשְׂרָה.

You are One, there is none to compare or consort with You. Without beginning, without end, all power and all order come from You.

Vehu Eili vechai go'ali,
vetsur chevli be'eit tzarah.
Vehu nisi umanos lee
menat kosi beyom ekra.

וְהוּא אֵלִי וְחַי · גֹּאֲלִי,
וְצוּר חֶבְלִי · בְּעֵת צָרָה.
וְהוּא נִסִּי · וּמָנוֹס לִי
מְנָת · כּוֹסִי · בְּיוֹם אֶקְרָא.

You are my God, my living redeemer, You are my rock in time of distress; You are my banner and my refuge, You fill my cup when I cry to You.

Beyado afkid ruchi,
be'eit ishan ve'a'ira.
Ve'im ruchi geviyati,
Adonai li velo ira.

בְּיָדוֹ אַפְקִיד רוּחִי,
בְּעֵת אִישַׁן וְאָעִירָה.
וְעִם רוּחִי · גְּוִיָּתִי,
יְיָ לִי וְלֹא אִירָא.

Into Your hands I entrust my spirit, When I sleep and when I wake; And with my spirit, my body, too: You are with me, I shall not fear.

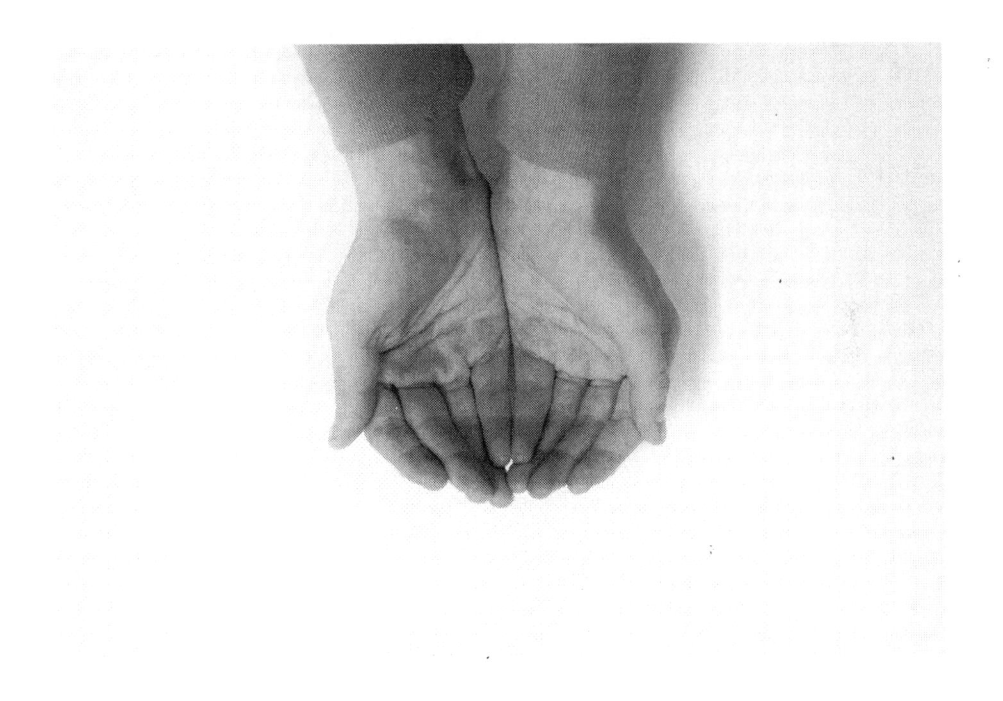

This piyyut *(hymn) has been a regular part of Jewish daily, Shabbat, and festival prayer since 1500 C.E. It has been attributed to Solomon ibn Gabirol (1021–1058), to Rav Hai Gaon (939-1038) and even to the Talmudic sage Yohanan ben Zakkai.*

Avodah Service

This adaptation of the ancient Avodah service is a guided meditation which may be read aloud.

Today we create atonement with our words. But once upon a time, atonement was achieved through the actions of the High Priest. When the Temple fell, the rabbis preserved the story of the ritual. Today we remember how we used to atone.

Make sure you're seated comfortably: feet on the floor, seat firmly planted. Stretch a little if you need to; relax your neck and shoulders. If you're comfortable doing so, close your eyes.

We are in Jerusalem, city of white stone, City of David. It's just before dawn on the day before Yom Kippur. You are the High Priest, the *Kohen ha-Gadol,* and you have risen early. A flock of faithful have gathered around you, and they accompany you to the eastern gate. It's still dark. Stars are sprinkled across the sky.

A group of elders has gathered to remind you how to light the incense within the Holy of Holies. You realize again just how risky this ritual is. You can't help trembling. You don't feel worthy.

All day long you relearn the rites. The other priests gather around you. They tell stories and sing songs to keep you awake all night.

Now the sun is just beginning to rise on Yom Kippur, pinking the hills and the walls of the city. They spread a linen veil over you to conceal you. You remove your clothes, immerse in a mikveh of living waters, and change into golden robes.

You wash your hands and feet and prepare the daily offering. With help from one of your colleagues, you make the offering to God, burning the animal on the altar. You burn the incense and the smoke rises to God. Smell the charred meat and the incense.

Again they spread out a white veil to conceal you. You take off your clothes again, immerse again, and change into white linen garments. You approach your own bull, large and fat, snorting and stamping its hooves. You place your hands on its head and you confess your own sins, withholding nothing in your heart. Place your hands on the head of this powerful bull and confess everywhere that you have missed the mark in the last year.

And you say: O God, I have sinned! I and my household have done wrong! I beg of you, by Your holy name, forgive, pardon, and grant atonement for our sins. As it is written in Torah,

Ki bayom hazeh y'chaper ale-ichem l'taher etchem, mikol chatateichem lifnei Havayah!	כִּי-בַיּוֹם הַזֶּה יְכַפֵּר עֲלֵיכֶם, לְטַהֵר אֶתְכֶם מִכֹּל חַטֹּאתֵיכֶם לִפְנֵי הויה!

For on this day I will make atonement for you and purify you from all of your sins/ missings-of-the-mark before God!

Everyone is standing in the courtyard around you. When they hear you say God's holiest name, they fall on their faces and say

Baruch shem k'vod malchuto l'olam va'ed.	בָּרוּךְ שֵׁם כְּבוֹד מַלְכוּתוֹ לְעוֹלָם וָעֶד.

Through time and space, Your glory shines, Majestic One!

You say to them: "You shall be cleansed!" Hear your voice thunder forth. Know that everyone here believes you.

Now you go to the eastern end of the courtyard. You see two goats, purchased with funds from the whole community. You reach for the box held by one of your junior colleagues which holds two lots: one bears God's name, and one says "For Azazel." Shake the box, then stick your hand in and withdraw the lots. Attach them to the goats and call out God's name. On the goat which is meant for Azazel, you tie a crimson thread. Lead it to the gate from where it will be sent forth. Secure it there for now.

Now you confess the sins of the priests. And you say: O God, we have sinned! I and my household, Your priests, have done wrong! I beg of you, by Your holy name, forgive, pardon, and grant atonement for our sins. As it is written in Torah,

Ki bayom hazeh y'chaper ale-ichem l'taher etchem, mikol chatateichem lifnei Havayah!	כִּי-בַיּוֹם הַזֶּה יְכַפֵּר עֲלֵיכֶם, לְטַהֵר אֶתְכֶם מִכֹּל חַטֹּאתֵיכֶם לִפְנֵי הויה!

For on this day I will make atonement for you and purify you from all of your sins/ missings-of-the-mark before God!

Everyone is standing in the courtyard around you. When they hear you say God's holiest name, they fall on their faces and say

Baruch shem k'vod malchuto l'olam va'ed.	בָּרוּךְ שֵׁם כְּבוֹד מַלְכוּתוֹ לְעוֹלָם וָעֶד.

Through time and space, Your glory shines, Majestic One!

You say to them: "You shall be cleansed!" Hear your voice thunder forth. Know that everyone here believes you.

Now you fetch the sharpest knife in the temple precinct. Slaughter the bull, quickly, so that it does not suffer. Collect its blood in a basin, and put that basin on a stand, full of steaming blood.

Slaughter the goat which received the lot "for Adonai." Collect its blood lovingly in another holy basin. Mix the two bowls of blood, take them to the Golden Altar, and sprinkle the blood: once, twice, thrice, four times, five times, six times, seven times.

Return to the goat you tied near the gate, and confess the sins of the entire people. And you say: O God, we have sinned! I and my household, Your entire community, have done wrong! I beg of you, by Your holy name, forgive, pardon, and grant atonement for our sins. As it is written in Torah,

Ki bayom hazeh y'chaper aleichem l'taher etchem, mikol chatateichem lifnei Havayah!	כִּי-בַיּוֹם הַזֶּה יְכַפֵּר עֲלֵיכֶם, לְטַהֵר אֶתְכֶם מִכֹּל חַטֹּאתֵיכֶם לִפְנֵי הויה!

For on this day I will make atonement for you and purify you from all of your sins/ missings-of-the-mark before God!

Everyone is standing in the courtyard around you. When they hear you say God's holiest name, they fall on their faces and say

Baruch shem k'vod malchuto l'olam va'ed.	בָּרוּךְ שֵׁם כְּבוֹד מַלְכוּתוֹ לְעוֹלָם וָעֶד.

Through time and space, Your glory shines, Majestic One!

You say to them: "You shall be cleansed!" Hear your voice thunder forth. Know that everyone here believes you.

Send the scapegoat out into the wilderness. Watch it bound across the rocks and hills. It takes the sins of the entire community with it.

Return to the altar. Here you're going to burn parts of the bull, and parts of the goat. The air smells like charring meat; smell the smoke and the burning flesh. Here you read from Torah, in front of the altar and the sacrifice.

Now you wash your hands and feet again. They hold up the linen veil again. Immerse yourself in the mikveh a third time.

Now you will enter the sanctuary, and in your golden garments once more, you'll burn an incense offering and light the holy lamps. Smell the incense, sweet and strong. Remove your clothes and immerse in the sanctuary mikveh, going under the water five times. Each time the waters receive you it is like returning to the divine womb.

When you emerge, it feels as though you have been born again. Your beautiful face is like the rising sun. You can feel that all of the sins of the community, all of the sins of the priesthood, all of your household sins, all of your own sins have been washed away.

Everyone gathers around you, singing and dancing, and they escort you home. They are filled with joy. Thanks to you and the work you have done today, the whole community is cleansed. God is the mikveh of Israel; God purifies and cleanses us; God has made us clean like the angels of the morning.

And you sing this song which is one long holy Name of the One:

Source of Mercy!
With loving strength
Untie our tangles.
Through time and space
Your glory shines
Majestic One!

Ana bakoach
gedulat yemincha
tatir tzrurah.

Baruch sheim
kavod malchuto
le'olam va'ed.

אָנָּא בְּכֹחַ
גְּדֻלַּת יְמִינְךָ
תַּתִּיר צְרוּרָה.

בָּרוּךְ שֵׁם
כְּבוֹד מַלְכוּתוֹ
לְעוֹלָם וָעֶד.

All of this occurred when the Temple was on its foundation.

All of this is happening right now.

Take three deep breaths and slowly return to the here and now.

Yom Kippur Afternoon Service

We remove the Torah from the Ark while singing

Hareini M'kabel Alai

□ הֲרֵינִי מְקַבֵּל עָלַי
אֶת מִצְוַת הַבֹּרֵא
וְאָהַבְתָּ לְרֵעֲךָ כָּמוֹךָ
לְרֵעֲךָ כָּמוֹךָ!

□ Hareini m'kabel alai
Et mitzvat ha-borei
V'ahavta l'reakha camokha,
l'reakha camokha!

(Behold, I take upon myself the mitzvah of the Creator: to love my neighbor as myself!)

The blessings before and after Torah are on p. 124.

Yom Kippur Afternoon Torah Reading

Leviticus 19:9-18

First aliyah:

וּבְקֻצְרְכֶם אֶת־קְצִיר אַרְצְכֶם
לֹא תְכַלֶּה פְּאַת שָׂדְךָ לִקְצֹר
וְלֶקֶט קְצִירְךָ לֹא
תְלַקֵּט׃ וְכַרְמְךָ לֹא תְעוֹלֵל
וּפֶרֶט כַּרְמְךָ לֹא תְלַקֵּט לֶעָנִי
וְלַגֵּר תַּעֲזֹב אֹתָם אֲנִי יְיָ
אֱלֹהֵיכֶם׃ לֹא תִּגְנֹבוּ
וְלֹא־תְכַחֲשׁוּ וְלֹא־תְשַׁקְּרוּ אִישׁ
בַּעֲמִיתוֹ׃

When you reap the harvest of your land, you shall not reap all the way to the edges of your field, or gather the gleanings of your harvest. You shall not pick your vineyard bare, or gather the fallen fruit of your vineyard; you shall leave them for the poor and the stranger. I am Adonai your God. You shall not steal; you shall not deal deceitfully or falsely with one another.

Second aliyah:

You shall not swear falsely by my name, profaning the name of your God: I am Adonai. You shall not defraud your fellow. You shall not commit robbery. The wages of a worker shall not remain with you until morning. You shall not insult the deaf, or place a stumbling block before the blind. You shall fear your God: I am Adonai.

וְלֹא־תִשָּׁבְעוּ בִשְׁמִי לַשָּׁקֶר
וְחִלַּלְתָּ אֶת־שֵׁם אֱלֹהֶיךָ אֲנִי יְיָ׃
לֹא־תַעֲשֹׁק אֶת־רֵעֲךָ וְלֹא תִגְזֹל
לֹא־תָלִין פְּעֻלַּת שָׂכִיר אִתְּךָ
עַד־בֹּקֶר׃ לֹא־תְקַלֵּל חֵרֵשׁ
וְלִפְנֵי עִוֵּר לֹא תִתֵּן מִכְשֹׁל
וְיָרֵאתָ מֵּאֱלֹהֶיךָ אֲנִי יְיָ׃

Third aliyah:

You shall not render an unfair decision; do not favor the poor or show deference to the rich; judge your neighbor fairly. Do not deal basely with your fellows. Do not profit by the blood of your neighbor: I am Adonai. You shall not hate your fellow in your heart. Reprove your neighbor but incur no guilt because of your neighbor. You shall not take vengeance or bear a grudge against your fellow. Love your neighbor as yourself: I am Adonai.

לֹא־תַעֲשׂוּ עָוֶל בַּמִּשְׁפָּט
לֹא־תִשָּׂא פְנֵי־דָל וְלֹא תֶהְדַּר
פְּנֵי גָדוֹל בְּצֶדֶק תִּשְׁפֹּט
עֲמִיתֶךָ׃ לֹא־תֵלֵךְ רָכִיל בְּעַמֶּיךָ
לֹא תַעֲמֹד עַל־דַּם רֵעֶךָ אֲנִי
יְיָ׃ לֹא־תִשְׂנָא אֶת־אָחִיךָ
בִּלְבָבֶךָ הוֹכֵחַ תּוֹכִיחַ
אֶת־עֲמִיתֶךָ וְלֹא־תִשָּׂא עָלָיו
חֵטְא׃ לֹא־תִקֹּם וְלֹא־תִטֹּר
אֶת־בְּנֵי עַמֶּךָ וְאָהַבְתָּ לְרֵעֲךָ
כָּמוֹךָ אֲנִי יְיָ׃

Haftarah Reading
The Book of Jonah

Blessing Before the Reading

Blessed are You, Adonai our God, source of all, who has chosen good prophets and has delighted in the faithful words they have spoken. Blessed are You Adonai, who continues to choose Torah, Moses, the people Israel, and prophets of truth and justice.

בָּרוּךְ אַתָּה יְיָ אֱלֹהֵינוּ מֶלֶךְ
הָעוֹלָם, אֲשֶׁר בָּחַר בִּנְבִיאִים
טוֹבִים, וְרָצָה בְדִבְרֵיהֶם
הַנֶּאֱמָרִים בֶּאֱמֶת, בָּרוּךְ
אַתָּה יְיָ, הַבּוֹחֵר בַּתּוֹרָה
וּבְמֹשֶׁה עַבְדּוֹ, וּבְיִשְׂרָאֵל
עַמּוֹ, וּבִנְבִיאֵי הָאֱמֶת וָצֶדֶק.

1.

The word of Adonai came to Jonah son of Amitai (Dove, son of Truth), saying, “Arise, go to Nineveh, that great city, and proclaim to it, for their wickedness has risen before Me.”

Jonah fled to Tarshish, away from Adonai. He went down to Yafo and found a ship going to Tarshish. He paid the fare and went down into the ship with the others to Tarshish, away from Adonai.

Adonai cast a great wind upon the sea and there was a great tempest upon the sea. The ship was in danger of breaking up.

וַיְהִי דְּבַר־יְיָ אֶל־יוֹנָה בֶן־אֲמִתַּי
לֵאמֹר: קוּם לֵךְ אֶל־נִינְוֵה
הָעִיר הַגְּדוֹלָה וּקְרָא עָלֶיהָ
כִּי־עָלְתָה רָעָתָם לְפָנָי: וַיָּקָם
יוֹנָה לִבְרֹחַ תַּרְשִׁישָׁה מִלִּפְנֵי יְיָ
וַיֵּרֶד יָפוֹ וַיִּמְצָא אָנִיָּה | בָּאָה
תַרְשִׁישׁ וַיִּתֵּן שְׂכָרָהּ וַיֵּרֶד בָּהּ
לָבוֹא עִמָּהֶם תַּרְשִׁישָׁה מִלִּפְנֵי
יְיָ: וַייָ הֵטִיל רוּחַ־גְּדוֹלָה
אֶל־הַיָּם וַיְהִי סַעַר־גָּדוֹל בַּיָּם
וְהָאֳנִיָּה חִשְּׁבָה לְהִשָּׁבֵר:

The sailors trembled and cried out in fright, each to his own god. They threw the ship's cargo into the sea to make it lighter. Jonah went down into the bowels of the ship, lay down and went to sleep.

וַיִּירְאוּ הַמַּלָּחִים וַיִּזְעֲקוּ אִישׁ
אֶל־אֱלֹהָיו וַיָּטִלוּ אֶת־הַכֵּלִים
אֲשֶׁר בָּאֳנִיָּה אֶל־הַיָּם לְהָקֵל
מֵעֲלֵיהֶם וְיוֹנָה יָרַד אֶל־יַרְכְּתֵי
הַסְּפִינָה וַיִּשְׁכַּב וַיֵּרָדַם׃

When the captain came close to Jonah he said, "What are you doing, sleeping? Get up! Cry out to your god! Perhaps the god will be kind to us and we will not perish!

וַיִּקְרַב אֵלָיו רַב הַחֹבֵל וַיֹּאמֶר
לוֹ מַה־לְּךָ נִרְדָּם קוּם קְרָא
אֶל־אֱלֹהֶיךָ אוּלַי יִתְעַשֵּׁת
הָאֱלֹהִים לָנוּ וְלֹא נֹאבֵד׃

The men said to each other, "Let us cast lots so we will know on whose account this evil has come upon us." They cast lots and the lot fell on Jonah.

וַיֹּאמְרוּ אִישׁ אֶל־רֵעֵהוּ לְכוּ
וְנַפִּילָה גוֹרָלוֹת וְנֵדְעָה בְּשֶׁלְּמִי
הָרָעָה הַזֹּאת לָנוּ וַיַּפִּלוּ גּוֹרָלוֹת
וַיִּפֹּל הַגּוֹרָל עַל־יוֹנָה׃ וַיֹּאמְרוּ
אֵלָיו הַגִּידָה־נָּא לָנוּ בַּאֲשֶׁר
לְמִי־הָרָעָה הַזֹּאת לָנוּ
מַה־מְּלַאכְתְּךָ וּמֵאַיִן תָּבוֹא מָה
אַרְצֶךָ וְאֵי־מִזֶּה עָם
אָתָּה׃ וַיֹּאמֶר אֲלֵיהֶם עִבְרִי
אָנֹכִי וְאֶת־יְיָ אֱלֹהֵי הַשָּׁמַיִם אֲנִי
יָרֵא אֲשֶׁר־עָשָׂה אֶת־הַיָּם
וְאֶת־הַיַּבָּשָׁה׃ וַיִּירְאוּ הָאֲנָשִׁים
יִרְאָה גְדוֹלָה וַיֹּאמְרוּ אֵלָיו
מַה־זֹּאת עָשִׂיתָ

They said to him, "Please, tell us—for you are the one on whose account this evil has come upon us—what has sent you? From where have you come? What is your country? From what people are you?"

He said to them, "I am a Hebrew and I worship Adonai, the God of Heaven, who made the sea and the land."

The men trembled in awe and terror, and they asked him, "What have you done?"

And when the men knew that he was fleeing from Adonai—for so he told them—they said to him, “What must we do to you to silence the sea around us?” For the sea was growing more stormy. He said to them, “Throw me in to silence the sea around you, for I know that this great storm came upon you because of me.”

כִּי־יָדְעוּ הָאֲנָשִׁים כִּי־מִלִּפְנֵי יְיָ
הוּא בֹרֵחַ כִּי הִגִּיד
לָהֶם: וַיֹּאמְרוּ אֵלָיו מַה־נַּעֲשֶׂה
לָּךְ וְיִשְׁתֹּק הַיָּם מֵעָלֵינוּ כִּי הַיָּם
הוֹלֵךְ וְסֹעֵר: וַיֹּאמֶר אֲלֵיהֶם
שָׂאוּנִי וַהֲטִילֻנִי אֶל־הַיָּם
וְיִשְׁתֹּק הַיָּם מֵעֲלֵיכֶם כִּי יוֹדֵעַ
אָנִי כִּי בְשֶׁלִּי הַסַּעַר הַגָּדוֹל
הַזֶּה עֲלֵיכֶם:

The men tried to row to return to dry land, but they could not, for the sea was growing more stormy around them.

וַיַּחְתְּרוּ הָאֲנָשִׁים לְהָשִׁיב
אֶל־הַיַּבָּשָׁה וְלֹא יָכֹלוּ כִּי הַיָּם
הוֹלֵךְ וְסֹעֵר עֲלֵיהֶם:

They cried out to Adonai, saying, “Please, Adonai, please do not let us perish on account of this man’s life. Do not hold us guilty of killing an innocent person! For You, O Adonai, as it pleased You, have brought this about!” And they threw Jonah into the sea, and the sea was stilled from its rage. The men were truly in great awe of Adonai. They offered a sacrifice to Adonai and they made vows.

וַיִּקְרְאוּ אֶל־יְיָ וַיֹּאמְרוּ אָנָּה יְיָ
אַל־נָא נֹאבְדָה בְּנֶפֶשׁ הָאִישׁ
הַזֶּה וְאַל־תִּתֵּן עָלֵינוּ דָּם נָקִיא
כִּי־אַתָּה יְיָ כַּאֲשֶׁר חָפַצְתָּ
עָשִׂיתָ: וַיִּשְׂאוּ אֶת־יוֹנָה וַיְטִלֻהוּ
אֶל־הַיָּם וַיַּעֲמֹד הַיָּם
מִזַּעְפּוֹ: וַיִּירְאוּ הָאֲנָשִׁים יִרְאָה
גְדוֹלָה אֶת־יְיָ וַיִּזְבְּחוּ־זֶבַח לַייָ
וַיִּדְּרוּ נְדָרִים:

2

Adonai brought a great fish to swallow Jonah, and Jonah remained in the fish's belly three days and three nights. Jonah prayed to Adonai his God from the belly of the fish. He said:

וַיְמַן יְיָ דָּג גָּדוֹל לִבְלֹעַ אֶת־יוֹנָה
וַיְהִי יוֹנָה בִּמְעֵי הַדָּג שְׁלֹשָׁה
יָמִים וּשְׁלֹשָׁה לֵילוֹת׃ וַיִּתְפַּלֵּל
יוֹנָה אֶל־יְיָ אֱלֹהָיו מִמְּעֵי
הַדָּגָה׃ וַיֹּאמֶר

In my trouble I called
to Adonai,
And God answered me.
From the belly of the
underworld I cried out,
And You heard my voice.
You cast me into the depths,
Into the heart of the sea.
The floods engulfed me.
All Your breakers and billows
Swept over me.
I thought I was driven away
Out of Your sight.
Would I ever gaze again
Upon Your holy Temple?
The waters closed in
up to my neck.
The deep engulfed me.
Weeds twined around my head.
I sank down to the base
of the mountains.
The bars of the earth closed
upon me forever.
Yet You brought my life up
from the pit,
Adonai my God!

קָרָאתִי מִצָּרָה לִי
אֶל־יְיָ
וַיַּעֲנֵנִי
מִבֶּטֶן שְׁאוֹל שִׁוַּעְתִּי
שָׁמַעְתָּ קוֹלִי׃
וַתַּשְׁלִיכֵנִי מְצוּלָה
בִּלְבַב יַמִּים
וְנָהָר יְסֹבְבֵנִי
כָּל־מִשְׁבָּרֶיךָ וְגַלֶּיךָ עָלַי עָבָרוּ׃
וַאֲנִי אָמַרְתִּי
נִגְרַשְׁתִּי מִנֶּגֶד עֵינֶיךָ אַךְ
אוֹסִיף לְהַבִּיט אֶל־הֵיכַל
קָדְשֶׁךָ׃
אֲפָפוּנִי מַיִם עַד־נֶפֶשׁ תְּהוֹם
יְסֹבְבֵנִי סוּף חָבוּשׁ לְרֹאשִׁי׃
לְקִצְבֵי הָרִים יָרַדְתִּי הָאָרֶץ
בְּרִחֶיהָ בַעֲדִי לְעוֹלָם
וַתַּעַל מִשַּׁחַת חַיַּי
יְיָ אֱלֹהָי

When my life was ebbing away,
I remembered Adonai
And my prayer came to You,
To Your holy Temple.
They who cling to empty folly
Forsake their own welfare.
But I, with spoken thanks,
Will make an offering to You.
What I have vowed
I will complete.
Deliverance is Adonai's.

בְּהִתְעַטֵּף עָלַי נַפְשִׁי
אֶת־יְיָ זָכָרְתִּי
וַתָּבוֹא אֵלֶיךָ תְּפִלָּתִי אֶל־הֵיכַל
קָדְשֶׁךָ׃
מְשַׁמְּרִים הַבְלֵי־שָׁוְא
חַסְדָּם יַעֲזֹבוּ׃ וַאֲנִי בְּקוֹל תּוֹדָה
אֶזְבְּחָה־לָּךְ אֲשֶׁר נָדַרְתִּי
אֲשַׁלֵּמָה יְשׁוּעָתָה לַייָ׃

Adonai commanded the fish, and it spewed Jonah out upon dry land.

וַיֹּאמֶר יְיָ לַדָּג וַיָּקֵא אֶת־יוֹנָה
אֶל־הַיַּבָּשָׁה׃

3

The word of Adonai came to Jonah a second time, saying, "Arise, go to Nineveh, that great city, and proclaim to it the proclamation I tell you." Jonah arose and went to Nineveh.

Jonah started out and entered the city—a day's journey—and proclaimed, saying, "Another forty days and Nineveh will be overthrown!"

וַיְהִי דְבַר־יְיָ אֶל־יוֹנָה שֵׁנִית
לֵאמֹר׃ קוּם לֵךְ אֶל־נִינְוֵה
הָעִיר הַגְּדוֹלָה וּקְרָא אֵלֶיהָ
אֶת־הַקְּרִיאָה אֲשֶׁר אָנֹכִי דֹּבֵר
אֵלֶיךָ׃ וַיָּקָם יוֹנָה וַיֵּלֶךְ
אֶל־נִינְוֵה כִּדְבַר יְיָ וְנִינְוֵה הָיְתָה
עִיר־גְּדוֹלָה לֵאלֹהִים מַהֲלַךְ
שְׁלֹשֶׁת יָמִים׃ וַיָּחֶל יוֹנָה לָבוֹא
בָעִיר מַהֲלַךְ יוֹם אֶחָד וַיִּקְרָא
וַיֹּאמַר עוֹד אַרְבָּעִים יוֹם וְנִינְוֵה
נֶהְפָּכֶת׃

The people of Nineveh had faith in God. They proclaimed a fast and both the great and the lowly put on sackcloth.

וַיַּאֲמִינוּ אַנְשֵׁי נִינְוֵה בֵּאלֹהִים
וַיִּקְרְאוּ־צוֹם וַיִּלְבְּשׁוּ שַׂקִּים
מִגְּדוֹלָם וְעַד־קְטַנָּם׃

The news reached the king of Nineveh. He rose from his throne, took off his robe, put on sackcloth and sat in ashes. He had the word cried through Nineveh, “By decree of the king and his nobles, neither person nor beast, flock nor herd, shall eat anything! They shall neither graze nor drink water! They shall be covered with sackcloth, person and beast, and cry to God with all their might. Let all turn back from their evil ways and from the violence they would do. Who knows? Perhaps God will relent and show compassion. Perhaps God will turn from anger so that we will not perish.”

וַיִּגַּע הַדָּבָר אֶל־מֶלֶךְ נִינְוֵה וַיָּקָם
מִכִּסְאוֹ וַיַּעֲבֵר אַדַּרְתּוֹ מֵעָלָיו וַיְכַס
שַׂק וַיֵּשֶׁב עַל־הָאֵפֶר׃
וַיַּזְעֵק וַיֹּאמֶר בְּנִינְוֵה מִטַּעַם הַמֶּלֶךְ
וּגְדֹלָיו לֵאמֹר הָאָדָם וְהַבְּהֵמָה
הַבָּקָר וְהַצֹּאן אַל־יִטְעֲמוּ מְאוּמָה
אַל־יִרְעוּ וּמַיִם אַל־יִשְׁתּוּ׃ וְיִתְכַּסּוּ
שַׂקִּים הָאָדָם וְהַבְּהֵמָה וְיִקְרְאוּ
אֶל־אֱלֹהִים בְּחָזְקָה וְיָשֻׁבוּ אִישׁ
מִדַּרְכּוֹ הָרָעָה וּמִן־הֶחָמָס אֲשֶׁר
בְּכַפֵּיהֶם׃ מִי־יוֹדֵעַ יָשׁוּב וְנִחַם
הָאֱלֹהִים וְשָׁב מֵחֲרוֹן אַפּוֹ וְלֹא
נֹאבֵד׃

God saw what they did, how they turned from their evil ways. God had compassion for them and relented from the pronounced punishment and did not carry it out.

וַיַּרְא הָאֱלֹהִים אֶת־מַעֲשֵׂיהֶם
כִּי־שָׁבוּ מִדַּרְכָּם הָרָעָה וַיִּנָּחֶם
הָאֱלֹהִים עַל־הָרָעָה אֲשֶׁר־דִּבֶּר
לַעֲשׂוֹת־לָהֶם וְלֹא עָשָׂה׃

4

This brought great displeasure to Jonah and it angered him. He prayed to Adonai, saying, “Please, Adonai, is this not the very thing I have been saying since I was in my country? This is why I fled earlier to Tarshish, because I knew that You are a gracious and compassionate God, slow to anger and showing great love—and that You would show compassion to evil! Now, Adonai, take my life from me, for I would rather die than live.”

וַיֵּרַע אֶל־יוֹנָה רָעָה גְדוֹלָה וַיִּחַר לוֹ׃ וַיִּתְפַּלֵּל אֶל־יְיָ וַיֹּאמַר אָנָּה יְיָ הֲלוֹא־זֶה דְבָרִי עַד־הֱיוֹתִי עַל־אַדְמָתִי עַל־כֵּן קִדַּמְתִּי לִבְרֹחַ תַּרְשִׁישָׁה כִּי יָדַעְתִּי כִּי אַתָּה אֵל־חַנּוּן וְרַחוּם אֶרֶךְ אַפַּיִם וְרַב־חֶסֶד וְנִחָם עַל־הָרָעָה׃ וְעַתָּה יְהוָֹה קַח־נָא אֶת־נַפְשִׁי מִמֶּנִּי כִּי טוֹב מוֹתִי מֵחַיָּי׃

Adonai said, “Are you really that angry?”

וַיֹּאמֶר יְיָ הַהֵיטֵב חָרָה לָךְ׃

Jonah left the city and settled down east of the city. He made himself a shelter there and sat under it in the shade so he could see what would happen to the city. And Adonai-God produced a plant which grew up over Jonah to be a shade over his head and save him from the sun’s harm. Jonah was happy about the plant—a great happiness.

וַיֵּצֵא יוֹנָה מִן־הָעִיר וַיֵּשֶׁב מִקֶּדֶם לָעִיר וַיַּעַשׂ לוֹ שָׁם סֻכָּה וַיֵּשֶׁב תַּחְתֶּיהָ בַּצֵּל עַד אֲשֶׁר יִרְאֶה מַה־יִּהְיֶה בָּעִיר׃ וַיְמַן יְיָ־אֱלֹהִים קִיקָיוֹן וַיַּעַל | מֵעַל לְיוֹנָה לִהְיוֹת צֵל עַל־רֹאשׁוֹ לְהַצִּיל לוֹ מֵרָעָתוֹ וַיִּשְׂמַח יוֹנָה עַל־הַקִּיקָיוֹן שִׂמְחָה גְדוֹלָה׃

But at the next sunrise, God produced a worm that attacked the plant so that it dried up.

וַיְמַן הָאֱלֹהִים תּוֹלַעַת בַּעֲלוֹת הַשַּׁחַר לַמָּחֳרָת וַתַּךְ אֶת־הַקִּיקָיוֹן וַיִּיבָשׁ׃

The sun blazed and God produced a hot east wind. The sun beat down on Jonah's head and he became faint. He wished for death, saying, "I would rather die than live."

God said to Jonah, "Are you really that angry about the plant?" He said, "I am so very angry that I could die."

Adonai said, "You cared about the plant, which you did not raise and did not grow, which came in a night and perished in a night. Shall I not care about Nineveh, that great city, that has in it more than a hundred and twenty thousand people who do not know their right hand from their left, and many beasts, as well?"

יְהִי | כִּזְרֹחַ הַשֶּׁמֶשׁ וַיְמַן אֱלֹהִים
רוּחַ קָדִים חֲרִישִׁית וַתַּךְ הַשֶּׁמֶשׁ
עַל־רֹאשׁ יוֹנָה וַיִּתְעַלָּף וַיִּשְׁאַל
אֶת־נַפְשׁוֹ לָמוּת וַיֹּאמֶר טוֹב
מוֹתִי מֵחַיָּי׃ וַיֹּאמֶר אֱלֹהִים
אֶל־יוֹנָה הַהֵיטֵב חָרָה־לְךָ
עַל־הַקִּיקָיוֹן וַיֹּאמֶר הֵיטֵב
חָרָה־לִי עַד־מָוֶת׃ וַיֹּאמֶר יְיָ אַתָּה
חַסְתָּ עַל־הַקִּיקָיוֹן אֲשֶׁר
לֹא־עָמַלְתָּ בּוֹ וְלֹא גִדַּלְתּוֹ
שֶׁבִּן־לַיְלָה הָיָה וּבִן־לַיְלָה
אָבָד׃ וַאֲנִי לֹא אָחוּס עַל־נִינְוֵה
הָעִיר הַגְּדוֹלָה אֲשֶׁר יֶשׁ־בָּהּ
הַרְבֵּה מִשְׁתֵּים־עֶשְׂרֵה רִבּוֹ אָדָם
אֲשֶׁר לֹא־יָדַע בֵּין־יְמִינוֹ לִשְׂמֹאלוֹ
וּבְהֵמָה רַבָּה׃

We Are Jonah

In Rabbi Eliezer's vision
Jonah entered the whale's mouth
as we enter a synagogue.
Light streamed in through its eyes.
Jonah approached the *bimah*, the whale's head.
Show me wonders, he said, as though
his own life weren't a miracle.

The whale obliged, swimming down
to the foundation stone,
the navel of creation
fixed deep beneath the land.
Tsk tsk, chided the fish:
you're beneath God's temple—
you should pray.

Prayer requires stillness.
Running away had always been
so easy. Sitting silent
in self-judgement — forget it!
But waves only churn the surface.
In the deep beneath the deep
Jonah was wholly present.

We all flee
from uncomfortable conversations
the drip of a hospital IV
the truths we don't want to own
the work we don't want to do.
Now we're in the belly of the whale,
someplace deep and strange.

God calls us to awareness:
to stand our ground
in the place where we are,
to do the work which needs doing.
To bring kindness and mercy
even to those who are unlike us.
Are we listening?

(Rabbi Rachel Barenblat)

Blessings After the Haftarah

Blessed are You, Adonai our God, source of all, rock of all time and space, righteous in every generation, the faithful God whose word is deed, who speaks and establishes, whose every word is truth and justice.

בָּרוּךְ אַתָּה יְיָ אֱלֹהֵינוּ מֶלֶךְ הָעוֹלָם, צוּר כָּל הָעוֹלָמִים, צַדִּיק בְּכָל הַדּוֹרוֹת, הָאֵל הַנֶּאֱמָן הָאוֹמֵר וְעֹשֶׂה, הַמְדַבֵּר וּמְקַיֵּם, שֶׁכָּל דְּבָרָיו אֱמֶת וָצֶדֶק.

You are faithful, Adonai our God, and faithful is Your word. Not a single word You have spoken goes unfulfilled, for You are God, faithful, just (and merciful). Blessed are You, Adonai our God, faithful in all ways.

נֶאֱמָן אַתָּה הוּא יְיָ אֱלֹהֵינוּ, וְנֶאֱמָנִים דְּבָרֶיךָ, וְדָבָר אֶחָד מִדְּבָרֶיךָ אָחוֹר לֹא יָשׁוּב רֵיקָם, כִּי אֵל מֶלֶךְ נֶאֱמָן (וְרַחֲמָן) אָתָּה. בָּרוּךְ אַתָּה יְיָ, הָאֵל הַנֶּאֱמָן בְּכָל דְּבָרָיו.

Be compassionate upon Zion, for it is a life-giving home for our people. Restore her soon. Blessed are You, Adonai, who brings rejoicing to Zion and her children.

רַחֵם עַל צִיּוֹן כִּי הִיא בֵּית חַיֵּינוּ, וְלַעֲלוּבַת נֶפֶשׁ תּוֹשִׁיעַ בִּמְהֵרָה בְיָמֵינוּ. בָּרוּךְ אַתָּה יְיָ, מְשַׂמֵּחַ צִיּוֹן בְּבָנֶיהָ.

Adonai our God, let us rejoice in the fulfillment of our dream of Elijah and David. Let messianic redemption come soon and bring joy to our hearts. Let us not be misled by false prophets, for You have promised that redemption's light shall never be extinguished.

שַׂמְּחֵנוּ יְיָ אֱלֹהֵינוּ בְּאֵלִיָּהוּ הַנָּבִיא עַבְדֶּךָ, וּבְמַלְכוּת בֵּית דָּוִד מְשִׁיחֶךָ, בִּמְהֵרָה יָבֹא וְיָגֵל לִבֵּנוּ, עַל כִּסְאוֹ לֹא יֵשֵׁב זָר וְלֹא יִנְחֲלוּ עוֹד אֲחֵרִים אֶת כְּבוֹדוֹ, כִּי בְשֵׁם קָדְשְׁךָ נִשְׁבַּעְתָּ לּוֹ, שֶׁלֹּא יִכְבֶּה נֵרוֹ לְעוֹלָם וָעֶד.

Blessed are You, Adonai, shield of David.	בָּרוּךְ אַתָּה יְיָ, מָגֵן דָּוִד.
We thank You for the Torah and worship, for the prophets, (for this Shabbat), and for this Day of Atonement that You have given us, Adonai our God (for holiness and rest,) for honor and splendor. We thank You for everything, Adonai our God. Let Your name ever be blessed by all that lives. Your word is true forever. Blessed are You, Adonai, source of all the earth, who sanctifies (Shabbat,) the people Israel and the Day of Atonement.	עַל הַתּוֹרָה, וְעַל הָעֲבוֹדָה, וְעַל הַנְּבִיאִים, (וְעַל יוֹם הַשַּׁבָּת הַזֶּה,) וְעַל יוֹם הַכִּפּוּרִם הַזֶּה, שֶׁנָּתַתָּ לָּנוּ יְיָ אֱלֹהֵינוּ, (לִקְדֻשָּׁה וְלִמְנוּחָה,) לְכָבוֹד וּלְתִפְאָרֶת. עַל הַכֹּל יְיָ אֱלֹהֵינוּ, אֲנַחְנוּ מוֹדִים לָךְ, וּמְבָרְכִים אוֹתָךְ, יִתְבָּרַךְ שִׁמְךָ בְּפִי כָּל חַי תָּמִיד לְעוֹלָם וָעֶד וּדְבָרְךָ אֱמֶת וְקַיָּם לָעַד. בָּרוּךְ אַתָּה יְיָ, מְקַדֵּשׁ (הַשַּׁבָּת וְ) יִשְׂרָאֵל וְיוֹם הַכִּפּוּרִם.

After returnng the Torah to the Ark

(singing Hareini M'kabel Alai *again or a niggun):*

turn to p. 206 for the Amidah

followed by p. 220 for Selichot, and then to p. 306 for Ne'ilah.

And/or: continue with the following poems

for silent reflection and contemplation.

Yom Kippur

You are asked to stand and bow your head,
consider the harm you've caused,
the respect you've withheld,
the anger misspent, the fear spread,
the earnestness displayed
in the service of prestige and sensibility,
all the callous, cruel, stubborn, joyless sins
in your alphabet of woe
so that you might be forgiven.
You are asked to believe in the spark
of your divinity, in the purity
of the words of your mouth
and the memories of your heart.
You are asked for this one day and one night
to starve your body so your soul can feast
on faith and adoration.
You are asked to forgive the past
and remember the dead, to gaze
across the desert in your heart
toward Jerusalem. To separate
the sacred from the profane
and be as numerous as the sands
and the stars of heaven.
To believe that no matter what
you have done to yourself and others
morning will come and the mountain
of night will fade. To believe,
for these few precious moments,

in the utter sweetness of your life.
You are asked to bow your head
and remain standing,
and say Amen.

(Philip Schultz)

Teshuvah

God and I collaborate
on revising the poem of myself.

I decide what needs polishing,
what to preserve and what to lose;

God reads my draft with pursed lips.
If I really mean it, God

sings a new song, one strong
as stone and serene as silk.

I want this year's poem
to be joyful. I want this year's poem

to be measured like flour,
to burn like sweet dry maple.

I want every reader
to come away more certain

that transformation is possible.
I'd like holiness

to fill my words
and my empty spaces.

On Rosh Hashanah it is written
and on Yom Kippur it is sealed:

who will be a haiku and who
a sonnet, who needs meter

and who free verse, who an epic
and who a single syllable.

If I only get one sound
may it be *yes*, may I be One.

(Rabbi Rachel Barenblat)

Al Chet Shechatati L'fanecha: For the sin I have sinned before You

I need to speak these words aloud
and to know that the universe hears them.
I get caught in old patterns and paradigms;
I am stubborn and hard-headed.
In the last year I have missed the mark
more than I want to admit.

Forgive me, Source of all being,
for the sin I have sinned before You

By allowing my body to be an afterthought
too often and too easily;
By not walking, running, leaping, climbing
or dancing although I am able;
By eating in my car and at my desk,
mindlessly and without blessing;
By not embracing those who needed it,
not allowing myself to be embraced;
By not praising every body's beauty,
with our quirks and imperfections.

By letting my emotions run roughshod
over the needs of others;
By poking at sources of hurt
like a child worrying a sore tooth;
By revealing my heart before those
who neither wanted nor needed to see it;
By hiding love, out of fear of rejection,
instead of giving love freely;
By dwelling on what's internal
when the world is desperate for healing.

By indulging in intellectual argument
without humility or consideration;
By reading words of vitriol,

cultivating hot indignation;
By eschewing intellectual discomfort
that might prod me into growing;
By living in anticipation,
and letting anxiety rule me;
By accepting defeatist thinking
and the comfortable ache of despair.

By not being awake and grateful,
despite uncountable blessings;
By not being sufficiently gentle,
with my actions or with my language;
By being not pliant and flexible,
but obstinate, stark, and unbending;
By not being generous with my time,
with my words or with my being;
By not being kind to everyone
who crosses my wandering path.

For all of these, eternal Source of forgiveness
Help me know myself to be pardoned
Help me feel in my bones that I'm forgiven
Remind me I'm always already at/one with You.

(Rabbi Rachel Barenblat)

Ne'ilah / The Closing of the Gates

Before the gate has been closed,
before the last question is posed,
before I am transposed.
Before the weeds fill the gardens,
before there are no pardons,
before the concrete hardens.

Before all the flute-holes are covered,
before things are locked in the cupboard,
before the rules are discovered.
Before the conclusion is planned,
before God closes his hand,
before we have nowhere to stand.

(Yehuda Amichai)

At the Closing of the Gates

At the closing of the gates
At the turning of the day
We turn our hearts to You
and You won't turn away.

(Rabbi Irwin Keller)

Ne'ilah

The hinge of the year
the great gates opening
and then slowly slowly
closing on us.

I always imagine those gates
hanging over the ocean
fiery over the stone grey
waters of evening.

We cast what we must
change about ourselves
onto the waters flowing
to the sea. The sins,

errors, bad habits, whatever
you call them, dissolve.
When I was little I cried
out *I! I! I! I want, I want.*

Older, I feel less important,
a worker bee in the hive
of history, miles of hard
labor to make my sweetness.

The gates are closing
The light is failing
I kneel before what I love
imploring that it may live.

So much breaks, wears
down, fails in us. We must
forgive our broken promises—
their sharp shards in our hands.

(Marge Piercy)

Open the Gates

פִּתחוּ לִי שַׁעֲרֵי צֶדֶק אַבֹא בָם אוֹדֶה יָהּ.

Open for me the gates of righteousness
And I will enter them, praising God.

פְּתַח לָנוּ שַׁעַר בְּעֵת נְעִילַת שַׁעַר כִּי פָנָה יוֹם.

Open the gate for us, now when the gates are closing,
for the day is passing.

הַיּוֹם יִפְנֶה. הַשֶּׁמֶשׁ יָבוֹא וְיִפְנֶה. נָבוֹאָה שְׁעָרֶיךָ.

The day is passing. The sun goes and turns.
Let us enter Your gates.

Please, God, spare.	אָנָּא אֵל נָא.
Forgive...	שָׂא נָא.
Pardon...	סְלַח נָא.
Acquit...	מְחַל נָא.
Absolve....	חֲמָל נָא.
Have mercy...	רַחֵם נָא.
Clear us completely.	כַּפֵּר נָא.
Help us overcome sin and wrongdoing.	כְּבֹשׁ חֵטְא וְעָוֹן.

Open for us a gate

One after another things
are happening to me which
at a different time
would illuminate me
with the light of joy.
And I would walk beautiful,
careful, lest they be
extinguished,
carrying back and forth
humble gratitude.

But in this setting
they are summer's lightning,
sparks—
and when they vanish
the clouds are even darker
and in the stifling air
no sign of rain.

Heaven stands sealed.
Open for us a gate.

בְּזֶה אַחַר זֶה קוֹרִים לִי
מִקְרִים שֶׁבְּעֵת אַחֶרֶת
הָיוּ מַדְלִיקִין בִּי אֶת כָּל
פְּנָסֵי הַשִּׂמְחָה.
וְהָיִיתִי הוֹלֶכֶת יָפָה,
זְהִירָה, פֶּן יִכְבּוּ,
וְנוֹשֵׂאת בִּי הָלֹךְ וְנַשֹּׂא
הַכְנָעַת הוֹדָיָה.

אֲבָל עַל הָרֶקַע הַזֶּה
הֲלֹא הַם בִּרְקֵי–קַיִץ,
הֲזִיזִים –
וּבְהֵעָלְמָם
הֶעָבִים כֵּהִים עוֹד יוֹתֵר
וּמַחֲנָק
אֵין צִפִּיָּה לְגֶשֶׁם.

הַשָּׁמַיִם עוֹמְדִים אֲטוּמִים.
פְּתַח לָנוּ שַׁעַר.

(Lea Goldberg, translated by Rabbi Rachel Barenblat)

Eil Nora Alila / God of Awe

Eil nora alila, Eil nora alila,
Ha-m'tzi lanu m'chilah,
bi-sh'at ha-ne'ilah.

אֵל נוֹרָא עֲלִילָה, אֵל נוֹרָא עֲלִילָה,
הַמְצִיא לָנוּ מְחִילָה, בִּשְׁעַת הַנְּעִילָה.

God of awe and God of might,
God of awe and God of might,
Grant us pardon in this hour
As Your gates draw closed this night.

We have struggled all day long
Aspiring toward Your lofty height;
We are fearful in our prayer
As Your gates draw closed this night.

Pouring out our hearts we pray
That the sentence You will write
Will hold pardon for our sins
As Your gates draw closed this night.

God, our refuge strong and sure,
You know this is our human plight;
Seal our destiny for joy
As Your gates draw closed this night.

Grant us favor, show us grace;
Help us listen for what's right
And choose in ways which draw You near
As Your gates draw closed this night.

The generations from which we come
Strong in faith walked in Your light.
As of old, renew our days,
As Your gates draw closed this night.

Gather us from where we've scattered
Let us glimpse life through Your sight;
Bless the cycle of this year
As Your gates draw closed this night.

May we all, both old and young,
Look for gladness and delight
In the many years to come,
As Your gates draw closed this night.

May the angels Wonder, Strength
Comfort, and Your shining Light*
Accompany us as evening falls,
As Your gates draw closed this night.

(Translation adapted from Rabbi David de Sola Pool.)

Ashrei Chant

Ashrei yoshvei veitecha Od y'hallelucha selah	אַשְׁרֵי יוֹשְׁבֵי בֵיתֶךָ, עוֹד יְהַלְלוּךָ סֶּלָה:	Joyous, dwelling in the One! Home is in my heart.

(English words, melody by Rabbi Hanna Tiferet Siegel)

**In the liturgy for the bedtime shema, it is traditional to call upon four angels: Michael (Who Is Like God), Gavriel (God's Strength), Uriel (God's Light) and Raphael (God's Healing) to watch over us as we sleep. These angels' names have been simplified in this El Nora Alila variation to Wonder, Strength, Comfort, and Light.*

Preparing for the Final *Amidah*

Day is waning.
The gates of Yom Kippur are beginning to swing shut.
What do you need to say to God
as this intense day draws to its close?
What do you need to pour out before the One
Who hears all prayer?

Amidah

Adonai sefatai tiftach
ufi yagid tehilatecha.

אֲדֹנָי שְׂפָתַי תִּפְתָּח
וּפִי יַגִּיד תְּהִלָּתֶךָ:

Eternal God, open my lips
that my mouth may declare Your praise.

Avot v'Imahot: Our Ancestors

Baruch atah Adonai Eloheinu
v'Elohei avoteinu v'imoteinu,
elohei Avraham, elohei
Yitzchak, elohei Ya'akov,
elohei Sarah, elohei Rivkah,
elohei Leah, v'elohei Rachel.
Ha'el hagadol hagibor v'hanora
Eil elyon, gomeil chasadim
tovim v'koneh hakol v'zocheir
chasei avot v'imahot, umeivi
go'el livnei veneihem lema'an
shemo b'ahavah.

בָּרוּךְ אַתָּה יְיָ אֱלֹהֵינוּ וֵאלֹהֵי
אֲבוֹתֵינוּ וְאִמּוֹתֵינוּ, אֱלֹהֵי
אַבְרָהָם, אֱלֹהֵי יִצְחָק, וֵאלֹהֵי
יַעֲקֹב, אלֹהֵי שָׂרָה, אלֹהֵי
רִבְקָה, אלֹהֵי לֵאָה, וֵאלֹהֵי
רָחֵל. הָאֵל הַגָּדוֹל הַגִּבּוֹר
וְהַנּוֹרָא, אֵל עֶלְיוֹן, גּוֹמֵל
חֲסָדִים טוֹבִים, וְקוֹנֵה הַכֹּל,
וְזוֹכֵר חַסְדֵי אָבוֹת ואמהות,
וּמֵבִיא גוֹאֵל לִבְנֵי בְנֵיהֶם לְמַעַן
שְׁמוֹ בְּאַהֲבָה:

Blessed are You, Adonai our God and God of our ancestors, God of Abraham, God of Isaac, God of Jacob; God of Sarah, God of Rebecca, God of Rachel and God of Leah; the great, mighty, and awesome God, God on high, who does deeds of loving kindness, who is the Source of all, and who remembers the steadfast love of our ancestors, who lovingly brings redemption to their children's children for Your name's sake.

זָכְרֵנוּ לְחַיִּים, מֶלֶךְ חָפֵץ בַּחַיִּים, וְכָתְבֵנוּ בְּסֵפֶר הַחַיִּים, לְמַעַנְךָ אֱלֹהִים חַיִּים.

Zochreinu lechayim melech chafeitz bachayim, vekotveinu beseifer ha-chayyim le ma'ancha Elohim chayyim.

מֶלֶךְ עוֹזֵר וּמוֹשִׁיעַ וּמָגֵן: בָּרוּךְ אַתָּה יְיָ, מָגֵן אַבְרָהָם וְאֶזְרַת שָׂרָה:

Melech ozeir u-moshia u-magen. Baruch Atah Adonai, magein Avraham v'ezrat Sarah.

Remember us for life, creator Who delights in life, and inscribe us in the book of life for Your own sake, O God of life.

Ruler, helper, redeemer, and protector, blessed are You Adonai, Abraham's shield and Sarah's strength.

Gevurot: God's Strength

אַתָּה גִּבּוֹר לְעוֹלָם אֲדֹנָי, מְחַיֵּה מֵתִים אַתָּה, רַב לְהוֹשִׁיעַ: מוֹרִיד הַטָּל:

Atah gibor l'olam Adonai, mechayeh meitim atah rav l'hoshia. Morid ha-tal.

You are our eternal strength, Adonai. Your saving power gives life that transcends death. You bring the dew of the field.

מְכַלְכֵּל חַיִּים בְּחֶסֶד, מְחַיֵּה מֵתִים בְּרַחֲמִים רַבִּים, סוֹמֵךְ נוֹפְלִים, וְרוֹפֵא חוֹלִים, וּמַתִּיר אֲסוּרִים, וּמְקַיֵּם אֱמוּנָתוֹ לִישֵׁנֵי עָפָר, מִי כָמוֹךָ בַּעַל גְּבוּרוֹת וּמִי דּוֹמֶה לָּךְ, מֶלֶךְ מֵמִית וּמְחַיֶּה וּמַצְמִיחַ יְשׁוּעָה:

Mechalkel chayyim b'chesed, m'chayeh meitim b'rachamim rabim, somech noflim, v'rofeh cholim, umatir asurim, um'kayem emunato lishenei afar. Mi chamocha ba'al gevurot? U-mi domeh lach? Melech meimit u'm'chayeh, umatzmiach yeshuah.

מִי כָמְוֹךָ אַב הָרַחֲמִים, זוֹכֵר יְצוּרָיו לְחַיִּים בְּרַחֲמִים:

Mi chamocha av harachaman, zocheir yetzurav l'chayyim b'rachamim.

וְנֶאֱמָן אַתָּה לְהַחֲיוֹת מֵתִים. בָּרוּךְ אַתָּה יְיָ, מְחַיֵּה הַמֵּתִים:

V'ne'eman atah le'ha-chayot meitim. Baruch atah Adonai, mechayeh hameitim.

You sustain the living with kindness, in Your great mercy You bestow eternal life. You support the fallen, heal the sick, and free the captive. You keep Your faith with us beyond life and death. There is none like You, our source of strength, the ruler of life and death, the source of our redemption.

Who is like You, source of mercy, Who mercifully remembers Your creatures for life?

Our faith is with You, the God Who brings eternal life. Blessed are You, Adonai, Who gives life which transcends death.

שְׁמַע נָא, סְלַח נָא הַיּוֹם,
עֲבוּר כִּי פָּנָה יוֹם,
וּנְהַלֶּלְךָ נוֹרָא וְאָיוֹם, קָדוֹשׁ.

Hear us, forgive us this day,
For the day is fading.
We offer prayer
To the holy God of our awe and wonder.

פִּתְחוּ לָנוּ שַׁעֲרֵי־צֶדֶק, נָבוֹא בָם נוֹדֶה יָּהּ.
דְּלָתֶיךָ דָּפַקְנוּ רַחוּם וְחַנּוּן
נָא אַל תְּשִׁיבֵנוּ רֵיקָם מִלְּפָנֶיךָ.

Open for us the gates of righteousness.
Let us enter them, God of our thanks.
Open wide the gates of mercy and grace.
Do not turn us aside in emptiness.

Kidushat Hashem: Making the Name Holy

You are holy,
and Your name is holy,
and holy ones praise You
always, *selah*.

אַתָּה קָדוֹשׁ וְשִׁמְךָ קָדוֹשׁ
וּקְדוֹשִׁים בְּכָל יוֹם יְהַלְלוּךָ,
סֶּלָה.

And so
May fear and concern
be instilled in all living beings,
deep concern for all created.
All creation should be in awe,
all of life humbled before You.
May all of creation form
a single bond to do Your will.
We know that You alone rule
that Your strength is justice
and Your awesome being
transcends all which You
have created.

וּבְכֵן
תֵּן פַּחְדְּךָ יְיָ אֱלֹהֵינוּ, עַל כָּל
מַעֲשֶׂיךָ, וְאֵימָתְךָ עַל כָּל מַה
שֶּׁבָּרָאתָ, וְיִירָאוּךָ כָּל
הַמַּעֲשִׂים וְיִשְׁתַּחֲווּ לְפָנֶיךָ כָּל
הַבְּרוּאִים, וְיֵעָשׂוּ כֻלָּם אֲגֻדָּה
אַחַת לַעֲשׂוֹת רְצוֹנְךָ בְּלֵבָב
שָׁלֵם, כְּמוֹ שֶׁיָּדַעְנוּ יְיָ אֱלֹהֵינוּ,
שֶׁהַשִּׁלְטָן לְפָנֶיךָ, עֹז בְּיָדְךָ
וּגְבוּרָה בִּימִינֶךָ, וְשִׁמְךָ נוֹרָא
עַל כָּל מַה שֶּׁבָּרָאתָ.

And so
May honor be granted
to Your people,
Praise to those who feel awe
and hope to those
who seek You
and voice sincere yearnings.
May there be joy
throughout the land
and joyfulness for the
inhabitants of Your city.
May the light of joy and justice
shine forth in our lifetime.

וּבְכֵן
תֵּן כָּבוֹד, יְיָ לְעַמֶּךָ, תְּהִלָּה
לִירֵאֶיךָ וְתִקְוָה טוֹבָה
לְדוֹרְשֶׁיךָ, וּפִתְחוֹן פֶּה
לַמְיַחֲלִים לָךְ, שִׂמְחָה לְאַרְצֶךָ
וְשָׂשׂוֹן לְעִירֶךָ, וּצְמִיחַת קֶרֶן
לְדָוִד עַבְדֶּךָ, וַעֲרִיכַת נֵר
לְבֶן־יִשַׁי מְשִׁיחֶךָ, בִּמְהֵרָה
בְיָמֵינוּ.

And so
When such a day arrives
those who struggled for justice
will be first to rejoice;
the upright will be glad;
the faithful will sing with joy;
injustice will close its mouth;
evil will vanish like smoke;
falsehoods will depart from the
earth.

וּבְכֵן
צַדִּיקִים יִרְאוּ וְיִשְׂמָחוּ, וִישָׁרִים
יַעֲלֹזוּ, וַחֲסִידִים בְּרִנָּה יָגִילוּ,
וְעוֹלָתָה תִּקְפָּץ־פִּיהָ, וְכָל
הָרִשְׁעָה כֻּלָּהּ כְּעָשָׁן תִּכְלֶה, כִּי
תַעֲבִיר מֶמְשֶׁלֶת זָדוֹן מִן
הָאָרֶץ.

Sacred Oneness will govern
all things; Mount Zion
will be among Your resting-
places, as will Your holy city,
the city of Shalom, Jerusalem.
As it is written in these holy
words: "Adonai will reign
forever, Your God, O Zion, for
all generations, halleluyah."

וְתִמְלֹךְ, אַתָּה יְיָ לְבַדֶּךָ, עַל כָּל
מַעֲשֶׂיךָ, בְּהַר צִיּוֹן מִשְׁכַּן
כְּבוֹדֶךָ, וּבִירוּשָׁלַיִם עִיר
קָדְשֶׁךָ, כַּכָּתוּב בְּדִבְרֵי קָדְשֶׁךָ:
יִמְלֹךְ יְיָ לְעוֹלָם, אֱלֹהַיִךְ צִיּוֹן
לְדֹר וָדֹר: הַלְלוּיָהּ.

You are holy,
Your name is holy
And there is no God besides
You, as it is written:
"The Eternal, the power of all
creation, is elevated through
justice, God's holiness
sanctified through
acts of justice."
Blessed is the Ineffable One,
the sacred Power.

קָדוֹשׁ אַתָּה וְנוֹרָא שְׁמֶךָ, וְאֵין
אֱלוֹהַּ מִבַּלְעָדֶיךָ, כַּכָּתוּב:
וַיִּגְבַּהּ יְיָ צְבָאוֹת בַּמִּשְׁפָּט,
וְהָאֵל הַקָּדוֹשׁ נִקְדַּשׁ בִּצְדָקָה.
בָּרוּךְ אַתָּה, יְיָ, הַמֶּלֶךְ הַקָּדוֹשׁ.

Kidushat Hayom: Sanctifying This Day

אַתָּה בְחַרְתָּנוּ עִם כָּל הָעַמִּים,
אָהַבְתָּ אוֹתָנוּ וְרָצִיתָ בָּנוּ,
וְרוֹמַמְתָּנוּ מִכָּל הַלְּשׁוֹנוֹת,
וְקִדַּשְׁתָּנוּ בְּמִצְוֹתֶיךָ, וְקֵרַבְתָּנוּ
מַלְכֵּנוּ לַעֲבוֹדָתֶךָ, וְשִׁמְךָ הַגָּדוֹל
וְהַקָּדוֹשׁ עָלֵינוּ קָרָאתָ.

You have delighted in us
among all the peoples,
loving us, desiring us, elevating
us and sanctifying us
with mitzvot,
drawing us near to serve You,
that Your great holy Presence
might be known to us.

וַתִּתֶּן לָנוּ, יְיָ אֱלֹהֵינוּ, בְּאַהֲבָה
אֶת יוֹם
(הַשַּׁבָּת הַזֶּה וְאֶת יוֹם) תְּרוּעָה
(בְּאַהֲבָה) מִקְרָא קֹדֶשׁ, זֵכֶר
לִיצִיאַת מִצְרָיִם.

With love, we have been given
(on Shabbat) this Shabbat and
this Day of Atonement
for renouncing our wrongs,
for asking for forgiveness,
for cleansing, for
reconciliation.

A day of holy gathering
reminding us of our liberation
from the straits of
enslavement.

Rachamana: Merciful One!

Rachamana d'anei l'ani-yei aneina!

Rachamana d'ani litbirei liba, aneina, aneina!

רַחֲמָנָא דְעָנֵי לַעֲנִיֵּי עֲנֵינָא!

רַחֲמָנָא דְעָנֵי לִתְבִירֵי לִבָּא עֲנֵינָא, עֲנֵינָא!

O Merciful One who answers those in need, answer us!

O Merciful One who answers the broken-hearted, answer us!

Ya'aleh v'yavo: May These Ascend

Our God
and God of our ancestors:
allow memory to ascend,
to come, to reach us.
May our memory
and our ancestors' memory
and the memory of the dream
of a messianic time,
and the memory of the vision
of Jerusalem as a city of peace,
and the memories of all of Your
people of the House of Israel,
be before You.
On this day
may these memories,
these dreams of redemption,
inspire graciousness,
lovingkindness,
and compassion in us,
for life and for peace,
on this Yom Kippur.

אֱלֹהֵינוּ
וֵאלֹהֵי אֲבוֹתֵינוּ וְאִמּוֹתֵינוּ,
יַעֲלֶה וְיָבֹא, וְיַגִּיעַ וְיֵרָאֶה,
וְיֵרָצֶה וְיִשָּׁמַע,
וְיִפָּקֵד וְיִזָּכֵר
זִכְרוֹנֵנוּ וּפִקְדוֹנֵנוּ,
וְזִכְרוֹן אֲבוֹתֵינוּ וְאִמּוֹתֵינוּ,
וְזִכְרוֹן מָשִׁיחַ בֶּן־דָּוִד עַבְדֶּךָ,
וְזִכְרוֹן יְרוּשָׁלַיִם עִיר קָדְשֶׁךָ,
וְזִכְרוֹן כָּל עַמְּךָ
בֵּית יִשְׂרָאֵל לְפָנֶיךָ
לִפְלֵיטָה וּלְטוֹבָה,
לְחֵן וּלְחֶסֶד וּלְרַחֲמִים, לְחַיִּים
וּלְשָׁלוֹם,
בְּיוֹם הַכִּפּוּרִים הַזֶּה.

Remember us, Adonai our
God, for goodness. Count us in
for blessing. Save us with life.
Shower us with salvation
and with compassion;
be merciful to us; enfold us
in the compassion we knew
before we were born.
For You are our merciful
parent and sovereign.

זָכְרֵנוּ, יְיָ אֱלֹהֵינוּ בּוֹ לְטוֹבָה,
וּפָקְדֵנוּ בוֹ לִבְרָכָה, וְהוֹשִׁיעֵנוּ
בוֹ לְחַיִּים; וּבִדְבַר יְשׁוּעָה
וְרַחֲמִים חוּס וְחָנֵּנוּ, וְרַחֵם
עָלֵינוּ וְהוֹשִׁיעֵנוּ, כִּי אֵלֶיךָ
עֵינֵינוּ, כִּי אֵל מֶלֶךְ חַנּוּן וְרַחוּם
אָתָּה.

Our God
and God of our generations:
shine Your glory on all
creation.
Remind us that You cherish
all who live on this earth,
here and everywhere.
You are our Creator;
You formed us; You breathe
life into us in every moment.
You are King/Queen
of all creation.

אֱלֹהֵינוּ וֵאלֹהֵי אֲבוֹתֵינוּ, מְלוֹךְ
עַל כָּל הָעוֹלָם כֻּלּוֹ בִּכְבוֹדֶךָ,
וְהִנָּשֵׂא עַל כָּל הָאָרֶץ בִּיקָרֶךָ,
וְהוֹפַע בַּהֲדַר גְּאוֹן עֻזֶּךָ, עַל כָּל
יוֹשְׁבֵי תֵבֵל אַרְצֶךָ, וְיֵדַע כָּל
פָּעוּל כִּי אַתָּה פְעַלְתּוֹ, וְיָבִין
כָּל יָצוּר כִּי אַתָּה יְצַרְתּוֹ,
וְיֹאמַר כֹּל אֲשֶׁר נְשָׁמָה בְאַפּוֹ,
יְיָ אֱלֹהֵי יִשְׂרָאֵל מֶלֶךְ, וּמַלְכוּתוֹ
בַּכֹּל מָשָׁלָה.

Our God
and God of our generations:
(accept our rest with mercy)
help us make ourselves holy
with Your mitzvot; give us
a portion of Your Torah's
sweetness; grant us
Your goodness, help us rejoice
in Your salvation
(and on this Shabbat which is
also a holiday, help us be
mindful of both, and to wholly
rest as befits Your people
who yearn to sanctify Your
name).

אֱלֹהֵינוּ וֵאלֹהֵי אֲבוֹתֵינוּ, (רְצֵה
בִמְנוּחָתֵנוּ) קַדְּשֵׁנוּ בְּמִצְוֹתֶיךָ
וְתֵן חֶלְקֵנוּ בְּתוֹרָתֶךָ, שַׂבְּעֵנוּ
מִטּוּבֶךָ וְשַׂמְּחֵנוּ בִּישׁוּעָתֶךָ
(וְהַנְחִילֵנוּ, יְיָ אֱלֹהֵינוּ, בְּאַהֲבָה
וּבְרָצוֹן שַׁבַּת קָדְשֶׁךָ, וְיָנוּחוּ
בָהּ יִשְׂרָאֵל מְקַדְּשֵׁי שְׁמֶךָ).

וְטַהֵר לִבֵּנוּ לְעָבְדְּךָ בֶּאֱמֶת, כִּי אַתָּה אֱלֹהִים אֱמֶת, וּדְבָרְךָ אֱמֶת וְקַיָּם לָעַד. בָּרוּךְ אַתָּה, יְיָ, מֶלֶךְ עַל כָּל הָאָרֶץ, מְקַדֵּשׁ (הַשַּׁבָּת וְ) יִשְׂרָאֵל וְיוֹם הַכִּפּוּרִים.

Purify our hearts to serve You in truth, for You are God of truth and your truth endures forever.
Blessed are You, Adonai, ruler over all the earth,
Who sanctifies (Shabbat and) Israel and this Day of Atonement.

Avodah: Worship

רְצֵה, יְיָ אֱלֹהֵינוּ, בְּעַמְּךָ יִשְׂרָאֵל וּבִתְפִלָּתָם, בְּאַהֲבָה תְקַבֵּל וּתְהִי לְרָצוֹן תָּמִיד עֲבוֹדַת יִשְׂרָאֵל עַמֶּךָ.

May it be Your will, Adonai our God, that You accept our rest and take pleasure in our prayers. Accept the service of our hearts and our lips which we mean to offer in love. May the offerings of our hearts always bring You joy in Your people.

וְתֶחֱזֶינָה עֵינֵינוּ בְּשׁוּבְךָ לְצִיּוֹן בְּרַחֲמִים. בָּרוּךְ אַתָּה יְיָ, הַמַּחֲזִיר שְׁכִינָתוֹ לְצִיּוֹן.

May Your presence return to Zion speedily and with compassion. Blessed are You, Adonai, Whose presence returns to Zion and fills all creation.

Yom Kippur is a day to remove our *kapparot*, our coverings, the masks and stories which conceal our true selves.

(*Rabbi David Ingber*)

Hoda'ah: Giving Thanks

We are grateful before You, that You are our God and God of our generations, for ever. You are the rock of our lives, the shield of our salvation; You, only You, from generation to generation we sing praises. For our lives which are in Your keeping; for our souls of which You take daily account; for all of the miracles which You perform for us, and all of the wonders and goodnesses which You bring forth in every era and in every day, evening and morning and afternoon; for the goodness of Your compassion; for all of these things we could never thank You enough.

מוֹדִים אֲנַחְנוּ לָךְ, שָׁאַתָּה
הוּא, יְיָ אֱלֹהֵינוּ וֵאלֹהֵי
אֲבוֹתֵינוּ, לְעוֹלָם וָעֶד, צוּר
חַיֵּינוּ, מָגֵן יִשְׁעֵנוּ, אַתָּה הוּא
לְדוֹר וָדוֹר נוֹדֶה לְּךָ וּנְסַפֵּר
תְּהִלָּתֶךָ. עַל חַיֵּינוּ הַמְּסוּרִים
בְּיָדֶךָ, וְעַל נִשְׁמוֹתֵינוּ הַפְּקוּדוֹת
לָךְ, וְעַל נִסֶּיךָ שֶׁבְּכָל יוֹם עִמָּנוּ,
וְעַל נִפְלְאוֹתֶיךָ וְטוֹבוֹתֶיךָ
שֶׁבְּכָל עֵת, עֶרֶב וָבֹקֶר
וְצָהֳרָיִם, הַטּוֹב כִּי לֹא כָלוּ
רַחֲמֶיךָ, וְהַמְרַחֵם כִּי לֹא תַמּוּ
חֲסָדֶיךָ מֵעוֹלָם קִוִּינוּ לָךְ.

For all of these we bless and elevate Your name, our Sovereign and Source, forever and ever.

וְעַל כֻּלָּם יִתְבָּרַךְ וְיִתְרוֹמַם
שִׁמְךָ מַלְכֵּנוּ תָּמִיד לְעוֹלָם וָעֶד.

And we thank You for inscribing us, the children of Your covenant, into the book of life.

וּכְתוֹב לְחַיִּים טוֹבִים כָּל בְּנֵי
בְרִיתֶךָ.

All that lives praises Your name in truth, our God and our help. Blessed are You, Adonai, for Your goodness and for the many wonders which merit our thanks.

וְכֹל הַחַיִּים יוֹדוּךָ סֶּלָה, וִיהַלְלוּ
אֶת שִׁמְךָ בֶּאֱמֶת, הָאֵל
יְשׁוּעָתֵנוּ וְעֶזְרָתֵנוּ סֶלָה. בָּרוּךְ
אַתָּה יְיָ, הַטּוֹב שִׁמְךָ וּלְךָ נָאֶה
לְהוֹדוֹת.

Birkat Shalom: Peace

שָׁלוֹם רָב עַל יִשְׂרָאֵל עַמְּךָ
תָּשִׂים לְעוֹלָם, כִּי אַתָּה הוּא
מֶלֶךְ אָדוֹן לְכָל הַשָּׁלוֹם. וְטוֹב
בְּעֵינֶיךָ לְבָרֵךְ אֶת עַמְּךָ
יִשְׂרָאֵל, בְּכָל עֵת וּבְכָל שָׁעָה
בִּשְׁלוֹמֶךָ.

Shalom rav al Yisrael amcha
tasim le'olam, ki atah hu
melech adon l'chol hashalom.
V'tov b'einecha levarech et
amcha Yisrael, b'chol eit
u'vchol sha'ah bishlomecha.

בְּסֵפֶר חַיִּים, בְּרָכָה וְשָׁלוֹם
וּפַרְנָסָה טוֹבָה, נִזָּכֵר וְנִכָּתֵב
לְפָנֶיךָ, אֲנַחְנוּ וְכָל עַמְּךָ בֵּית
יִשְׂרָאֵל, לְחַיִּים טוֹבִים
וּלְשָׁלוֹם.

B'sefer chayyim, bracha
v'shalom, ufarnasah tovah,
n'zacher v'nikatev l'fanecha,
anachnu v'chol amcha beit
Yisrael, l'chayyim tovim
u'l'shalom.

בָּרוּךְ אַתָּה יְיָ, עוֹשֵׂה הַשָּׁלוֹם.

Baruch atah, Adonai, oseh ha-
shalom.

May there be abundant peace for Israel Your people, always; for You are the sovereign of peace. Let it be good in Your eyes to bless Your people Israel, in every time and in every hour, with Your peace.

In the book of life, blessing, peace and of making a good living may we be remembered and written before You: us, and all of Your people in our many communities, for a good life and for peace.

Blessed are You, Adonai, maker of peace.

Meditations After Prayer

אֱלֹהַי, נְצוֹר לְשׁוֹנִי מֵרָע.
וּשְׂפָתַי מִדַּבֵּר מִרְמָה:
וְלִמְקַלְלַי נַפְשִׁי תִדֹּם, וְנַפְשִׁי
כֶּעָפָר לַכֹּל תִּהְיֶה. פְּתַח לִבִּי
בְּתוֹרָתֶךָ, וּבְמִצְוֹתֶיךָ תִּרְדּוֹף
נַפְשִׁי.

Elohai n'tzor l'shoni mera
usfatai m'daber mirmah
v'limkallelai nafshi tidom
v'nafshi ke'afar l'kol tihiyeh.
Petach libi ba-Toratecha,
uv'mitzvotecha tirdof nafshi.

God, keep my tongue from evil
and my lips from speaking deceit.
Before those who slander me, I will hold my tongue;
I will practice humility.
Open my heart to Your Torah,
and connect my heart to Your mitzvot.

יִהְיוּ לְרָצוֹן אִמְרֵי פִי וְהֶגְיוֹן לִבִּי
לְפָנֶיךָ, יְיָ צוּרִי וְגוֹאֲלִי.
עֹשֶׂה שָׁלוֹם בִּמְרוֹמָיו הוּא
יַעֲשֶׂה שָׁלוֹם עָלֵינוּ וְעַל כָּל
יִשְׂרָאֵל, וְעַל כָּל יוֹשְׁבֵי תֵבֵל,
וְאִמְרוּ אָמֵן:

Yihiyu l'ratzon imrei fi
v'hegyon libi l'fanecha
Adonai tzuri v'goali.

Oseh shalom bimromav,
hu ya'aseh shalom, aleinu
v'al kol yisrael, v'al kol yoshvei
tevel, v'imru Amen.

May the words of my mouth
and the meditations of my heart
be acceptable to You, O God,
my rock and my redeemer.

May the One Who makes peace in the heavens
make peace for us, for all Israel
and for all who dwell on earth.
And let us say: Amen.

Adon HaSelichot : Master of Repentance

Master of forgiveness, examiner of hearts, Revealer of depths, declarer of righteousness, We have sinned before You. Have mercy on us!	Adon haselichot, Bochen levavot, Golah amukot, Doveir tzedakot, Chatanu lefanecha. Rachem aleinu!	אֲדוֹן הַסְּלִיחוֹת, בּוֹחֵן לְבָבוֹת, גֹּלָה עֲמֻקוֹת, דּוֹבֵר צְדָקוֹת. חָטָאנוּ לְפָנֶךָ. רַחֵם עָלֵינוּ!
The One who dwells in wonders, Ancient One of mercy, Who remembers our ancestors' covenant and examines inward parts, We have sinned before You. Have mercy on us!	Hadur baniflaot, Vatik benachamot, Zocheir berit avot, Chokeir kelayot, Chatanu lefanecha. Rachem aleinu!	הָדוּר בַּנִּפְלָאוֹת, וָתִיק בְּנֶחָמוֹת, זוֹכֵר בְּרִית אָבוֹת, חוֹקֵר כְּלָיוֹת. חָטָאנוּ לְפָנֶךָ. רַחֵם עָלֵינוּ!
The One who is good and benefits all life, who knows all that is hidden, Subduer of transgressions, wrapped in righteousness, We have sinned before You. Have mercy on us!	Tov umeitiv labriot, Yodei'a kol nistarot, Koveish avonot, Loveish tzedakot, Chatanu lefanecha. Rachem aleinu!	טוֹב וּמֵטִיב לַבְּרִיּוֹת, יוֹדֵעַ כָּל נִסְתָּרוֹת, כּוֹבֵשׁ עֲווֹנוֹת, לוֹבֵשׁ צְדָקוֹת. חָטָאנוּ לְפָנֶךָ. רַחֵם עָלֵינוּ!

The Thirteen Attributes

☐ יְיָ, יְיָ, אֵל רַחוּם וְחַנּוּן, אֶרֶךְ
אַפַּיִם, וְרַב חֶסֶד וֶאֱמֶת: נֹצֵר
חֶסֶד לָאֲלָפִים, נֹשֵׂא עָוֹן
וָפֶשַׁע וְחַטָּאָה, וְנַקֵּה:

☐ Adonai, Adonai, El rachum vechanun, erech apayim, verav chesed ve'emet, notseir chesed la'alafim, nosei avon, vafesha, vechata'ah, venakeih.

Adonai, Adonai, God of mercy and grace, patient, loving and faithful. Who extends love to the thousandth generation, forgiving transgression, rebellion and sin, and granting pardon.

Singable English:

☐ Yod Hay, Vav Hay, Compassion and Tenderness,
Patience, Forebearance, Kindness, Awareness.
Bearing love from age to age,
Lifting guilt and mistakes and making us free.

"בְּשֵׁם אֱלֹהִים הָרַחֲמָן וְהָרַחוּם."

"In the name of God, the Merciful, the Compassionate."

Sh'ma Koleinu: Hear Our Voice

שְׁמַע קוֹלֵנוּ, יְיָ אֱלֹהֵינוּ, חוּס
וְרַחֵם עָלֵינוּ, וְקַבֵּל בְּרַחֲמִים
וּבְרָצוֹן אֶת תְּפִלָּתֵנוּ.
הֲשִׁיבֵנוּ יְיָ אֵלֶיךָ וְנָשׁוּבָה,
חַדֵּשׁ יָמֵינוּ כְּקֶדֶם.

Sh'ma koleinu, Adonai
eloheinu, chus v'rachem
aleinu, v'kabel b'rachamim
u'v'ratzon et t'filateinu.
Hashiveinu Adonai elecha
v'nashuva, chadesh yameinu
k'kedem.

Hear our voice, Adonai our God. Be merciful with us and accept our prayer. Return us, Adonai, to You and we will be returned. Renew our days, as in days of old.

אַל תַּשְׁלִיכֵנוּ מִלְּפָנֶיךָ, וְרוּחַ קָדְשְׁךָ אַל תִּקַּח מִמֶּנּוּ.
אַל תַּשְׁלִיכֵנוּ לְעֵת זִקְנָה, כִּכְלוֹת כֹּחֵנוּ אַל תַּעַזְבֵנוּ.
אַל תַּעַזְבֵנוּ, יְיָ אֱלֹהֵינוּ, אַל תִּרְחַק מִמֶּנּוּ. עֲשֵׂה עִמָּנוּ אוֹת
לְטוֹבָה, וְיִרְאוּ שׂוֹנְאֵינוּ וְיֵבֹשׁוּ, כִּי אַתָּה יְיָ עֲזַרְתָּנוּ וְנִחַמְתָּנוּ.
כִּי לְךָ יְיָ הוֹחָלְנוּ, אַתָּה תַעֲנֶה, אֲדֹנָי אֱלֹהֵינוּ.

Do not cast us away,
Do not take Your holy spirit from us.

Do not cast us away in our old age,
When our strength is gone, do not abandon us.

Do not abandon us, Adonai our God.
Do not be distant from us.

Give us a sign of Your goodness to drive away our trouble.
You are Adonai, our help and comfort.

You will answer.
For You we wait, our source, our God.

Ki Anu Amecha: We Are Your People

כִּי אָנוּ עַמֶּךָ, וְאַתָּה אֱלֹהֵינוּ.
אָנוּ בָנֶיךָ וְאַתָּה אָבִינוּ.
אָנוּ עֲבָדֶיךָ, וְאַתָּה אֲדוֹנֵינוּ.
אָנוּ קְהָלֶךָ, וְאַתָּה חֶלְקֵנוּ.
אָנוּ נַחֲלָתֶךָ, וְאַתָּה גּוֹרָלֵנוּ.
אָנוּ צֹאנֶךָ, וְאַתָּה רוֹעֵנוּ.
אָנוּ כַרְמֶךָ, וְאַתָּה נוֹטְרֵנוּ.
אָנוּ פְעֻלָּתֶךָ וְאַתָּה יוֹצְרֵנוּ.
אָנוּ רַעְיָתֶךָ, וְאַתָּה דוֹדֵנוּ.
אָנוּ סְגֻלָּתֶךָ, וְאַתָּה קְרוֹבֵנוּ.
אָנוּ עַמֶּךָ, וְאַתָּה מַלְכֵּנוּ.
אָנוּ מַאֲמִירֶיךָ, וְאַתָּה
מַאֲמִירֵנוּ.

Ki anu amecha ve'atah Eloheinu. Anu vanecha ve'atah avinu. Anu avdecha, ve'atah adoneinu. Anu kehalecha, ve'atah chelkeinu. Anu nachalatecha, ve'atah goraleinu. Anu tzonecha, ve'atah ro'einu. Anu charmecha, ve'atah notreinu. Anu fe'ulatecha, ve'atah yotzreinu. Anu rayatecha, ve'atah dodeinu. Anu segulatecha, ve'atah keroveinu.
Anu amecha, ve'atah malkeinu.
Anu ma'amirecha, ve'ata ma'amireinu.

We are Your people,
and You our holy source.
We are Your children, and You our parent.
We are Your helpers,
and You our guiding spirit.
We are Your body,
and You our designer.
We are Your images,
and You our true essence.
We are Your flock,
and You our shepherd.
We are Your plantings, and You our gardener.
We are Your creation, and You our origin.
We are Your companions, and You our beloved.
We are Your treasure, and You delight in us.
We are Your people,
and You are our sovereign.
We solely favor You,
and You recognize us.

Vidui: Confessional Prayers

We knock on our hearts, imploring them to open.

אֱלֹהֵינוּ וֵאלֹהֵי אֲבוֹתֵינוּ, תָּבֹא
לְפָנֶיךָ תְּפִלָּתֵנוּ, וְאַל תִּתְעַלַּם
מִתְּחִנָּתֵנוּ, שֶׁאֵין אָנוּ עַזֵּי פָנִים
וּקְשֵׁי עֹרֶף, לוֹמַר לְפָנֶיךָ יְיָ
אֱלֹהֵינוּ וֵאלֹהֵי אֲבוֹתֵינוּ,
צַדִּיקִים אֲנַחְנוּ וְלֹא חָטָאנוּ,
אֲבָל אֲנַחְנוּ וַאֲבוֹתֵינוּ חָטָאנוּ.

Our God and God of our ancestors, accept our prayer and do not hide from us. We are not so hard-hearted and stiff-necked to say before You, Adonai, that we are righteous and pure. Rather, we confess that we have sinned.

□ אָשַׁמְנוּ, בָּגַדְנוּ, גָּזַלְנוּ,
דִּבַּרְנוּ דֹפִי. הֶעֱוִינוּ,
וְהִרְשַׁעְנוּ, זַדְנוּ, חָמַסְנוּ,
טָפַלְנוּ שֶׁקֶר. יָעַצְנוּ רָע,
כִּזַּבְנוּ, לַצְנוּ, מָרַדְנוּ, נִאַצְנוּ,
סָרַרְנוּ, עָוִינוּ, פָּשַׁעְנוּ, צָרַרְנוּ,
קִשִּׁינוּ עֹרֶף. רָשַׁעְנוּ, שִׁחַתְנוּ,
תִּעַבְנוּ, תָּעִינוּ, תִּעְתָּעְנוּ.

□ Ashamnu, bagadnu, gazalnu, dibarnu dofi. He'evinu, vehirshanu, zadnu, chamasnu, tafalnu shaker. Ya'atsnu ra, kizavnu, latsnu, maradnu, ni'atsnu, sararnu, avinu, pashanu, tzararnu, kish inu oref. Rashanu, shichatnu, ti'avnu, ta'inu, titanu.

We have abused, betrayed, conspired, deceived, endangered, flattered, gossiped, hated, insulted, jeered, kept grudges, lied, mocked, neglected, oppressed, perverted, quarreled, rebelled, stolen, threatened, undermined, vilified, wasted, and yielded to temptation.

Ashamnu (Singable English)

Who are we? We're light and truth and infinite wisdom, eternal goodness. Yet we've **A**bused, we've **B**etrayed, we've been **C**ruel, we've **D**estroyed. We've **E**mbittered, we have **F**alsified, we have **G**ossiped, we have **H**ated. We've **I**nsulted, we have **J**eered, we have **K**illed, we have **L**ied.

Sweep it out! Throw it out! Wipe it out! Clean it all out!

At our core, we're light and truth and infinite wisdom, eternal goodness. Yet we have **M**ocked, we've **N**eglected, we've **O**ppressed, we have **P**erverted. We have **Q**uarreled, we've been **R**acist, we have **S**tolen, we've Transgressed. We've been **U**nkind, we've been **V**iolent, we've been **W**icked, we've been **X**enophobic.

Sweep it out! Throw it out! Wipe it out! Clean it all out!

Al Chet: for the sins we have sinned

For the sin we have sinned against You by
not caring for the earth
and the sin we have sinned against You by
not caring for its inhabitants

For the sin we have sinned against You by
numbing ourselves to the news
and the sin we have sinned against You by
using the news to numb ourselves

For the sin we have sinned against You by
not paying attention to Your creation
and the sin we have sinned against You by
misusing the earth we've been given:

וְעַל כֻּלָּם, אֱלוֹהַּ סְלִיחוֹת, סְלַח לָנוּ, מְחַל לָנוּ, כַּפֶּר לָנוּ.

Ve'al kulam, Elo'ah selichot, selach lanu, mechal lanu, kaper lanu.

For all of these—God of forgiveness— forgive us, pardon us, grant us atonement.

For the sin we have sinned against You by not being kind
and the sin we have sinned against You by
not cultivating compassion

For the sin we have sinned against You by
not expressing love
and the sin we have sinned against You by
expressing love in inappropriate ways

For the sin we have sinned against You by
puffing ourselves up with pride
and the sin we have sinned against You by
believing that we are worthless:

וְעַל כֻּלָּם, אֱלוֹהַּ סְלִיחוֹת, סְלַח לָנוּ, מְחַל לָנוּ, כַּפֶּר לָנוּ.

Ve'al kulam, Elo'ah selichot, selach lanu, mechal lanu, kaper lanu.

For all of these—God of forgiveness— forgive us, pardon us, grant us atonement.

For the sin we have sinned against You by
arguing and confrontation
and the sin we have sinned against You by
generating heat instead of light

For the sin we have sinned against You by
not seeing the best in each other
and the sin we have sinned against You by
not seeing the best in ourselves

For the sin we have sinned against You by
not making time to care for our souls
and the sin we have sinned against You by
believing that nothing we do matters:

וְעַל כֻּלָּם, אֱלוֹהַּ סְלִיחוֹת, סְלַח לָנוּ, מְחַל לָנוּ, כַּפֶּר לָנוּ.

Ve'al kulam, Elo'ah selichot, selach lanu, mechal lanu, kaper lanu.

For all of these—God of forgiveness— forgive us, pardon us, grant us atonement.

This is the season
for *tikkun ha-sulam*,
repairing the ladder
which connects
heaven and earth.
Each of us
has been climbing
toward our yearnings;
now we approach
the last rung.
What alignment work
do you need
to do right now
in order for blessing
to flow freely?
What can you repair
in your body, heart,
mind, and soul
so that God's light
can shine in you
and your light can shine
into creation?

Ne'ilah

"Wherever we stand to lift our eyes to heaven, that place is a Holy of Holies." —S. Ansky

The sun descending setting
on the roof of the synagogue.
The cantor faces the open Ark.
His exhausted voice sounds hoarse.
My lips are dry, my mouth bitter,
My irritable tongue feels
a burning sensation, sends flash signals
to my brain, while my stomach blows shofar.
A realization: what it is like to be hungry...
The sanctuary doors are closed,
I feel like Jonah in the whale's belly.
A thousand people pray here
and I feel lonely, uncertain.
After a day full of prayers
a thunderstorm of psalms, poems,
an avalanche of biblical passages
showering my God
with compliments, praise, petition, lamentations,
exhausted from memorial chants,
confession of sins never committed
I reach the last page of the Machzor.
I close my eyes, frightened by the thought
that the liturgy I have been chanting all day
is not sincere, the words not mine.
Angels, hell, paradise, seem far away.
Now in the last moments before
the Ark is closed, I pray:
Simple words, children, people, earth,
sunshine, health, love, peace:
God—I say—make me wise enough
to care about others who are hungry,
good enough to share my love
with the less fortunate in this world.

(Herman Taube)

Avinu Malkeinu / Imeinu Malkateinu

Our Father, our King, help us make this year a new beginning.
Our Mother, our Queen, help us grow when life is hard.

Our Source and our Destiny, teach us to accept what we must.
Our Guide and our Truth, teach us to change what we must.

Our Father, our King, teach us how to face disease and death.
Our Mother, our Queen, teach us how to enjoy the gifts of life.

Our Source and our Destiny, teach us how to make peace.
Our Guide and our Truth, teach us how to help our people.

Our Father, our King, teach us how to help all humanity.
Our Mother, our Queen, let us find pardon for our wrongdoings.

Our Source and our Destiny, let us return to You, completely.
Our Guide and our Truth, teach us to help those who are ill.

Our Father, our King, let us write our names in the Book of Life.
Our Mother, our Queen, help us to find meaningful work.

Our Source and our Destiny, help us to find inner freedom.
Our Guide and our Truth, help us to learn how to love.

Our Father, our King, receive our prayers.
Our Mother, our Queen, teach us how to be good partners.

Our Source and our Destiny, teach us how to be good parents.
Our Guide and our Truth, teach us how to be good children.

Our Father, our King, teach us how to be good friends.
Our Mother, our Queen, teach us how to be good Jews.

Our Source and our Destiny, teach us how to be good people.
Our Guide and our Truth, teach us to be one with You.

Avinu malkeinu, grant us justice and bring us salvation,
Grant us justice and loving kindness and bring us salvation!

(The full text of Avinu Malkeinu follows.)

Avinu malkeinu, chatanu l'fanecha.

אָבִינוּ מַלְכֵּנוּ חָטָאנוּ לְפָנֶיךָ.

Avinu Malkeinu, we have sinned before You.

Avinu malkeinu, ein lanu melech eleh atah.

אָבִינוּ מַלְכֵּנוּ אֵין לָנוּ מֶלֶךְ אֶלָּא אָתָּה.

Avinu Malkeinu, we have no ruler but You.

Avinu malkeinu, chadesh aleinu shanah tovah.

אָבִינוּ מַלְכֵּנוּ חַדֵּשׁ עָלֵינוּ שָׁנָה טוֹבָה.

Avinu Malkeinu, renew us for a good year.

Avinu malkeinu, kaleh kol tzar u-mastin me'aleinu.

אָבִינוּ מַלְכֵּנוּ כַּלֵּה כָּל צַר וּמַשְׂטִין מֵעָלֵינוּ.

Avinu Malkeinu, rid us of persecution.

Avinu malkeinu, caleh dever v'cherev v'ra'av v'shvi u-mashchit v'avon.

אָבִינוּ מַלְכֵּנוּ כַּלֵּה דֶּבֶר וְחֶרֶב וְרָעָב וּשְׁבִי וּמַשְׁחִית וְעָוֹן.

Avinu Malkeinu, rid us of sickness, sword, hunger & destruction.

Avinu malkeinu, slach u'mchal l'chol avonoteinu.

אָבִינוּ מַלְכֵּנוּ סְלַח · וּמְחַל לְכָל עֲוֹנוֹתֵינוּ.

Avinu Malkeinu, forgive us all our sins.

Avinu malkeinu, kotveinu (*ne'ilah:* chotmeinu) b'sefer g'ulah v'yeshua.

אָבִינוּ מַלְכֵּנוּ כָּתְבֵנוּ (חָתְמֵנוּ)
בְּסֵפֶר גְּאֻלָּה וִישׁוּעָה.

Avinu Malkeinu, inscribe (seal) us in the Book of Redemption.

Avinu malkeinu, kotveinu (*ne'ilah:* chotmeinu) b'sefer parnassah v'chalkalah.

אָבִינוּ מַלְכֵּנוּ כָּתְבֵנוּ (חָתְמֵנוּ)
בְּסֵפֶר פַּרְנָסָה וְכַלְכָּלָה.

Avinu Malkeinu, inscribe (seal) us in the Book of Prosperity.

Avinu malkeinu, kotveinu (*ne'ilah:* chotmeinu) b'sefer s'lichah u-m'chilah.

אָבִינוּ מַלְכֵּנוּ כָּתְבֵנוּ
(חָתְמֵנוּ) בְּסֵפֶר סְלִיחָה
וּמְחִילָה.

Avinu Malkeinu, inscribe (seal) us in the Book of Forgiveness.

Avinu malkeinu, chus v'rachem aleinu.

אָבִינוּ מַלְכֵּנוּ חוּס וְרַחֵם עָלֵינוּ.

Avinu Malkeinu, have mercy upon us.

Avinu malkeinu, kabel b'rachamim u'v'ratzon et t'filateinu.

אָבִינוּ מַלְכֵּנוּ קַבֵּל בְּרַחֲמִים
וּבְרָצוֹן אֶת תְּפִלָּתֵנוּ.

Avinu Malkeinu, accept our prayers in mercy.

Avinu malkeinu, na al tashivenu reikam milfanecha.

אָבִינוּ מַלְכֵּנוּ נָא אַל תְּשִׁיבֵנוּ
רֵיקָם מִלְּפָנֶיךָ.

Avinu Malkeinu, do not turn us away from You empty-handed.

Avinu malkeinu, z'chor ki afar anachnu.

אָבִינוּ מַלְכֵּנוּ זְכֹר כִּי עָפָר
אֲנָחְנוּ.

Avinu Malkeinu, remember that we are dust.

Avinu malkeinu, chamol aleinu v'al olaleinu v'tapenu.

אָבִינוּ מַלְכֵּנוּ חֲמֹל עָלֵינוּ וְעַל
עוֹלָלֵינוּ וְטַפֵּנוּ.

Avinu Malkeinu, have mercy on us and our children.

Avinu malkeinu, aseh l'ma'an harugim al shem kodshecha.

אָבִינוּ מַלְכֵּנוּ עֲשֵׂה לְמַעַן הֲרוּגִים עַל שֵׁם קָדְשֶׁךָ.

Avinu Malkeinu, act for the sake of those who died to sanctify Your name.

Avinu malkeinu, aseh l'ma'anecha im lo l'ma'aneinu.

אָבִינוּ מַלְכֵּנוּ עֲשֵׂה לְמַעַנְךָ אִם לֹא לְמַעֲנֵנוּ.

Avinu Malkeinu, act for Your sake if not ours.

□ Avinu malkeinu, chanenu va'anenu, ki ein banu ma'asim, aseh imanu tzedakah vachesed v'hoshienu.

□אָבִינוּ מַלְכֵּנוּ, חָנֵּנוּ וַעֲנֵנוּ, כִּי אֵין בָּנוּ מַעֲשִׂים,
עֲשֵׂה עִמָּנוּ צְדָקָה וָחֶסֶד וְהוֹשִׁיעֵנוּ.

Avinu malkeinu, be gracious and answer us,
for we have little merit.
Treat us generously and with kindness, and be our help.

If you've just davened the full Avinu Malkeinu on ***Rosh Hashanah morning****, continue on p. 117.*

If you've just davened the full Avinu Malkeinu at ***Kol Nidre****, continue on p. 237.*

If you've just davened the full Avinu Malkeinu at ***Ne'ilah****, continue on the next page.*

Shema Yisrael!

One time: Hear O Israel, Adonai is our God, Adonai is One!

☐ Shema Yisrael:
Adonai Eloheinu
Adonai echad!

☐שְׁמַע יִשְׂרָאֵל, יְיָ אֱלֹהֵינוּ,
יְיָ אֶחָד:

*Three times: Through time and space, Your glory shines,
Majestic One!*

☐ Baruch sheim kevod
malchuto le'olam va'ed!

☐ בָּרוּךְ שֵׁם כְּבוֹד מַלְכוּתוֹ
לְעוֹלָם וָעֶד.

*Seven times: Adonai is God!
(God far away is God deep within!
Transcendence and Immanence are One!)*

☐ Adonai Hu Ha-elohim!

☐ יְיָ הוּא הָאֱלֹהִים!

TEKIAH GEDOLAH! תקיעה גדולה

Havdalah: Declaring the New Day

Hold up the glass of wine.

בָּרוּךְ אַתָּה יְיָ, אֱלֹהֵינוּ מֶלֶךְ
הָעוֹלָם, בּוֹרֵא פְּרִי הַגָּפֶן.

Baruch Atah Adonai
eloheinu melech ha'olam
borei p'ri hagafen.

Blessed are You, Adonai our God, sovereign of all worlds, Who creates the fruit of the vine.

Hold up the spices, then pass them around and inhale their sweetness.

בָּרוּךְ אַתָּה יְיָ, אֱלֹהֵינוּ מֶלֶךְ
הָעוֹלָם, בּוֹרֵא מִינֵי בְשָׂמִים:

Baruch Atah Adonai
eloheinu melech ha'olam
borei minei besamim.

Blessed are You, Adonai our God, source of all being, Who creates various spices.

Hold up the braided candle and see your radiance reflected there.

בָּרוּךְ אַתָּה יְיָ, אֱלֹהֵינוּ מֶלֶךְ
הָעוֹלָם, בּוֹרֵא מְאוֹרֵי הָאֵשׁ:

Baruch Atah Adonai
eloheinu melech ha-olam
borei me-orey ha-esh.

Blessed are You, Adonai our God, enlivener of all worlds, Who creates the lights of fire.

Baruch Atah Adonai eloheinu melech ha-olam hamavdil beyn kodesh lechol, beyn or le-choshech, beyn Yisrael l'amim, beyn yom hashevi'i lesheshet yemey ha-ma'aseh. Baruch Atah Adonai, ha-mavdil u-m'gasher beyn kodesh lechol.

בָּרוּךְ אַתָּה יְיָ, אֱלֹהֵינוּ מֶלֶךְ
הָעוֹלָם, הַמַּבְדִּיל בֵּין קֹדֶשׁ
לְחוֹל, בֵּין אוֹר לְחֹשֶׁךְ, בֵּין
יִשְׂרָאֵל לָעַמִּים, בֵּין יוֹם
הַשְּׁבִיעִי, לְשֵׁשֶׁת יְמֵי
הַמַּעֲשֶׂה: בָּרוּךְ אַתָּה יְיָ,
הַמַּבְדִּיל וּמְגַשֵּׁר בֵּין קֹדֶשׁ
לְחוֹל:

Blessed are You, Adonai our God, source of all being, Who separates between holy and ordinary, between light and dark, between different communities, between the seventh day and the ordinary week. A fountain of blessings are You, Who separates and bridges between holy time and ordinary time.

Eliahu HaNavi / Miriam HaNeviah

Eliyahu hanavi, Eliyahu hatishbi, Eliyahu (3x) hagiladi. Bimheira beyameinu, yavo eleinu, im moshiach ben David (2x)

אֵלִיָּהוּ הַנָּבִיא, אֵלִיָּהוּ הַתִּשְׁבִּי,
אֵלִיָּהוּ, אֵלִיָּהוּ, אֵלִיָּהוּ הַגִּלְעָדִי.
בִּמְהֵרָה בְּיָמֵינוּ יָבֹא אֵלֵינוּ,
עִם מָשִׁיחַ בֶּן דָּוִד, עִם מָשִׁיחַ
בֶּן דָּוִד.

Miriam ha-n'vi'ah oz v'zimrah b'yadah. Miriam tirkod itanu l'taken et ha-olam. Bimheirah v'yameinu hi t'vi'einu, El mei ha-y'shuah (2x)

מִרְיַם הַנְּבִיאָה עֹז וְזִמְרָה
בְּיָדָהּ, מִרְיַם תִּרְקֹד אִתָּנוּ
לְתַקֵּן אֶת הָעוֹלָם.
בִּמְהֵרָה בְּיָמֵנוּ הִיא תְּבִיאֵנוּ
אֶל מֵי הַיְשׁוּעָה, אֶל מֵי
הַיְשׁוּאָה!

Elijah, the prophet; Elijiah, the Tishbite; Elijah, the Giladi!
Come quickly in our days and bring messianic transformation.

Miriam the prophet, strength and song in her hand;
Miriam, dance with us to increase the song of the world!
Miriam, dance with us in order to repair the world.
Soon she will bring us to the waters of redemption!

(second verse by R' Leila Gal Berner)

If Yom Kippur falls on Shabbat, end havdalah with:

Shavua Tov

Shavua tov! (repeat 8x)

שבוע טוב!

Shavua tov, a week of peace
May gladness reign, and joy increase! (repeat)

My deep thanks go to:

Rabbi Jeff Goldwasser (www.rebjeff.com): mentor, collaborator, teacher, and friend, whose *B'Kol Shofar* inspired and formed the backbone of this machzor;

Harriet Goren (www.gorenjudaica.com) for help with the cover design for the right-to-left edition;

Congregation Beth Israel (www.cbiweb.org) in North Adams, MA for giving me a place to "pray-test" much of this liturgy;

The CBI machzor committee for their suggestions;

The teachers in the ALEPH rabbinic ordination program, in whose name I give over these teachings;

The many artists, poets, liturgists, and rabbis who granted generous permission to reprint their work;

This *machzor*'s many beta-readers, among them Rabbi Megan Doherty, Rabbi Cynthia Hoffman, Rabbi David Markus, student hazzan Randall Miller, and rabbinic student David Curiel, who read multiple drafts and offered wise advice and cogent commentary;

All those who have read and commented at Velveteen Rabbi since I began blogging about Judaism there in 2003;

My lifelong *hevruta* partner Rabbi David Markus, whose presence in my life blesses me;

And most of all, my husband Ethan Zuckerman and our son Drew, who are endlessly supportive of my spiritual path, and who graciously share me with those to whom I tend.

For what is praiseworthy in this *machzor*, the abovementioned people merit credit. The mistakes remain entirely my own.

Rabbi Rachel Barenblat, 5775

NOTES/SOURCES

p. 9, Photograph by Mel G., www.flickr.com/photos/mellysphotos/1381729807/ Creative Commons.

p. 10, "Head of the Year," Myra Sklarew, from the *New Kehilla Machzor*. Reprinted with permission.

p. 12, Photograph of soaring bird, Karen Kelly. Reprinted with permission.

p. 13 "As we bless," Faith Rogow (c 1990). Reprinted with permission.

p. 15, Illustration of earth, heavens, and firmament, anonymous, 1745; in the public domain. Source: Wikimedia Commons.

p. 17, "An Unending Love," Rabbi Rami Shapiro, rabbirami.com. Reprinted with permission.

p. 20, Image source www.hanefesh.com/edu/Tzitzit_Shawl_Prayer.htm

p. 21, "This way you will be mindful," Rabbi Zalman Schachter-Shalomi. Reprinted with permission.

p. 23, Fern border, Johnny Automatic; licensed under Creative Commons.

p. 25, Hashkivenu chant, Rabbi Hanna Tiferet Siegel, from *Seeds of Wonder.* Reprinted with permission.

p. 25, Photograph by Rabbi Rachel Barenblat, 2013. Reprinted with permission.

p. 27, Shofar photograph by Metanya, from www.flickr.com/photos/government_press_office/7969002640/, licensed under Creative Commons.

p. 28, "Door to President's Office, Old Stone Capitol Building," A. D. White Architectural Photographs, Cornell University Library. Reprinted with permission.

p. 32, Hineni, David Markus. Reprinted with permission.

p. 35, Hamsa shviti, Heather Levy. Reprinted with permission.

p. 40, "And so...", adapted from the *New Kehila Machzor*, ed. Rabbi David Shneyer. Reprinted with permission.

p. 43, Photograph by Rabbi Rachel Barenblat, 2008. Reprinted with permission.

p. 49, Photograph by Rabbi Rachel Barenblat, 2008. Reprinted with permission.

p. 53, "And Then, And Then," from Judy Chicago's "Merger Poem." Reprinted with permission.

p. 58, "Each of us has a name," Zelda; originally published in *Al Tirchak* (*Be not far*), 1974. In the public domain.

p. 61, Photograph by Josh Bousel. Creative Commons.

p. 63, Photograph by flickr user origami48616. Reprinted with permission.

p. 66, "Rosh Hashanah," Rabbi Lewis Eron. Reprinted with permission.

p. 68, Photograph by Rabbi Rachel Barenblat, 2013. Reprinted with permission.

p. 73, "Daily Miracles," Rabbi Rachel Barenblat, from *Open My Lips* (Ben Yehuda Press 2014.) Reprinted with permission.

p. 73, Eyeglasses photograph by Scott Miller. Creative Commons.

p. 76, Baruch She'amar image by salempearce, www.flickr.com/photos/salempearce/8183918243/ Creative Commons.

p. 77, Emanation image, from Wikimedia Commons.
p. 80, "Ashrei," Rabbi Hana Tiferet Siegel, from *Seeds of Wonder.* Reprinted with permission.
p. 81, "Psalm 150," Rabbi Goldie Milgram. Reprinted with permission.
p. 81, Woodcut of musicians by Mary Azarian. Reprinted with permission.
p. 82, "Melech," Rabbi Marcia Prager. Reprinted with permission.
p. 83, "Shochen Ad," transl. Rabbi Daniel Siegel, from *Kol Koreh* machzor. Reprinted with permission.
p. 85, Photograph by Rabbi Rachel Barenblat, 2008. Reprinted with permission.
p. 89, "More Love," Shaker Hymn, public domain.
p. 89, Image by Johnny Automatic; licensed under Creative Commons.
p. 92, Shema mandala by Jackie Olenick, www.jackieolenickart.com/blog/judaic-art-the-amazing-shema/ Reprinted with permission.
p. 95, Photograph by David Curiel. Reprinted with permission.
p. 96, "Shema," from *Machzor Kol Koreh*, ed. Rabbi Daniel Siegel. Reprinted with permission.
p. 96, From Rodger Kamenetz's *The Jew in the Lotus*, Harper San Francisco, 1994.
p. 97, "Redemption," Rabbi Jeff Goldwasser, from *B'kol Shofar*. Reprinted with permission.
p. 99, "Without Ceasing," Rabbi Rachel Barenblat, from *Open My Lips* (Ben Yehuda 2014). Reprinted with permission.
p. 106, Hamsa, Max Dashu, from users.lmi.net/maxdashu/cards/hamsa.html
p. 109, Photograph by Rabbi Rachel Barenblat, 2008. Reprinted with permission.
p. 115, "We address the Parent of the Universe," from the New *Kehilla Machzor.* Reprinted with permission.
p. 117, Photograph by Rabbi Rachel Barenblat, 2008. Reprinted with permission.
p. 121, "13 attributes," from the *Beyt Tikkun Machzor*.
p. 125, Mi Sheberach by Debbie Friedman.
p. 123, Photograph by Len Radin, 2012; reprinted with permission.
p. 132, "Inheritance," Haim Gouri, translated by Rachel Barenblat. The original Hebrew poem appears in *Shoshanat Ruchot* / Compass Rose, 1960.
p. 133, "The ram's horn," Rabbi Jill Hammer, first published in *Zeek*. Awaiting reprint permission.
P. 134, "For I will consider your dog Molly," David Lehman, reprinted with permission.
p. 136, from "The Akedah Cycle," Rachel Barenblat, from *70 faces: Torah poems* (Phoenicia Publishing, 2011). Reprinted with permission.
p. 149, Haftarah blessing poem, Rabbi Rachel Barenblat. Reprinted with permission.
p. 150, Woodcut by Loren Kantor, http://woodcuttingfool.blogspot.com. Reprinted with permission.
p. 151, "Who By Fire," Leonard Cohen, from *The Essential Leonard Cohen*. Awaiting reprint permission from Sony.

p. 152, "The moving finger writes, " from the Rubáiyát of Omar Khayyám, translated by Edmund FitzGerald. Written 1048–1131. Public domain.
p. 153, "On Rosh Hashanah...," Rabbi Elliot Ginsburg. With permission.
p. 156, "The secret meanings," from *Or Yesharim;* translation Rabbi Rachel Barenblat. Public domain.
p. 156, key photograph by Brenda Clarke, www.flickr.com/photos/brenda-starr/3509344402/ Creative Commons.
p. 157, Painting of child's pose by Sandy Haight, www.etsy.com/listing/58806178/extended-childs-pose-original-sumie Reprinted with permission.
p. 158, Shofar service poems, Rabbi Rachel Barenblat, from *B'Kol Shofar*, Congregation Beth Israel, 2010. Reprinted with permission.
p. 161, "Where we are," Rabbi Rachel Barenblat, from *What Stays* (Bennington Writing Seminars Alumni Chapbook Series), 2002. Reprinted with permission.
p. 163, Woodcut illustration, from the Amsterdam edition of *Minhagim*, published by Solomon ben Joseph Proop in 1707. In the public domain.
p. 165, "Said the Baal Shem...," Rabbi Zalman Schachter-Shalomi, from *All Breathing Life* (Gaon Books). Reprinted with permission.
p. 166, Woodcut by Jonathan Gibbs, www.centralillustration.com/illustrators/jonathan-gibbs Reprinted with permission.
p. 167, Photograph of Chora Church, Istanbul, Turkey, 1903. Brooklyn Museum Archives. In the public domain.
p. 171, Prayer for Israel, Rabbi Arik Ascherman. Licensed under Creative Commons.
p. 174, "It's upon us," Rabbinic Pastor Shayndel Kahn. Reprinted with permission.
p. 177, "Psalm 27," Alicia Ostriker, from *Days of Awe*. Reprinted with permission.
p. 180, Selichot meditation, adapted from Ari Dolgin, from OpenSiddur. Creative Commons.
p. 181, Decorative image from karenswhimsy.com/art-border-clip.shtm. In the public domain.
p. 182, "This prayer before Yom Kippur, Rabbi Burt Jacobson. Reprinted with permission.
p. 185, "Return Again," Rabbi Shlomo Carlebach. In the public domain.
p. 186, Photograph by Rabbi Rachel Barenblat, 2008. Reprinted with permission.
p. 189, "Bar'chu, Dear One," adapted by Lev Friedman from a Sufi chant. Reprinted with permission.
p. 191, hamsa by Heather Levy. Reprinted with permission.
p. 195, Latter paragraphs of the shema, Rabbi Zalman Schachter-Shalomi, from *All Breathing Life Adores Your Name* (Gaon Books). Reprinted with permission.
p. 201, "Hashkivenu," Rabbi Hanna Tiferet Siegel, from *Seeds of Wonder.* It is reprinted with permission.
p. 203, Hand Carved Front Doors of Trinity Episcopal Church in Atchison, Kansas. In the US National Archives. In the public domain.

p. 205, This shviti, drawn by anonymous sofer Ba'al HaKochav, was found at the Open Siddur project and licensed under Creative Commons.
p. 212, Photograph by Rabbi Rachel Barenblat, 2008. Reprinted with permission.
p. 217, This papercut of Mishlei (Proverbs) 20:27 by artist Anna Kronick, akronick.wordpress.com. Reprinted with permission.
p. 219, Trash can image from MIT-images, http://www.flickr.com/photos/mit-libraries/3445920258/ Creative Commons.
p. 226, "Ashamnu," from the *Beyt Tikkun Machzor*.
p. 226, "Ki Hineh Kachomer," translated by Rabbi Zalman Schachter-Shalomi, from *All Breathing Life Adores Your Name* (Gaon Books). Reprinted with permission.
p. 227, Photograph by Walt Stoneburner. Creative Commons.
p. 234, "Our Father, Our King / Our Mother, Our Queen" is adapted from Rabbi Burt Jacobson. Reprinted with permission.
p. 234, "Singable refrain," by Rabbi Burt Jacobson, from the *Aquarian Minyan Machzor.* Reprinted with permission.
p. 236, "*Ein banu ma'asim*" Rabbi David Seidenberg, from neohasid.org/torah/ein_banu/. Reprinted with permission.
p. 237, Photograph by Rabbi Rachel Barenblat, 2008. Reprinted with permission.
p. 246, "Psalm 27," Rabbi Zalman Schachter-Shalomi, from *I Breathing Life Adores Your Name* (Gaon Books). Reprinted with permission.
p. 246, Decorative border from karenswhimsy.com/art-border-clip.shtm. In the public domain.
p. 248, Hamsa image by Danial Roushankar, from mymzone.com/blog/hamsa-a-universal-sign-of-protection/nps_hamsa/ Reprinted with permission.
p. 253, Poem by Rumi, translated by Coleman Barks, from *The Illuminated Rumi* (Broadway Books). Reprinted with permission from Coleman Barks.
p. 253, Photograph from here: http://gpacarts.wordpress.com/2011/05/26/scottish-fingerprints-on-world-music Reprinted with permission.
p. 256, Photograph by Rabbi Rachel Barenblat, 2006. Reprinted with permission.
p. 260, "Life after death," Laura Gilpin, from *The Hocus-Pocus of the Universe*, Doubleday. In the public domain.
p, 261, "What the Living Do," Marie Howe, from *What the Living Do*, WW Norton. Reprinted with permission from the poet.
p. 262, "Kaddish," Alan Elyshevitz, from *Beloved on the Earth: 150 Poems of Grief and Gratitude*, Holy Cow Press.
p. 267, "Eli Eli" ("Halikha l'Caesaria"), Hannah Szenes. In the public domain.
p. 270, Photograph by JDENredden. Licensed under Creative Commons.
p. 276, "Ein Od Milvado"by Julie Seltzer (http://www.etsy.com/shop/HebrewCalligraphyArt) Reprinted with permission.

p. 277, Photograph by Rabbi Rachel Barenblat, 2008. Reprinted with permission.

p. 281, Photograph by Glen Bledsoe, aka flickr user PhotoAtelier. Licensed under Creative Commons.
p. 287, "Ana B'Koach" translated by Rabbi Zalman Schachter-Shalomi, from *All Breathing Life* (Gaon Books). Reprinted with permission.
p. 297, Jonah and the whale, from www.kidscd.co.uk/Jonah-Colouring-Pages.html
p. 301, "Hashiveinu" excerpt, Kohenet Ilana Joy Streit, reprinted with permission.
p. 303, "Teshuvah,"Rabbi Rachel Barenblat, from *Open My Lips* (Ben Yehuda, 2014) Reprinted with permission.
p. 303, "Al Chet," Rabbi Rachel Barenblat, from *Open My Lips* (Ben Yehuda, 2014) Reprinted with permission.
p. 306, "Before," Yehuda Amichai. In the public domain.
p. 306, "At the closing of the gates," Rabbi Irwin Keller. Reprinted with permission.
p. 307, "Ne'ilah," Marge Piercy. Awaiting reprint permission.
p. 308, Gate photograph by Javier Kohen. Creative Commons.
p. 310, "Ashrei," Rabbi Hanna Tiferet Siegel, from *Seeds of Wonder*. Reprinted with permission.
p. 311, Shviti art restored by Andrew Meit, from the Royal Library of Denmark's Simonsen Manuscripts Collection. Shared at Open Siddur. Licensed under Creative Commons.
p. 318, Photograph by Rabbi Rachel Barenblat, 2008. Reprinted with permission.
p. 320, This teaching from Rabbi David Ingber was given-over orally at a Yom Kippur retreat at Elat Chayyim / Isabella Freedman. Reprinted with permission.
p. 325, Bismillah calligraphy. In the public domain.
p. 330, "Ashamnu," from the *Beyt Tikkun Machzor*.
p. 330, Illustration cropped from M. Bihn & J. Bealings illustration, 1922. From Wikimedia Commons. In the public domain.
p. 333, Ladder image: Eiserne Leiter zum Steineberg in der Nagelfluhkette, from Wikimedia Commons. In the public domain.
p. 334, "Ne'ilah," Herman Taube, from *Looking Back, Going Forward: New & Selected Poems*.
p. 335, "Our Father, Our King / Our Mother, Our Queen," Rabbi Burt Jacobson. Reprinted with permission.
p. 341, Havdalah photograph by Karen Kelly. Reprinted with permission.

Made in the USA
Lexington, KY
13 September 2015